University Success

WRITING

INTERMEDIATE TO HIGH-INTERMEDIATE

Tim Dalby and Kristin Dalby
Series Editor: Maggie Sokolik
Authentic Content Contributor: Ronnie Hess II

Pearson

University Success Writing, Intermediate to High-Intermediate Level

Pearson Education, 221 River Street, Hoboken, NJ 07030

Staff credits: The people who made up the *University Success* team, representing content development, design, manufacturing, marketing, multimedia, project management, publishing, rights management, and testing, are Pietro Alongi, Stephanie Callahan, Kimberly Casey, Tracey Cataldo, Sara Davila, Dave Dickey, Gina DiLillo, Warren Fischbach, Nancy Flaggman, Lucy Hart, Sarah Henrich, Gosia Jaros-White, Niki Lee, Amy McCormick, Jennifer Raspiller, Robert Ruvo, Katarzyna Skiba, Kristina Skof, Katarzyna Starzynska-Kosciuszko, Joanna Szyszynska, John Thompson, Paula Van Ells, Joseph Vella, Rebecca Wicker, and Natalia Zaremba.

Project coordination: Robyn Brinks Lockwood

Project supervision: Debbie Sistino

Contributing editors: Lida Baker, Eleanor Barnes, Andrea Bryant, Barbara Lyons, Leigh Stolle, and Sarah Wales-McGrath

Cover image: Oleksandr Prykhodko / Alamy Stock Photo

Video research: Constance Rylance

Video production: Kristine Stolakis, assisted by Melissa Langer

Text composition: EMC Design Ltd

Library of Congress Cataloging-in-Publication Data

A catalog record for the print edition is available from the Library of Congress.

Printed in the United States of America

ISBN-10: 0-13-465321-1

ISBN-13: 978-0-13-465321-1

1 18

Contents

Welcome to *University Success*

INTRODUCTION

University Success is a new academic skills series designed to equip intermediate- to transition-level English learners with the reading, writing, and oral communication skills necessary to succeed in courses in an English-speaking university setting. The blended instructional model provides students with an inspiring collection of extensive authentic content, expertly developed in cooperation with five subject matter experts, all "thought leaders" in their fields. By utilizing both online and in-class instructional materials, *University Success* models the type of "real life" learning expected of students studying for a degree. *University Success* recognizes the unique linguistic needs of English language learners and carefully scaffolds skill development to help students successfully work with challenging and engaging authentic content.

SERIES ORGANIZATION: *THREE STRANDS*

This three-strand series, **Reading**, **Writing**, and **Oral Communication**, includes five distinct content areas: The Human Experience, Money and Commerce, The Science of Nature, Arts and Letters, and Structural Science, all popular fields of study among English language learners. The three strands are fully aligned across content areas and skills, allowing teachers to utilize material from different strands to support learning. Teachers can delve deeply into skill development in a single area, or provide additional support materials from other areas for richer development across the four skills.

THE *UNIVERSITY SUCCESS* APPROACH: *AN AUTHENTIC EXPERIENCE*

This blended program combines the utility of an interactive student book, online learner lab, and print course to create a flexible approach that adjusts to the needs of teachers and learners. Its skill-based and step-by-step instruction enables students to master essential skills and become confident in their ability to perform successfully in academic degree courses taught in English. Students at this level need to engage with content that provides them with the same challenges native speakers face in a university setting. Many English language learners are not prepared for the quantity of reading and writing required in college-level courses, nor are they properly prepared to listen to full-length lectures that have not been scaffolded for them. These learners, away from the safety of an ESL classroom, must keep up with the rigors of a class led by a professor who may be unaware of the challenges a second-language learner faces. Strategies for academic success, delivered via online videos, help increase students' confidence and ability to cope with the challenges of academic student and college culture. *University Success* steps up to the podium to represent academic content realistically with the appropriate skill development and scaffolding essential for English language learners to be successful.

PUTTING STUDENTS ON THE PATH TO *UNIVERSITY SUCCESS*

Intensive skill development and extended application—tied to specific learning outcomes—provide the scaffolding English language learners need to become confident and successful in a university setting.

Global Scale of English	10	20	30	40	50	60	70	80	90

CEFR	<A1	A1	A2 +	B1 +	B2 +	C1	C2

INTERMEDIATE TO HIGH-INTERMEDIATE LEVEL

B1–B1+ | 43–58

Authentic content with careful integration of essential skills, the Intermediate to High-Intermediate level familiarizes students with real-world academic contexts.

INTENSIVE SKILL PRACTICE

Intensive skill practice tied to learning objectives informed by the Global Scale of English

AUTHENTIC CONTENT

- Readings: 200–2,000 words
- Lectures: 15–20 minutes
- Multiple exposures and chunking

EXPLICIT VOCABULARY INSTRUCTION

- Pre- and post-reading and listening vocabulary tasks
- Glossing of receptive vocabulary
- Recycling throughout each part and online

SCAFFOLDED APPROACH

Multiple guided exercises focus on comprehension, application, and clarification of productive skills.

VOCABULARY STRATEGIES

Vocabulary strategy sections focus on form, use, and meaning.

GRAPHIC ORGANIZERS

Extensive integration of graphic organizers throughout to support note-taking and help students process complex content.

ADVANCED LEVEL

B2–B2+ | 59–75

Challenging, authentic content with level-appropriate skills, the Advanced level prepares students to exit the ESL safety net.

INTENSIVE SKILL PRACTICE

Intensive skill practice tied to learning objectives informed by the Global Scale of English

AUTHENTIC CONTENT

- Readings: 200–3,000 words
- Lectures: 20 minutes

EXPLICIT VOCABULARY INSTRUCTION

- Pre- and post-reading and listening vocabulary tasks
- Glossing of receptive vocabulary
- Recycling throughout each part and online

MODERATELY SCAFFOLDED

Guided exercises focus on comprehension, application, and clarification of productive skills.

VOCABULARY STRATEGIES

Vocabulary strategy sections focus on form, use, and meaning to help students process complex content.

TRANSITION LEVEL

B2+–C1 | 68–80

A deep dive for transition-level students, the Transition level mirrors the academic rigor of college courses.

INTENSIVE SKILL PRACTICE

Intensive skill practice tied to learning objectives informed by the Global Scale of English

AUTHENTIC CONTENT

Readings and lectures of significant length:

- 200–3,500-word readings
- 25-minute lectures

CONTENT AND FLUENCY VOCABULARY APPROACH

- No direct vocabulary instruction
- Online vocabulary practice for remediation

Key Features

UNIQUE PART STRUCTURE

University Success employs a unique three-part structure, providing maximum flexibility and multiple opportunities to customize the content. The series is "horizontally" aligned to teach across a specific content area and "vertically" aligned to allow a teacher to gradually build skills.

Each part is a self-contained module allowing teachers to customize a non-linear program that will best address the needs of students. Parts are aligned around science, technology, engineering, arts, and mathematics (STEAM) content relevant to mainstream academic areas of study.

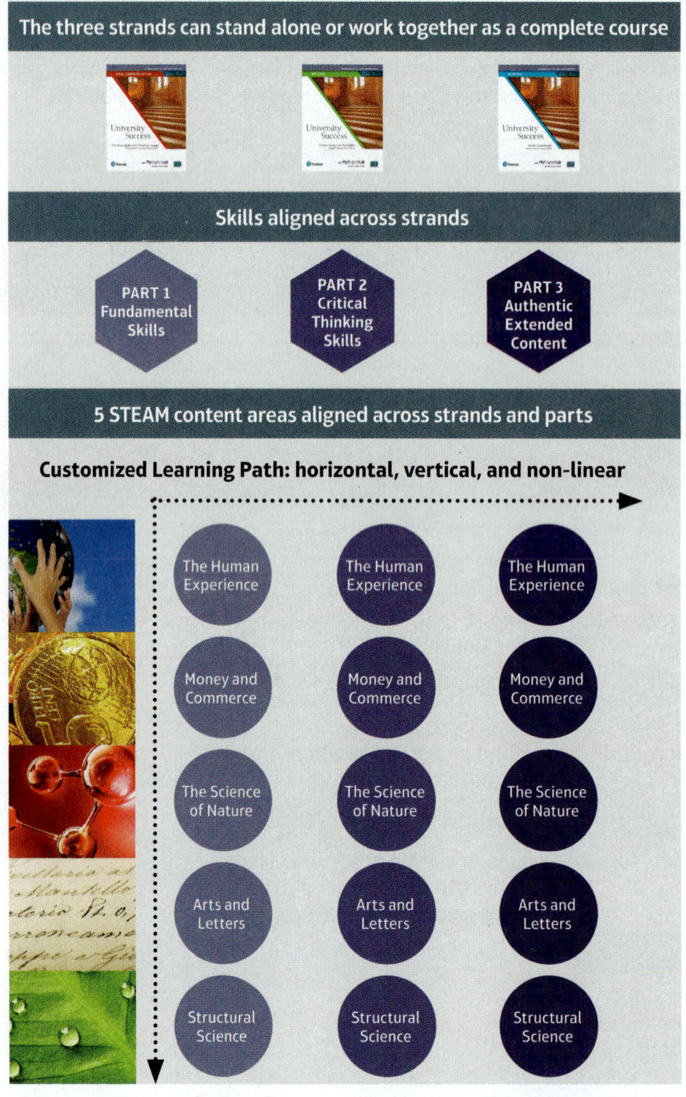

THE THREE PARTS AT A GLANCE

Parts 1 and 2 focus on the fundamental writing and critical thinking skills most relevant for students preparing for university degrees. In Part 1 and Part 2, students work with comprehensive skills that include:

- Understanding assignments and using the academic writing process
- Developing and integrating ideas
- Presenting and supporting facts and opinions
- Using narrative and descriptive writing
- Paraphrasing and summarizing

Part 3 introduces students to extended practice with the skills. Content created by top university professors provides students with a challenging experience that replicates the authentic experience of studying in a mainstream university class.

PART 1

Fundamental Writing Skills

THE HUMAN EXPERIENCE Bioethics — THE AC
MONEY AND COMMERCE Business and Design — IDEA DE
THE SCIENCE OF NATURE Zoology — EXTEND
ARTS AND LETTERS History — NARRAT
STRUCTURAL SCIENCE Chemical Engineering — EDITINC

Part 1 is designed to build fundamental sk… academic content. Practice activities tied t… on understanding the function and applic…

PART 2

Critical Thinking Skills

CT AND OPINION 170
TEGRATING IDEAS FROM SOURCES 206
OCESS WRITING 238
YLE AND GENRE 268
ESENTING NUMERICAL INFORMATION 304

…pplication of the skills that require critical thinking. …rning outcomes in each unit require a deeper level …ntent.

169

PART 3

Extended Writing

THE HUMAN EXPERIENCE Bioethics — WRITING AS A BIOETHICIST 342
MONEY AND COMMERCE Business and Design — WRITING AS A BUSINESSPERSON 356
THE SCIENCE OF NATURE Zoology — WRITING AS A SCIENTIST 370
ARTS AND LETTERS History — WRITING AS A HISTORIAN 382
STRUCTURAL SCIENCE Chemical Engineering — WRITING AS A CHEMICAL ENGINEER 396

Part 3 presents authentic content written by university professors. Academically rigorous application and assessment activities allow for a synthesis of the skills developed in Parts 1 and 2.

341

PART 1 AND PART 2

Student Book

MyEnglishLab

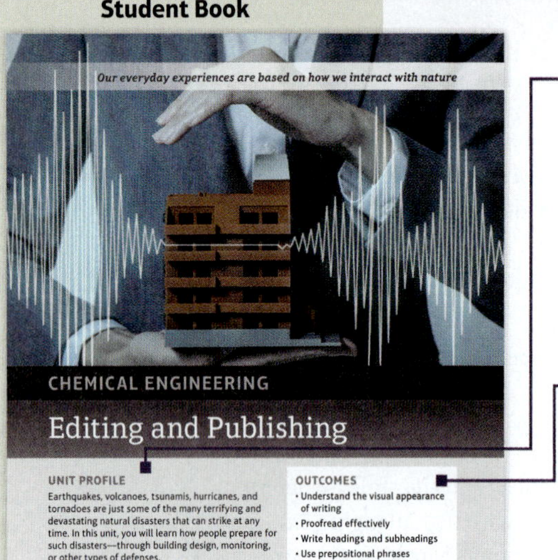

A **unit profile** outlines the content.

Outcomes aligned with the Global Scale of English (GSE) are clearly stated to ensure student awareness of skills.

Skill Self-assessments provide opportunities for students to identify skill areas for improvement and provide teachers with information that can inform lesson planning.

Professors provide a **preview** and a **summary** of the content.

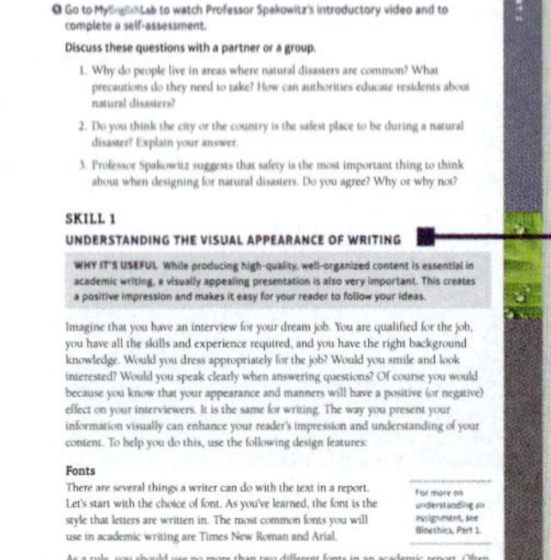

Why It's Useful sections highlight the need for developing skills and support transfer of skills to mainstream class content.

A **detailed presentation** facilitates intensive development of the skills. Follow-up exercises enhance skill understanding and conclude with a productive writing task.

Additional **practice online** encourages the application of skills.

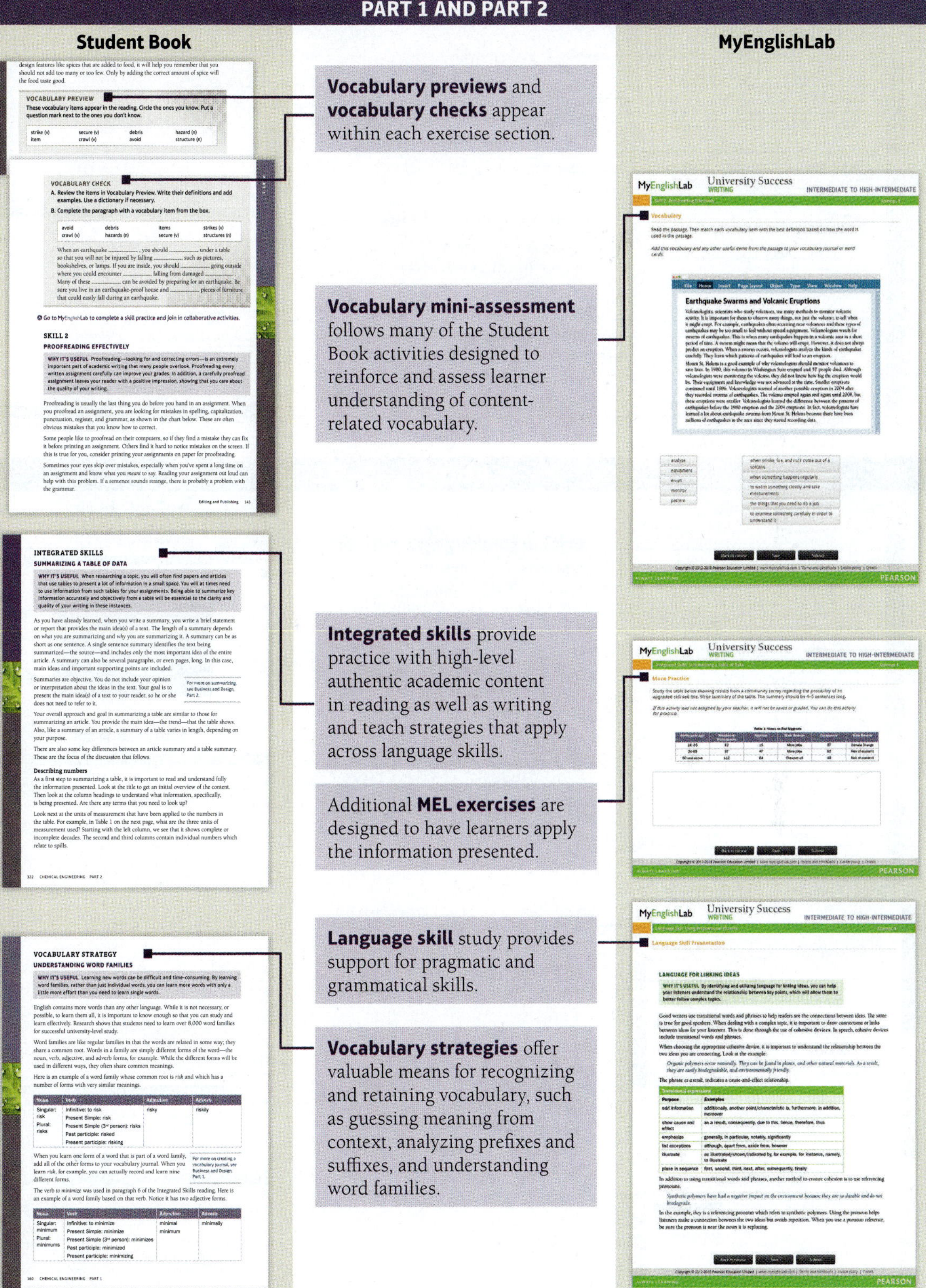
PART 1 AND PART 2
Student Book
MyEnglishLab
Vocabulary previews and vocabulary checks appear within each exercise section.
Vocabulary mini-assessment follows many of the Student Book activities designed to reinforce and assess learner understanding of content-related vocabulary.
Integrated skills provide practice with high-level authentic academic content in reading as well as writing and teach strategies that apply across language skills.
Additional MEL exercises are designed to have learners apply the information presented.
Language skill study provides support for pragmatic and grammatical skills.
Vocabulary strategies offer valuable means for recognizing and retaining vocabulary, such as guessing meaning from context, analyzing prefixes and suffixes, and understanding word families.

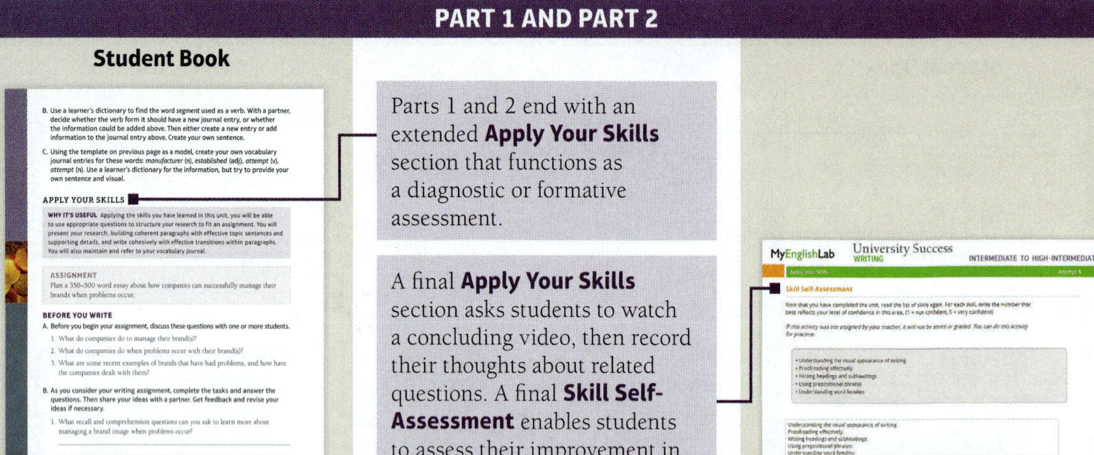

PART 1 AND PART 2

Student Book

Parts 1 and 2 end with an extended **Apply Your Skills** section that functions as a diagnostic or formative assessment.

A final **Apply Your Skills** section asks students to watch a concluding video, then record their thoughts about related questions. A final **Skill Self-Assessment** enables students to assess their improvement in unit skill areas.

PART 3

Student Book

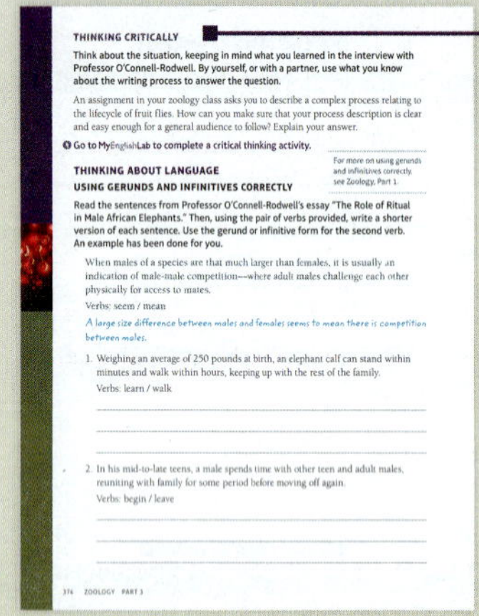

MyEnglishLab

Critical thinking activities ask learners to engage at a deep level with the content and prompt thought about specific real-world applications.

The Interview sections allow students to view professors discussing their own writing processes. Follow-up includes a comprehension check and a **Thinking Critically** activity.

Guided research activities form the basis of the culminating **writing assignments**.

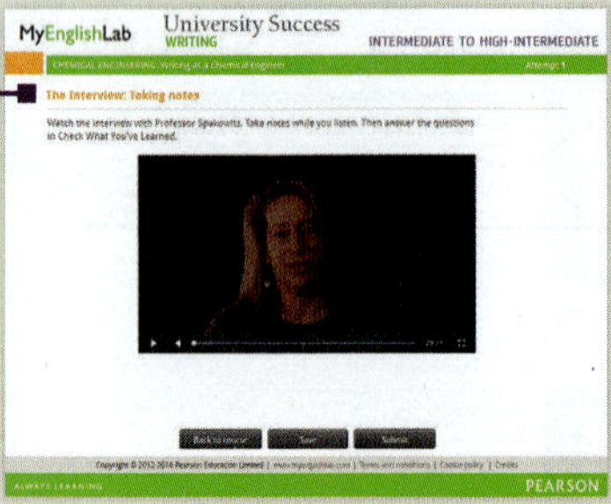

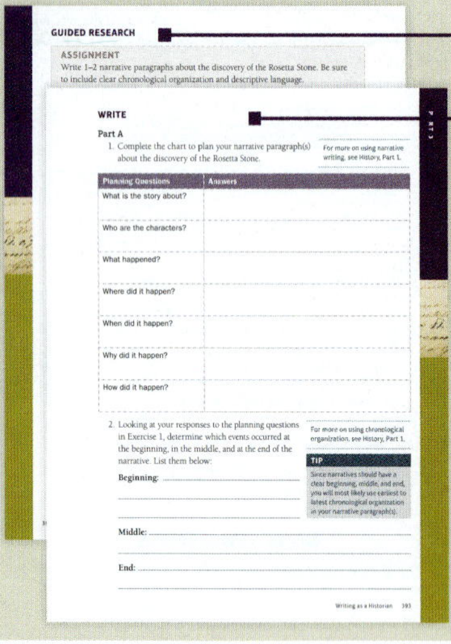

The writing assignment is built upon a thematically relevant **reading** written by the professor who has been interviewed, allowing students to dive deeper into the content.

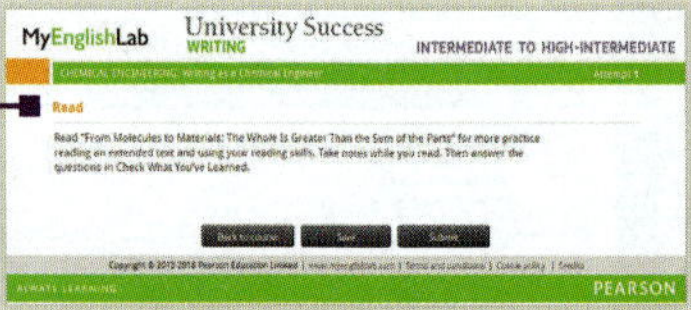

STRATEGIES FOR ACADEMIC SUCCESS AND SOFT SKILLS

Strategies for academic success and soft skills, delivered via online videos, help increase students' confidence and ability to cope with the challenges of academic study and college culture. Study skills include how to talk to professors during office hours and time management techniques.

TEACHER SUPPORT

Each of the three strands is supported with:

- Comprehensive **downloadable teaching notes** in MyEnglishLab that detail key points for all of the specialized, academic content in addition to tips and suggestions for how to teach skills and strategies.
- **An easy-to-use online learning management system** offering a flexible gradebook and tools for monitoring student progress
- Essential tools, such as **video scripts** and **course planners**, to help in lesson planning and follow-up.

ASSESSMENT

University Success provides a package of assessments that can be used as precourse diagnostics, midcourse assessments, and final summative assessments. The flexible nature of these assessments allows teachers to choose which assessments will be most appropriate at various stages of the program. These assessments are embedded in the student book and are available online in MyEnglishLab.

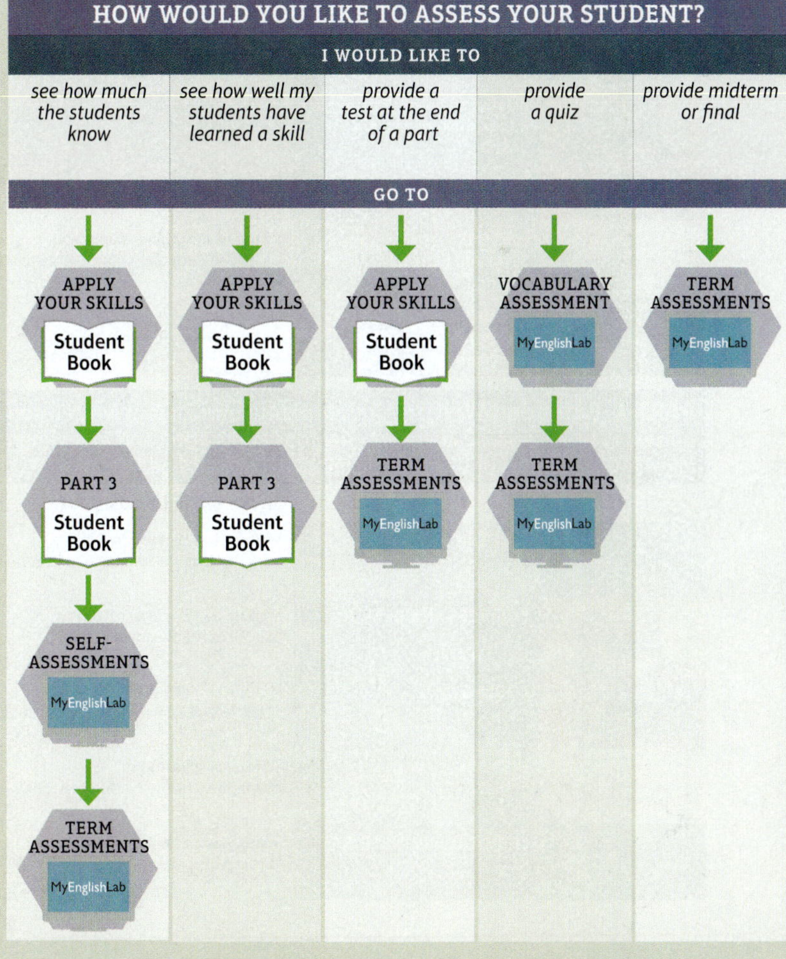

Scope and Sequence

PART 1 Fundamental Writing Skills is designed to build fundamental skills step-by-step through exploration of rigorous academic content.

	Fundamental Skills
BIOETHICS **The Academic Writing Process**	Understanding an assignment Using the academic writing process
BUSINESS AND DESIGN **Idea Development**	Using questions to guide your research Building paragraphs and connecting ideas
ZOOLOGY **Extended Writing**	Writing an introduction Writing a conclusion
HISTORY **Narratives**	Using narrative writing Writing a biography
CHEMICAL ENGINEERING **Editing and Publishing**	Understanding the visual appearance of writing Proofreading effectively

PART 2 Critical Thinking Skills moves from skill building to application of the skills that require critical thinking.

	Fundamental Skills
BIOETHICS **Fact and Opinion**	Stating an argument Supporting an argument with examples
BUSINESS AND DESIGN **Integrating Ideas from Sources**	Identifying keywords Paraphrasing ideas
ZOOLOGY **Process Writing**	Describing a process Using process language
HISTORY **Style and Genre**	Writing a descriptive paragraph Using compare-and-contrast organization
CHEMICAL ENGINEERING **Presenting Numerical Information**	Creating tables Using numbers in writing

PART 3 Extended Writing presents authentic content written and delivered by university professors. Academically rigorous application and assessment activities allow for a synthesis of the skills developed in Part 1 and Part 2.

	Interviews and Readings
BIOETHICS	Writing as a Bioethicist "Whole Genome Sequencing: Uses and Challenges"
BUSINESS AND DESIGN	Writing as a Businessperson "So What is a Business Model?"
ZOOLOGY	Writing as a Scientist "The Role of Ritual in Male African Elephants"
HISTORY	Writing as a Historian "Changing History by Accident: How Accidents Can Uncover Important Archaeological Finds"
CHEMICAL ENGINEERING	Writing as a Chemical Engineer "From Molecules to Materials: The Whole is Greater Than the Sum of the Parts"

Integrated Skills	Language Skills	Vocabulary Strategy	Apply Your Skills
Taking effective notes	Using *-ing* and *-ed* adjectives correctly	Understanding register	Plan a 250–300 word paragraph on the advantages and disadvantages of using gene editing in people.
Identifying topic sentences	Using conjunctions to connect ideas	Creating a vocabulary journal	Plan a 350–500 word essay about how companies can successfully manage their brands when problems occur.
Understanding and using thesis statements	Using gerunds and infinitives correctly	Determining meaning from context	Plan a well-researched 2–3 page paper that answers these questions: Why are African elephants being poached? How is poaching harming elephant social structure? What is being done to prevent poaching?
Using chronological organization	Using narrative tenses	Understanding affixes	Plan a 300–500 word narrative essay about the history of Angkor Wat, or a 300–500 word biography of the explorer who made Angkor Wat popular in the West.
Writing headings and subheadings	Using prepositional phrases	Understanding word families	Plan a 500–700 word report that explains a design solution for disaster-resistant housing in a developing country.

Integrated Skills	Language Skills	Vocabulary Strategy	Apply Your Skills
Reading and responding to a persuasive essay	Using hedging structures	Understanding collocation	Plan a 250–300 word paragraph discussing whether or not gene drive should be used outside a laboratory.
Summarizing	Using reporting verbs	Using synonyms	Plan a 200–300 word summary of the article "Product Wars," from Business and Design, Part 1.
Summarizing a process	Using causative verbs	Using a dictionary to expand vocabulary	Plan a 150–300 word explanation of the process of one form of elephant communication: visual, tactile, or chemical.
Identifying style and tone	Using compare-and-contrast language	Using adjectives	Plan a well-researched 300–500 word essay comparing and contrasting the discovery of the Varna Necropolis and the Terracotta Army.
Summarizing a table of data	Knowing how and when to use the passive voice	Creating word cards	Plan to write a 500-word report on the destruction of the Aral Sea.

Research / Assignment
Write a detailed outline of a persuasive essay discussing whether or not people should be encouraged to have their whole genome sequenced.
Summarize the section about Target Corporation's business model from Juli Sherry's essay "So What Is a Business Model?"
Write a short essay about a ritual that male elephants use to maintain social bonds.
Write 1 to 2 narrative paragraphs about the discovery of the Rosetta Stone.
Write 1 to 2 paragraphs about a synthetic material—a material that has been invented—rather than produced naturally.

A Note from Maggie Sokolik

Series Editor for *University Success Writing*

Intermediate to high-intermediate EAP students are often at a critical point in their studies; further work in English will help them to advance towards their academic plans. Although they have reached a level of success and proficiency in their English language studies, students at this level will often lack exposure to the types of writing used in academic settings. *University Success Writing* introduces them to the academic skills and vocabulary needed to continue to grow into academic writers. To help students with this continued development as they prepare for academic study, *University Success Writing* showcases writing instruction and assignments in a way that aligns with how academic writing is taught at the university and across disciplines. The focus is on inquiry-based and research writing, on writing in the subject areas, and on critical and creative thinking that results in strong content development.

University Success Writing, Intermediate to High-Intermediate Level, breaks down, explains, and carefully scaffolds the processes involved in academic writing tasks. This helps students understand how they can plan writing assignments in different disciplines and build essays they can be proud of. The intermediate to high-intermediate level of *University Success* is ideal because it provides content that is appropriate and authentic, exposing learners to materials at the college level and helping them to understand the rationales behind academic writing. It also prepares them to think about and meet their academic goals. The materials acknowledge students' needs as they move to more advanced levels of English by providing strong scaffolding that includes targeted grammar review and is complemented by useful learning tips and interesting, informative culture notes. Once they complete this level, students can easily move into the higher levels, where they will succeed with less scaffolding and continue crossing the bridge to academic study.

PART 1—FUNDAMENTAL WRITING SKILLS

In the first five units of *University Success Writing Intermediate to High-Intermediate Level*, each of the five main subject areas, Bioethics, Business and Design, Zoology, History, and Chemical Engineering, is used to provide authentic content for skill-based learning as well as an introduction to some of the elements of research-based writing. While students at this level have most likely started learning the steps in the writing process, they have not had enough time to practice those skills as they develop their own ideas within an academic context. This level allows for substantial practice, breaking academic tasks into manageable, recognizable tasks. It also focuses on vocabulary development as a key component of successful writing.

PART 2—CRITICAL THINKING SKILLS

The next five units continue the exploration of the topics from Part 1 from a new angle. Students are invited to think critically about ideas, and are then challenged with engaging writing tasks, including: critically reading texts to evaluate sources, integrating both fact and opinion to support an idea, using descriptive and narrative writing techniques to develop effective essays, and practicing ways to propose and present ideas, both in writing and through use of graphics. In fact, this level of *University Success Writing* makes extensive use of graphic organizers to support the tasks of academic writing, including note-taking and outlining.

PART 3—EXTENDED WRITING

Part 3 begins with interviews with Stanford professors about their own writing processes and habits. These interviews provide students with a unique opportunity to hear professors explain how they get their ideas, carry out research, and then develop their writing. It also shows students what professors expect from student writing in different disciplines. These interviews are followed by opportunities for students to engage in critical thinking, analysis, and discussion of authentic situations based on assignments in the subject areas. After additional review of the language skills from Parts 1 and 2, students complete a culminating writing task that is preceded by extensive guided research. The writing task builds upon a thematically relevant reading written by the professor who has been interviewed and uses the featured language skills. Students thus have a final opportunity for practice that will help them participate in inquiry-based research and writing.

SUBJECT MATTER EXPERTS

Henry T. (Hank) Greely is the Deane F. and Kate Edelman Johnson Professor of Law and Professor by courtesy of Genetics at Stanford University. He directs Stanford's Center for Law and the Biosciences and its Program on Neuroscience in Society. The author of *The End of Sex*, he serves as President of the International Neuroethics Society and on the Committee on Science, Technology, and Law of the National Academy of Sciences and the NIH Multi-Council Working Group on the BRAIN Initiative.

Juli Sherry is the Design Lead at Worldview Stanford, where she develops hybrid courses and learning experiences for professionals. She facilitates sessions on Design Thinking, creating visualizations and experiences to communicate complex ideas and expose students to potential futures including drones, food substitutes, and wearable technologies. As a business strategist, designer, and entrepreneur, she develops strategic brands for small businesses and startups to help drive her clients' businesses into the future.

Caitlin O'Connell-Rodwell is an adjunct professor at Stanford University School of Medicine. She has studied elephants for the last 25 years, authored seven popular books and dozens of scientific papers and magazine articles about elephants, and was the focus of the award-winning Smithsonian documentary *Elephant King*. She taught creative science writing for Stanford and *The New York Times*, and has won numerous awards for her writing. She currently blogs for National Geographic from her field site in Namibia.

Award-winning archaeologist and author **Patrick Hunt** has taught at Stanford University for 25 years. He directed the Stanford Alpine Archaeology Project from 1994 to 2012 and continues to conduct research in the region. Hunt is a National Geographic Expeditions Expert and a National Lecturer for the Archaeological Institute of America as well as an elected Fellow of the Royal Geographical Society. In addition to publishing over 100 articles, he is the author of 20 published books including the best-seller *Ten Discoveries That Rewrote History* and most recently, *Hannibal*.

Andrew Spakowitz is a professor in the Department of Chemical Engineering at Stanford University, where he established a theoretical and computational lab that develops physical models to understand and control critical biological processes and cutting-edge materials applications. In 2009, he was awarded the NSF CAREER Award for work in modeling DNA in living cells. In addition to his research and teaching programs, Professor Spakowitz established an outreach program that developed a comprehensive science lab curriculum for high school students who are being treated for cancer or other illnesses.

SERIES EDITORS

Robyn Brinks Lockwood teaches courses in spoken and written English at Stanford University in the English for Foreign Students graduate program and is the program education coordinator of the American Language and Culture undergraduate summer program. She is an active member of the international TESOL organization, serves as Chairperson of the Publishing Professional Council, and is a past chair of the Materials Writers Interest Section. She is a frequent presenter at TESOL regional and international conferences. Robyn has edited and written numerous textbooks, online courses, and ancillary components for ESL courses and TOEFL preparation.

Maggie Sokolik holds a BA in Anthropology from Reed College, and an MA in Romance Linguistics and Ph.D. in Applied Linguistics from UCLA. She is the author of over 20 ESL and composition textbooks. She has taught at MIT, Harvard, Texas A&M, and currently UC Berkeley, where she is Director of College Writing Programs. She has developed and taught several popular MOOC courses in English language writing and literature. She is the founding editor of *TESL-EJ*, a peer-reviewed journal for ESL / EFL professionals, one of the first online journals. Maggie travels frequently to speak about grammar, writing, and instructor education. She lives in the San Francisco Bay area, where she and her husband play bluegrass music.

Lawrence J. Zwier is an Associate Director of the English Language Center, Michigan State University. He holds a bachelor's degree in English Literature from Aquinas College, Grand Rapids, MI, and an MA in TESL from the University of Minnesota. He has taught ESL / EFL at universities in Saudi Arabia, Malaysia, Japan, Singapore, and the US. He is the author of numerous ELT textbooks, mostly about reading and vocabulary, and also writes nonfiction books about history and geography for middle school and high school students. He is married with two children and lives in Okemos, Michigan.

Acknowledgments

We would like to thank the many people at Pearson who contributed toward making this book a reality. We'd like to give a special mention to Sara Davila for connecting us with this project and for all she has done to make it what it is. Thanks to Niki Cunnion for her rapid responses, help, and advice throughout, Rebecca Wicker and Eleanor Barnes, for seeing the book through to production, and Natalia Cebulska and Kasia (Katarzynska) Skiba, for making the MEL content work as well as it does. We are grateful to Amy McCormick for putting such a great team together. Thanks are also due to Debbie Sistino for her sustained guidance and patience, for keeping us on our toes, and keeping the project moving along. We thank Ronnie Hess for his contributions to the Integrated Skills sections. Finally, an extra special thank you is necessary for Barbara Lyons, our Development Editor. Her expertise, patience, and careful attention to detail have helped to turn this book from a collection of ideas into what you see now.

We would like to thank also the many students and teachers on several continents whom we have been fortunate to meet throughout our careers. They have helped us continue to grow and develop our craft. Every day in the classroom we learn something new, and this book reflects many of those lessons.

We have enjoyed working together closely and collaboratively for many years. We used our writing of this book as an opportunity to teach our wonderful children, Aiden and Julien, how to clean their own rooms, engage in yard work, and entertain themselves while their parents spent many hours hard at work. Thank you, boys, for all your support over this past year! —*Tim Dalby* and *Kristin Dalby*

Reviewers

We would like to thank the following reviewers for their many helpful comments and suggestions:

Jamila Barton, North Seattle Community College, Seattle, WA; **Joan Chamberlin**, Iowa State University, Ames IA; **Lyam Christopher**, Palm Beach State College, Boynton Beach, FL; **Robin Corcos**, University of California, Santa Barbara, Goleta, CA; **Tanya Davis**, University of California, San Diego, CA; **Brendan DeCoster**, University of Oregon, Eugene, OR; **Thomas Dougherty**, University of St. Mary of the Lake, Mundelein, IL; **Bina Dugan**, Bergen County Community College, Hackensack, NJ; **Priscilla Faucette**, University of Hawaii at Manoa, Honolulu, HI; **Lisa Fischer**, St. Louis University, St. Louis, MO; **Kathleen Flynn**, Glendale Community College, Glendale, CA; **Mary Gawienowski**, William Rainey Harper College, Palatine, IL; **Sally Gearhart**, Santa Rosa Junior College, Santa Rosa, CA; **Carl Guerriere**, Capital Community College, Hartford, CT; **Vera Guillen**, Eastfield College, Mesquite, TX; **Angela Hakim**, St. Louis University, St. Louis, MO; **Pamela Hartmann**, Evans Community Adult School, Los Angeles Unified School District, Los Angeles, CA; **Shelly Hedstrom**, Palm Beach State University, Lake Worth, FL; **Sherie Henderson**, University of Oregon, Eugene, OR; **Lisse Hildebrandt**, English Language Program, Virginia Commonwealth University, Richmond, VA; **Barbara Inerfeld**, Rutgers University, Piscataway, NJ; **Zaimah Khan**, Northern Virginia Community College, Loudon Campus, Sterling, VA; **Tricia Kinman**, St. Louis University, St. Louis, MO; **Kathleen Klaiber**, Genesee Community College, Batavia, NY; **Kevin Lamkins**, Capital Community College, Hartford, CT; **Mayetta Lee**, Palm Beach State College, Lake Worth, FL; **Kirsten Lillegard**, English Language Institute, Divine Word College, Epworth, IA; **Craig Machado**, Norwalk Community College, Norwalk, CT; **Cheryl Madrid**, Spring International Language Center, Denver, CO; **Ann Meechai**, St. Louis University, St. Louis, MO; **Melissa Mendelson**, Department of Linguistics, University of Utah, Salt Lake City, UT; **Tamara Milbourn**, University of Colorado, Boulder, CO; **Debbie Ockey**, Fresno City College, Fresno, CA; **Diana Pascoe-Chavez**, St. Louis University, St. Louis, MO; **Kathleen Reynolds**, William Rainey Harper College, Palatine, IL; **Linda Roth**, Vanderbilt University ELC, Greensboro, NC; **Minati Roychoudhuri**, Capital Community College, Hartford, CT; **Bruce Rubin**, California State University, Fullerton, CA; **Margo Sampson**, Syracuse University, Syracuse, NY; **Sarah Saxer**, Howard Community College, Ellicott City, MD; **Anne-Marie Schlender**, Austin Community College, Austin, TX; **Susan Shields**, Santa Barbara Community College, Santa Barbara, CA; **Barbara Smith-Palinkas**, Hillsborough Community College, Dale Mabry Campus, Tampa, FL; **Sara Stapleton**, North Seattle Community College, Seattle, WA; **Lisa Stelle**, Northern Virginia Community College Loudon, Sterling, VA; **Jamie Tanzman**, Northern Kentucky University, Highland Heights, KY; **Jeffrey Welliver**, Soka University of America, Aliso Viejo, CA; **Mark Wolfersberger**, Brigham Young University, Hawaii, Laie, HI; **May Youn**, California State University, Fullerton, CA

PART 1

Fundamental Writing Skills

Part 1 is designed to build fundamental skills step by step through exploration of rigorous, academic content. Practice activities tied to specific learning outcomes in each unit focus on understanding the function and application of the skills.

How advances in biosciences raise legal, social, and ethical concerns

BIOETHICS

The Academic Writing Process

UNIT PROFILE

Gene editing is a widespread, controversial technique used to make changes at the genetic level of a living organism. In this unit, you will learn about a gene editing technique called CRISPR, and how it is being used to solve problems like keeping yogurt fresh, making vaccines safe, and growing human organs. You will also consider some of the possible ethical problems that using CRISPR may cause.

OUTCOMES

- Understand an assignment
- Use the academic writing process
- Take effective notes
- Use *-ing* and *-ed* adjectives correctly
- Understand register

You will plan a 250–300 word paragraph on the advantages and disadvantages of using gene editing in people. What are the benefits and what are the possible ethical problems? Your paragraph should be typed and follow standard formatting guidelines.

For more about **BIOETHICS**, see 2 3. See also R and OC **BIOETHICS** 1 2 3.

GETTING STARTED

Go to MyEnglishLab to watch Professor Greely's introductory video and to complete a self-assessment.

Discuss these questions with a partner or a group.

1. Genes contain the codes that are passed down from our parents. They decide what we look like, how our bodies develop, and what our personalities are like. What do you know about genes? What do you know about problems that are caused when genes go wrong? Are there genetic diseases that you are familiar with?
2. If you could edit your genes to make yourself smarter, stronger, or more attractive, would you? Why or why not? Are there other things about yourself that you would like to change by gene editing?
3. Professor Greely suggests that CRISPR is one of the most exciting advances in biosciences in recent years. Do you agree? Why or why not?

SKILL 1

UNDERSTANDING AN ASSIGNMENT

WHY IT'S USEFUL Knowing how to understand an assignment is important because the assignment tells you exactly what your instructor expects. Understanding this can save you time and effort. Misunderstanding an assignment can lead to frustration, not to mention poor grades.

An assignment usually provides a lot of information. Some of this information is explicit, or stated very clearly. However, some of the information may be implicit, or not stated directly. As a student, you need to understand all the information in the assignment and, if you don't, you need to seek help.

An assignment can have several parts, but they can usually be grouped into two main categories: what to do and how to do it.

What to do

This part of the assignment provides the question(s) that you need to answer or the task(s) that you must complete. The task(s) could specify the type or structure of the writing you need to do, for example writing an essay or only a paragraph. The task(s) may also indicate the organization type, such as a cause-and-effect essay or a problem-solution paragraph. The topic is also included as part of the assignment.

Here is an example of a task:

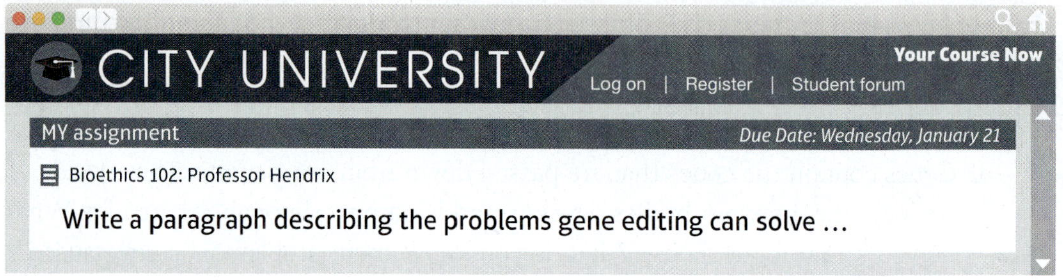
CITY UNIVERSITY

Your Course Now

Log on | Register | Student forum

MY assignment — Due Date: Wednesday, January 21

Bioethics 102: Professor Hendrix

Write a paragraph describing the problems gene editing can solve …

Some information in the task is explicit; it clearly tells you what is needed. Other information is implicit; the task assumes you already understand some information.

	Explicit Information	Implicit Information
Structure	Paragraph	Paragraphs should have a topic sentence and several supporting sentences.
Organization	Problems	Solutions will at least be mentioned because problem and solution go together.
Topic	Gene editing	The problems will be genetic problems because gene editing is used to change the genetic makeup of a living organism, not fix your computer!

How to do it

The "how to do it" part of the assignment tells you how your instructor expects to receive your work. It may include details such as length, page size, format, and the hand-in date (along with any penalties for late submission!). Look at the example below.

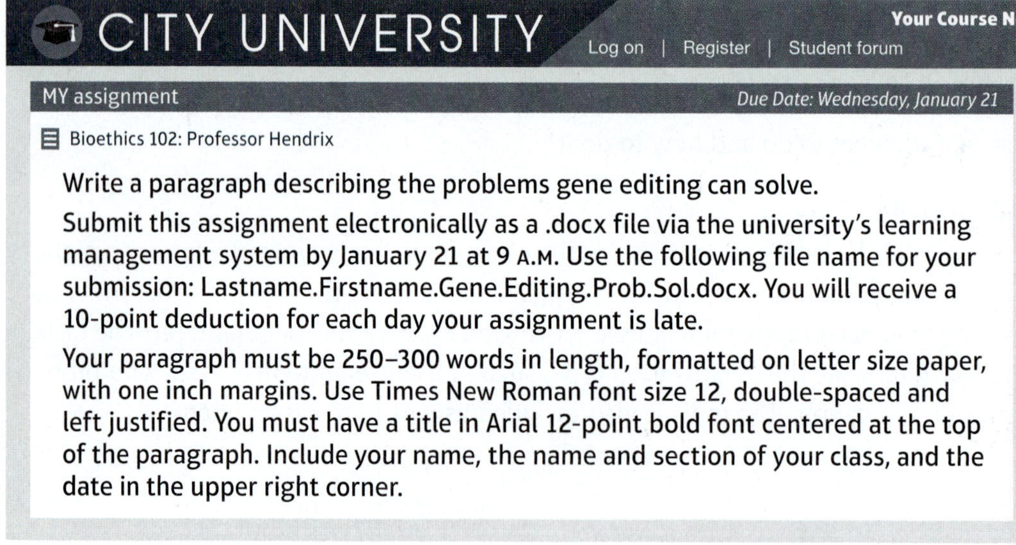
CITY UNIVERSITY

Your Course Now

Log on | Register | Student forum

MY assignment — Due Date: Wednesday, January 21

Bioethics 102: Professor Hendrix

Write a paragraph describing the problems gene editing can solve.

Submit this assignment electronically as a .docx file via the university's learning management system by January 21 at 9 A.M. Use the following file name for your submission: Lastname.Firstname.Gene.Editing.Prob.Sol.docx. You will receive a 10-point deduction for each day your assignment is late.

Your paragraph must be 250–300 words in length, formatted on letter size paper, with one inch margins. Use Times New Roman font size 12, double-spaced and left justified. You must have a title in Arial 12-point bold font centered at the top of the paragraph. Include your name, the name and section of your class, and the date in the upper right corner.

There are a lot of instructions which need to be followed; otherwise, your instructor may return your work as incomplete. Let's look at each instruction and break it down into what it tells you explicitly and what it assumes you already know.

TIP

Assignments may not always be so specific about how to format your paper. You should talk to your instructor about the preferred style. Your institution's writing center may also be able to advise you on style and presentation of your assignments.

	Explicit Information	Implicit Information
Length	250–300 words	If you write something shorter or longer, you may be penalized. You should know how to use word count tools.
Submission type	.docx file via learning management system	If you don't use Microsoft® Word, you need to convert the file to the correct format. You don't need to print the assignment on paper, but you need to understand how to use the learning management system.
File name	Lastname.Firstname.Gene.Editing.Prob.Sol.docx	Last name means family name. First name means given name.
Deadline	January 21 at 9 A.M.	The instructor can tell the exact time that you upload your assignment.
Penalty	You will receive a 10-point deduction for each day your assignment is late.	Don't wait until the last minute to upload the document. Unexpected problems could result in a lower grade.
Format	All assignments must be formatted on letter paper, with one inch margins. Use Times New Roman font size 12, double-spaced and left justified. Your paragraph must have a title in Arial 12-point font centered at the top of the paragraph and in bold. Include your name, the name and section of your class, and the date in the upper right corner.	Though there is variation, these guidelines describe typical standards for formatting an academic paper in an American university.

CULTURE NOTE

Computers brought from other countries may have word processing software with standard defaults that are different from U.S. standards. For example, the paper size may automatically default to A4. You may need to change settings to follow these guidelines.

VOCABULARY PREVIEW

These vocabulary items appear in the reading. Circle the ones you know. Put a question mark next to the ones you don't know.

gene	create	organ	pancreas	insulin	diabetes	controversial

EXERCISE 1

A. Read the background information about animal-human chimeras and the related assignment. Then answer the comprehension questions.

MY assignment — *Due Date: Friday, January 30*

Bioethics 102: Professor Hendrix

Background: A chimera is an organism made up of genes from two different species. Imagine that there was a way for scientists to create a human organ in animals. For example, what if scientists could put a human pancreas in sheep? There are many uses for this kind of animal-human chimera. The pancreas is a very important organ in humans. It helps us digest food by creating a hormone called insulin. If the pancreas doesn't work correctly, this results in a disease that many people suffer from, diabetes. Scientists could make more advances in understanding and treating diseases like diabetes if the animal models they use had actual human organs.

However, this kind of research is controversial. One reason why some people are uncomfortable with animal-human chimeras is scientists aren't sure if the human genes would be in only the targeted organ. What if human genes developed in a sheep's brain? Would the sheep still be a sheep or would it be human? These are the kinds of ethical questions that scientists are trying to answer.

Assignment: Is it a good idea for scientists to create animal-human chimera to be used in medical research? Why or why not? Write a 200–250 word paragraph and use standard formatting. Give more than one reason for your answer. Upload your document by January 30, 5 P.M. No late assignments accepted.

Glossary

Hormone: a chemical in your body

Ethical: connected with principles of what is right and wrong

1. What is a chimera?

2. How could a chimera be used to help people?

3. What is controversial about using a chimera for medical research?

B. Now complete the chart. With a partner, discuss the missing information you have supplied.

Information	Explicit	Implicit
1. Structure	A paragraph	
2. Organization		I shouldn't take both sides.
3. Topic		This is not about the mythical creature called the "chimera."
4. Length	200–250 words	
5. Submission type		This must mean upload to the university's learning management system. The file type is not specified but the LMS only accepts .doc or .docx files. I don't need to print it.
6. Deadline	January 30, 5 P.M.	
7. Penalty		If I hand in the assignment late, I won't get credit. I need to be sure that I upload it on time.
8. Format	Standard formatting	

C. How can you be sure that you completely understand an assignment like the one above? What should you do if you don't completely understand an assignment? Discuss your ideas with a partner.

EXERCISE 2

A. Read the assignments and match each one with a description of the submission. Then discuss your answers with a partner.

Assignment

.... 1. Organ donation is a serious issue. There is a long waiting list of people who need transplants, and a shortage of donors. Explain how animal-human chimera could be used to address this shortage.

.... 2. Animal-human chimera could be created to grow an organ, such as a pancreas, for human transplants. However, it is possible that human genes will appear in other parts of the chimera. Discuss the concerns people might have about this.

.... 3. Organ donation is a serious issue. There is a long waiting list of people who need transplants, and a shortage of donors. Discuss possible solutions to this problem.

.... 4. Medical research is often publicly funded. Some people believe animal-human chimera research should be publicly funded while others disagree. Discuss both sides of this issue and give your own opinion.

Submission Description

a. reasons why people might not want to use organs from animal-human chimera for transplants

b. reasons why animal-human chimera research could benefit society and reasons why people might not approve of this research

c. explanation of how animal-human chimera could help solve organ donation problems and an explanation of how paying donors or their families could help solve organ donation problems

d. explanation of how animal-human chimera could help solve organ donation problems

B. Now that you understand how to assess the explicit and implicit information in an assignment, look at the assignment on the next page. Read the four submissions and decide which one best answers the assignment question. Use the checklists after the submissions to help you. An example has been done for you.

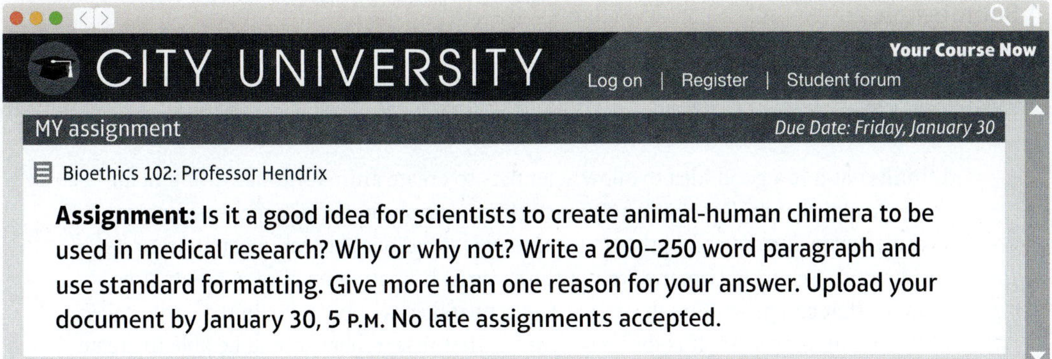

Submission 1:

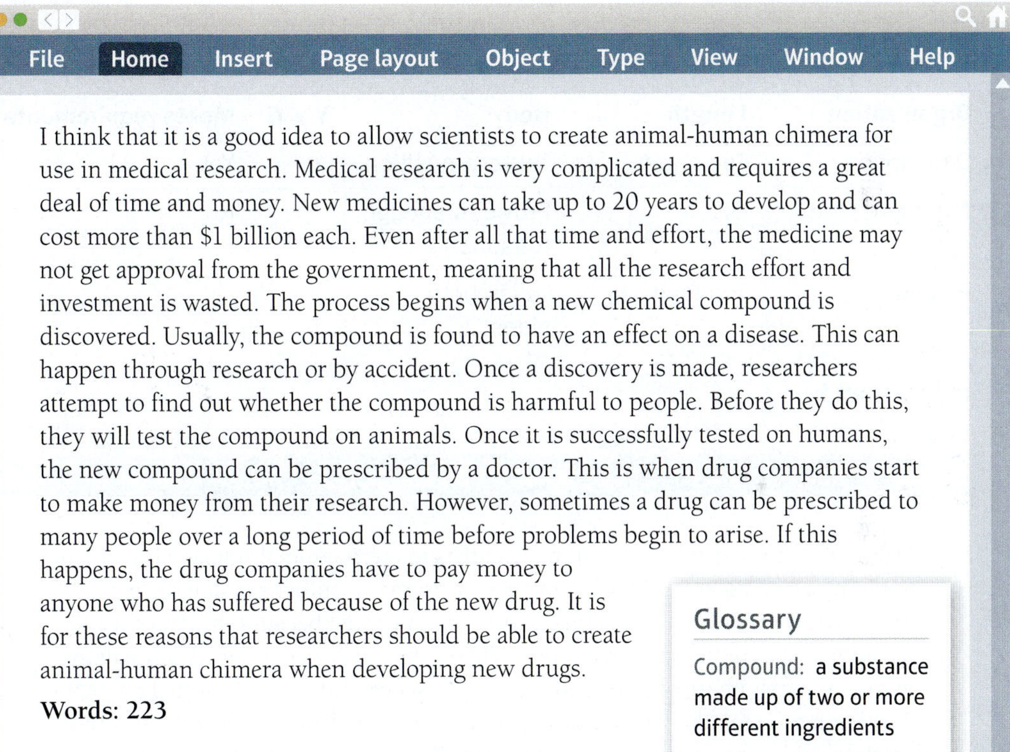

Submission 1 Checklist

Organization		Length		Body	Y / N	Meets requirements	
Description		Too short		Takes a position	Y	Yes	
Argument		OK	✗	Provides enough reasons	N	No	✗
Process	✗	Too long		Takes both sides	N		

Submission 2:

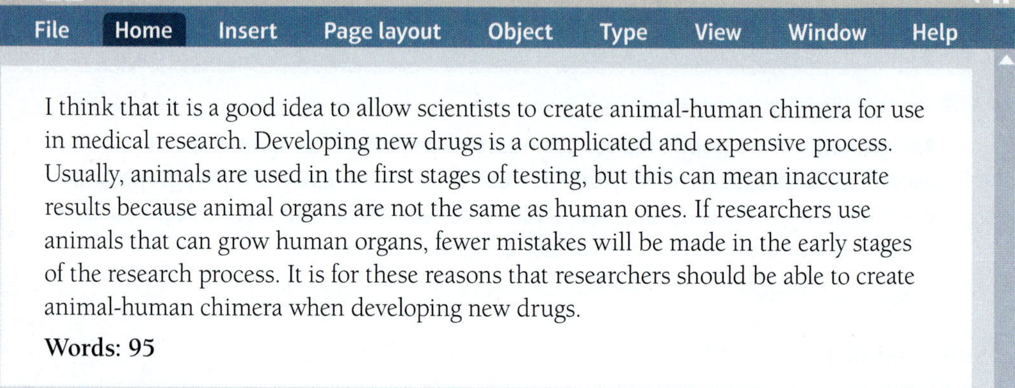

I think that it is a good idea to allow scientists to create animal-human chimera for use in medical research. Developing new drugs is a complicated and expensive process. Usually, animals are used in the first stages of testing, but this can mean inaccurate results because animal organs are not the same as human ones. If researchers use animals that can grow human organs, fewer mistakes will be made in the early stages of the research process. It is for these reasons that researchers should be able to create animal-human chimera when developing new drugs.

Words: 95

Submission 2 Checklist

Organization		Length		Body	Y / N	Meets requirements	
Description		Too short		Takes a position		Yes	
Argument		OK		Provides enough reasons		No	
Process		Too long		Takes both sides			

Submission 3:

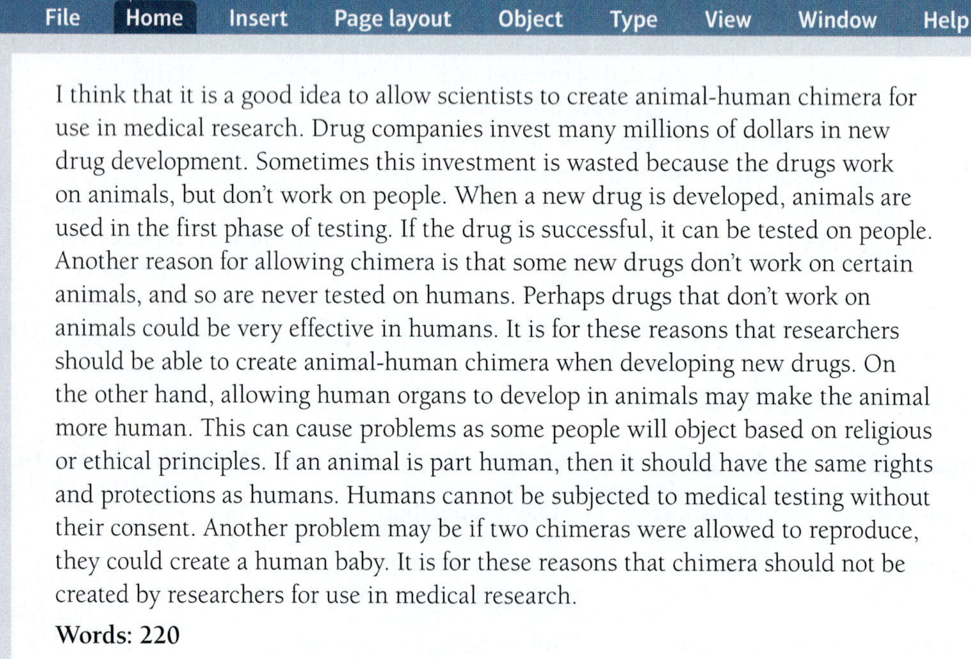

I think that it is a good idea to allow scientists to create animal-human chimera for use in medical research. Drug companies invest many millions of dollars in new drug development. Sometimes this investment is wasted because the drugs work on animals, but don't work on people. When a new drug is developed, animals are used in the first phase of testing. If the drug is successful, it can be tested on people. Another reason for allowing chimera is that some new drugs don't work on certain animals, and so are never tested on humans. Perhaps drugs that don't work on animals could be very effective in humans. It is for these reasons that researchers should be able to create animal-human chimera when developing new drugs. On the other hand, allowing human organs to develop in animals may make the animal more human. This can cause problems as some people will object based on religious or ethical principles. If an animal is part human, then it should have the same rights and protections as humans. Humans cannot be subjected to medical testing without their consent. Another problem may be if two chimeras were allowed to reproduce, they could create a human baby. It is for these reasons that chimera should not be created by researchers for use in medical research.

Words: 220

Submission 3 Checklist

Organization		Length		Body	Y / N	Meets requirements	
Description		Too short		Takes a position		Yes	
Argument		OK		Provides enough reasons		No	
Process		Too long		Takes both sides			

Submission 4:

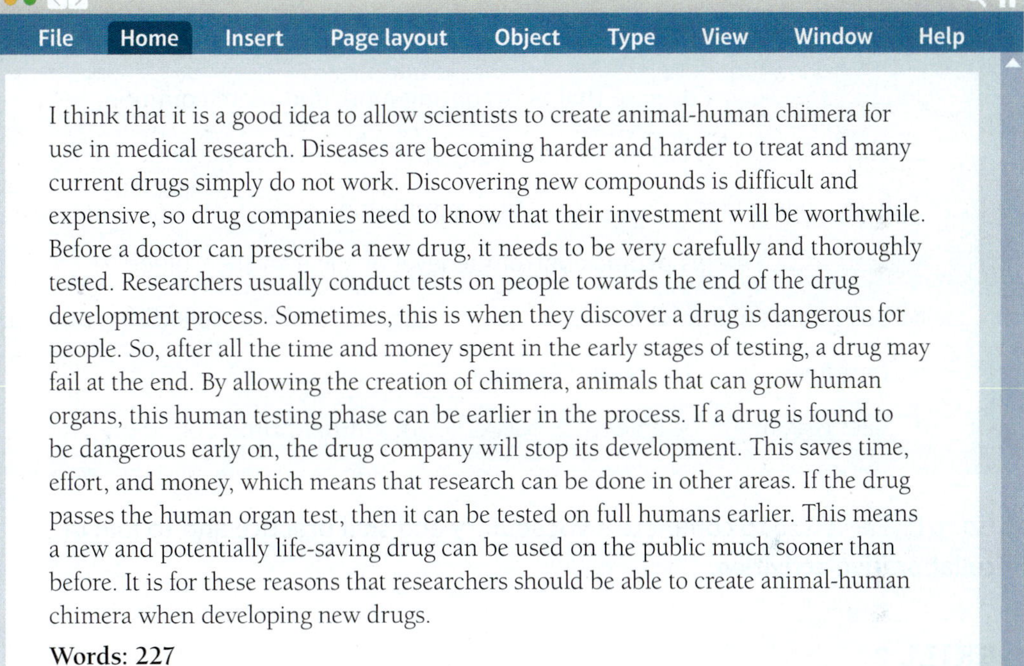

I think that it is a good idea to allow scientists to create animal-human chimera for use in medical research. Diseases are becoming harder and harder to treat and many current drugs simply do not work. Discovering new compounds is difficult and expensive, so drug companies need to know that their investment will be worthwhile. Before a doctor can prescribe a new drug, it needs to be very carefully and thoroughly tested. Researchers usually conduct tests on people towards the end of the drug development process. Sometimes, this is when they discover a drug is dangerous for people. So, after all the time and money spent in the early stages of testing, a drug may fail at the end. By allowing the creation of chimera, animals that can grow human organs, this human testing phase can be earlier in the process. If a drug is found to be dangerous early on, the drug company will stop its development. This saves time, effort, and money, which means that research can be done in other areas. If the drug passes the human organ test, then it can be tested on full humans earlier. This means a new and potentially life-saving drug can be used on the public much sooner than before. It is for these reasons that researchers should be able to create animal-human chimera when developing new drugs.

Words: 227

Submission 4 Checklist

Organization		Length		Body	Y / N	Meets requirements	
Description		Too short		Takes a position		Yes	
Argument		OK		Provides enough reasons		No	
Process		Too long		Takes both sides			

C. Compare your answers with a partner and discuss any differences. Decide together how you would change the submissions to meet the assignment criteria, referring to your checklists.

EXERCISE 3

Write your own answer to the assignment question. Include five words from the Vocabulary Check.

VOCABULARY CHECK

A. Review the items in Vocabulary Preview. Write their definitions and add examples. Use a dictionary if necessary.

B. Complete each sentence with a vocabulary item from the box.

controversial	create	diabetes	genes	insulin	organs	pancreas

1. .... is a disease that is becoming more and more common.
2. The .... is a part of the body that helps with digestion.
3. Parents pass their .... to their children.
4. .... helps people control the level of sugar in their blood.
5. Designing an animal is a .... idea that many people disagree with.
6. Your heart, liver, lungs, and skin are all ....
7. Scientists might be able to .... an animal-human chimera.

Go to MyEnglishLab to complete a vocabulary and skill practice and to join in collaborative activities.

SKILL 2

USING THE ACADEMIC WRITING PROCESS

WHY IT'S USEFUL When you are given a writing assignment, it can be difficult to know where to start. By using the academic writing process, you break the assignment down into separate, manageable steps that make it easier to proceed. Also, by following all the steps, you can significantly improve the quality of your writing.

A good academic writer knows that each step in the writing process requires different skills. The early stages require thinking skills. For example, you may need to read a lot to really understand your subject and you will need to sort out and organize your information and ideas. Later, after you have written your first draft, you will apply editing and proofreading skills to revise your work. Collaboration—sharing ideas with other students and giving feedback to each other—will also be important. Above all, remember that the writing process is not linear; in other words, one step does not always lead directly to the next. Sometimes you will have to go back a few steps and start again or go back to an earlier stage, as shown in the diagram below.

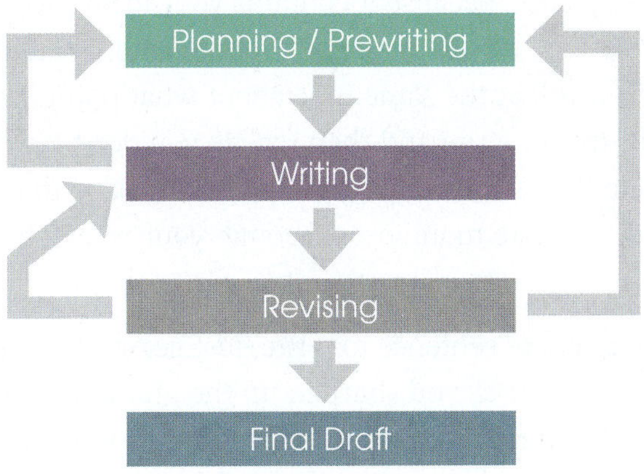

PART 1

Planning and prewriting

Before you actually start to write, it's important to follow the first step in the academic writing process: planning and prewriting. In this step, you will do more thinking and researching than writing. The writing you do will be mostly in the form of notes and outlines.

Step	When:	What you do:
Planning	Start this step as soon as you get a writing assignment.	Determine the purpose of the writing assignment by asking yourself: • What is the task? • Who is my audience? • What type of writing or structure is needed? • How will I find information about the topic?
Prewriting	Start this step after you have some ideas about how you will handle the writing task.	• Brainstorm all possible kinds of information you can provide; choose the best ideas from your brainstorming. • Do research on your topic. • Take notes while you read. • Make an outline of the ideas you will present in carrying out the writing assignment.

TIP

Brainstorming is a way to produce many ideas about a topic. It can be done individually, but is often done in a group. Group brainstorming can lead to more ideas because individuals can build on each other's ideas.

For more on using questions to guide your research, see Business and Design, Part 1.

Writing

Once you have finished planning and prewriting, you are ready to begin writing a first draft. The outline you prepared in the prewriting stage organizes your writing task and breaks it into smaller pieces. Because it contains your ideas grouped and presented in a logical order, you can concentrate on creating clear sentences and effective paragraphs, rather than trying to think at the same time about what points you need to make. Sometimes you will start to write and then realize you don't have enough ideas or examples to complete the task. When this happens, go back to the planning and prewriting stage and generate more ideas through your research.

Sometimes the hardest part of the assignment is starting the first draft. Don't wait until you've thought of the perfect sentence to write, just get started. You will go back and improve your sentences later as you sharpen up the grammar and vocabulary. Good writers don't expect the first draft to be perfect. You can improve a first draft, but you can't do anything if you don't have a first draft!

Look at the incomplete outline and early stages of a first draft written in response to the assignment shown. Notice how the outline and first draft are incomplete. The writer still needs to do more research to find support for the assignment. This will involve going back to the planning and prewriting stage.

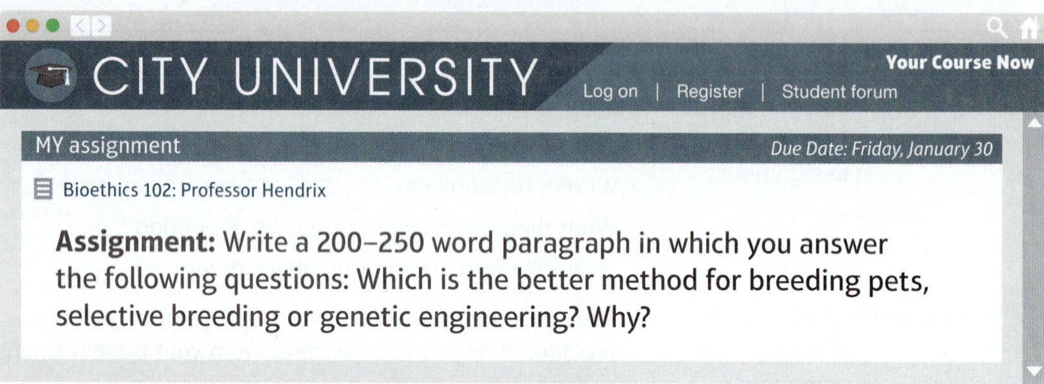

New pet designs: genetically engineered micropigs with a cat

Incomplete Paragraph Outline

I. Problems with selective breeding

  A. Can harm animals

  B. . . .

  C. . . .

II. Benefits of new genetic engineering techniques over selective breeding

  A. Healthier pets

  B. Faster

  C. . . .

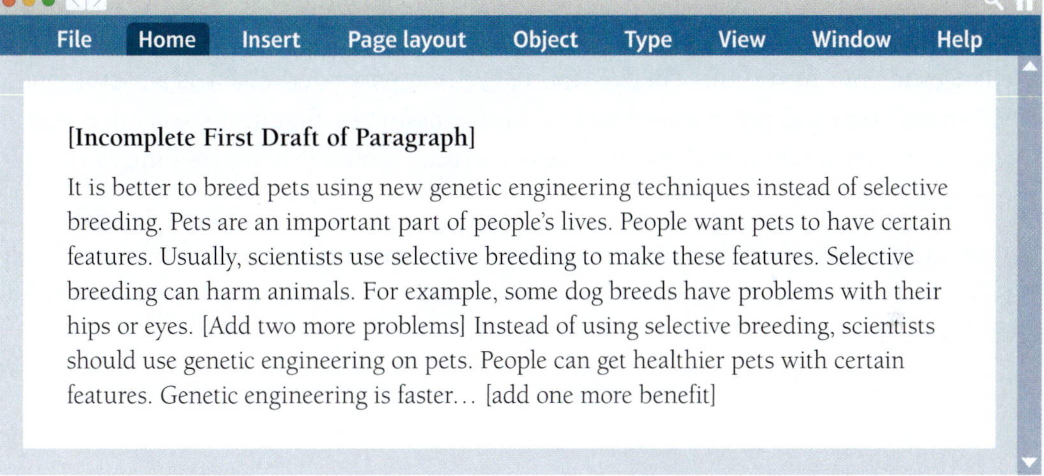

[Incomplete First Draft of Paragraph]

It is better to breed pets using new genetic engineering techniques instead of selective breeding. Pets are an important part of people's lives. People want pets to have certain features. Usually, scientists use selective breeding to make these features. Selective breeding can harm animals. For example, some dog breeds have problems with their hips or eyes. [Add two more problems] Instead of using selective breeding, scientists should use genetic engineering on pets. People can get healthier pets with certain features. Genetic engineering is faster… [add one more benefit]

Revising / editing

The final step in the academic writing process is revising and editing. It's a step you will need to repeat more than once.

Revise your ideas first, without worrying too much about grammar and vocabulary; there's no point fixing the grammar in a sentence or paragraph that is going to be changed or removed. Once you've dealt with ideas that don't work, you may need to add additional and more-effective ideas. If so, follow the planning and prewriting steps once more.

When you have included all the ideas you think you need, check and correct the grammar and make sure also that your vocabulary choices are accurate. Once this process is complete, you have another new draft, which may need to be revised and edited once more.

For more on proofreading effectively, see Chemical Engineering, Part 1.

Good writers go through this revision process as often as necessary before they submit their assignment. Remember, you don't necessarily have to revise the whole paper each time. You may choose instead to revise and edit each paragraph until you are happy with it, before moving on to the next. Many writers revise and edit the introduction and conclusion last. That way, they know that the first and last paragraphs match the final draft of the body of the paper.

For more on writing an introduction and a conclusion, see Zoology, Part 1.

Another important part of revising and editing is peer review. Peer review is when you show your draft to someone else, such as a classmate, and ask for feedback. Peer review is very useful at the revision stage because you will discover, before you submit the assignment for a grade, if someone else can follow your ideas. If your classmate has problems understanding what you mean, your instructor will too. Your classmate can offer advice about how to make your ideas clearer and then you can make changes in your next draft. There is another reason why peer review is a useful tool. When you read and provide feedback on your classmates' first drafts you are exposed to and become familiar with many styles of writing which you yourself might use in future assignments.

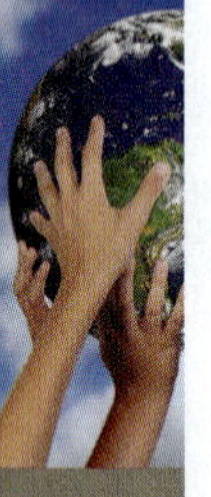

When you are satisfied that you can't make your paper any better (or when the deadline is so close that you risk losing points on your grade), save your document and hand it in as directed.

The chart below summarizes the final step—revising and editing—of the academic writing process.

Step	Focus on:	What you do:
Revising	Ideas	Ask yourself: • Do the ideas make sense? • Do the ideas fit together in an orderly, logical way?
Editing	Grammar Vocabulary	• Check for grammatical errors. • Make sure your vocabulary is precise.

EXERCISE 4

A. Look at this list of activities that make up the writing process. Decide which stage of the writing process they belong to. Write *PP* (planning and prewriting), *W* (writing), and *RE* (revising and editing).

.... 1. Writing the introduction

.... 2. Making sure proper nouns are capitalized

.... 3. Doing research in the library

.... 4. Talking with your classmates about how to answer the assignment question

.... 5. Saving the document, naming it correctly, and uploading it for the instructor to read

.... 6. Reading the assignment question

.... 7. Highlighting important sections in your reading

.... 8. Changing an adjective from the *-ing* form to the *-ed* form

.... 9. Reading and commenting on your classmate's paper

.... 10. Writing an outline of your paper

.... 11. Realizing that a word you've used is not academic and should be changed

.... 12. Writing a good topic sentence

B. Discuss the questions with a partner.

1. Are you used to following the various steps listed above in your own academic writing? Which steps are you already familiar with?
2. Are there others that you will need to start including in your writing? How can you do this?

VOCABULARY PREVIEW

These vocabulary items appear in the reading. Circle the ones you know. Put a question mark next to the ones you don't know.

process (n)	selective	breed (n, v)	desirable	produce (v)	research (n)

EXERCISE 5

A. Read the background paragraphs about selective breeding and genetically engineered animals and then read the assignment. Complete the chart and the related planning / prewriting questions that follow.

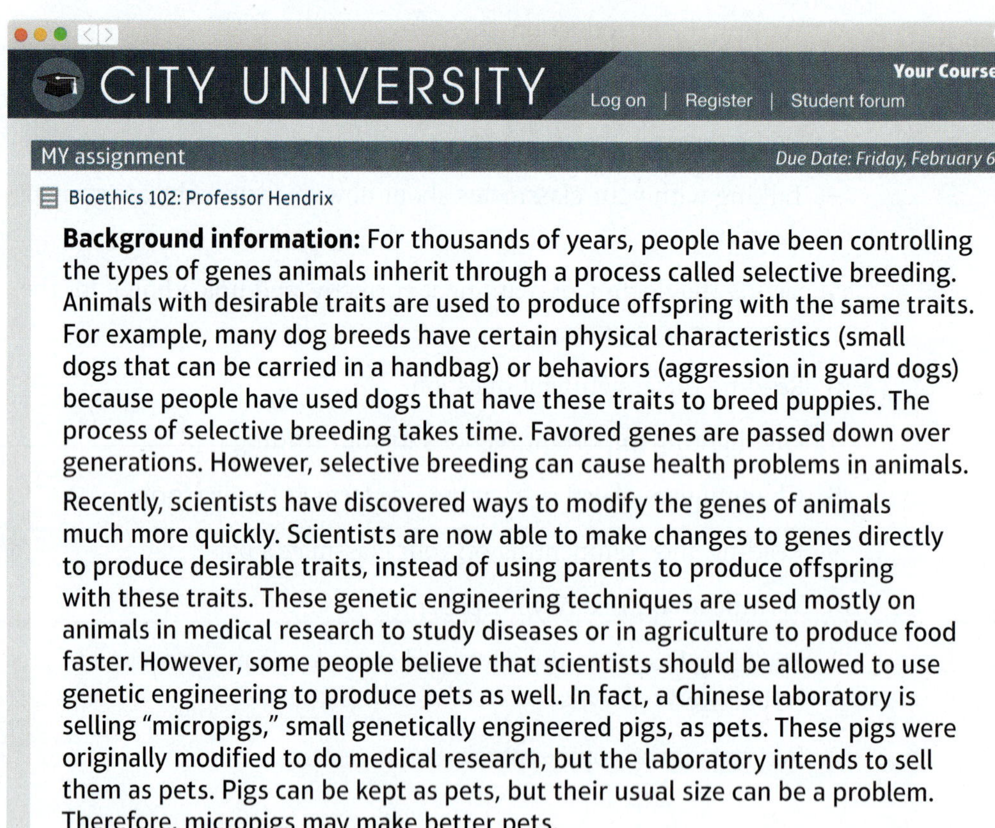

Background information: For thousands of years, people have been controlling the types of genes animals inherit through a process called selective breeding. Animals with desirable traits are used to produce offspring with the same traits. For example, many dog breeds have certain physical characteristics (small dogs that can be carried in a handbag) or behaviors (aggression in guard dogs) because people have used dogs that have these traits to breed puppies. The process of selective breeding takes time. Favored genes are passed down over generations. However, selective breeding can cause health problems in animals.

Recently, scientists have discovered ways to modify the genes of animals much more quickly. Scientists are now able to make changes to genes directly to produce desirable traits, instead of using parents to produce offspring with these traits. These genetic engineering techniques are used mostly on animals in medical research to study diseases or in agriculture to produce food faster. However, some people believe that scientists should be allowed to use genetic engineering to produce pets as well. In fact, a Chinese laboratory is selling "micropigs," small genetically engineered pigs, as pets. These pigs were originally modified to do medical research, but the laboratory intends to sell them as pets. Pigs can be kept as pets, but their usual size can be a problem. Therefore, micropigs may make better pets.

Assignment: Write a 200–250 word paragraph in which you answer the following questions: Which method is better to breed pets, selective breeding or genetic engineering? Why?

Glossary

Trait: a characteristic of someone. A trait can be physical, such as hair color, or behavioral, such as cats cleaning themselves

Offspring: children of people or young of animals

Modify: to make small changes to something in order to make it better or more suitable

THE WRITING PROCESS: STEP 1 PLANNING / PREWRITING	
Planning Questions	**Answers**
1. What is the task?	
2. Who is my audience?	
3. What kind of writing is it?	
4. How am I going to find out more about the writing topic?	
5. What is my position on this topic?	

B. Read the assignment again. Write down your answers to the questions, referring to online sources for any additional information you need. Then take turns confirming the information with a partner.

1. What is selective breeding? Why is it used? How does it work?

   ....

2. What is genetic engineering? How is it different from selective breeding?

   ....

3. Why do scientists genetically modify the genes of animals?

   ....

4. What are some problems with each method?

   ....

C. Work in a small group. Decide which method you favor for breeding pets: selective breeding or genetic engineering. For 10 minutes, brainstorm as many reasons as you can to support your answer. Write down all ideas, even if they seem silly and add everyone's ideas to the chart.

Why .... is a better method to breed pets

D. How did brainstorming help you get more ideas about the topic? What is the next step in the prewriting stage? Share your ideas with a partner.

EXERCISE 6

A. Write a 200–250 word paragraph to answer to the assignment question. Include five words from the Vocabulary Check.

B. Work with a partner. Read each other's paragraph and complete the peer review form.

Questions	Yes	No	Notes
Does the writing address the assignment task?	☐	☐	
Is the structure of the writing clear?	☐	☐	
Can you identify the writer's position on this topic?	☐	☐	
Are the ideas clear and easy to understand?	☐	☐	
Do the ideas fit together in an orderly, logical way?	☐	☐	
Are any ideas missing?	☐	☐	
Is the vocabulary precise?	☐	☐	
Are there any grammatical errors?	☐	☐	
Are there any other comments you would like to make?	☐	☐	

C. Discuss each other's comments and then revise your draft.

VOCABULARY CHECK

A. Review the items in Vocabulary Preview. Write their definitions and add examples. Use a dictionary if necessary.

B. Choose the sentence that correctly expresses the meaning of each underlined vocabulary item.

1. a. Selective means to be careful about the things you choose.

   b. Selective means to be careless about the things you choose.

2. a. A breed is a particular type of gene.

   b. A breed is a particular type of animal.

3. a. When there is something you want, it is <u>desirable</u>.

   b. When there is something that you don't want, it is <u>desirable</u>.

4. a. Doing things in the correct order is a <u>process</u>.

   b. Doing things in any order is a <u>process</u>.

5. a. Carrying out an experiment is a type of <u>research</u>.

   b. Telling someone what you know is a type of <u>research</u>.

6. a. To <u>produce</u> is to buy something.

   b. To <u>produce</u> is to create something.

Go to MyEnglishLab to complete a vocabulary and skill practice and to join in collaborative activities.

INTEGRATED SKILLS

TAKING EFFECTIVE NOTES

WHY IT'S USEFUL Being able to take good notes is an essential skill for a student in higher education. You will be expected to read a lot of material covering different subject areas and to complete assignments based on what you have read. By reviewing your notes, rather than rereading course material, you save time and effort writing an assignment or studying for a test. In addition, taking notes increases your understanding of the content.

There are several ways to take notes. Some are quick, but are less effective. Others take longer, but will be more useful. The type of note-taking you do will depend largely on the type of reading you are doing and how you might need to use the information later on.

Highlighting

This is probably the quickest form of note-taking. All you need to do is highlight, or even underline, areas of the text that you think are useful. This can be done on paper, or on an electronic copy of the text. You can make highlighting even more useful by using different colors to show where different ideas occur in a text. Blue could be used to highlight facts and yellow could be used to identify examples, for instance. Additionally, different colors can be used to keep track of different topics in the same text. Yellow could be used to highlight uses of genetically modified plants and green could be used to highlight uses of genetically modified animals.

The problem with this form of note-taking is that you can end up highlighting too much. Also, you will still need to refer to the original text later on. For good notes (see below), highlighting usually is the first stage in the process. Look at the example.

> People have been changing the genetic makeup of plants and animals for centuries through a process known as selective breeding. When a plant shows a trait that is useful, such as a brighter red rose, it is used to breed other roses that are bright red. Other, less bright red roses are left to die. The same idea can be applied to animals. If a dog shows a lot of aggression, it may be bred with another aggressive dog to make a dog that is useful as an attack dog.

Glossary

Aggression: angry or violent behavior or feelings

Margin notes

Writing notes in the white space around a text, or writing comments in an electronic document, is more effective than simple highlighting. When you write questions, comments, or references to other texts, you are engaged with the reading. The more engaged you are, the more effective your notes will be and the more you will remember.

However, taking margin notes, like highlighting or underlining, requires you to refer back to the original reading. The notes can also get quite messy on a page. This lack of organization may make it difficult to use the notes later on without having to reread the article. Look at the example.

> TALENs and zinc fingers are methods of changing genes in plants and animals that were developed in the 20th century. They have been used successfully in some species, but not in others.
>
> *I need to know more about "TALENs" and "zinc fingers"*

Creating an outline

Outlining is a more time-consuming, but more effective form of note-taking. When you create an outline, you show the ideas in the reading in an organized way. As a note-taker, you may at times choose to organize the ideas in a different order from the way they are presented.

To create an outline, identify the main ideas of the reading. These will become the headings in your outline. Under each heading, write down the key related points.

While outlining will take longer, it should save you from having to read an entire article again. Creating an outline is particularly useful when you need to use an article as the basis for writing an assignment or to study for a test. Look at the example outline.

I. Types of gene editing
- A. Selective breeding
  - 1. Oldest form of gene editing
  - 2. Used on both plants and animals
- B. TALENs
- C. Zinc Fingers
- D. CRISPR

Outlines use a combination of numbers and letters to show the relationship between the ideas. The more specific the information, the further right it goes. The level of detail you include in your outline depends on how you will use the information.

TIP

When you write down key points from an article to create an outline, use your own words. Paraphrase the author's ideas rather than copying directly the language of the original text. Using your own words helps you understand the ideas better and helps you avoid accidental plagiarism when you use information from your outline in your own writing.

For more on paraphrasing ideas, see Business and Design, Part 2.

VOCABULARY PREVIEW

These vocabulary items appear in the reading. Circle the ones you know. Put a question mark next to the ones you don't know.

edit	alter	species	cell	agriculture
technique	DNA	protein	potential	complex

EXERCISE 7

A. Read the article about CRISPR, a method of editing genes, and study the related diagrams. Then answer the comprehension questions.

APPLICATIONS OF CRISPR

1 CRISPR, a gene editing technique introduced in 2012, is taking biology by storm. Researchers are already using CRISPR to alter the DNA of many different species. This new technique may allow biologists to make more accurate changes to genes more quickly than ever before. Plus, this technique is far cheaper than other gene-editing methods.

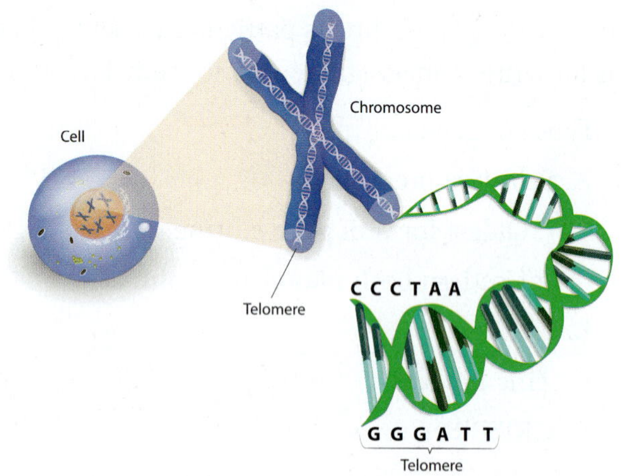

2 CRISPR is a form of gene editing, a practice where scientists change an organism's genes at the molecular level. Selective breeding accomplishes the same thing, but gene editing is faster because you don't need to wait years to breed generations. CRISPR is special because, unlike other forms of gene editing, such as TALENs and zinc fingers, it allows precise segments of DNA to be changed or removed, even in living organisms. For example, scientists know what causes some diseases, such as cystic fibrosis. Using CRISPR, they could target the exact part of a specific gene which causes the disease and repair it. This could wipe out the disease in just a few years.

3 To modify a gene using CRISPR, scientists need three things: RNA, which is similar to DNA, but has a different job; a protein called Cas9; and new DNA. When scientists want to edit the broken gene, they inject RNA into the cell. The RNA goes to the gene which the scientists want to edit and carries the protein with it. The protein makes a cut, like scissors, in the precise part of the gene that is broken. Then scientists add new DNA to the gene. The new DNA has the correct information and joins the cell where the cut was made. The gene repairs itself.

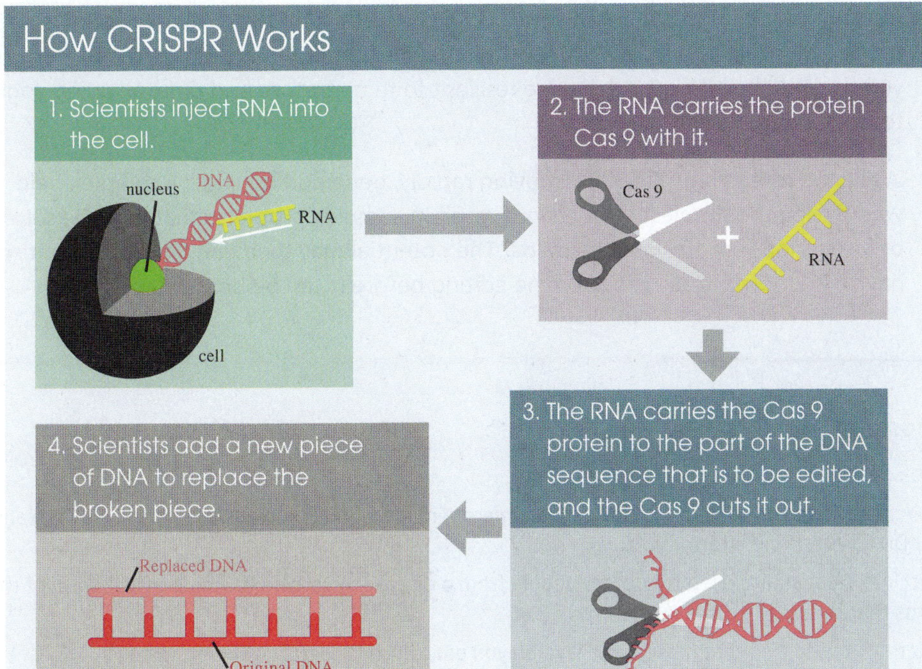

4 CRISPR has potential benefits when it comes to agriculture. Gene editing can be used to improve disease resistance in crops or livestock. Other forms of gene editing have already been used to make tomatoes stay fresh and help pigs fight respiratory disease. However, CRISPR is much faster and cheaper. Plant and animal breeders could rapidly respond to a crisis. For example, the problems facing honeybees may be solvable using CRISPR.

5 CRISPR's ease of use in agriculture worries some environmental advocates, though. There is a widespread fear that a modified plant or animal could accidently become a kind of invasive species, harming ecosystems. Because of this, researchers are careful not to release modified species before they have been fully studied.

6 Another use of CRISPR is in the development of vaccines. Since vaccines are often made using chicken eggs, people with egg allergies cannot get them. It may be possible to remove allergens from eggs by using CRISPR. Only a tiny amount of a chicken's DNA results in the proteins which cause egg allergies. Individual eggs can be edited for use in vaccines. While this might seem reasonable on a small scale, it could be much more efficient to alter the entire species, or at least one particular breed of chicken.

(Continued)

7 Another area that may benefit from CRISPR is the dairy industry. Dairy products, such as yogurt, could have a longer shelf life. Through CRISPR editing, the bacteria in yogurt could be altered to be more resilient to temperature and time, allowing yogurt to last longer in the refrigerator.

8 While the research on CRISPR is moving rapidly, gene editing is still a complex field where even the simplest of questions result in complex problems that must be solved before serious progress can be made. The potential may seem limitless, but scientists have a lot more to learn about gene editing before it can be broadly applied.

Glossary

Biology: the scientific study of living things

RNA: This is short for "ribonucleic acid," a molecule made from amino acids. It acts like a messenger for DNA by carrying information.

Vaccine: a substance used to protect people from a disease. A vaccine contains a weak form of the virus that causes the disease.

Allergy: a condition that makes you ill when you eat, touch, or breathe something

Dairy: made from milk

1. What is CRISPR?

....

2. What is it used for?

....

....

3. What are the advantages and disadvantages of using CRISPR?

....

....

B. Reread the article, looking specifically for information to help you answer this writing prompt: *Explain what gene editing is, especially CRISPR, and the best application of this technology.* Highlight or underline the information you think is important for this task.

C. Work with a partner. Compare the information you highlighted and discuss why you chose to highlight it. If you find a part of the text that causes confusion, write a question or comment in the margin. Here's an example from the last sentence in paragraph 4:

For example, the problems facing honeybees may be solvable using CRISPR.	What is the honeybee problem and why is it important? How can CRISPR solve it? I need to find more information on this.

D. Now you have a general understanding of the article. For example, you know that CRISPR is a kind of gene editing and that gene editing means making changes to a plant's or an animal's genes. Read the article again, and fill in the missing information. Then compare your answers with a partner.

I. Advantages of CRISPR compared to ....
   A. More accurate
   B. ....
   C. Less ....
II. How CRISPR works
   A. .... goes into a damaged gene
   B. .... cuts the broken part
   C. New DNA ....
      1. Correct information
      2. ....
III. Possible ....
   A. Agriculture
      1. Resist .... – tomatoes / pigs
      2. Respond to crisis – ....
   B. People
      1. .... – cystic fibrosis
      2. ....
      3. Improve shelf life of food – ....
IV. .... with CRISPR
   A. ....
      ....
   B. Many unknown problems

VOCABULARY CHECK

A. Review the items in Vocabulary Preview. Write their definitions and add examples. Use a dictionary if necessary.

B. Complete the paragraph with vocabulary items from the box.

agriculture	cell	DNA	potential	species
altered	complex	edit	protein	technique

CRISPR is a new .... that can be used to .... genes. Cas9 is a .... which is injected into a .... using RNA. The use of CRISPR can bring many .... benefits. For example, it can be used to make advances in .... by changing certain .... of tomatoes. However, the use of gene editing may cause .... problems because the .... that is .... by CRISPR is passed on to the next generation.

Go to MyEnglishLab to complete a vocabulary and skill practice and to join in collaborative activities.

LANGUAGE SKILL

USING *-ING* AND *-ED* ADJECTIVES CORRECTLY

WHY IT'S USEFUL Adjectives, used well, can help to make a paper more interesting and informative by adding descriptive detail. The correct use of *-ing* and *-ed* adjectives is essential because these adjectives are commonly used in academic writing.

Go to MyEnglishLab for the Language Skill presentation and practice.

VOCABULARY STRATEGY

UNDERSTANDING REGISTER

WHY IT'S USEFUL Awareness of the register of words and expressions—the context in which they are commonly used—is an important skill that helps you, as a writer, to pick the right words for the right occasion.

Language register changes depending on the situation. For example, you use some words in everyday English that you wouldn't use in academic English. Neutral words and expressions can be used in all kinds of situations while others are appropriate only in some contexts.

One way to understand register is to think about greetings. You might say, "Hey, what's up?" to your roommate, but you wouldn't want to say that to your biology professor. The register is too informal. Instead, you might say, in a more formal register, "Hello, how are you?"

Register isn't limited to spoken English. In written English, for example, you might send a text message or a chat to your friend in language you wouldn't use for your research assignment. In academic English, a neutral or formal register is required. Look at these general guidelines.

GENERAL GUIDELINES

- Do not use contractions – a short form of one or more words. Instead, write out the word(s) in full.

  it's → it is

  don't → do not

- Do not use written forms of spoken English. Sometimes in informal writing people write words the way they are pronounced. Do not do this in academic English.

  gonna → going to

  wanna → want to

- Do not use informal words. Replace these with a neutral or formal word. There are many examples of informal words and replacements.

  There are a lot of ways to use CRISPR. → There are many ways to use CRISPR.

  Genes carry lots of information. → Genes carry a great deal / a large amount of information.

  CRISPR research is really expensive. → CRISPR research is extremely expensive.

  The results were awesome! → The results were excellent.

  The price went up. → The price increased.

Technical English

Another category of register is technical English. There are many types of technical English. These are specialized words that belong to certain subjects or that have a specific meaning within a specialized field. These words are often called *terms*. One example of a technical term is *CRISPR*. It is a word that biologists would know because it is related to their work. However, a person without specialized knowledge would not know what this term means. Did you know it before you started this unit?

When deciding whether or not to use technical English in your writing, think about your readers. If they share technical knowledge in a specialized field or subject, using technical words is appropriate. However, if your readers do not share this type of knowledge, use technical English carefully. Do not use technical words unless there is no better expression to use. When you use a technical word for a general audience, do not expect your readers to know its meaning. Instead, always provide a short definition the first time you use it.

Being aware of register

When you are learning a new word or expression, note any information that is provided about register. For example, learner's dictionaries often point out if a word is only used in formal or informal registers. Learner's dictionaries also point out if a word is technical. For example, if you look up the word *register*, some learner's dictionaries include the term *linguistics*. This means the word *register* is a technical term used in the field of linguistics, the study of language. Noting down this kind of information will help you understand when to use a word, and when not to use it.

Try to notice different registers. When reading a text that comes from an academic source, look for more formal language. When reading a text that comes from a less academic source, like a magazine or a blog, look for examples of more informal language. When reading information about a specialized subject, try to identify examples of technical English. Building awareness of register takes time, but it is time well spent because you will know which words to use in different situations.

EXERCISE 8

A. What registers would you expect to find in each type of writing listed below? Write *N* (neutral), *F* (formal), *I* (informal), and *T* (technical). There may be more than one answer for each one.

.... 1. An email to a professor

.... 2. A newspaper article

.... 3. An email to a family member

.... 4. An academic essay

.... 5. A biology laboratory report

.... 6. A cover letter with a job application

.... 7. A magazine article

.... 8. A finance report

.... 9. A text to your roommate

.... 10. A textbook

B. Match each formal word or expression to a neutral or informal word or expression.

	Formal	Neutral or Informal
....	1. however	a. let go
....	2. increase	b. but
....	3. alter	c. bad
....	4. a great deal of	d. smart
....	5. completely	e. find out
....	6. children	f. go up
....	7. release	g. totally
....	8. negative	h. lots of
....	9. discover	i. change
....	10. intelligent	j. kids

C. Read the email from a student to his biology professor. It is written in the wrong register. Find six places where the register should be changed by using neutral, formal, or technical words or expressions. Rewrite the email in the correct register.

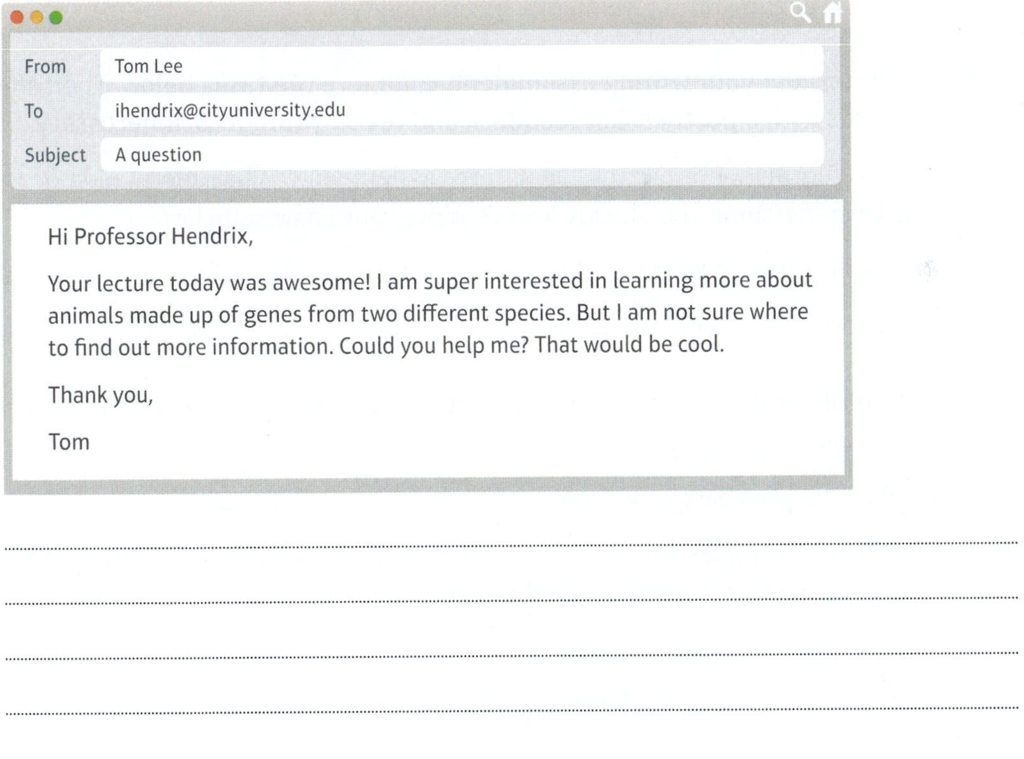
From Tom Lee

To ihendrix@cityuniversity.edu

Subject A question

Hi Professor Hendrix,

Your lecture today was awesome! I am super interested in learning more about animals made up of genes from two different species. But I am not sure where to find out more information. Could you help me? That would be cool.

Thank you,

Tom

....

....

....

....

....

APPLY YOUR SKILLS

WHY IT'S USEFUL By applying the skills you have learned in this unit, you will be able to assess a writing assignment and to follow the steps of the academic writing process to respond appropriately and fully, using suitable vocabulary.

ASSIGNMENT

Plan a 250–300 word paragraph on the advantages and disadvantages of using gene editing in people. What are the benefits and what are the possible ethical problems? Your paragraph should be typed and follow standard formatting guidelines.

BEFORE YOU WRITE

A. Before you begin your assignment, discuss these questions with one or more students.

1. Do your genes make you who you are?
2. Would you want to edit your genes if you had a disability?
3. Would you want to edit your children's genes to prevent an inherited condition from developing or to give them a special ability?

B. As you consider your writing assignment, complete the tasks below. Then share your ideas with a partner. Get feedback and revise your ideas, if necessary.

1. What information is clearly stated in the assignment? What information does your instructor assume you already know? Write your answers below.
   a. explicit information: ....
   b. implicit information: ....
2. Think about the possible applications of gene editing you have read about for use in people.
   a. List the possible applications: ....
   b. What techniques will you use to generate ideas about the advantages and disadvantages of using gene editing in people? ....
   ....
   c. Use the organizer on the next page to help you organize your ideas.

Advantages	Disadvantages

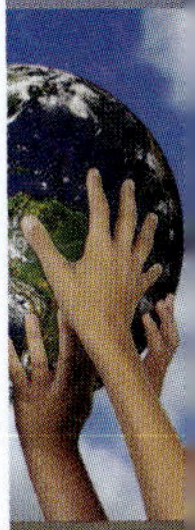

3. How will you find out more information about gene editing in people? How will you take notes?

....

....

C. Review the Unit Skills Summary on the next page. As you plan the writing task, apply the skills you learned in this unit.

UNIT SKILLS SUMMARY

Understand an assignment

- Make sure that you understand the explicit and implicit information concerning the desired structure, organization, and topic as well as the expected format.

Use the academic writing process

- Take a structured, step-by-step approach to writing an academic essay, working your way through the planning and prewriting, writing, and revising and editing stages.

Take effective notes

- Take effective notes, writing and organizing the important information from your reading.

Write *-ing* and *-ed* adjectives correctly

- Use *-ing* and *-ed* adjectives correctly, distinguishing between each form.

Understand register

- Recognize that some words are neutral, informal, formal, or technical.

THINKING CRITICALLY

As you think about your assignment, use the information from the earlier sections of the unit to answer the questions. Discuss your answers with one or more students and revise your ideas if necessary.

1. How would you compare the use of gene editing in agriculture and the use of gene editing in people?
2. Use an example to explain why a person might want to use gene editing on himself or herself. Why might someone else object to this use of gene editing?

THINKING VISUALLY

Look at the image and discuss with a partner how it might relate to human gene editing. Does it show an advantage or a disadvantage?

"Diversity is good. Pass it down."

THINKING ABOUT LANGUAGE

Read the film review and underline the adjectives ending in *-ed* or *-ing*. Highlight technical words, that is, words that are only used in the world of the movie. Then discuss with a partner how the use of *-ing* and *-ed* adjectives and technical vocabulary makes the film review more interesting.

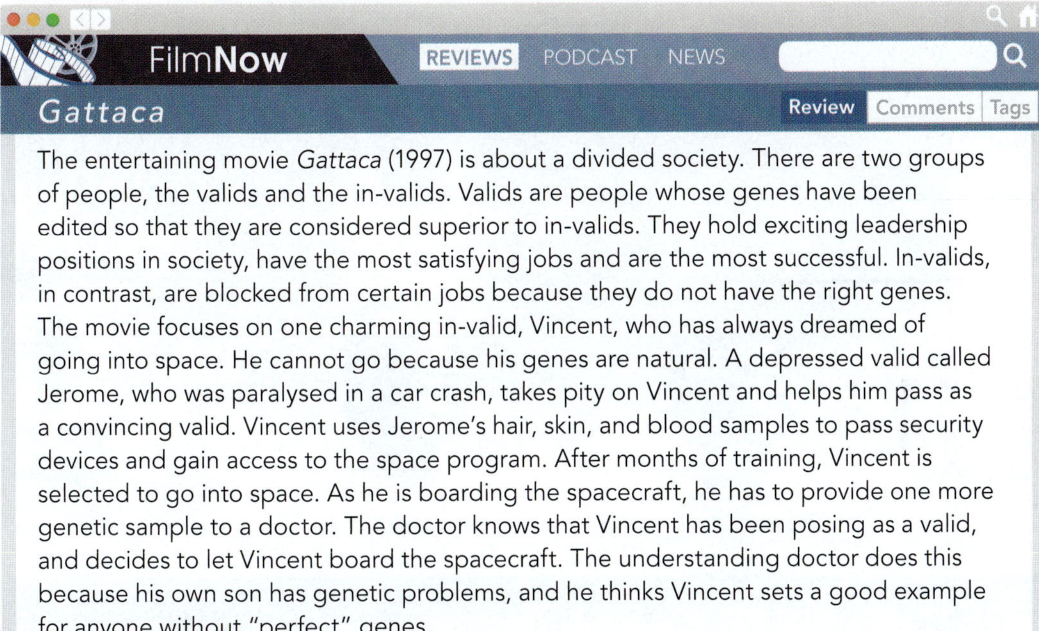

The entertaining movie *Gattaca* (1997) is about a divided society. There are two groups of people, the valids and the in-valids. Valids are people whose genes have been edited so that they are considered superior to in-valids. They hold exciting leadership positions in society, have the most satisfying jobs and are the most successful. In-valids, in contrast, are blocked from certain jobs because they do not have the right genes. The movie focuses on one charming in-valid, Vincent, who has always dreamed of going into space. He cannot go because his genes are natural. A depressed valid called Jerome, who was paralysed in a car crash, takes pity on Vincent and helps him pass as a convincing valid. Vincent uses Jerome's hair, skin, and blood samples to pass security devices and gain access to the space program. After months of training, Vincent is selected to go into space. As he is boarding the spacecraft, he has to provide one more genetic sample to a doctor. The doctor knows that Vincent has been posing as a valid, and decides to let Vincent board the spacecraft. The understanding doctor does this because his own son has genetic problems, and he thinks Vincent sets a good example for anyone without "perfect" genes.

WRITE

A. Look again at the writing assignment and at your lists from Before You Write and Thinking Visually on the advantages and disadvantages of using gene editing in people. Think about your plans for finding additional information.

B. Research the topic and take effective notes. Discuss your notes and ideas with others and make any needed adjustments.

C. Write an outline of your paragraph.

BEYOND THE ASSIGNMENT

Write a well-researched, 250–300 word paragraph on the advantages and disadvantages of using gene editing in people. What are the benefits and what are the possible ethical problems? Your paragraph should be typed and follow standard formatting guidelines. Use all the skills you learned in this unit.

Go to MyEnglishLab to watch Professor Greely's concluding video and to complete a self-assessment.

BUSINESS AND DESIGN

Idea Development

UNIT PROFILE

Managing how people feel about a company or product is called brand management. The brand is the image, logo, and experience that you connect to the company. Brand management is not an exact science. Sometimes things can go very wrong, and when they do, the costs can be enormous. Understanding who your customers are, what they want, and how much they are willing to pay for your brand are all important parts of brand management.

OUTCOMES

- Use questions to guide your research
- Build paragraphs and connect ideas
- Identify topic sentences
- Use conjunctions to connect ideas
- Create a vocabulary journal

You will plan a 350–500 word essay about how companies can successfully manage their brands when problems occur.

For more about **BUSINESS AND DESIGN**, see 2 3.
See also [R] and [OC] **BUSINESS AND DESIGN** 1 2 3.

PART 1

GETTING STARTED

Go to MyEnglishLab to watch Juli Sherry's introductory video and to complete a self-assessment.

Discuss these questions with a partner or a group.

1. Brands are everywhere. Which brands are you most familiar with? What's the difference between a product and a brand? What's the difference between a company and a brand?
2. Companies spend millions of dollars every year to establish, maintain, and promote their brands. Why are brands so important? Are you "loyal" to brands?
3. The instructor suggests that brand strategy helps businesses develop a stronger relationship with their customers. Do you agree? Why or why not?

SKILL 1

USING QUESTIONS TO GUIDE YOUR RESEARCH

WHY IT'S USEFUL When you are presented with an academic writing assignment on an unfamiliar topic, asking good, appropriate questions at the outset can guide your reading and research as well as the writing process itself. This approach helps you to proceed efficiently and to produce a well-organized, accurate piece of work.

As you have learned, when you are presented with a writing assignment on an unfamiliar topic, there are key steps to follow in the research process:

For more on understanding an assignment and using the academic writing process, see Bioethics, Part 1.

Step 1: You will need to read widely to get a basic understanding of the subject. Your reading will help you discover the technical or specialist vocabulary that is needed, as well as the key issues, arguments, or themes that may be relevant to your assignment.

Step 2: As you become more knowledgeable about your topic, you will begin to take a position and, in turn, narrow your search so that you can look for evidence in the form of examples, facts, and opinions, to support what you want to say.

Step 3: Depending on the assignment, you may also need to find evidence for your arguments and counterarguments. Sometimes you will find so many sources of information that you will need to decide which sources to keep and which to reject.

Step 4: As you write, you will need to integrate the information you have found into your own arguments, using your sources to support what you want to say in a clear, coherent manner.

Asking good questions, which will have different functions at different stages of your research, is key to preparing a high-quality written assignment. The question process will usually be essential at the first two steps of the research process—the focus of our discussion here—but may also be important at later stages of your research, depending on the assignment.

Using questions to remember and understand information

Take a look at the assignment that a student must prepare for her business class:

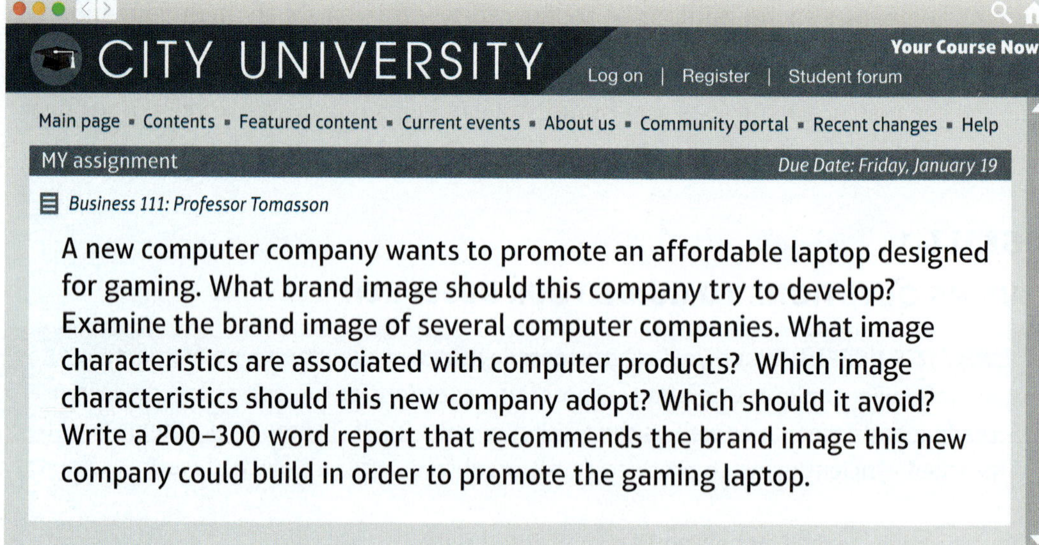

To do the assignment well, the student needs, as a first step, to become more knowledgeable about some of the key terms and themes. She can do this by thinking about what she needs to know and forming questions to direct her research. Her initial questions will help her (1) remember assignment-related information that she already knows and (2) comprehend the assignment's terms and themes, which she may be less familiar with. Look at the questions on the next page that she developed and at the responses she provided in her notes. Are there any other questions you think she should have asked? Could you answer all of her questions, or would you need to do some research—as the student herself did?

For more on identifying key words, see Business and Design, Part 2.

Glossary

Customize: to change something to make it more suitable for a particular person or purpose

Skill	Example questions	Student notes
Recall: This type of question helps you remember basic information.	What is a brand? What is a brand image? Which technology companies make laptops?	Brand = The name a company gives to a product it makes Brand image = The idea or impression customers have about a particular brand Companies = Apple®, Lenovo®, Dell®
Comprehension: This type of question helps you understand information.	What brand image does each company have? What image characteristics are similar between the companies? Which are different?	Brand Image Apple: Associated with sense of style; innovation; expensive products Lenovo: Flexible products; fast at adapting to new technology; less expensive products Dell: Customized products; good relationship with customers

Using questions to apply and organize information

By reading and researching, the student has answered her initial questions and has begun to learn more about her topic. She is now ready to apply her new information specifically to the assignment and to examine and organize it so that it will be easier to use in her writing. See below the two types of questions she can ask at this stage. How many of her questions can you answer? As you can see, the student has begun to answer some of the questions in her notes.

Skill	Example questions	Student notes
Application: This type of question helps you use what you have learned in a different way.	What kind of image would best apply to a new gaming laptop? Which of the image characteristics of existing brands could apply to the new laptop? Which of the image characteristics should be avoided?	Important image characteristics Less expensive—gamers may not have a lot of money to spend on the product.
Examination: This type of question helps you analyze information.	What causes a computer brand to be successful? What are some image characteristics of successful computer brands? What image characteristics might lead to a branding failure?	Successful computer brands Apple's brand image of having stylish products contributes to its success—its customers care about looking stylish.

Now that the student has asked good questions and sought answers at different stages, she can build on what she has learned and her own assessment of the information, responding to the assignment with an appropriate level of depth and supporting her suggestions with examples. She can also propose alternative solutions and give reasons why they will or will not work.

EXERCISE 1

A. Read the assignment. Then follow the directions to ask initial questions that can guide your research, using the Ford Edsel—marketed in the 1950s—as an example of a failed product.

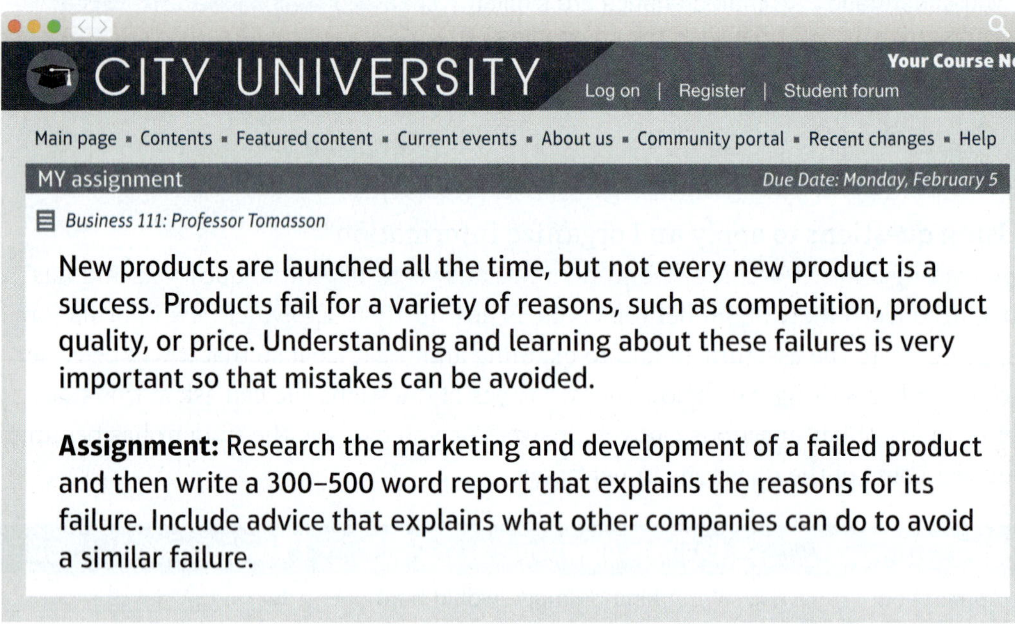

Now, decide what you need to know about the failure of the marketing and development of the Ford Edsel. Write down three recall questions and three comprehension questions to guide the initial stage of your research.

B. Compare your questions with a partner. Make any necessary changes in your lists.

VOCABULARY PREVIEW

These vocabulary items appear in the reading. Circle the ones you know. Put a question mark next to the ones you don't know.

launch (v)	rival (n)	advanced	recession
executive	conduct (v)	deliver	

EXERCISE 2

A. As part of your research, read the blog explaining the failure of the Ford Edsel. Then answer the comprehension questions.

The Ford Edsel

Few people have heard about the Ford Edsel. Even fewer decided to purchase one when the vehicle was launched in 1957. Why was this, and what lessons are there for today's branding executives?

Ford was one of the "big three" motor companies in the United States, along with General Motors and Chrysler (now known as Fiat Chrysler), and competition between them was fierce. Each company produced models that served a particular section of the market. For instance, the Lincoln® brand of Ford vehicles was aimed at people who wanted luxury cars and could afford to pay for them. The Cadillac® brand, from General Motors, was aimed at the same people.

In the 1950s, Ford was losing ground to its two main rivals and needed a new brand to compete. In 1955, market research began into a new brand of car. Design experts were hired to find out what the American public wanted in a new car, using a series of polls. Company executives conducted rigorous market research to help design the car, and several advanced new features were added. Over $250 million was spent developing the new brand, which was to be delivered through its own dealership network and in a variety of models. It was heavily advertised as "the car of the future."

It failed. Ford lost over $350 million on the Edsel, which ceased production in 1960, just three years after it was launched. There were several reasons for the failure of the Edsel. Although the Ford Motor Company had promised a car of the future, the Edsel turned out to be a fairly ordinary car. Ford's advertising overpromised and underdelivered. Pricing was a major factor. The Edsel was priced at around the same level as a luxury car, like the Ford Mercury® brand, and it used a lot of gas. In 1957, there was a recession, and money was tight for most people. Also, although market research had been conducted, Ford's executives didn't really listen to what the consumer wanted. Instead, they went with their hunches and designed a car they *thought* the American public would buy. In addition, the car was badly made. Stories of oil leaks, trunks that wouldn't open, and buttons that couldn't be pressed spread rapidly.

(Continued)

The Edsel was an overpriced, badly designed, and poorly manufactured vehicle launched at the wrong time to a consumer who did not want it. Any study of major product failures shows that any one of these problems can be enough to sink a product or a brand. The Ford Edsel managed to hit them all.

Glossary

Hunch: a feeling you have that something is true or that something will happen, even if you have no information or proof

1. Why was the Edsel produced?

   ....

2. Who was it aimed at?

   ....

3. Why did it fail?

   ....

B. Look again at your questions from Exercise 1, Part B on page 40. Which ones does this blog answer? Are there others for which you still need to do some research?

C. Now that you understand the writing assignment, create one or more application questions and one or more examination questions you can use to guide the next stage of your research.

D. Discuss your questions with two or more classmates. Add any questions you did not have to your list. How do these questions differ from the questions you developed at the beginning stage of your research on the Edsel?

E. Research the answers to your application and examination questions. Share your research with your classmates.

EXERCISE 3

A. Using the information you already have on the Ford Edsel and the answers to your questions from Exercise 2, write your answer to the assignment question in Exercise 1, Part A on page 40. Use four words from the Vocabulary Check in your response.

B. Work with a partner. Read each other's report and complete the peer review form. Discuss your comments.

Questions	Yes	No	Notes
Does the writing address the assignment task?	☐	☐	
Is the structure of the writing clear?	☐	☐	
Are the ideas clear and easy to understand?	☐	☐	
Do the ideas fit together in an orderly, logical way?	☐	☐	
Were at least four words from the Vocabulary Check used?	☐	☐	
Are there any grammatical errors?	☐	☐	
Are there any other comments you would like to make?	☐	☐	

C. Revise your draft based on the feedback you have received.

VOCABULARY CHECK

A. Review the items in the Vocabulary Preview. Write their definitions and add examples. Use a dictionary if necessary.

B. Complete the paragraph with vocabulary items from the box.

advanced	conduct (v)	deliver	executives
launches (v)	recession	rivals (n)	

Before designing a new product, it is important for a company to .... market research. The data gathered allow company .... to determine if the new product is the right one for the market. This research is especially important if a company has .... who are designing similar products. Products with .... technology will be profitable only if these are features that the public wants. Even if a company does market research before it .... a product, unpredictable events can impact its success. For example, the United States entered a .... when the Edsel hit the market. The car was too expensive for Americans who were worried about money. Another reason why the Edsel was not successful is that the car did not .... on its promises. There were many problems with the design of the car.

Go to MyEnglishLab to complete vocabulary and a skill practice and join in collaborative activities.

SKILL 2

BUILDING PARAGRAPHS AND CONNECTING IDEAS

WHY IT'S USEFUL Knowing how to write paragraphs that have clear main ideas and well-organized supporting details is essential for clear, readable academic writing. Connecting ideas smoothly within and between sentences and paragraphs also helps your reader to follow your ideas easily.

Academic writing is divided into paragraphs, each focused on one main idea. There are different kinds of paragraphs in academic writing, and the kind you write depends on your purpose. For example, a paragraph might focus on the description of a process or on developing an argument. It might describe an item or focus on similarities between two items. Whatever their focus, all paragraphs have distinct parts: a topic sentence and supporting details. A good writer connects the ideas within and between sentences and paragraphs by using cohesive devices.

Topic sentences

The topic sentence is very important because it announces the main idea of a paragraph. It is often, though not always, the first or second sentence of a paragraph. Look at the topic sentence below and think about the qualities of a good topic sentence.

Creating an international brand is an important strategy for modern businesses.

On the basis of this topic sentence, how do you expect that the paragraph will be developed? What is the likely focus?

The topic of this sentence is "creating an international brand." The writer could say many things about "creating an international brand" but will focus on the idea that doing so "is an important strategy for modern businesses." The writer would develop this paragraph by explaining *why* creating an international brand is an important strategy. It is very important that the focus of your topic sentence be an idea that can be developed and supported, or you will run into problems. For this reason, your topic sentence should present an idea that is not just a fact or a specific detail.

Supporting details

Once you have a clear topic sentence for a paragraph, develop it with supporting details. Supporting details give more specific information about the idea you are focusing on. The type of supporting details you use will depend on what kind of paragraph you are writing. In a paragraph that describes a process, the supporting details would most likely be explanations of the steps in the process. In a paragraph that develops an argument, the supporting details would be reasons that explain why you hold a certain position. Facts, examples, and statistics can also be used to give more information about your focus.

It's important that *all* of your supporting details relate to the topic and focus that you expressed in the topic sentence. If the supporting details do not support the topic sentence, your paragraph will be confusing and hard for your reader to follow. A student has listed some possible supporting details for the topic sentence shown below and decided that two do not fit. Why do you think he made the two deletions?

The original recipe for Coca-Cola® is behind the company's success.

1. The recipe was unchanged and well-known until 1985 when the company changed it.
2. ~~The recipe is kept secret so that competitors do not copy it.~~
3. When Coca-Cola changed its recipe, consumers were angry and protested.
4. Coca-Cola received 1500 complaints per day about the change to the recipe.
5. ~~Coca-Cola spent $4 million developing the new recipe.~~
6. Coca-Cola brought back the original recipe; three months later, consumers were relieved and sales went up.

One way you can make sure that your supporting details are on topic is to connect the ideas in the supporting details to one another. Connecting ideas in this way is called building cohesion.

Building cohesion

When a paragraph is cohesive, it is unified. That means all the ideas are related to each other, and each idea connects to previous ideas and information. There are certain words, phrases, or techniques that we use to show the relationship between ideas. These are called cohesive devices. You can think of them as the glue that makes ideas stick together. There are three main cohesive devices: transition signals, pronouns, and repetition of key terms.

Transition signals: Transition signals are words or phrases that link ideas together and show the relationship between them. Some people like to think of transition signals as bridges: You leave one idea and go to the next. In order to use transition signals effectively, you must know what you are trying to signal. Notice how each transition signal in the examples below has a different meaning.

Meaning	Transition Signals	Example
Adding related Information	In addition Also As well as not only...but also	**In addition** to making a cola drink, Coca-Cola sells other soft drinks and juices.
Showing similarities	Likewise Similarly In the same way Equally / Identically	Coca-Cola produces a variety of beverages, including soft drinks and juices. **Likewise**, PepsiCo® produces a range of beverages that includes soft drinks, teas, and bottled water.
Showing contrasts	However Although Despite / In spite of In contrast	In blind taste tests, people prefer Pepsi®. **However**, people tend to choose Coke® when they know which beverage they are drinking.
Explaining effect	As a result (of) Consequently Therefore For this reason	**As a result of** its simplicity in marketing, Coca-Cola is one of the world's most valuable brands.
Concluding	On the whole Ultimately In short Overall	**On the whole**, Coca-Cola is one of the world's most successful brands.

Be alert when you use transition signals. You must understand how to use transition words and phrases correctly. The grammar patterns and common collocations for the signals vary. Also, it is important to understand that transition signals can be overused. Do not attempt to use one in every sentence.

For more on using compare-and-contrast language, see History, Part 2.

Using pronouns: Pronouns are words that are used in place of a noun. Use of pronouns helps you avoid unnecessary repetition. Writing is also made more cohesive by using pronouns because pronouns enable you to refer back to previously mentioned nouns or ideas. This helps you link ideas both within and between sentences, as a student writer has done in the sentences on the next page.

Coca-Cola changed to a new recipe in 1985. **It** returned to its original recipe since consumers did not like the new **one**. **They** were relieved and sales increased.

Note that in this example, *it* refers to the company, Coca-Cola, *one* refers to the recipe, and *they* refers to consumers.

CULTURE NOTE

Although companies are often referred to using singular pronouns and verb forms in American English, in British English, companies are referred to using plural pronouns and verb forms. For instance, in British English, the example above would read: "Coca-Cola changed to a new recipe in 1985. They returned to their original recipe since consumers did not like the new one."

In the paragraph below, the pronoun *This* in the last sentence refers back to an idea, the unchanged logo and bottle style. Can you identify the other pronouns in this paragraph and the nouns to which they refer?

A key factor of Coca-Cola's international success is brand recognition. Coca-Cola's logo has remained unchanged since 1923 so people all over the world have had almost 100 years to become familiar with it. Coca-Cola has used the same style of bottle to package its drink since 1916, and this bottle is almost as well known as the logo. This is why Coca-Cola has one of the most recognizable brands in the world.

Repeating key terms: To write cohesively and vary your language, use synonyms for key terms when appropriate. In the paragraph below, there are three sets of repeated key terms. Can you identify them? How do they help to relate the sentences and ideas within the paragraph?

For more on using synonyms and identifying keywords, see Business and Design, Part 2.

Coca-Cola's international marketing strategy has been a huge success. Coke is one of the most recognized words in the world. Coca-Cola is sold in many countries around the world. The company's logo is the best-known logo in the world. More than 10,000 bottles or cans of the soft drink are consumed each second. This beverage company is one of the most valuable brands in the world, worth over $58 billion.

By using a variety of key terms, the writer has made his writing more interesting and more cohesive. He has done this in the following way:

- The first set of synonyms related to the company Coca-Cola, for example, Coca-Cola = the company = this beverage company.
- The second set has the meaning of "well known": most recognized = best known.
- The third set refers to the beverage Coca-Cola, for example, Coke = Coca-Cola = soft drink.

EXERCISE 4

A. Match the terms on the left with the correct explanation on the right. Then compare your answers with a partner.

.... 1. paragraph

.... 2. topic sentence

.... 3. topic

.... 4. focus

.... 5. supporting details

.... 6. cohesive devices

.... 7. transition signal

.... 8. pronoun

.... 9. repeated key terms

a. certain words, phrases, or techniques that are used to show the relationship between ideas

b. the subject of a paragraph

c. a word that is used in place of a noun or an idea

d. a section of writing about one main idea

e. important words and their synonyms used throughout a paragraph

f. a sentence that announces the main idea of your paragraph

g. details that give more specific information about the ideas you are focusing on

h. a word or phrase that links ideas together and shows the relationship between them

i. what the writer will say about the topic of a paragraph

B. Discuss the questions with a partner.

1. Do your paragraphs use topic sentences and supporting details?
2. Which of the cohesive devices above do you already use to show the relationship between your ideas?
3. Which will you need to start using, and how can you do this?

VOCABULARY PREVIEW

These vocabulary items appear in the reading. Circle the ones you know. Put a question mark next to the ones you don't know.

tradition	inspiration	astronaut	cushion (n)	innovation

EXERCISE 5

A. Read the online article about the Nike® brand and answer the questions. Then discuss your responses with a partner.

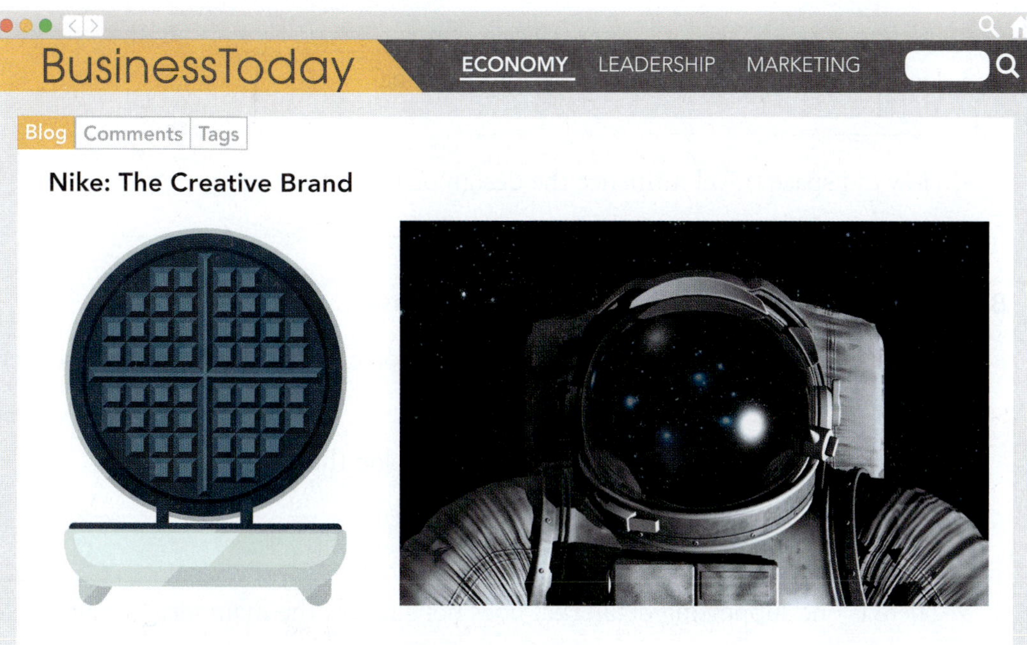

Nike: The Creative Brand

The Nike brand has long been connected with creativity. Nike has a tradition of using new ideas to make products. This company has been selling cutting-edge sports products since 1971. Bill Bowerman, who is the co-founder of Nike, got the idea for one of Nike's early shoe designs while making waffles for breakfast. He looked at the waffle iron and realized he could use it to make the soles of running shoes with a better grip. These shoes are known as Nike Waffle Trainers®. Similarly, the idea for Nike Air Max® Shoes came from an unusual place. Its inspiration was space travel. To make these top-selling shoes, Nike used blow rubber molding, a technique originally used to create helmets for astronauts, to insert gas-filled bags into the sole of the shoe. As a result of the air cushion, this shoe is very comfortable. Michael Jordan is well known for promoting Nike shoes. Overall, Nike's customers have come to expect innovation from the Nike brand and the products deliver it.

Glossary

Grip: the ability to hold firmly

Sole: the bottom of a shoe that touches the ground

Waffle: a flat cake with a pattern of square holes in it, often eaten for breakfast in the United States

CULTURE NOTE

Michael Jordan was a professional basketball player who played in the National Basketball Association (NBA) League between 1984 and 2003. He was named the second greatest athlete of the twentieth century by Associated Press in 1999, and he is one of the richest former athletes in the United States.

1. What is the Nike brand known for?

2. How is Bill Bowerman connected to Nike?

3. How did a waffle influence the design of a shoe?

4. How did space travel influence the design of a shoe?

B. Now read the article again and complete the tasks.

1. Write the topic sentence below. Underline the topic and double underline the focus.

2. In general, how do the supporting details develop the focus?

3. There is one supporting detail that does not support the main idea. Write it below.

4. What transition signals are used in the article? Complete the chart.

Transition Signal	Meaning

5. Find four examples of pronouns and the word(s) each replaces. Complete the chart.

Pronoun	Word or Idea Replaced

6. Complete the set of repeated, related key terms:

creativity = ... = ... = ...

C. With a partner, decide which of these supporting details should be added to the paragraph about the Nike brand. After you decide, determine where in the paragraph you would place it and explain why.

1. One example that illustrates how Nike has shown creativity in its advertisements is that it was the first company to use a Beatles song in a television commercial.
2. Showing even more creativity, the designers showed off the air cushions by putting a "window" on the side of the shoe.

EXERCISE 6

A. Complete the tasks to build a paragraph for the topic sentence below.

1. Go online to find supporting details.
2. Find and use at least one transition signal and one set of repeated key terms in your paragraph.
3. Be sure to use pronouns appropriately throughout.
4. Make sure that you include three vocabulary items from the Vocabulary Check.

Topic sentence: Nike promotes its brand through creative advertising.

B. Exchange paragraphs with a partner and complete the peer review form. Discuss each other's comments.

Questions	Yes	No	Notes
Do all of the supporting details support the topic sentence?	☐	☐	
Did the writer use at least one transition signal?	☐	☐	
Can you identify repeated key terms?	☐	☐	
Has the writer used pronouns appropriately?	☐	☐	
Did the writer include words from the Vocabulary Check?	☐	☐	

C. Based on your partner's suggestions, rewrite your paragraph.

VOCABULARY CHECK

A. Review the items in the Vocabulary Preview. Write their definitions and add examples. Use a dictionary if necessary.

B. Complete each sentence with a vocabulary item from the box.

astronauts	cushion (n)	innovation	inspiration	tradition

1. The ...., or idea, for products can come from unusual places.
2. Technology used to design equipment for .... on their space missions is sometimes used to design new products.
3. Some companies are skilled at developing new ideas and are known for .... in a particular industry.
4. It is comfortable to walk in shoes with a ....
5. Companies who have a long history of making profitable products are said to have a .... of success.

Go to MyEnglishLab to complete a vocabulary and skill practice and to join in collaborative activities.

INTEGRATED SKILLS

IDENTIFYING TOPIC SENTENCES

WHY IT'S USEFUL Identifying topic sentences as you read an article helps you to recognize and understand the writer's message efficiently. In addition, being able to identify topic sentences in your reading can inform how you write. Being aware of the role and importance of topic sentences, enables you to write clearer topic sentences in your assignments.

As you have learned in Skill 2, a topic sentence announces the main idea of a paragraph. Good writers include clear topic sentences to guide their readers, and good readers are able to identify topic sentences quickly as they read. Identifying topic sentences in a longer reading not only helps you find the main idea of each paragraph, but it can also help you see how the main ideas lead to the thesis, or main point, of the article.

PART 1

Placement of topic sentences

In academic writing, topic sentences are usually placed at the beginning of a paragraph, as the first or second sentence, as in the example below.

> Audi is one of three well-known German luxury car makers. **It is a company that consistently pushes the luxury car industry to develop technologically.**

In this example, the topic sentence is the second sentence. The reader can expect the rest of the paragraph to develop the main idea—Audi encourages technological innovation in the luxury car industry—by explaining how the company does this.

Sometimes, a writer starts a paragraph with an idea that *seems* to be the main idea. This idea is developed to a certain extent in the first few sentences of the paragraph. However, the writer then includes a sentence that changes the direction of the idea. In this case, the topic sentence is located near the middle of the paragraph, as in the example below.

> Luxury car buyers enjoy the speed their cars allow them to achieve. One of the first questions many buyers will ask the salesperson is "How long does it take this car to get from 0 to 60 miles (96.5 km) per hour?" In addition, they often boast about how quickly their car can go. **However, research shows the car's design and style are often what customers really care about.**

In this example, the topic sentence is the fourth sentence. In the first few sentences, the main idea seems to be that speed is the most important factor that consumers consider when buying a luxury car. The fourth sentence changes the direction of the paragraph. It starts with the word *however*, a clear signal to the reader that the direction is going to change since *however* signals contrast. The reader can expect the rest of the paragraph to develop the true main idea: Design is the most important factor that luxury car buyers consider when buying a luxury car.

For more on using compare-and-contrast language, see History, Part 2.

A writer can also end a paragraph with the topic sentence. The supporting details are given first, and the reader is led to the main idea. The main idea is delayed until the end of the paragraph after the supporting details have been provided.

> Modern drivers want to be able to connect to their smartphones in their cars so they can easily access information stored in the device. Because of this, the inside of a modern luxury car looks very different than it did a decade ago. The dashboard of these cars can resemble touch screen tablets. Drivers want to be able to access their music, and passengers may want to access video. It is undeniable that navigation apps found on most smartphones help drivers get from point A to point B. Using voice control to access contact lists and make calls is also important to many car owners. **Luxury carmakers need to focus on in-car connectivity to attract future consumers.**

In this example, the topic sentence is the last sentence of the paragraph. The supporting details are provided first. The reader learns how modern drivers rely on their smartphones. Several reasons are provided that show why they would want to be able to connect their smartphone to their car. The reader is not at all surprised by the main idea in the last sentence of the paragraph: in-car connectivity is an important focus for luxury carmakers.

VOCABULARY PREVIEW

These vocabulary items appear in the reading. Circle the ones you know. Put a question mark next to the ones you don't know.

established (adj)	manufacturer	niche
segment (n)	attempt (n)	convinced (adj)

EXERCISE 7

A. Read the blog about product wars, which occur when two companies launch a similar product, but only one can be successful. Then answer the comprehension questions.

BusinessToday ECONOMY LEADERSHIP MARKETING

Blog Comments Tags

Product Wars

1 All businesses use advertising to market their products, and advertising is a powerful force. The power of marketing explains why having the "best" product does not guarantee that one company will be more successful than another. In recent years, many large, established businesses have faced sudden competition from smaller startups. These new companies may not have an established business's design and development experience, but they are often quite skilled at marketing. Underdog companies often find an underserved customer base and market toward them aggressively. The "best" quality product can easily be displaced by great marketing. Product wars are often won by companies that know who their customers are and what they want.

2 Every company claims to provide customers with the best possible product, but what actually makes one product better than a competitor's is not always clear. In the late 1970s and early 1980s, Sony® was convinced that its Betamax® home

recording technology was clearly the superior format. Competitor JVC's VHS® player had both a lower picture and lower sound quality compared to the high-tech Betamax. However, customers, especially in the United States, disagreed. Not only were VHS players considerably cheaper, they also allowed users to record almost twice as much footage to a tape. Users could record entire movies to a single cassette, something that made a slightly higher picture quality seem irrelevant. This demonstrates the first lesson of a product war: The better product is the product the customer actually wants, NOT simply the more technologically advanced.

3 It may seem easy to figure out what a customer wants. If a company makes headphones, for example, it knows that the customer is going to want the best sound quality available for the price. While this may seem like good logic, understanding a customer's wants can be more complicated. It took some businesses a surprisingly long time to realize that different customers want different things. This is something headphones manufacturer Bose® learned the hard way. Overnight, the company went from industry leader to second place, realizing that they had only been serving one market segment and not the whole market.

4 Beats by Dre™, a headphone company co-founded by musician-producer Dr. Dre and producer Jimmy Iovine, saw the headphone market as ripe for disruption. Most consumers settled for whatever headphones came packaged with their devices. High-end headphones were a niche market for dedicated enthusiasts. By releasing bass heavy headphones with all the marketing savvy of musical promotion, Beats headphones came to dominate the high-end headphone market soon after they entered production.

5 Bose, the industry leader for decades, was challenged by this development. Attempts to sell customers on a better listening experience based on rigorous product testing fell flat against a social media focused marketing campaign. No one in the headphone sector could compete with Beats' marketing and image. Bose still had a great product and the loyalty of their original customer base, but Beats had opened a niche market to a wider range of consumers. Through strategic marketing and a glamorous, celebrity endorsed image, Beats was selling headphones to a new group of customers. Bose was only selling a product, while Beats sold luxury and lifestyle.

6 Even some established, billion-dollar companies owe their success to thinking like an underdog. Apple, the computer manufacturer that had previously led the pack in MP3 players and smartphones, recently found itself the leader in a new niche: expensive watches. An industry led for a long time by brands like Rolex® and Omega® suddenly found itself competing with a tech giant. A large company had successfully "invaded" a previously stable niche, finding great success in doing so. Apple had brought an enormous, established customer base into a product area that had previously seemed to be, if anything, for the very wealthy upper class only.

(Continued)

7 It is difficult to determine whether the Apple Watch®, a tech gizmo that extended the use of a smartphone, is "better" than the carefully crafted analog products of brands like Rolex. A direct comparison is, of course, highly subjective. Apple was clearly better at marketing to a large variety of customers, though interestingly, Apple recently dialed back attempts to break into the highest priced markets. Two- to five-hundred-dollar watches are Apple's top sellers, but thousand-dollar watches and above belong to old companies like Rolex. It just goes to show that each customer's taste is subjective. Learning how to create the "best" product for a market segment and income level is still the heart of good business strategy.

Glossary

Underdog: the business in a product war that is not expected to succeed

Footage: a length of film

Subjective: influenced by your own opinions and feelings rather than facts

1. How can new, or less-known, companies compete with older, well-known companies?

....

2. Why did Sony think its product was better than JVC's product?

....

3. Why did JVC win its product war?

....

....

4. What lesson did Beats teach Bose?

....

5. How did Apple use the "underdog approach" to enter the luxury watch industry?

....

6. Has Apple won the luxury watch product war?

....

B. Reread the blog and underline the topic sentence in each paragraph. Then answer these questions. What is the main idea of the blog? How do the topic sentences lead to the main idea? Compare and discuss your answers and ideas with a partner and discuss any differences.

C. Now you're ready to write your own paragraphs. Choose one of these pairs of competitors: Nike vs. Reebok®, Netflix® vs. Hulu®, Uber® vs. Lyft®, Facebook® vs. Snapchat®. Research the rivalry between their products. Write two paragraphs, 150–200 words each, about the competition. Place your topic sentence in each paragraph in a different position. Include three words from the Vocabulary Check.

D. Share your paragraphs with a partner. Use the peer-review questions to evaluate each other's work and to offer revision suggestions.

Questions	Yes	No	Notes
Can you identify the topic sentence in each paragraph?	☐	☐	
Did the writer choose the most effective placement for each topic sentence?	☐	☐	
Did the writer include three words from the Vocabulary Check?	☐	☐	
Are there any other comments you would like to make?	☐	☐	

E. Rewrite your paragraphs based on the feedback you received.

VOCABULARY CHECK

A. Review the items in the Vocabulary Preview. Write their definitions and add examples. Use a dictionary if necessary.

B. Choose the sentence that correctly paraphrases the meaning of each underlined vocabulary item.

1. a. The company was <u>convinced</u>, or certain, that its product would be a success.
   b. The company was <u>convinced</u>, or uncertain, that its product would be a success.
2. a. If a company finds a new <u>niche</u> market, it has a new type of customer that likes everything.
   b. If a company finds a new <u>niche</u> market, it has a new type of customer with specific interests.

(Continued)

3. a. An established company is a new company that has just started.

   b. An established company is a company that has been in operation for a long period of time.

4. a. An attempt can be successful or unsuccessful.

   b. An attempt is always successful.

5. a. A manufacturer makes products.

   b. A manufacturer buys products.

6. a. A segment, or all, of the population likes the new product.

   b. A segment, or part, of the population likes the new product.

Go to MyEnglishLab to complete a vocabulary and skill practice and to join in collaborative activities.

LANGUAGE SKILL

USING CONJUNCTIONS TO CONNECT IDEAS

WHY IT'S USEFUL Conjunctions create a relationship between your ideas. They add cohesion to your ideas, and help you avoid writing too many short, choppy sentences. This makes your writing smoother, enabling your reader to follow your ideas more easily.

Go to MyEnglishLab for the Language Skill presentation and practice.

VOCABULARY STRATEGY

CREATING A VOCABULARY JOURNAL

WHY IT'S USEFUL Creating a vocabulary journal helps you build on your current knowledge by adding new words, meanings, and forms as you meet them. This journal is a lasting record of your journey as a language learner.

Read Jiwon's thoughts about her language-learning experience at a university in the United States on the next page.

I've always been a hard-working language learner. I studied hard, and got a good TOEFL score. Now that I am here, my language learning has not stopped. There are, of course, many new words and phrases that I have to learn. But there are also words I thought I knew, which are being used in new and interesting ways. Every time I see a new word, or a new meaning of a familiar word, I write it in my vocabulary journal. When I have free time, I find out more about the word. I could not manage all this new knowledge without my vocabulary journal. It will keep helping me as I progress as a business major.

A language learner's experience

As you can see, Jiwon uses her vocabulary journal to learn new words and to learn new meanings, or uses, for familiar words. It is her personalized learner's dictionary, which also serves as a record of her experiences as a language learner.

Creating a vocabulary journal

The first step in creating a good vocabulary journal is finding a good notebook. It should not be too big—otherwise, it is heavy and awkward to carry—and it should not be too small—otherwise, it won't last very long. A standard composition notebook can be a good choice for most people. Alternatively, you could find something you can personalize. Whatever you find, try to find something that you will enjoy spending time with.

What to include: include in your vocabulary journal only key information that is fairly easy to find. When you come across a new word during a lecture or your research, simply write the word—and the sentence or phrase where you found it—as a new entry in your journal. When you have more time, add relevant information, which you can find in a good learner's dictionary.

For more on using a dictionary to expand vocabulary, see Zoology, Part 2.

Look at the complete vocabulary journal entry for the word *niche* from paragraph 4 of the Integrated Skills reading. This entry includes the sentence from that article, along with other useful information. For some words, it can be difficult to find good synonyms or antonyms, and creating a good visual can take time. It will not therefore always be practical to include each of these elements in your entry.

Subject Area: business

Word: niche

Part of Speech: adjective

Definition: A small group of people with particular needs or interests that companies try to sell specific products to.

Sentence: Most consumers settled for whatever headphones came packaged with their devices; high-end headphones were a niche market for dedicated enthusiasts.

Visual:

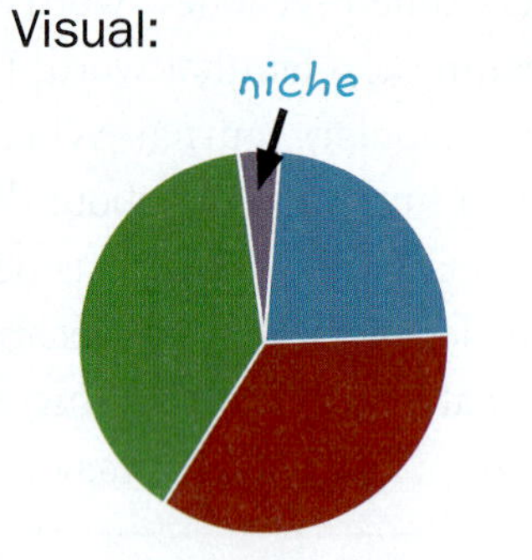

Synonym(s): very small section
very small segment

Antonym(s): mass

Initially, the word *niche* was used as an adjective in the Integrated Skills reading. However, in paragraph 6, the same word is used in a different way, as a noun. In a case like this, it is not necessary to create a completely new entry. Instead, you can simply write in the new part of speech and a new sentence as shown below.

Part of Speech: adjective + noun

Sentence: Most consumers settled for whatever headphones came packaged with their devices; high-end headphones were a niche market for dedicated enthusiasts. – adj

Apple, the computer manufacturer that had previously led the pack in MP3 players and smartphones, recently found itself the leader in a new niche: expensive watches. – noun

Because the noun and adjective forms of *niche* have similar meanings, it was possible to add new information to an existing entry. However, in many cases, when the word changes form, or you see or hear an existing word with a new meaning, it is best to create a new entry. This avoids making your vocabulary journal too messy. Since it is your journal, you can decide which approach is best for you.

Learning new words takes time and effort. Some research suggests that a new word must come to your attention more than twenty times before you can really use it well. As you see words that are in your journal, but you have not fully learned yet, you can use your vocabulary journal as a quick reference.

TIP

Writing in an actual book is preferable to creating an electronic vocabulary journal. Research shows that the process of writing text on a page will help you remember the information much more quickly than typing, or cutting and pasting information on a screen.

PART 1

EXERCISE 8

A. Look at these entries for the word *segment* from a vocabulary journal and write them in the correct place in the template that follows. Create your own visual.

- one of the parts that something is divided into
- whole
- noun
- segment
- part
- Overnight, the company went from industry leader to second place, realizing that they had only been serving one market segment and not the whole market.
- business

Subject Area:	
Word:	Part of Speech:
Definition:	
Sentence:	
Synonyms:	Visual:
Antonyms:	

B. Use a learner's dictionary to find the word *segment* used as a verb. With a partner, decide whether the verb form should have a new journal entry, or whether the information could be added above. Then either create a new entry or add information to the journal entry above. Create your own sentence.

C. Using the template on previous page as a model, create your own vocabulary journal entries for these words: *manufacturer* (n), *established* (adj), *attempt* (v), *attempt* (n). Use a learner's dictionary for the information, but try to provide your own sentence and visual.

APPLY YOUR SKILLS

WHY IT'S USEFUL Applying the skills you have learned in this unit, you will be able to use appropriate questions to structure your research to fit an assignment. You will present your research, building coherent paragraphs with effective topic sentences and supporting details, and write cohesively with effective transitions within paragraphs. You will also maintain and refer to your vocabulary journal.

ASSIGNMENT

Plan a 350–500 word essay about how companies can successfully manage their brands when problems occur.

BEFORE YOU WRITE

A. Before you begin your assignment, discuss these questions with one or more students.

1. What do companies do to manage their brand(s)?
2. What do companies do when problems occur with their brand(s)?
3. What are some recent examples of brands that have had problems, and how have the companies dealt with them?

B. As you consider your writing assignment, complete the tasks and answer the questions. Then share your ideas with a partner. Get feedback and revise your ideas if necessary.

1. What recall and comprehension questions can you ask to learn more about managing a brand image when problems occur?

....

....

....

2. Research and find answers to your questions in #1.

3. What application and examination questions can you ask to help you further develop your response to the assignment?

C. **Review the Unit Skills Summary. As you plan the writing task, apply the skills you learned in this unit.**

UNIT SKILLS SUMMARY

Use questions to guide your research

- Ask appropriate questions at different stages of the research process.
- Develop questions at the outset to help guide your research as you deepen and broaden your knowledge of the topic.
- Continue to develop questions to help you apply and organize the information from your research.

Build paragraphs and connecting ideas

- Write topic sentences that can be developed with supporting details in well-organized paragraphs.
- Use cohesive devices carefully to connect ideas within and between your sentences.

Identify topic sentences

- Identify, as you read, the topic sentence of each paragraph.
- Be alert about the placement of topic sentences, as both a reader and a writer.
- Understand how the topic sentences lead to the thesis, or main point, of the article.

Use conjunctions to connect ideas

- Use coordinating conjunctions to combine words, phrases, and clauses.
- Use subordinating conjunctions to connect a dependent clause to an independent clause.
- Use paired conjunctions to show a strong relationship between two ideas.

Create a vocabulary journal

- Recognize important words and add them to your journal.
- Create useful entries that will help you learn and remember how to use new words.

THINKING CRITICALLY

As you think about your writing assignment, discuss the questions with one or more students.

1. What factors cause brand failures?
2. What are some examples of brand or product successes? What factors led to those successes?

THINKING VISUALLY

Think of the brands that each of these images reminds you of. Write down three words or phrases that you associate with each one. Discuss your ideas with a partner. Have these brands had any problems? If so, how did the company respond to them?

THINKING ABOUT LANGUAGE

Read the interview with a brand strategist about the importance of public relations in brand management. Underline the conjunctions. Then, with a partner, decide whether the conjunctions are coordinating, subordinating, or paired. Then complete a vocabulary journal entry for the term *public relations*.

PART 1

Managing Your Brand with PR

Public relations, the relationship between a company and ordinary people, is an important part of brand management. *Business for You* (BFY) Magazine talks to Thomas Park, brand strategist, to find out how companies can use PR to promote a brand and what to do if there is a PR problem.

BFY: What is public relations (PR), and why is it important for a company?

Thomas Park: Public relations is the relationship you, as a business, build with the public. All businesses want ordinary people, whether they are customers or not, to have a good image of their company. PR refers to how a company delivers the information the public needs in order to form an image of it, preferably a good image!

BFY: How can companies best use PR to manage brands?

Thomas Park: A successful brand tells a story. Since people like stories, a company should use PR to tell them a good, believable story about the brand. If companies provide the right kind of information to the public, people will understand and remember it. As long as the story tells people what your company stands for and what motivates your employees, that story becomes the message behind the brand. This message is sometimes also known as brand promise. PR helps your company deliver the brand promise.

BFY: In the real world, problems happen, and sometimes a company has a problem with one of its products. How can PR be used to respond when a problem occurs?

Thomas Park: You're right—problems can and do happen in the business world. For example, a product can fail in some way. When this happens, there are three things a company should do to avoid a PR nightmare. The first is to admit that there is a problem rather than try to hide it. Even though this may seem like the safest reaction, hiding can cause bigger problems than just admitting there is one. Next, a company should take responsibility even if the problem was partially caused by others. Finally, a company can both resolve a problem and actually benefit from it. This is a likely outcome when people are happy with how a company responds to the problem. For instance, a company can not only refund people for a faulty product, but also give them a gift certificate. The response becomes part of the brand story.

WRITE

A. Look again at the writing assignment and your answers to the questions in Before You Write, Thinking Critically, and Thinking VIsually.

B. Research the topic and take notes. Discuss your notes and ideas with others and make adjustments as needed. Write an outline of your essay.

BEYOND THE ASSIGNMENT

Write a 350–500 word essay about how companies can successfully manage their brands when problems occur. Use all the skills you learned in this unit.

Go to MyEnglishLab to watch Juli Sherry's concluding video and to complete a self-assessment.

ZOOLOGY

Extended Writing

UNIT PROFILE

Millions of elephants once roamed across the plains of Africa. Now, there are fewer than half a million left. Elephants are in danger in three ways: climate change is affecting their environment; more people are using the land for farms; the ivory in elephants' tusks is worth millions of dollars, so people kill them to get rich. But people are finding new ways to help elephants and to help the world understand that they are worth more than money.

OUTCOMES

- Write an introduction
- Write a conclusion
- Understand and use thesis statements
- Use gerunds and infinitives correctly
- Determine meaning from context

You will plan a well-researched, 2–3 page paper that answers three questions about the poaching of elephants. Your paper should have an introduction with a thesis statement, three body paragraphs with topic sentences, and a suitable conclusion.

For more about **ZOOLOGY**, see 2 3. See also R and OC **ZOOLOGY** 1 2 3.

GETTING STARTED

Go to MyEnglishLab to watch Professor O'Connell-Rodwell's introductory video and to complete a self-assessment.

Discuss these questions with a partner or group.

1. What do you know about elephants? How many different types of elephants do you know about? Where do they live?
2. Have you ever seen an elephant? Was it in a zoo, a safari park, or in the wild?
3. Professor O'Connell-Rodwell suggests that there is hope for elephants' survival. Do you agree? Why or why not?

SKILL 1

WRITING AN INTRODUCTION

WHY IT'S USEFUL Writing an effective introduction helps to provide your readers with the overview and information they need to approach your paper. Ideally, the introduction will also engage their attention so that they will want to keep reading.

Imagine arriving late to a movie theater and missing the first ten minutes of a movie. Most likely this would make it difficult for you to fully understand and enjoy the movie. An introduction to an essay serves a similar function—it sets the scene. It provides enough information to guide readers toward the body of your paper and helps them understand why you are writing on a given topic. A good introduction also engages readers so that they want to read the rest of your paper.

TIP

You may have learned to use a "hook" to get your reader's attention when writing an essay. While this technique may be appropriate in some forms of writing, academic essays do not contain a "hook." That means you should avoid starting your paper with questions and avoid idioms such as "every coin has two sides." Instead of using a hook, you can engage your reader with an interesting fact related to the topic.

How to write an effective introduction

Students often ask how long an introduction should be. While there is no definite answer, a useful guideline to follow is that your introduction should be around 10–15 percent of the length of the paper. So, if you are writing an 800-word essay, your introduction should be roughly 80–120 words. The longer the paper, the longer the introduction will be. Although an introduction appears at the start of a paper, it is important to note that it does not have to be the first thing you write. In fact, many good writers wait until they have completed their main body paragraphs before writing an introduction. That way they can make sure that the introduction fits the essay.

Regardless of the length, an effective introduction has three main parts: a general overview, some sentences focused on the topic of the paper, and a thesis statement. We'll discuss the first two parts in this section. In the Integrated Skills section, we'll deal with the final part, the thesis statement, which tells the reader the main points of your paper. You can think of the introduction like a funnel:

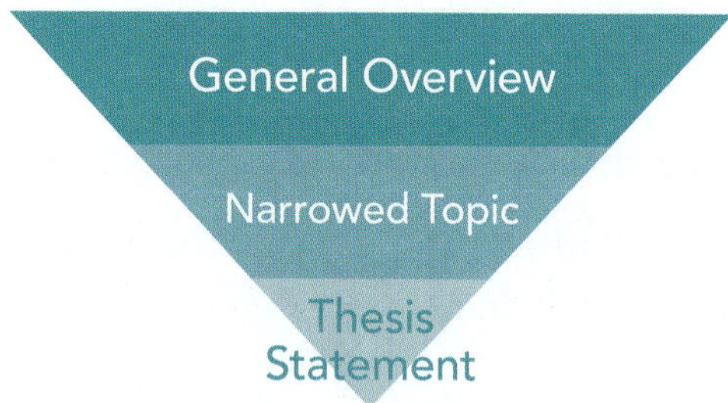

Let's look at how this works in practice. A student has been given the assignment shown below to write about how elephants are damaging farms in Africa and how farmers are responding.

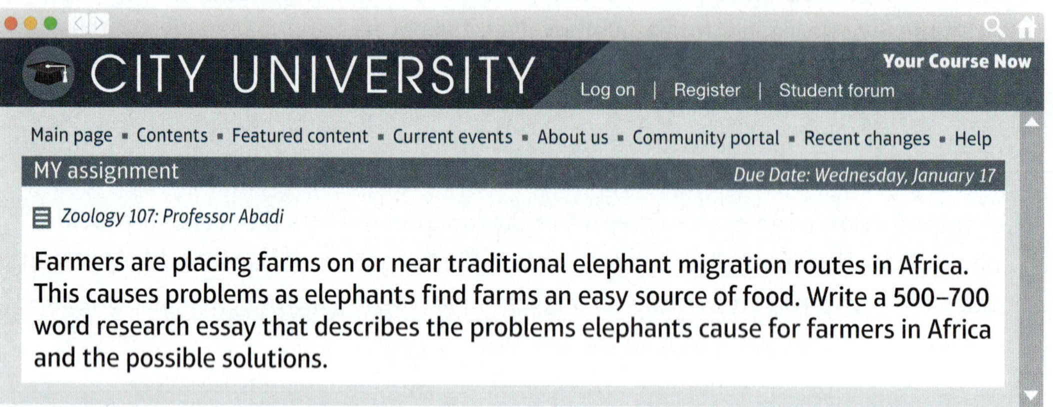
CITY UNIVERSITY

Your Course Now

Log on | Register | Student forum

Main page ▪ Contents ▪ Featured content ▪ Current events ▪ About us ▪ Community portal ▪ Recent changes ▪ Help

MY assignment — *Due Date: Wednesday, January 17*

Zoology 107: Professor Abadi

Farmers are placing farms on or near traditional elephant migration routes in Africa. This causes problems as elephants find farms an easy source of food. Write a 500–700 word research essay that describes the problems elephants cause for farmers in Africa and the possible solutions.

After doing some research, the student has decided that this is a problem-solution paper. She will need to examine the causes of the problem and then evaluate possible solutions. Look at the outline of her paper:

I. Causes of the problem
   A. Population Growth
   B. Climate Change
II. How farmers deal with the problem
   A. Noise
   B. Electric fences
   C. Killing elephants

III. Beehive fences
  A. The research
  B. The fences
IV. Additional benefits
  A. Honey
  B. More productive farms

Once the writer completed the body of her essay based on her outline, she wrote the introduction shown below. The first part, the overview of the topic, is highlighted in yellow. The second part, highlighted in green, narrows the topic. The thesis statement is the final sentence. Does the writer effectively follow the pattern shown in the diagram above?

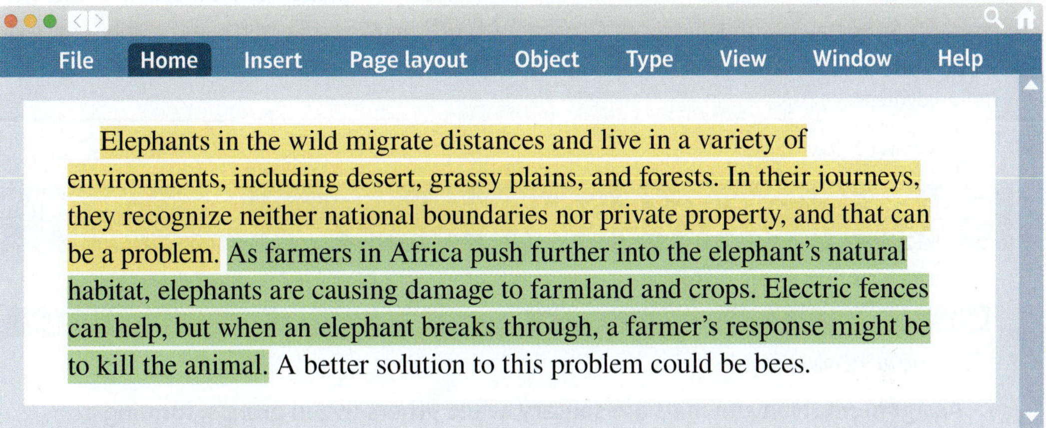

Elephants in the wild migrate distances and live in a variety of environments, including desert, grassy plains, and forests. In their journeys, they recognize neither national boundaries nor private property, and that can be a problem. As farmers in Africa push further into the elephant's natural habitat, elephants are causing damage to farmland and crops. Electric fences can help, but when an elephant breaks through, a farmer's response might be to kill the animal. A better solution to this problem could be bees.

In the first part of her introduction, the writer has introduced the nature of elephants and some general information about how they live. Her second part is more specific, focusing on how elephants and farmers come into contact, the problems this causes, and the current solutions that farmers have. Third, note that the thesis follows quite naturally from the rest of the introduction.

CULTURE NOTE

As well as losing habitat, African elephants are hunted for the ivory in their tusks. From a population that used to be in the millions, there are now fewer than 500,000 elephants in Africa. A worldwide ban on ivory sales has helped, but African elephants are still at risk. Asian elephants suffer from the same problems, but they are much fewer in number. Because Asian elephants are smaller, they are often put to work in local communities. There are thought to be fewer than 40,000 wild elephants left.

VOCABULARY PREVIEW

These vocabulary items appear in the reading. Circle the ones you know. Put a question mark next to the ones you don't know.

lifetime	cooperate	bond (n)	calf	wise	survive

EXERCISE 1

A. A student has written an essay about elephant families in response to the following assignment. Read the body of the essay, for which there is not yet an introduction or conclusion. Then answer the comprehension questions.

Glossary

Solitary: spending time alone

Interact: to do things with others

Socialization: spending time with others for enjoyment

Matriarch: the leader of the group, who is female

Harsh: unpleasant or difficult conditions to live in

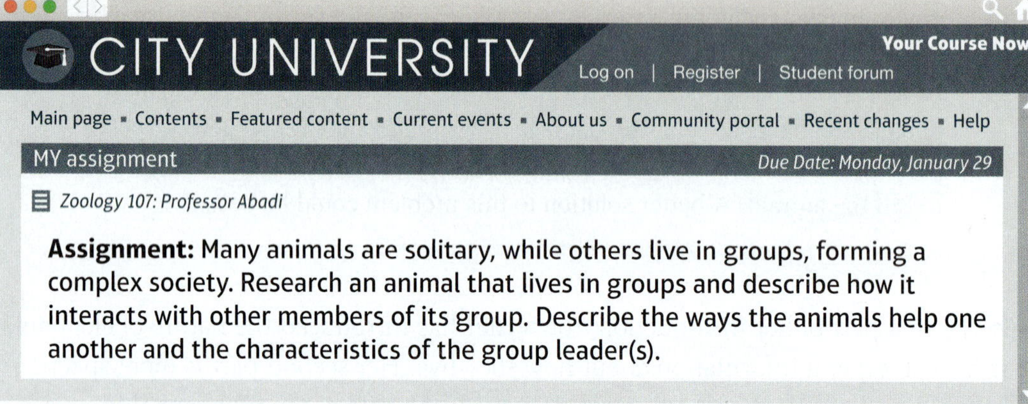

Assignment: Many animals are solitary, while others live in groups, forming a complex society. Research an animal that lives in groups and describe how it interacts with other members of its group. Describe the ways the animals help one another and the characteristics of the group leader(s).

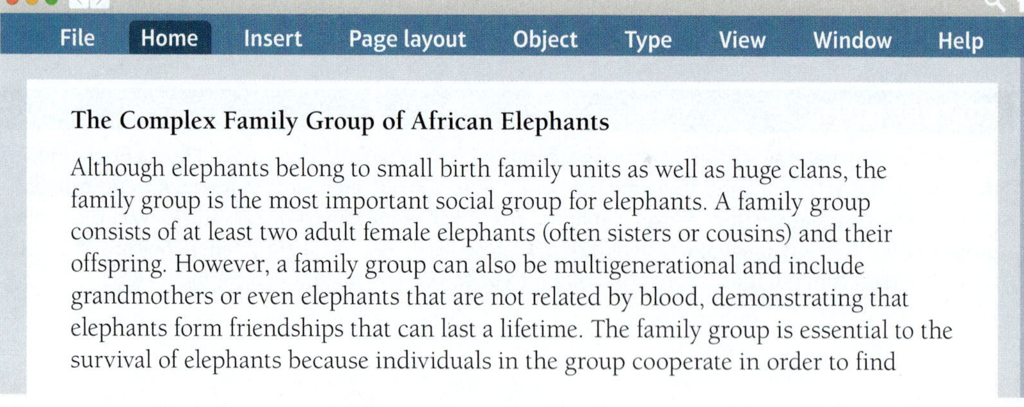

The Complex Family Group of African Elephants

Although elephants belong to small birth family units as well as huge clans, the family group is the most important social group for elephants. A family group consists of at least two adult female elephants (often sisters or cousins) and their offspring. However, a family group can also be multigenerational and include grandmothers or even elephants that are not related by blood, demonstrating that elephants form friendships that can last a lifetime. The family group is essential to the survival of elephants because individuals in the group cooperate in order to find food and water, care for the young, defend themselves against enemies, and make any other necessary decisions. Important and lasting bonds are formed between members in the family group. Female siblings often live together their whole lives.

Such strong bonds between individuals are formed through the socialization that occurs in the family groups. Like in human societies, elephants help one another learn how to live in a group. For example, elephant calves play together to learn how to behave and understand their status in the group. Calves learn from adults how to find food. Female adults teach each other how to raise young. For instance, a new mother may receive help from her older sister who has already had calves. That same new mother might enlist the help of younger females who have not yet had calves, and they will be better prepared to care for their future young.

The glue that holds the family group together is the matriarch. The matriarch is the leader of the family group. She has the strongest influence on the others, and the health of the family group in large part depends on how good she is at leading and how much experience she has. Like people, elephants have different personalities. Some are outgoing; others are shy. Some are likable; others are aggressive. Research indicates that successful matriarchs have good social skills and are confident and wise. Experience contributes to wisdom. Additional studies show that family groups with more experienced matriarchs are healthier. This may be because matriarchs remember where good watering holes are in times of drought and thus prevent a needless journey in harsh conditions. The glue holding the bonded individuals together can come apart with the death of a matriarch. In fact, when a matriarch dies, family groups sometimes split up.

1. Who can be a member of an elephant family group?

....

2. In what ways do members of the elephant family group help each other?

....

3. What are some characteristics of a successful elephant matriarch?

....

B. Complete the outline of the student's essay.

I.
    A.
    B.
II.
    A.
    B.
    C.
III.
    A.
    B.

C. This student has waited to write the introduction until the rest of the essay is completed. Referring to the body and outline of the essay, look at three draft introductions and decide which one is best suited to the essay. Discuss your choice with a partner.

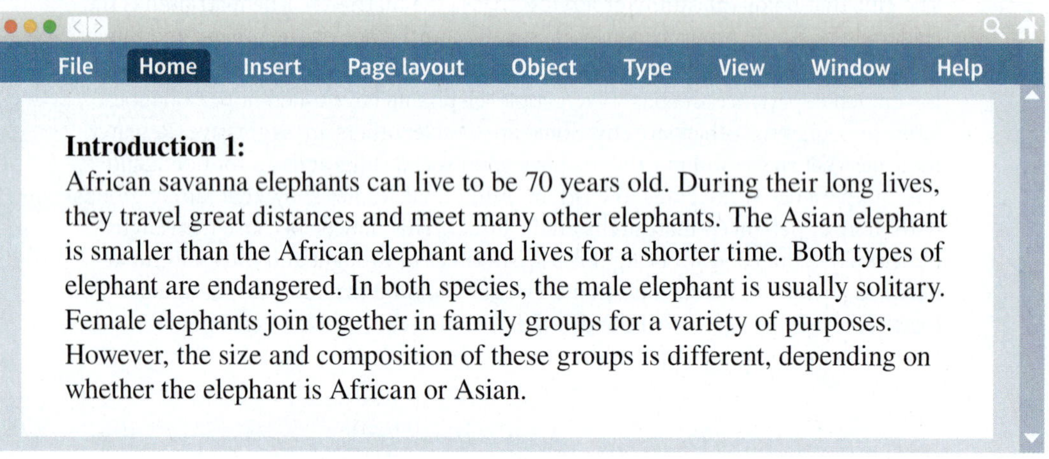

Introduction 1:
African savanna elephants can live to be 70 years old. During their long lives, they travel great distances and meet many other elephants. The Asian elephant is smaller than the African elephant and lives for a shorter time. Both types of elephant are endangered. In both species, the male elephant is usually solitary. Female elephants join together in family groups for a variety of purposes. However, the size and composition of these groups is different, depending on whether the elephant is African or Asian.

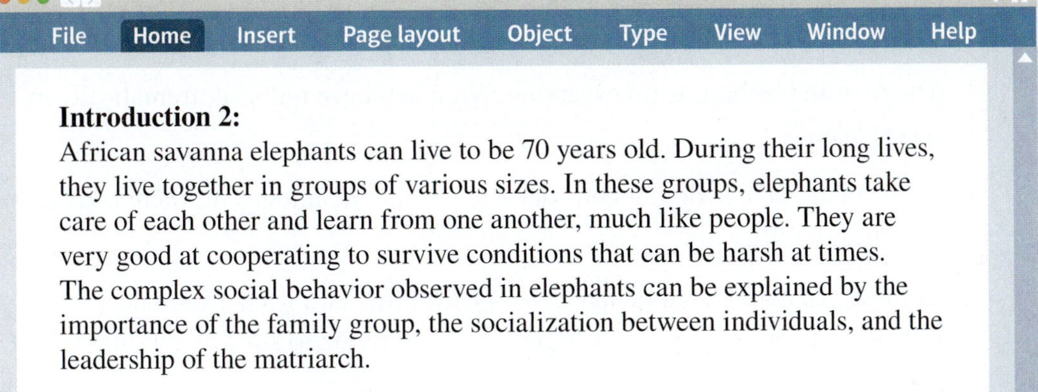

Introduction 2:
African savanna elephants can live to be 70 years old. During their long lives, they live together in groups of various sizes. In these groups, elephants take care of each other and learn from one another, much like people. They are very good at cooperating to survive conditions that can be harsh at times. The complex social behavior observed in elephants can be explained by the importance of the family group, the socialization between individuals, and the leadership of the matriarch.

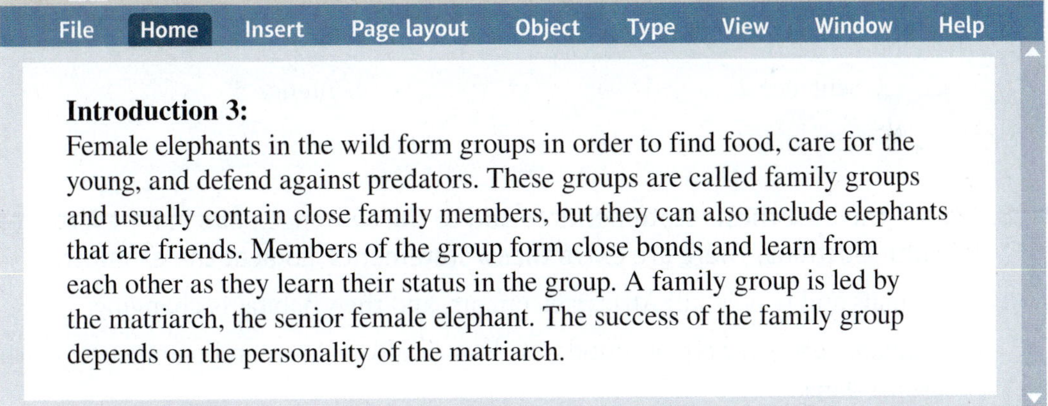

Introduction 3:
Female elephants in the wild form groups in order to find food, care for the young, and defend against predators. These groups are called family groups and usually contain close family members, but they can also include elephants that are friends. Members of the group form close bonds and learn from each other as they learn their status in the group. A family group is led by the matriarch, the senior female elephant. The success of the family group depends on the personality of the matriarch.

EXERCISE 2

A. The following sentences have been taken from the draft introductions in Exercise 1, Part C. The sentences below provide a general topic overview. The sentences on the next page narrow the topic. Match the sentences that go together. An example has been done for you on the next page.

1. African savanna elephants can live to be 70 years old. During their long lives, they live together in groups of various sizes.
2. In order for animals to survive and cooperate in the wild, communication is vital.
3. When most people think of an elephant, they think of the majestic African elephant.
4. Many animals in the wild are endangered. Some are threatened by other animals, some by their environment, and some by contact with humans.
5. Some mammals, like the great apes, are considered to have human-like intelligence because of their ability to use tools and solve problems.

a. While many animals communicate only through sound, elephants have several methods of communication.

b. The African elephant is no exception. Numbers have reduced dramatically in recent years.

c. While many people do not consider elephants to be intelligent, there is increasing evidence that they are.

d. In these groups, elephants take care of each other and learn from one another, much like people. They are very good at cooperating to survive conditions that can be harsh at times.

e. However, there are two main types of elephant, the African and the Asian.

...d... Sentence 1

.... Sentence 2

.... Sentence 3

.... Sentence 4

.... Sentence 5

B. Choose the best thesis statements to add to the sentence pairs in Part A to create five introductions. There are extra thesis statements. Look at the example.

1. Animals and people kill African elephants, and their habitat is changing.
2. Elephants use a variety of sounds, such as rumbles, roars, and trumpets to warn against danger.
3. Other mammals that are intelligent include dolphins, which can communicate over long distances, cats, which have great memories, and squirrels, which can solve complex problems.
4. Although larger than their Asian cousins, the African elephant is similar in many ways. There are also several key differences.
5. Animals and people kill Asian elephants, and their habitat is changing.
6. The ability to form complex family groups, use tools, and pass on knowledge to their offspring suggest that elephants have high levels of intelligence.
7. As well as sound, elephants communicate visually and through touch.
8. The complex social behavior observed in elephants can be explained by the importance of the family group, the socialization between individuals, and the leadership of the matriarch.

...8... Introduction 1

.... Introduction 2

.... Introduction 3

.... Introduction 4

.... Introduction 5

EXERCISE 3

A. Look at the thesis statement and outline below prepared in response to the assignment. Using your knowledge about elephant family groups and your research, write the general overview and the sentences narrowing the focus for an introduction. Use the thesis statement provided for the end of your introduction. Include three words from the Vocabulary Check.

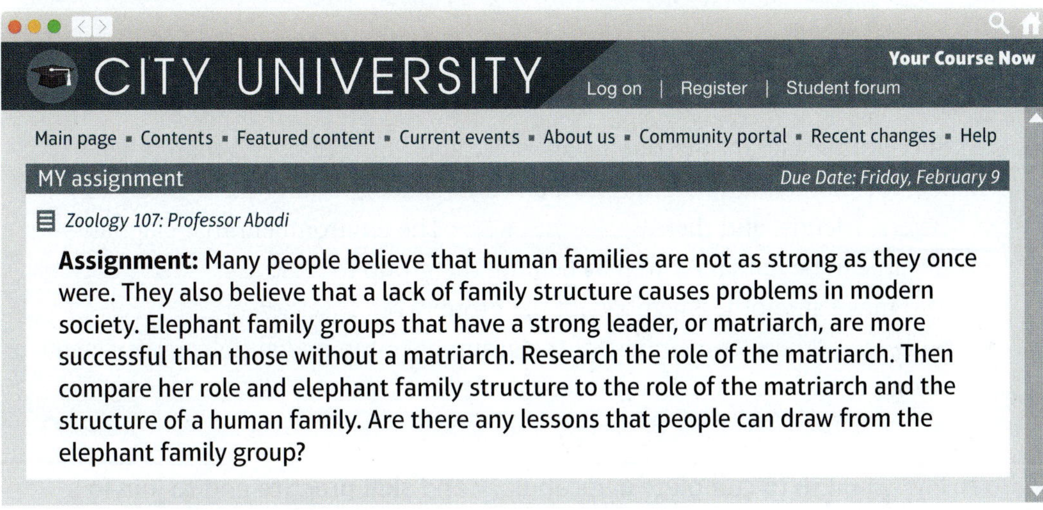

Assignment: Many people believe that human families are not as strong as they once were. They also believe that a lack of family structure causes problems in modern society. Elephant family groups that have a strong leader, or matriarch, are more successful than those without a matriarch. Research the role of the matriarch. Then compare her role and elephant family structure to the role of the matriarch and the structure of a human family. Are there any lessons that people can draw from the elephant family group?

Thesis statement: There are many lessons that humans can learn by understanding the role that elephant matriarchs play in the family group.

I. Matriarchs are often the oldest and wisest of the elephants.

II. Matriarchs remember where to find food and water.

III. Family groups with a strong matriarch live longer and are more successful.

IV. Matriarchs know better how to deal with danger.

B. Work with a partner. Read and discuss each other's introductions and complete the peer review form.

Questions	Yes	No	Notes
Is there a general overview of the topic?	☐	☐	
Are there two or more specific sentences to narrow the topic?	☐	☐	
Did the writer include three words from the Vocabulary Check?	☐	☐	

C. Revise your draft, taking your partner's suggestions into account.

VOCABULARY CHECK

A. Review the items in the Vocabulary Preview. Write their definitions and add examples. Use a dictionary if necessary.

B. Complete the paragraph with vocabulary items from the box.

bond (n)	calves	cooperate	lifetime	survive	wiser

Successful elephant matriarchs are older and .... than other members of the family group, which can include grandmothers, mothers, sisters, friends, and their .... The environment that elephants live in can be harsh. As well as helping the group to .... , they also make sure other members of the group work together, or .... , with each other. As members of the group have fun and socialize, they create a strong .... that can last a ....

Go to MyEnglishLab to complete a vocabulary and skill practice and to join in collaborative activities.

SKILL 2

WRITING A CONCLUSION

WHY IT'S USEFUL An effective conclusion reminds your readers of the main points you have made and provides a final thought that will make them continue to think about your paper.

Writing a conclusion can be difficult. You have introduced the topic, narrowed it, and outlined the main points in your introduction. You have developed your main points in the body of the paper. It can be challenging to get to the end of the body and write an effective conclusion because it may seem that you have nothing more to say. In fact, however, a skillfully written conclusion can reinforce the points you have made throughout your paper while prompting your reader to think further about your ideas. It can make the difference between a satisfactory paper and an excellent one.

How to write an effective conclusion

To write an effective conclusion, follow two steps. First, reiterate, or restate, the main points of your paper. It is tempting to do this by simply repeating or paraphrasing the thesis statement. However, this is not the most effective approach. Instead, use these tips to reinforce the points you want your reader to remember.

- Use new wording to explain the main points again.
- Do not put all the main points in one sentence. Instead, use a few sentences.
- Consider, if appropriate, referring to the main points of your paper in a different order from how they appeared in the body. This reordering can freshen what you have to say.
- Do not add any new points or important details to this part of the conclusion. You should be reiterating only ideas that you have already developed in the body of your paper.

TIP

Avoid using phrases like *in conclusion, in summary*, or *in a nutshell* to start your conclusion. Instead, just reiterate your main points.

The second step in writing an effective conclusion is crafting the final thought, which is expressed in the last sentence or two of the paper. This final thought should ensure that your reader continues to think about your chosen topic and the main points you have made. In the final thought, you can take the reader in a slightly different direction in order to encourage further thought on the topic. There are several techniques you can use to write a final thought, and the one you choose to follow depends a great deal on the kind of paper you have written. The chart below shows various techniques and an explanation of when each technique might be effective as a final thought for your paper.

Final Thought Technique	When You Might Use It
Recommendation	If your paper has focused on the negative effects of a phenomenon, your final thought could be a recommendation that shows how these effects could be avoided. Example: More money should be given to farmers to help them build beehive fences.
Warning	If your paper talks about a problem and solution, your final thought could be a warning about what might happen if the solution you outlined is not followed. Example: More elephants will be shot and killed if farmers do not build beehive fences.
Prediction	If your paper has focused on the benefits of doing something, your final thought could be a prediction that extends the ideas in your paper. Example: If farmers embrace sustainable solutions, like beehive fences that benefit people and are less damaging to the elephants, we have a better chance of saving these majestic animals from extinction.

Why it matters	If your paper has been an explanation or analysis of a phenomenon and none of the above techniques fits, think of another way to explain to your reader why the points of your paper matter. Example: Building beehive fences is a cheap and sustainable way to help elephants and farmers, too.
Return to introduction	If you included an idea in the general overview section of your introduction that is worth echoing, you can return to this idea in your final thought. Example: Beehive fences are one boundary that elephants will recognize and not cross.

Let's look at how writing a conclusion works in practice. In Skill 1, we saw a student's outline and introduction for a paper on problems that elephants cause for farmers in Africa and the possible solutions. Read the body paragraphs of her paper to get an idea of the main points that should be reiterated in the conclusion.

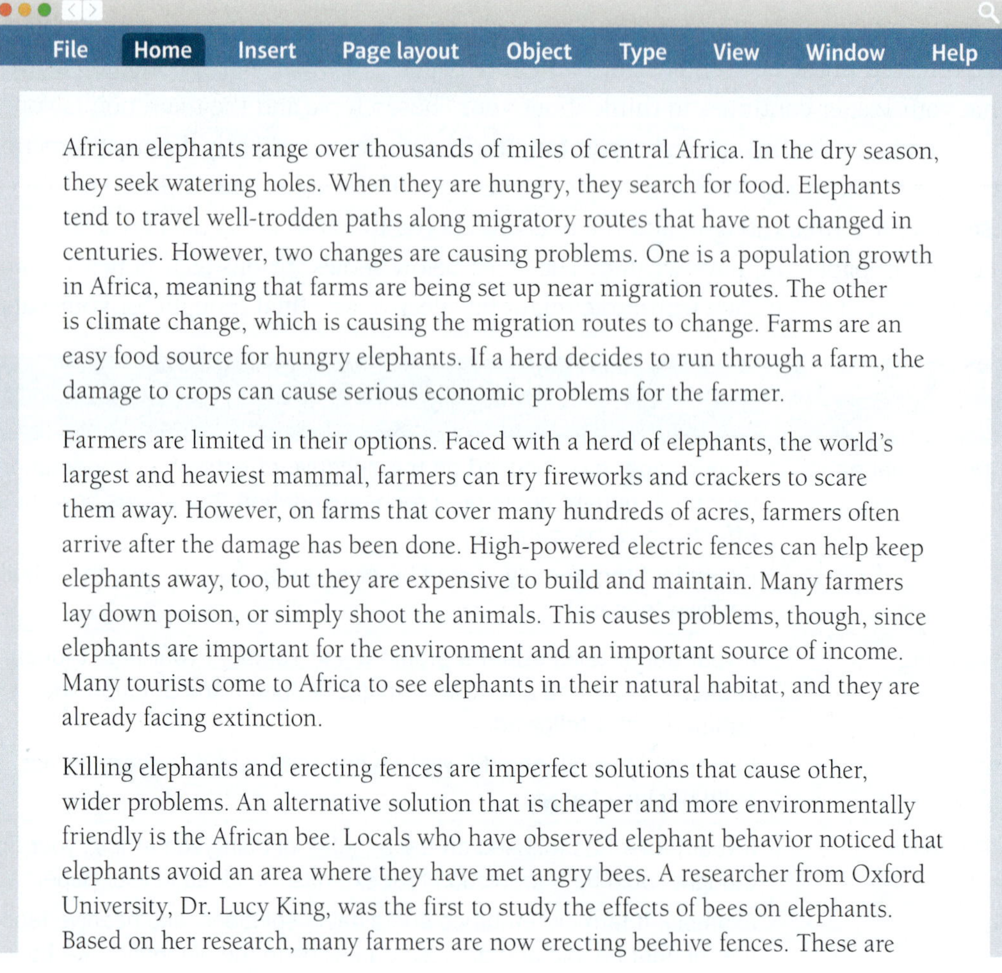

African elephants range over thousands of miles of central Africa. In the dry season, they seek watering holes. When they are hungry, they search for food. Elephants tend to travel well-trodden paths along migratory routes that have not changed in centuries. However, two changes are causing problems. One is a population growth in Africa, meaning that farms are being set up near migration routes. The other is climate change, which is causing the migration routes to change. Farms are an easy food source for hungry elephants. If a herd decides to run through a farm, the damage to crops can cause serious economic problems for the farmer.

Farmers are limited in their options. Faced with a herd of elephants, the world's largest and heaviest mammal, farmers can try fireworks and crackers to scare them away. However, on farms that cover many hundreds of acres, farmers often arrive after the damage has been done. High-powered electric fences can help keep elephants away, too, but they are expensive to build and maintain. Many farmers lay down poison, or simply shoot the animals. This causes problems, though, since elephants are important for the environment and an important source of income. Many tourists come to Africa to see elephants in their natural habitat, and they are already facing extinction.

Killing elephants and erecting fences are imperfect solutions that cause other, wider problems. An alternative solution that is cheaper and more environmentally friendly is the African bee. Locals who have observed elephant behavior noticed that elephants avoid an area where they have met angry bees. A researcher from Oxford University, Dr. Lucy King, was the first to study the effects of bees on elephants. Based on her research, many farmers are now erecting beehive fences. These are simple, cheap fences that have beehives hung on rope at regular intervals. If an elephant disturbs the fence, the beehive is disturbed, and the bees swarm. Elephants warn other members of the pack to avoid the area.

Although bees can also harm the farmers, they are unlikely to attack unless they are disturbed. Farmers with beehives fences gain two additional benefits. Bees produce honey, and the market in elephant-friendly honey is booming. Additionally, research shows that farms with nearby bees are more productive.

Glossary

Beehive: a wooden box built for bees to live in

By following the steps outlined above, the writer has crafted a conclusion for her paper. For the first step, highlighted in yellow, she reiterates the main points of the paper. The second step, highlighted in green, provides the reader with a final thought. Can you identify the technique she used for her final thought?

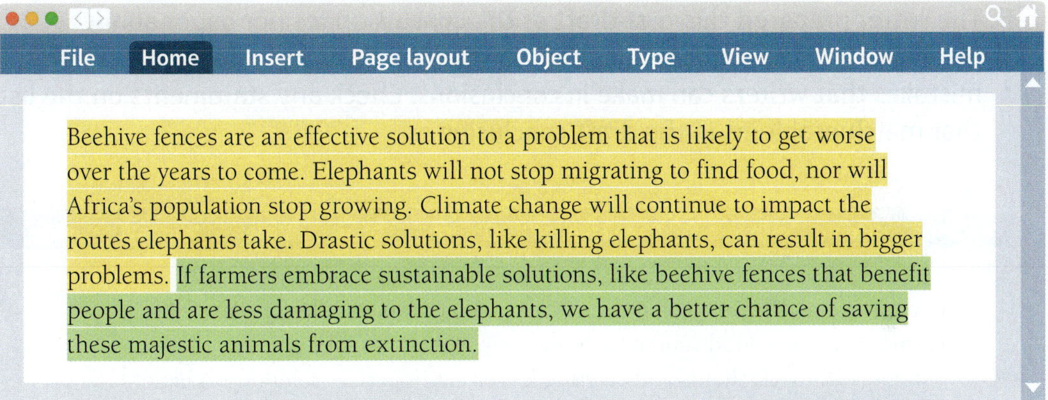

Beehive fences are an effective solution to a problem that is likely to get worse over the years to come. Elephants will not stop migrating to find food, nor will Africa's population stop growing. Climate change will continue to impact the routes elephants take. Drastic solutions, like killing elephants, can result in bigger problems. If farmers embrace sustainable solutions, like beehive fences that benefit people and are less damaging to the elephants, we have a better chance of saving these majestic animals from extinction.

Notice, in step 1, how the main points are presented in a different order from how they are presented in the body of the text, using slightly different wording. In step 2, a prediction is incorporated into the final thought. The reader can see that this paper is important because understanding the main points may help save elephants.

VOCABULARY PREVIEW

These vocabulary items appear in the reading. Circle the ones you know. Put a question mark next to the ones you don't know.

poison (n)	habitat	alternative	observe	interval	disturb

EXERCISE 4

A. Reread the student paper about beehive fences and answer the questions.

1. Why do elephants sometimes damage farms?

   ....

2. How might fireworks stop elephants from damaging farms?

   ....

3. Why isn't using fireworks an effective solution?

   ....

4. Why don't more farmers use electric fences?

   ....

5. How can beehive fences solve the problem?

   ....

B. The writer prepared this first draft of the conclusion for her paper about elephants and the damage they cause. Read the draft and the list of potential mistakes that writers can make in conclusions. Check any statements on the list that match problems in the draft conclusion.

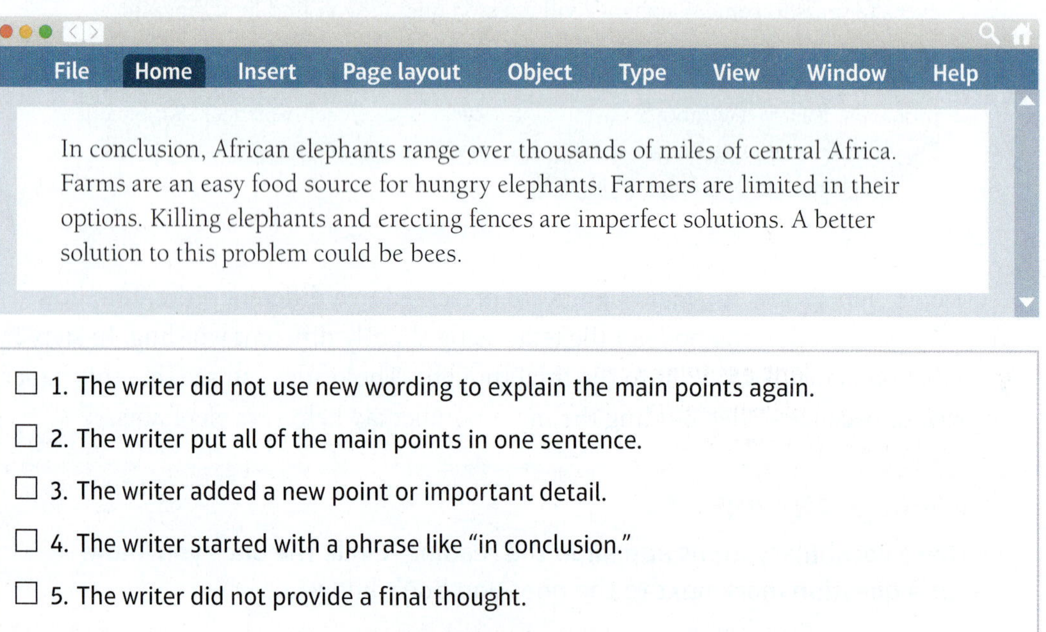

- ☐ 1. The writer did not use new wording to explain the main points again.
- ☐ 2. The writer put all of the main points in one sentence.
- ☐ 3. The writer added a new point or important detail.
- ☐ 4. The writer started with a phrase like "in conclusion."
- ☐ 5. The writer did not provide a final thought.
- ☐ 6. The writer did not answer the question "Why is this paper important?"

EXERCISE 5

In Exercise 1, Part A, on pages 70 and 71, you read the draft of a student paper about elephant family groups. Then in Part C, on pages 72 and 73, you chose the best introduction for the essay. Reread the introduction and body paragraphs in those sections. Then look at the drafts of four possible conclusions and decide which one is most appropriate. Explain your choice as well what is wrong with the other three drafts, referring to the checklist in the exercise above. Discuss your conclusions with a partner.

1. In summary, elephants live in many groups, but family groups are the most important. In family groups, adult female elephants cooperate to survive. Their children form strong bonds through socialization. The matriarch has the strongest influence and determines the health of the family group. Conservationists should be aware of the social complexities of elephant society in order to help elephants survive.
2. While socialization is important in family groups, the matriarch is the most important individual because she makes all the decisions. Without her guidance, individual elephants might be lost. Her leadership is key to helping family groups escape the threat of hunters. If matriarchs are not protected, family groups could be at risk.
3. Elephants are social animals living in groups led by wise and confident females. Individuals in family groups take care of each other and teach younger members how to survive. The socialization that occurs creates bonds that may last a lifetime. These gentle giants are not all that different from the people who both help and harm them today. Understanding how elephant families function can help us save these endangered animals.
4. In conclusion, the complex social behavior observed in elephants can be explained by the importance of the family group, the socialization between individuals, and the leadership of the matriarch. Any new elephant habitat should be designed with family groups in mind.

EXERCISE 6

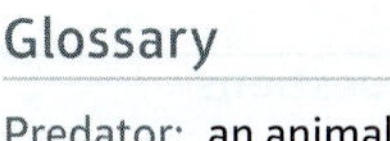

Glossary

Predator: an animal that kills and eats other animals

A. Read the student essay and write a suitable conclusion. Refer to the topic sentences in bold.

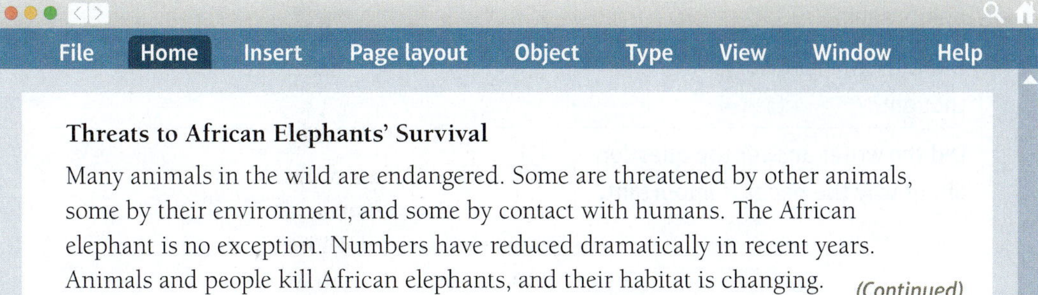

Threats to African Elephants' Survival

Many animals in the wild are endangered. Some are threatened by other animals, some by their environment, and some by contact with humans. The African elephant is no exception. Numbers have reduced dramatically in recent years. Animals and people kill African elephants, and their habitat is changing.

(Continued)

Even though elephants do not technically have any natural predators, a careless calf separated from its family group can be hunted by an especially hungry lion or snatched by a crocodile while playing in a river. Lions usually attack in a pack and target a young elephant from behind. Male lions are bigger and are, therefore, more likely to be a threat. Older, more experienced matriarchs can tell the difference between male and female lion roars and can better protect their family group if male lions come near. However, not every elephant family group is led by such a matriarch. Regardless of the effectiveness of matriarchs, elephants need to drink, and unlucky calves can be targeted by crocodiles at watering holes.

While elephants do not have any natural animal predators, people can and do kill them for sport or for their valuable ivory. Some countries allow hunters to pay a fee to hunt elephants for sport. They argue that the money earned from this practice helps local communities. However, this is debatable and results in fewer elephants. Elephants are not only killed as a sport, they are also killed for their ivory tusks. Although the international trade of ivory has been illegal since 1990, this has not stopped people from killing them just to take their tusks. There is still a large demand for ivory in some places, and there are also hunters who would love to add an elephant to their list of kills, putting elephants at risk.

People also threaten elephants by taking their habitat and contributing to climate change, which impacts both the food and water supply of elephants. People have started to use elephant habitat as farmland. This practice not only takes away important migratory routes, but can also cause conflict between farmers and elephants, which may result in elephant deaths. Even if farmers were not allowed to use elephant habitat, climate change may cause a shortage of food and fresh water for elephants. When temperatures are higher than usual, plants do not grow, and watering holes dry up. Without enough food and water, elephants could die in larger numbers.

B. Work with a partner. Read each other's conclusion and complete the peer review form. Discuss your comments.

Questions	Yes	No	Notes
Did the writer use new wording in the conclusion to explain the main points again?	☐	☐	
Did the writer provide a final thought?	☐	☐	
Did the writer answer the question about why the paper is important?	☐	☐	

C. Revise your draft, taking your partner's suggestions into account.

VOCABULARY CHECK

A. Review the items in the Vocabulary Preview. Write their definitions and add examples. Use a dictionary if necessary.

B. Complete each sentence with a vocabulary item from the box.

alternative	disturb	habitat	intervals	observing	poison (n)

1. As the human population grows, people are taking over the natural .... of some animals.
2. If you .... a beehive, you may get chased by a swarm of angry bees.
3. .... can kill or harm both people and animals.
4. Minutes are 60-second .... that make up one hour.
5. In order to learn about animal behavior, scientists spend many hours .... them.
6. Beehive fences are an .... solution to electric fences.

Go to MyEnglishLab to complete a vocabulary and skill practice and to join in collaborative activities.

INTEGRATED SKILLS

UNDERSTANDING AND USING THESIS STATEMENTS

WHY IT'S USEFUL Understanding a thesis statement, as a reader, and creating an effective thesis statement, as a writer, are vital skills for dealing with multiparagraph papers.

What is a thesis statement?

Like a good topic sentence at the paragraph level, a good thesis statement provides the main idea of an essay or paper and gives the reader an overview of the supporting points that will be presented. As you have already seen, the thesis statement is usually one or two sentences long and appears at the end of an introduction. Besides expressing the writer's point of view, it outlines the points that will be covered in the same order they are presented in the essay.

In Introduction 2 on page 73, the student used this thesis statement:

> The complex social behavior observed in elephants can be explained by the importance of the family group, the socialization between individuals, and the leadership of the matriarch.

Looking again at the essay, we can see that the points presented in the thesis statement are covered in the same order. The first paragraph talks about how important the family group is in elephant society. The second shows how elephants socialize within a group, and the third shows the leadership role played by the matriarch:

The Complex Family Group of African Elephants

African savanna elephants can live to be 70 years old. During their long lives, they live together in groups of various sizes. In these groups, elephants take care of each other and learn from one another, much like people. They are very good at cooperating to survive conditions that can be harsh at times. The complex social behavior observed in elephants can be explained by the importance of the family group, socializing between individuals, and the leadership of the matriarch.

Although elephants belong to small birth family units as well as huge clans, the family group is the most important social group for elephants. A family group consists of at least two adult female elephants—often sisters or cousins—and their offspring …

Such strong bonds between individuals are formed through the socialization that occurs in the family groups. Like in human societies, elephants help one another learn how to live in a group …

The glue that holds the family group together is the matriarch. The matriarch is the leader of the family group …

Elephants are social animals living in groups led by wise and confident females. Individuals in family groups take care of each other and teach younger members how to survive. The socialization that occurs creates bonds that may last a lifetime. These gentle giants are not all that different from the people who both help and harm them today. Understanding how elephant families function can help us save these endangered animals.

Writing effective thesis statements

Let's look at some further examples of thesis statements:

> Many elephants are kept in zoos.

This is a simple fact and does not show any specific details or the position the writer is taking. We do not know whether the writer thinks this is positive or negative, or what the paper is going to be about. A better thesis statement would include more detail, as in the example that follows:

> Many elephants are kept in zoos as a way to save them from the dangers they face in the wild.

This is a better thesis statement because the writer's position is now clear. This essay will argue that zoos are necessary because of the dangers that elephants face in the wild. However, it is still too general because there is no indication of what those dangers are. Add details to the thesis statement to show the points that will be covered in the paper:

> Many elephants are kept in zoos as a way to save them from the dangers they face in the wild, such as conflicts with farmers, illegal poaching, and the destruction of their environment.

Glossary

Poaching: hunting and killing an animal illegally

This thesis statement provides enough detail and is a guide to the essay to come. You can expect to read about three main topics related to the dangers elephants face in the wild, and in this order—conflicts with farmers, people who illegally hunt them, and destruction of the elephants' environment.

Using thesis statements in your reading and research

For more on using questions to guide your research, see Business and Design, Part 1.

Use your knowledge of the position and function of thesis statements to facilitate your reading and research. A good way to quickly know whether an article or text will be useful for you is to find and read the thesis statement. If it is relevant to your topic, you can continue reading. If not, you can move on.

For example, a student was given an assignment to write about elephants kept in large, open-air safari parks. She needed to find out whether safari parks have any positive or negative effects on the general elephant population. She found several articles and located the thesis statement in each one. As you can see below, just by looking at the thesis statements, she determined that some articles were clearly not useful for this assignment.

1. Safari parks are healthier environments than zoos because there is space for elephants to roam and enough variety to keep them entertained.
2. While safari parks provide a safe haven for elephants and protect them against illegal poaching, they are still unnatural environments and cause elephants harm.
3. ~~Safari parks are a great place for people to learn about animals of all kinds because they are close to major population centers and help people see animals in a more natural environment.~~
4. Safari parks provide an opportunity for people to engage with elephants in a more natural environment than a zoo. By providing this engagement, safari parks encourage people to help protect endangered elephants in the wild.
5. ~~Drive-through safari parks have a long history in the United States and are often associated with animals of sub-Saharan Africa.~~

Thesis statements 1, 2, and 4 showed promise. Article number 1 would provide a comparison with zoos in terms of the space that elephants have to live in and the kinds of activities that they can do to avoid boredom. Article number 2 would show some of the disadvantages of safari parks, while still showing the need to protect elephants that are endangered. Article number 3 seemed to be a very general text about animals in safari parks, whereas article number 4 was much more specific to elephants and how safari parks can encourage people to help protect them. Article number 5 was going to be about the history of safari parks, which might be of general interest, but would not be a major part of this student's assignment.

CULTURE NOTE

A safari, or wildlife, park is a large open-air zoo that is divided into sections that contain different types of animals. Many safari parks can be driven through, so you can get close to elephants, rhinos, and even monkeys—though some will steal your windshield wipers. The first safari park to open outside Africa was at Longleat, in the United Kingdom, in 1966. The United States has more than ten safari parks.

VOCABULARY PREVIEW

These vocabulary items appear in the reading. Circle the ones you know. Put a question mark next to the ones you don't know.

suffer	captivity	bruise (n)	isolation
condition (n)	lack (n)	territory	

EXERCISE 7

A. Read the article about elephants that are kept in zoos. Then answer the comprehension questions.

Capturing Majesty

1 My fondest childhood memories involve visiting the zoo with my family. That early desire to view wild creatures up close is what inspired me to become a zoologist. Those memories are tinged with sadness, now—as an adult I realize just how inadequate those old zoo habitats were. The elephants, especially, were suffering. This cruelty was not intentional. Zookeepers at the time may have known the elephants were uncomfortable, but only recently have we come to understand just how mentally and physically damaged elephants are by poor zoo conditions. Elephants in captivity live shorter lives and act out with stress behaviors never seen in wild elephants. Even a lack of social life takes a toll on these creatures. Elephants are not suited to captivity because zoos are unable to provide healthy food or appropriate exercise. Elephants in zoos are often bored and lonely, or stressed because they do not get along with other elephants they share an environment with.

2 If you have ever cared for a pet, you know how important it is to select appropriate foods and to play with it for exercise. Even we humans, masters of our environment, need to eat healthy foods and engage in physical activity. Elephants are formidable, rugged creatures that, in nature, travel long distances. Elephants eat a variety of plants. It is difficult for zookeepers to replicate this diet. Elephants eating bland, nutritionally poor food tend to overeat, causing many to become overweight. A lack of exercise—they have nothing to do—leads to poor overall health. Even the terrain poses an issue. Wild elephants walk on soft ground; an elephant's feet can easily support the creature's weight, but they run into trouble with hard ground. Zoo elephants walk over the same area, again and again, packing the dirt down with their weight over time. The full weight of an elephant walking over hard ground can easily injure the foot, leading to bruises, circulation problems, and infection. As disturbing as this is, what happens in the mind of zoo elephants can easily be worse.

3 Imagine never going more than one kilometer from your house for the rest of your life. Most people would, eventually, find themselves bored. With nothing new to do and no new territory to explore, each day would come to seem like all the rest. Elephants, being incredibly intelligent animals, find boredom to be just as stressful as humans. Wild elephants travel tremendous distances, crossing national borders and going from forest, to desert, to savannah. Zoo elephants, comparatively, have very little to amuse themselves with. This is one of the leading causes of stress behaviors like rocking back and forth—a response to trauma and boredom that researchers have never documented in wild elephants despite years of observation. What makes this boredom even worse for elephants is the extreme social isolation that goes along with it.

Glossary

Stress behaviors: actions that are caused by feeling nervous

Separation anxiety: feeling anxious or worried when alone or taken away from someone you love

Acquaintance: someone you know, but do not know well

1. Why does the author think that "zookeepers at the time may have known the elephants were uncomfortable"?

....

2. Why does the author use human behavior to describe problems that elephants face in captivity?

....

3. Based on the author's arguments, what kind of zoo would meet an elephant's needs?

....

B. Underline the thesis statement in the article in Part A. Does the text follow the order specified? Circle the topic sentence of each paragraph and then draw arrows from the part of the thesis statement that matches each one.

C. Evaluate these alternative thesis statements for the article in Part A. Mark the thesis statement *OK* if you think it is a good alternative, *F*, if it is too factual, or *G* if it is too general.

.... 1. If zoos wish to keep elephants, they should provide adequate nutrition and exercise, along with a stimulating environment and compatible companions.

.... 2. Zoos are inappropriate environments for elephants.

.... 3. Elephants live in zoos.

.... 4. Zoos contain a wide variety of animals, including elephants.

.... 5. To survive in captivity, elephants require a combination of good food and exercise, mental stimulation, and companionship with other elephants.

.... 6. Zoos are a way of protecting endangered animals like elephants.

.... 7. There are many zoos in the United States.

.... 8. If zoos wish to encourage people to visit, they need to take better care of their elephants by providing better food and exercise, more stimulating activities, and suitable companions.

D. Read the assignments. Use your knowledge and the information from your research to create two possible thesis statements for each assignment. Make sure that each thesis statement shows a position and provides enough details.

Glossary

Scrutiny: when something is examined or watched very carefully

Assignment A:

CITY UNIVERSITY

Your Course Now

Log on | Register | Student forum

Main page ▪ Contents ▪ Featured content ▪ Current events ▪ About us ▪ Community portal ▪ Recent changes ▪ Help

MY assignment — *Due Date: Friday, February 16*

Zoology 107: Professor Abadi

Assignment: As researchers discover more and more about the social behavior of elephants, the practice of keeping them in captivity has come under scrutiny. What can zoos do to ensure that the elephants they keep are happy and healthy?

Thesis statement 1: ....

....

Thesis statement 2: ....

....

Assignment B:

Glossary

Sanctuary: a place where animals, often those who have been abused in some way or abandoned, go to spend the rest of their lives. They are cared for and protected. Sanctuaries may or may not be open to the public.

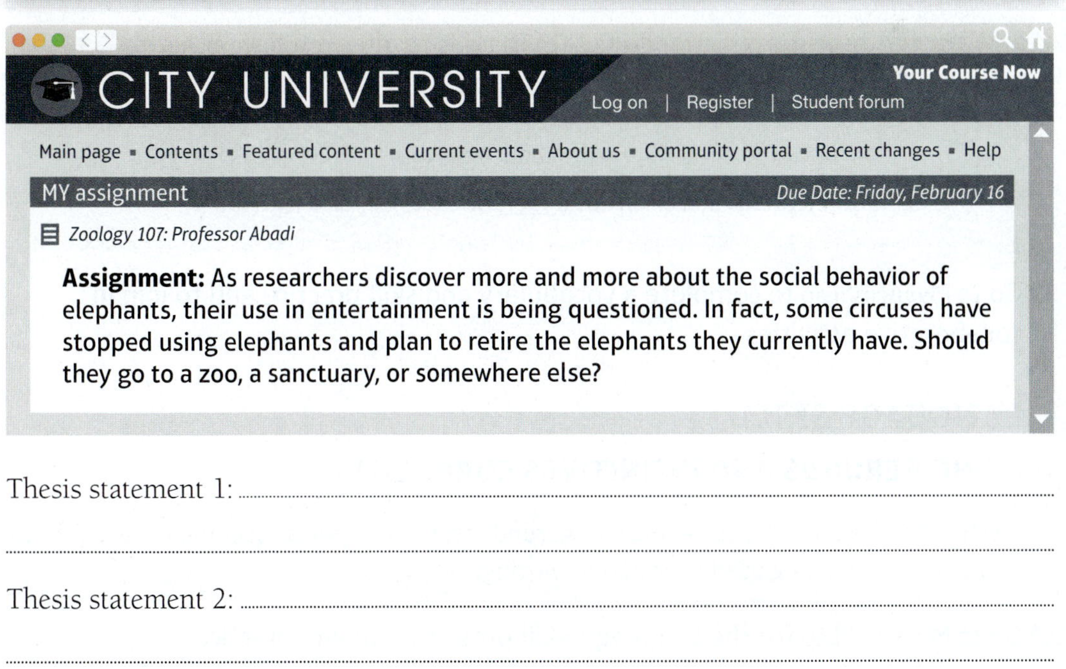

CITY UNIVERSITY

Your Course Now

Log on | Register | Student forum

Main page ▪ Contents ▪ Featured content ▪ Current events ▪ About us ▪ Community portal ▪ Recent changes ▪ Help

MY assignment — *Due Date: Friday, February 16*

Zoology 107: Professor Abadi

Assignment: As researchers discover more and more about the social behavior of elephants, their use in entertainment is being questioned. In fact, some circuses have stopped using elephants and plan to retire the elephants they currently have. Should they go to a zoo, a sanctuary, or somewhere else?

Thesis statement 1: ....

....

Thesis statement 2: ....

....

VOCABULARY CHECK

A. Review the items in the Vocabulary Preview. Write their definitions and add examples. Use a dictionary if necessary.

B. Choose the sentence that correctly shows the meaning of each underlined vocabulary item.

1. a. An animal that lives in captivity has a lot of space to explore.

   b. An animal that lives in captivity does not have a lot of space to explore.

2. a. An elephant that lives in isolation is surrounded by other elephants.

   b. An elephant that lives in isolation has no other elephants for company.

3. a. Elephants use their tusks to mark their territory, or the area that belongs to them.

   b. Elephants use their tusks to mark their territory, or the area that belongs to others.

4. a. The conditions, or surroundings, in a zoo are very different from those in the natural environment.

   b. The conditions, or meals, in a zoo are very different from those in the natural environment.

5. a. Elephants suffer in zoos because they don't have enough space.

   b. Elephants suffer in zoos because they are well looked after.

6. a. A bruise is a mark on the skin that forms after you have been hit.

   b. A bruise is a cut to the skin that forms after you have been hit.

7. a. If an elephant suffers from a lack of exercise, it is well rested.

   b. If an elephant suffers from a lack of exercise, it is unhealthy.

Go to MyEnglishLab to complete a vocabulary and skill practice and to join in collaborative activities.

LANGUAGE SKILL

USING GERUNDS AND INFINITIVES CORRECTLY

WHY IT'S USEFUL The correct use of gerunds and infinitives is essential because these forms are commonly used in academic writing.

Go to MyEnglishLab for the Language Skill presentation and practice.

VOCABULARY STRATEGY

DETERMINING MEANING FROM CONTEXT

WHY IT'S USEFUL Using context—nearby words and sentences—to determine the meaning of unknown words is an essential skill. Using context clues to figure out the meaning of new words makes you an efficient reader and helps you expand your vocabulary, which enables you to be more precise in your own writing.

While it is sometimes necessary to stop and look up the meaning of an unknown word, it is preferable not to interrupt your reading to refer to a dictionary repeatedly. Instead, you can often figure out what an unfamiliar word means by taking a look at the context—the surrounding words and sentences. The context may contain words you already know that can help you make sense of the new word or make an educated guess. The context may even help you determine meaning by providing a definition, a synonym, or a word or words with an opposite meaning.

Remember also to use the knowledge you already have when trying to determine meaning from context. For example, you can use your knowledge of grammar to determine what part of speech an unknown word is. This is a clue that can help you guess its meaning.

Let's look at some examples from texts you have read earlier to see how you might use context clues to determine meaning.

> Elephants tend to travel **well-trodden** paths along migratory routes that have not changed in centuries.

A student might not be sure what *well-trodden* means in this sentence, but by using context clues he or she can discover the following information:

- The item is acting like an adjective because it seems to be describing the word *paths*.
- In the second half of the sentence, *have not changed in centuries* shows that elephants have used the same paths for hundreds of years.
- A *well-trodden* path is probably a path that has been "used by many travelers for a long time."

In the next example, context clues in the sentences before and after the sentence with unknown words shed light on its meaning.

> Wild elephants will, in their lifetime, socialize with hundreds of other elephants. Zoo elephants seem to suffer from a lack of **social novelty**. Elephants in captivity simply don't get to meet new elephants or make dozens of friends.

A student not sure what *social novelty* means can use these context clues to help figure out the meaning:

- In the first sentence, the student learns that elephants "socialize with hundreds of other elephants" over the course of their lives. That must mean that wild elephants frequently meet new elephants.
- The third sentence contrasts—shows a difference—between elephants in captivity and wild elephants. It says that zoo elephants "don't get to meet new elephants." This is a second clue, related to the idea of "new."
- The word *novelty* is acting like a noun. The word *social* is describing it. The student is somewhat familiar with the word *social* and knows it is related to interacting with others.
- These clues help the student determine that *social novelty,* in this context, must mean "new ways to meet other elephants."

These clues show how you can use context to find the meaning of unknown items. This is an important strategy that requires practice. You may not be able to find enough clues to determine the meaning of every unknown item you encounter. However, with practice you will become skilled at using the surrounding words and sentences to give you enough meaning to continue reading without interrupting to check a dictionary.

EXERCISE 8

A. Read the excerpt from the article on elephants in captivity. Imagine that you are not sure what "appropriate foods" are. The possible context clues are underlined and numbered. Write down how you can use each clue to determine the meaning of "appropriate foods."

> If you have ever cared for a pet, then you know how important it is to select **appropriate foods**[1] and to play with it for exercise. Even we humans, masters of our environment, need to eat healthy foods[2] and engage in physical activity. Elephants are formidable, rugged creatures that, in nature, travel long distances. Elephants eat a variety of plants.[3] It is difficult for zookeepers to replicate this diet.[4] Elephants eating bland, nutritionally poor food[5] tend to overeat, causing many to become overweight.

1. ....

2. ....

3. ....

4. ....

5. ....

6. What are "appropriate foods" in this context? ....

....

....

B. Read the information about elephants. What context clues can help you determine the meaning of the items in bold? Underline the context clues and then explain to a partner how they help you.

1. Both Asian and African elephants have a **trunk**. Often we think of it like a nose since elephants do use it to smell and breathe. However, it is much more than a nose. Elephants use it to drink and make noise, like a mouth. They also use it to dig and pick things up, like hands and fingers.
2. Elephants can **snorkel**, and they don't need special equipment to do so. They can go underwater almost completely and still breathe. They just need to stick the tip of their trunk out of the water to breathe.
3. Elephants have a slow **pulse**. Unlike a small animal like a mouse whose heart beats very quickly, an elephant's heart beats slowly.
4. Some scientists believe that elephants may **pay homage** to their dead. People often bury their dead and mark the place so they can come back to visit and leave items such as flowers. Elephants have been observed showing strong interest in the bones of dead elephants. For example, they will often smell and touch dead elephants or their bones. They have even been observed trying to move or feed a dead relative. Scientists are not sure if this is a sign of respect or something else.
5. Humans have a **gestation period** of about nine months. Elephants, however, have the longest gestation period of all mammals. Female elephants are pregnant two and a half times longer than humans, with average pregnancies lasting about 22 months.

C. Using the context clues you discussed with a partner, write a definition for each term. Then compare your definition to the definition in a learner's dictionary.

1. trunk: ....
2. snorkel: ....
3. pulse: ....
4. pay homage: ....
5. gestation period: ....

APPLY YOUR SKILLS

WHY IT'S USEFUL By applying the skills you have learned in this unit, you will be able to put together a complete research paper, with an introduction, a conclusion, and well-formed body paragraphs that reflect a well-thought-out thesis statement. You will use gerunds and infinitives appropriately and thoughtfully in your writing.

ASSIGNMENT

Plan a well-researched 2–3 page paper that answers these questions:
Why are African elephants being poached? How is poaching harming elephant social structure? What is being done to prevent poaching? Your paper should have an effective introduction, including an appropriate thesis statement, and a suitable conclusion. It should also include three body paragraphs, each with a topic sentence and two or three supporting points.

BEFORE YOU WRITE

A. Before you begin your assignment, discuss these questions with one or more students.

1. What is poaching? What kinds of African animals are being poached?
2. What could be done to stop poaching?
3. What do you know about the social structure of elephant groups?

B. As you consider your writing assignment, complete the tasks. Then share your ideas with a partner. Get feedback and revise your ideas if necessary.

1. To prepare for your paper, find out the two main reasons why elephants are poached. List them below:

a. ....

b. ....

2. To help you organize the information you might include in this paper, answer the questions.

Problem

1. What is the problem?
2. What is causing the problem?
3. What is the impact of the problem?

Solution

1. What is a possible solution to the problem?
2. How does this solution help solve the problem?

3. Thinking about the parts of an essay that you have studied in this unit, discuss your answers to the questions below with a partner.

   a. What ideas will you include in your introduction?

   ....

   ....

   b. What could your thesis statement be?

   ....

   ....

   c. What kind of final thought might you provide in the conclusion?

   ....

   ....

C. Review the Unit Skills Summary. As you plan the writing task, apply the skills you learned in this unit.

UNIT SKILLS SUMMARY

Write an introduction

- Put together an introduction that begins with a general overview, narrows the topic, and includes a thesis statement.

Write a conclusion

- Provide in your conclusion an overview of your main points and add a closing comment.

Understand and use thesis statements

- End your introduction with a good thesis statement that indicates the main idea of your essay and a clear overview of the supporting points you will present.

Use gerunds and infinitives correctly

- Use gerunds and infinitives correctly, distinguishing between the two forms.

Determine meaning from context

- Use context clues to determine the meaning of unknown words to read efficiently and to expand your vocabulary for active use in your own writing.

THINKING CRITICALLY

As you think about your assignment, use the information from the earlier sections of the unit to answer the questions. Discuss your answers with one or more students and revise your ideas if necessary.

1. Poachers seeking ivory often target a matriarch. Why might that be?
2. Describe what an elephant family group might do with a calf that has just lost its mother to poachers. What might happen to the orphan? How might the orphan be raised?

THINKING VISUALLY

More and more elephants are being born without tusks. Why might this be? Is this a good development for elephants? Discuss your ideas with a partner.

THINKING ABOUT LANGUAGE

A. Read the article about using drones to stop poachers. Underline verb + gerund pairs and double underline verb + infinitive pairs. The first has been done for you.

STOP POACHERS WITH DRONES

Some conservationists recommend using drone technology to stop poachers. Now their use is being tested in several countries in Africa to see if it will be an effective solution to the increasingly severe poaching problem.

Poaching: A growing problem

Both elephants and rhinoceroses are the targets of poachers, who kill them for their valuable tusks or horns. Poachers are not easy to stop. There are often more poachers than there are park rangers, and the area where poachers may strike is huge. In addition, poachers usually strike at night when it is very difficult for rangers to patrol parks. Another reason why wildlife crime is on the rise is that the criminals are using more advanced technology to find and kill animals. Rangers risk getting hurt when they encounter poachers. Poachers can work in very organized groups using high-powered automatic weapons and even night vision goggles to help them find their prey in the dark. The solution to the poaching problem may be to fight technology with technology.

PART 1

High-tech Eyes in the Night Sky

Drones may be the technology we need to combat poachers. Drones, unmanned aerial vehicles, can go where people can't. These devices are too expensive to randomly position. Instead, operators send drones based on data that has been gathered over years of research on elephants. They predict where herds will be on a given night. If an operator spots poachers, rangers are alerted so they can stop the poachers.

Critics claim drones are not a viable solution that countries in Africa can realistically use for a long time. They cite high costs of operating and maintaining equipment and lack of drone operators. While these are certainly hurdles in the use of drone technology to stop poaching, they can be overcome. The more poachers that are caught using drones, the more data operators will have on when, where, and how poachers operate. Operators can learn to fly drones in areas even more likely to have poachers, with rangers nearby ready to stop them.

To avoid watching elephants and rhinoceroses become extinct, it is time to use drones to stop wildlife crime. We can't continue to let poachers get away with crime.

B. What context clues can you use to determine the meaning of these words: *rangers, randomly*? Discuss your answers with a partner.

WRITE

A. Look again at the writing assignment, your chart from Before You Write, and your conclusions from Thinking Critically and Thinking Visually. Determine how you might answer the assignment questions.

B. Continue to research the topic and take effective notes. Discuss your notes and ideas with others and make any needed adjustments.

C. Write an outline of your paper and make sure you have a clear thesis statement to guide your writing.

BEYOND THE ASSIGNMENT

Write a well-researched, 2–3 page paper that answers these questions: Why are African elephants being poached? How is poaching harming elephant social structure? What is being done to prevent poaching? Your paper should have an effective introduction, including an appropriate thesis statement, and a suitable conclusion. It should also include three body paragraphs, each with a topic sentence and two or three supporting points. Use all the skills you learned in this unit.

Go to MyEnglishLab to watch Professor O'Connell-Rodwell's concluding video and to complete a self-assessment.

HISTORY

Narratives

UNIT PROFILE

Archaeologists and explorers have made discoveries that changed our understanding of ancient people and places. Their finds have helped shape our knowledge of how our ancestors lived, what they believed in, and what they were capable of. Some of these people dedicated their lives to discovering the secrets of the past and telling their stories. In this unit, you will learn about several key discoveries as well as the people who made them.

OUTCOMES

- Use narrative writing
- Write a biography
- Use chronological organization
- Use narrative tenses
- Understand affixes

You will plan a 300–500 word narrative essay on one of two topics: either the history of Angkor Wat and its rediscovery, or the life of explorer Henri Mouhot, who made Angkor Wat famous in the West.

For more about **HISTORY**, see 2 3. See also W and OC **HISTORY** 1 2 3.

PART 1

GETTING STARTED

Go to MyEnglishLab to watch Dr. Hunt's introductory video and to complete a self-assessment.

Discuss these questions with a partner or a group.

1. Have you ever visited a historic site, or do you prefer to visit museums instead? Why? How are these experiences different?
2. How important is it to understand how people lived many thousands of years ago? How does such knowledge help us understand ourselves?
3. Dr. Hunt suggests that history is like a journey. Do you agree? Why or why not?

SKILL 1

USING NARRATIVE WRITING

WHY IT'S USEFUL Knowing how to write a narrative—to tell a story—is an important skill for many forms of writing, including academic writing. Understanding the elements involved in telling a story will help you write interesting narratives that bring history to life for your reader.

There are four main types of writing. The type you choose depends on your purpose for writing. While this section focuses on narrative writing, the chart below identifies the four broad categories of writing and the purpose of each one. Which type of writing are you most familiar with?

Type of Writing	Writer's Purpose
Expository	Informs readers about something. This type of writing can be used to explain an idea or a process, for example.
Persuasive	Persuades your readers to agree with you. This type of writing is often referred to as argumentative because you present an argument and support it.
Descriptive	Describes something in detail in a way that allows your reader to picture it. Descriptive writing can be about people, objects, places, or even experiences.
Narrative	Tells a story by explaining a series of events. Narrative writing shares certain elements with stories.

For more on stating an argument and supporting an argument with examples, see Bioethics, Part 2.

For more on writing a descriptive paragraph, see History, Part 2.

For more on describing a process, see Zoology, Part 2.

Narrative writing is a kind of storytelling. Storytelling is a common form of communication. Most people think of fiction when they hear the word *story*. It is true that narrative writing is used in fiction and poetry, but it is also used in nonfiction. Narratives can be very personal accounts of something that happened to the writer, or they can be more objective, explaining something that happened by focusing on the related events that took place. One of the main differences between narrative writing and expository or persuasive writing is that a narrative makes readers feel as if they are there, as much as possible, experiencing the events in the story. In fact, some historians use a form of narrative—known as narrative history—instead of a more analytical, expository format to help readers feel that they are experiencing a slice of history.

The elements of a story

Narratives stand out from other kinds of writing because they contain the elements of a story. When you write in narrative form, you will include some, if not all, of the elements explained in the chart below.

Story Element	Explanation
Narrator	A narrator is the person telling the story. If the narrator is part of the story, we say the story is told in the first person, and personal pronouns such as *I* or *me* are used. If the narrator is not a character, the story is told in third person, and pronouns like *he* or *she* are used.
Characters	Characters are the people in the story. The narrator helps the reader get to know the characters by describing them.
Setting	The setting is the place and / or time in which the events in a story happen.
Plot	Plot refers to the events in the narrative. Narratives, like stories, should have a clear beginning, middle, and end.

Let's look at two different approaches—narrative and expository—to the history assignment shown. Which of the two approaches do you find more compelling? Why? For what types of assignments might you choose to take a narrative approach?

For more on understanding an assignment, see Bioethics, Part 1.

Glossary

Mesopotamia: an ancient region between the Tigris and Euphrates rivers in the Middle East.

Scribe: scribes were members of ancient societies who copied texts.

Clay tablets: a piece of heavy, sticky earth used to record shapes and symbols of early language

Ancient Mesopotamia

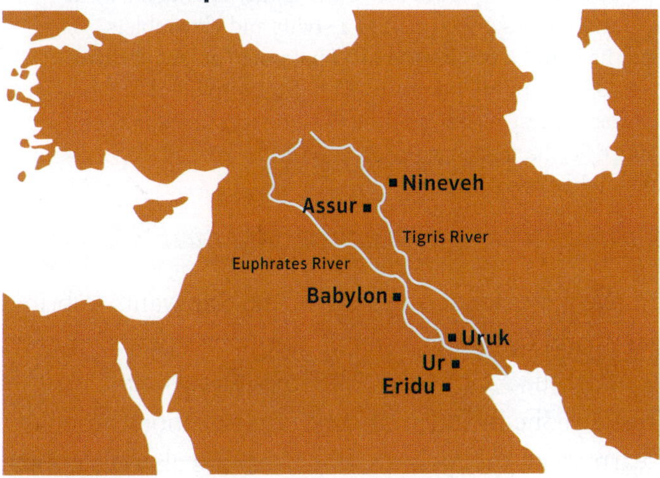

Student A: Narrative approach

A Day in the Life of a Mesopotamian Scribe

It was early in the day and although he had only been working for an hour, the scribe's fingers already ached from holding the stylus, the tool that he used to push letters into the clay tablet. The pain in his fingers reminded him of his scribe school days. Learning to read and write and do mathematics in ancient Mesopotamia was not something that all people got to do, and he knew he should be grateful. His job meant that he could provide material wealth for his family, and his own son would no doubt one day be a scribe as well. Maybe, if he worked hard enough, he would be Palace Scribe one day and help the king write his letters. So, he stretched his arms and returned to his work. At least today's work was interesting. Many of the tablets he had copied recently were legal texts concerning the sale of property in Nineveh, the city where he lived. However, today he was copying a story and one that he had heard before. In the story, a god told a man to build a boat and fill it with people and animals. A terrible storm came, and only the creatures in the boat survived. As he finished copying the tablet, he smiled and thought his young son and daughter might like to hear that story. He put away his tools and headed home.

Student B: Expository approach

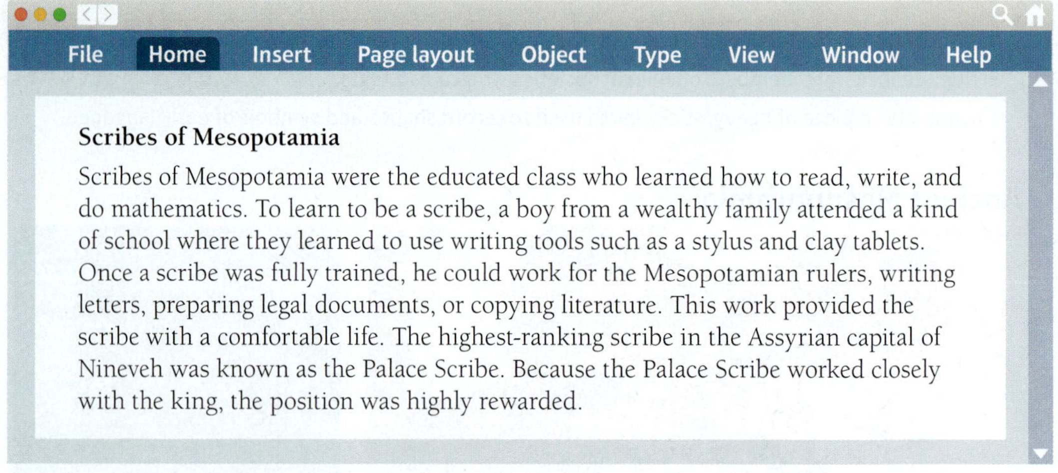

Student A decided to take a narrative approach to the assignment. She wants to bring the reader into the Mesopotamian world by telling a simple story of a scribe's day. She focuses the paragraph on the events of the scribe's day. The story has a simple plot: the beginning, middle, and end of his day. She included historical information throughout the narrative. For example, we learn about the tools a scribe used. We also learn that being a scribe was a good job reserved for men from wealthy families. The writer even mentions the kinds of texts that an Assyrian scribe might have worked on, such as legal documents and stories. This type of approach is appropriate when you want to tell a story to help your reader experience past events.

Student B took an expository approach to the assignment. He provides much of the same information as student A, but he informs the reader about Mesopotamian scribes by explaining a series of events. He is not concerned about giving the reader a sense of the scribe's world. This type of approach is appropriate when you want to inform your reader about a topic and explain related concepts.

Preparing to write a narrative

When you are planning to write a narrative, it is useful to gather information that answers these kinds of questions:

- What is this story about?
- Who are the characters?
- What happened? What are the main events?
- Where did these events happen?
- When did these events happen?
- Why did the characters do what they did?
- How did the characters do what they did?

For more on using questions to guide your research, see Business and Design, Part 1.

By answering these questions to the extent possible before you write, you will have gathered much of the information you need to tell an interesting story, with events that clearly signal a beginning, middle, and end.

VOCABULARY PREVIEW

These vocabulary items appear in the reading. Circle the ones you know. Put a question mark next to the ones you don't know.

treasure (n)	ancient	scholar	catalogue (n)
jewel	military	reputation	preserve (v)

EXERCISE 1

A. Read the assignment about the treasures of Ninevah and a student's response. Then answer the comprehension questions.

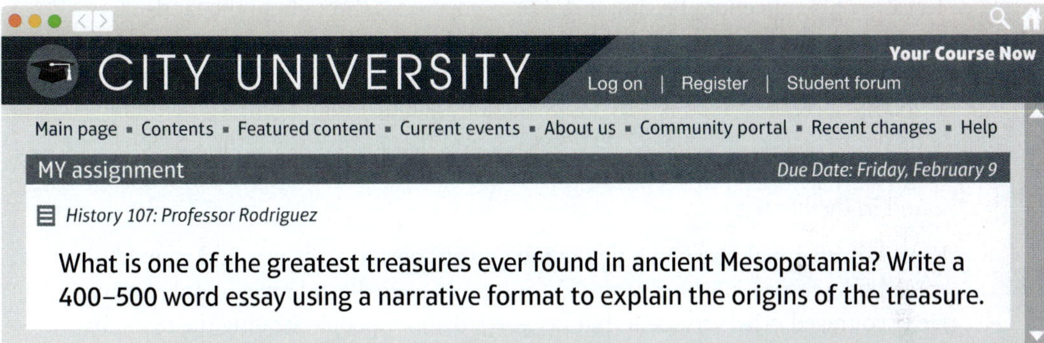

CITY UNIVERSITY

Your Course Now

Log on | Register | Student forum

Main page ▪ Contents ▪ Featured content ▪ Current events ▪ About us ▪ Community portal ▪ Recent changes ▪ Help

MY assignment — *Due Date: Friday, February 9*

History 107: Professor Rodriguez

What is one of the greatest treasures ever found in ancient Mesopotamia? Write a 400–500 word essay using a narrative format to explain the origins of the treasure.

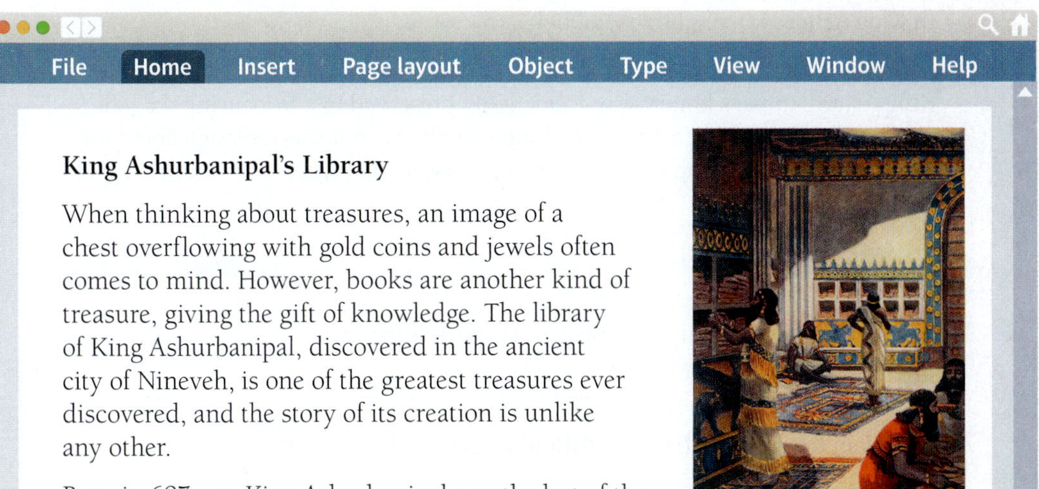

File | Home | Insert | Page layout | Object | Type | View | Window | Help

King Ashurbanipal's Library

When thinking about treasures, an image of a chest overflowing with gold coins and jewels often comes to mind. However, books are another kind of treasure, giving the gift of knowledge. The library of King Ashurbanipal, discovered in the ancient city of Nineveh, is one of the greatest treasures ever discovered, and the story of its creation is unlike any other.

Born in 687 BCE, King Ashurbanipal was the last of the great Assyrian kings, but he did not grow up expecting

(Continued)

to rule a military empire. Ashurbanipal surrounded himself with scholars, often religious priests, and learned from them. Unlike other kings of the time, he learned how to read, write, and do mathematics, and he absorbed much about the religious beliefs of the time. When Ashurbanipal's older brother died in 672 BCE and his father died a few years later, Ashurbanipal became king. This new role distracted him for a time, but he never stopped being a scholar and appreciating the arts.

Before he could return to scholarly learning, King Ashurbanipal had to focus on the military campaigns his father had started. Much like his father, grandfather, and great-grandfather before him, he did not think twice about killing or making slaves of his enemies. In this way, King Ashurbanipal helped spread Nineveh's reputation as a "city of blood." However, after defeating his enemies, King Ashurbanipal began building a treasure of knowledge: the world's first modern-day library. The knowledge he had gained both on and off the battlefield helped him understand that he could leave a great gift to the future.

To build this library, King Ashurbanipal did what modern librarians do. He purposely built a collection of texts, organized them by topic, and even made a library catalogue. King Ashurbanipal was the most powerful person in Assyria. To gather his collection, he simply wrote to governors throughout the lands of Mesopotamia, which were ruled by him, and demanded that they send texts to Nineveh. Then he had scribes copy them. The king was interested in many scholarly subjects, which is why his collection included many genres, including texts on medicine, law, magic, dictionaries, and literature. In fact, the Epic of Gilgamesh, perhaps the oldest written story in the world, was one of the treasures found in the library.

King Ashurbanipal also had a reputation as a supporter of the arts and wanted to spread knowledge. His library was not just a private collection meant only for him. He encouraged others to use it, but he worried about people stealing the texts. In modern libraries, users are discouraged from stealing with loud security systems. In King Ashurbanipal's library, a book curse was written on the texts, promising bad luck to anyone who stole them.

King Ashurbanipal's library was accidentally preserved in a fire during the fall of Nineveh, about 25 years after the king's death. Then it was forgotten about for two thousand years. The preserved texts are jewels that extend our knowledge of ancient history.

1. Why didn't Ashurbanipal expect to become king?

2. How was King Ashurbanipal different from other Assyrian kings?

3. What made the library of King Ashurbanipal similar to a modern library?

....

4. How did the king gather texts for his library?

....

5. What was the purpose of a book curse?

....

CULTURE NOTE

In many countries, the year is measured from the time it is believed Jesus Christ was born. The time before this event is sometimes known as BC (Before Christ). However, since many countries do not follow the Christian faith, the term BCE is becoming a common replacement. It means Before the Common Era. CE is used to show the Common Era, or the time after Christ. The letters AD (Anno Domini) are also frequently used to refer to the time after Christ.

BCE time is counted backwards, so King Ashurbanipal, who was born in 687 BCE, was around 15 years old when his brother died in 672 BCE.

Glossary

Empire: a group of countries or organizations that are all controlled by one person, government, etc.

Curse: magic words that bring someone bad luck

B. When planning the narrative, the student answered the planning questions below. Answer the questions yourself referring to the essay about King Ashurbanipal's library.

1. What is the story about?
2. Who are the characters?
3. What happened?
4. Where did it happen?
5. When did it happen?
6. Why did it happen?
7. How did it happen?

C. How would the student's response to the assignment about treasures of Nineveh have been different if he had used an expository approach instead of a narrative approach? Which approach would you have used for the assignment? Why? Discuss your ideas with a partner.

EXERCISE 2

A. When writing a narrative, the writer focuses on events to tell a story. A story has a beginning, middle, and end. Below are the events from the story about King Ashurbanipal's library, but in jumbled order. Put them in the correct order by numbering them from 1 to 10.

.... a. Ashurbanipal led battles around Mesopotamia.

.... b. Ashurbanipal let others use the library.

.... c. Ashurbanipal became king.

.... d. Ashurbanipal decided to build a library.

.... e. Scholars taught Ashurbanipal to read and write.

.... f. Ashurbanipal sent for clay tablets from all over Mesopotamia.

.... g. The library burned in a fire, and the texts were accidentally preserved.

.... h. Scribes copied tablets.

.... i. Ashurbanipal's brother and father died.

.... j. Ashurbanipal died.

B. Which events above are part of the beginning of the story? Which are part of the middle and the end? Go back and write *B*, *M*, or *E* next to each event, and then compare your answers with a partner. Discuss any differences.

EXERCISE 3

A. Write a narrative paragraph about finding a treasure. You may base your narrative on your own personal experience or on someone else's experience. Include three words from the Vocabulary Check. Begin by answering the planning questions.

1. What is the story about?
2. Who are the characters?
3. What happened?
4. Where did it happen?
5. When did it happen?
6. Why did it happen?
7. How did it happen?

B. Use the information from your planning questions to create a list of events for your narrative. Put the events in order and note which ones relate to the beginning, the middle, and the end of your story.

C. Write your narrative paragraph. Then exchange paragraphs with a partner and complete the peer review form. Discuss your comments.

Questions	Yes	No	Notes
Did the narrator describe the character(s)?	☐	☐	
Is the setting of the narrative clear?	☐	☐	
Is there a distinct beginning, middle, and end to the narrative?	☐	☐	
Did the writer include three words from the Vocabulary Check?	☐	☐	

D. Revise your draft, taking into account your partner's comments.

VOCABULARY CHECK

A. Review the items in the Vocabulary Preview. Write their definitions and add examples. Use a dictionary if necessary.

B. Choose the sentence that correctly paraphrases the meaning of each underlined vocabulary item.

1. a. A jewel is a kind of toy.

   b. A jewel is a valuable stone.

2. a. If you preserve something, you make it go away.

   b. If you preserve something, you make it last for a long time.

3. a. A reputation is the opinion that many people have about a person, a company, a place, etc.

   b. A reputation is how long a person, a company, a place, etc. has existed.

4. a. If something is ancient, it is very old.

   b. If something is ancient, many people want it.

5. a. A catalogue is a type of calendar.

   b. A catalogue is a type of list.

6. a. A treasure is something that is valuable.

   b. A treasure is something that is worthless.

(Continued)

7. a. A <u>scholar</u> is someone who knows a lot about fixing things.

   b. A <u>scholar</u> is someone who knows a lot about one or more academic subjects.

8. a. If a country is involved in a <u>military campaign</u>, it is recovering from a disaster.

   b. If a country is involved in a <u>military campaign</u>, it is at war.

Go to MyEnglishLab to complete a vocabulary and skill practice and to join in collaborative activities.

SKILL 2

WRITING A BIOGRAPHY

WHY IT'S USEFUL As part of your college course work, you may occasionally need to write a short biography of a historical figure. Knowing how to go about this task will ensure that you write an account of the person's life that is not only interesting, but also appropriate for the assignment.

Since a biography is a story about a person's life, your skills in narrative writing will be useful. Some biographies are entire books and present many detailed episodes of a person's life. While you are unlikely to be asked to write a book, you may be asked to write a short biography about a famous person. To write an interesting biography, follow the steps discussed below for planning and research, writing, and revision. These steps are similar to the steps of the general academic writing process.

For more on the academic writing process, see Bioethics, Part 1.

Planning and prewriting

If you have a choice about the subject of your biography, think carefully. Brainstorming different possibilities is a good idea. Also, consider these questions:

- How interested are you in the subject? The more interested you are, the easier it will be to plan and write the biography.
- How much information is available on the subject? If there is not enough information, it will be hard to research the person's life.
- Is the subject appropriate for the purpose of the assignment?

A student has been given the following assignment to write a biography. To start, he put together, by brainstorming, a list of archaeologists and their discoveries. Then he reviewed the list, asking himself the questions above, and added related notes.

Glossary

Archaeologist: a person who studies ancient societies by examining what remains of their buildings, tools, and places they were buried

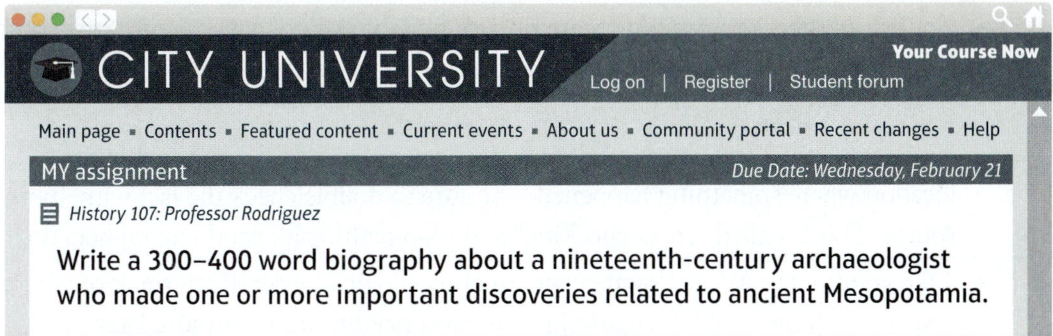

Archaeologists	Discoveries	Notes
Howard Carter	King Tut's tomb, Egypt —1920s	Wrong place and time period
Austin Henry Layard	Nimrud and Nineveh— 1840s–1850s	Appropriate—do more research
Hormuzd Rassam	Nineveh, Babylon— 1850s–1880s	Appropriate—do more research
Heinrich Schliemann	Troy, Greece—1870s	Wrong place
Henry Rawlinson	Behistun Rock, Babylon—1830s	Was he an archaeologist? Do more research.

The student saw that Carter and Schliemann would not be appropriate subjects for the assignment and removed them from his list. He did some preliminary research on Layard, Rassam, and Rawlinson. He determined that Rawlinson would not be appropriate for the assignment because he is more associated with learning Mesopotamian languages than with making significant discoveries. He was left with two choices and decided to write about Layard.

Researching your subject

After carefully choosing the subject of your biography, the next step is to do your research. Researching widely will help you gather the information you need, and it will help you verify that this information is accurate. Consider these tips when researching.

- Consult trusted sources. If you are unsure whether or not a website is trustworthy, ask your instructor. Don't forget that you can do research using books as well as online sources.
- When you find a fact about your subject—a date of birth, an important event, a location where something happened—be sure to double check the fact with another source. This is called "cross-checking" and is something all good biographers do.
- Take good notes. Write down events in chronological order. Keep track of where you got each piece of information in case you need to find out more later.

Take a look at the timeline made by the student writing about Austin Henry Layard to show events in the archaeologist's life.

March 5, 1817	Born in Paris
Childhood	Grew up mostly in Italy but educated in England
1833	Began to study law in England
1839	Left for a job (lawyer) in Ceylon (Sri Lanka) but traveled on land through Turkey and Persia (the Middle East)
1842	Got a job working with a diplomat in Constantinople (Istanbul)
1845	Returned to Iraq and began excavations of Nimrud
1849	Published a book, Nineveh and Its Remains – very popular!
1849	Began excavating Nineveh – Realized he mistook Nimrud for Nineveh when he discovered King Ashurbanipal's library
1852	Began political career – Elected to British Parliament
1853	Published another book, Discoveries among the Ruins of Nineveh and Babylon
1869	Began diplomatic career and worked in Spain and later Constantinople
1880	Retired and moved to Venice, Italy
July 5, 1894	Died in London, England

Make sure you use all resources available to you to help you understand the events in your subject's life. For example, the student, in making the timeline above, made use of online encyclopedias and maps to understand place names that have changed since Layard's lifetime. He learned that Ceylon is the old name for modern-day Sri Lanka and that the city of Constantinople is now known as Istanbul.

Writing

After you are satisfied you have done enough research to get a clear picture of your subject's life, begin the drafting process. Remember that a biography is a story about a person's life. It is not merely a long list of facts and events in chronological order. Since you will be limited as to what you can include, you will need to be selective about your information. You will be able to narrate only some episodes of the subject's life. It is therefore essential to have a main message, a thesis, that you want to communicate to your reader about your subject. Select examples and details about the subject's life that will help the reader understand your main message.

The biography assignment will help you determine the main message of the biography. Look again at the assignment above, which asks the student to write a biography about a nineteenth-century archaeologist who made one or more important discoveries related to ancient Mesopotamia. The main message of this biography will be connected to the subject's life as an archaeologist and to the Mesopotamian discoveries. This is not to say that no other information about the archaeologist's life should be included. However, other events should be combined and summarized.

Revising

As with any academic writing, you should revise the first draft of your biography before submitting it. If possible, seek feedback from a peer. You could ask a classmate to answer the following questions.

- Can you identify the main message of my biography?
- Do the events chosen support the central message?
- Were there enough examples and details to help you get a feel for the events?
- Can you follow the chronology of the subject's life? Were you confused about any parts of the subject's life?

You can incorporate changes based on your partner's feedback into your final draft. Don't forget to save enough time to proofread your final draft to catch careless mistakes.

EXERCISE 4

A. When you receive an assignment to write a biography, it is important to follow the writing process. Indicate the essential steps in each stage of the writing process.

Planning and Prewriting

1. ....

2. ....

3. ....

Writing

4. ....

5. ....

6. ....

Revising

7. ....

8. ....

9. ....

B. Have you ever written a biography? Who was it about? Did you follow the steps outlined above, or are there steps you didn't take but will want to be sure to include in the future? Discuss your answers with a partner.

VOCABULARY PREVIEW

These vocabulary items appear in the reading. Circle the ones you know. Put a question mark next to the ones you don't know.

adventure	ruins (n)	publish	archaeology
site (n)	diplomat	politics	

EXERCISE 5

A. Reread the student's notes about Austin Henry Layard on page 110. Then answer the questions.

1. What events in Layard's life are most relevant to the assignment and to the message the student needs to convey?

....

2. What kinds of examples and details should the student find out more about?

....

....

B. Now read the student's response to the History 107 assignment on page 109 and answer the comprehension questions.

Austen Henry Layard, Adventurer and Archaeologist in Ancient Mesopotamia

Austen Henry Layard was an adventurer and an archaeologist for a short time in his life. He contributed greatly to the understanding of ancient Mesopotamia through his discoveries at the sites of Nimrud and Nineveh. Born in Paris, in 1817, Layard grew up mostly in Italy but was educated in England. In 1833, he reluctantly began to study law with an uncle in London. Unhappy with this profession, but not sure what else to do, he took an offer to practice law in modern-day Sri Lanka. He was only 22 years old and decided to travel there over land on a horse. On his journey, he was determined to see archaeological sites such as the ruins of Petra. He overcame periods of illness from malaria and even continued on his adventures after being robbed several times. He became very interested in areas around modern-day Iraq. He even lived with nomadic tribes for a time, learning local customs and language.

By 1842, it was clear that he would not be going to Sri Lanka and instead went to modern-day Istanbul, Turkey, where he got a job working for a British diplomat. Layard's heart was still in Iraq, and he finally gained the diplomat's support to return there in 1845 to excavate Nimrud, a site near Mosul. Layard hired Hormuzd Rassam, a local, to help him organize the dig, and they became lifelong friends. The excavation uncovered extraordinary finds, such as an Assyrian palace and ivory plaques. Layard thought he had discovered the ancient Assyrian capital of Nineveh. He published a book, *Nineveh and Its Remains,* in 1849 before returning to excavate another nearby site later the same year. This second site was King Ashurbanipal's library—the true location of Nineveh.

(Continued)

Austen Henry Layard

Hormuzd Rassam

Layard continued to be an adventurous archaeologist until 1852 when he returned to England and entered politics. Reflecting on his adventures, he published another book, *Discoveries Among the Ruins of Nineveh and Babylon*. However, his career as an archaeologist had ended and he worked as a politician, and then as a diplomat, until he retired back to his childhood country of Italy, in 1880. Layard died in 1894 but left behind many discoveries in the world of archaeology.

Glossary

Reluctant: not wanting to do something

Nomadic tribe: a group of people who move from place to place rather than living in one place

Excavate: to dig up the ground, usually to look for items of archaeological interest

Plaque: a piece of flat metal or stone with writing on it, attached to a building to remind people of a famous event or person

1. Did Layard want to become a lawyer? How do you know?

   ....

2. What difficulties did Layard experience while traveling?

   ....

3. What does the student mean by "Layard's heart was still in Iraq"?

   ....

4. Why was 1849 an important year in Layard's career as an archaeologist?

   ....

5. What could be a reason why Layard retired to Italy?

   ....

C. What events in Layard's life did the student emphasize? What kinds of examples and details did the student include to help the reader experience these episodes? Which events did the student combine and briefly summarize? Compare and discuss your answers with a partner.

1. Emphasized events with examples and details

2. Combined and briefly summarized events

EXERCISE 6

A. A classmate chose Hormuzd Rassam as the subject of her biography. Do research and add 4–6 events to her chronological list.

	Date	Events in Hormuzd Rassam's Life
1.	1826	Born in Mosul, Iraq
2.		
3.	1845	Hired by Layard to excavate Nimrud
4.		
5.	1853	Discovered a plaque showing King Ashurbanipal hunting lions
6.		
7.	1876	Hired by British Museum to supervise excavations in Mesopotamia
8.		
9.	1910	Died

B. Based on your research, write a 200–300 word biography on Hormuzd Rassam. Include three words from the Vocabulary Check.

C. Work with a partner. Read each other's paragraphs and complete the peer review form. Discuss your comments.

Questions	Yes	No	Notes
Can you identify the central message of the biography?	☐	☐	
Do the events chosen support the central message?	☐	☐	
Were there enough examples and details to help you experience the events?	☐	☐	
Were you confused about any parts of the subject's life?	☐	☐	

D. Revise your draft, taking into account your partner's comments.

VOCABULARY CHECK

A. Review the items in the Vocabulary Preview. Write their definitions and add examples. Use a dictionary if necessary.

B. Complete the sentences with vocabulary items from the box.

adventure	archaeology	diplomat	politics
published	ruins (n)	site (n)	

1. Someone who likes .... enjoys exciting and unusual experiences.
2. A .... represents his or her government in a foreign country.
3. Training as a lawyer can be a good background for a job in ....
4. The study of .... helps us understand ancient societies.
5. The public are not allowed on the .... because there may be buried ....
6. After reluctantly returning home from his travels, Layard wrote and .... a book about his experiences.

Go to MyEnglishLab to complete a vocabulary and skill practice and to join in collaborative activities.

INTEGRATED SKILLS

USING CHRONOLOGICAL ORGANIZATION

WHY IT'S USEFUL Organizing information chronologically when you write provides your reader with a clear understanding of the sequence of events. It also gives you a logical basis for organizing your writing. When you are reading, recognizing chronological order will help you find information quickly.

Ordering events

Whether writing a narrative or a biography, putting events in chronological order requires you to understand when each event happened. There are three main methods of organization: earliest to latest, latest to earliest, and a combination of the two.

The first of these methods shows events in the order they occurred, while the second begins with the most recent event and works backwards through time. Many writers jump from one time period to another as they write. Careful use of sequencing language helps to show the order of events in this case.

Look at the excerpt from a newspaper article about a discovery made near Stonehenge, in southern England. Which form of organization is used?

Glossary

Excavation: the activity of digging up the ground, usually to look for items of historical interest

Mesolithic: Middle Stone Age: Approximately between 8000 BCE and 4000 BCE

Neolithic: New Stone Age: Approximately between 4000 BCE and 2000 BCE

MESOLITHIC HOUSE DISCOVERED

Our understanding of Stonehenge will need to be revised after yesterday's discovery of a house from the Mesolithic age. The house was built using stone and had a roof. There was also evidence that our Mesolithic ancestors warmed stones on the fire and then used them to heat the home—a type of storage heater. These discoveries suggest that people of the time were more advanced than previously thought.

David Jacques, the leader of the excavation team that made yesterday's discovery, has been studying Stonehenge and the surrounding area for the past ten years. He says that our previous understanding was that early humans traveled from Europe to what is now called Britain in the Neolithic age. However, this discovery shows that Mesolithic people were already living there, and they were quite capable of using tools to create long-lasting shelters.

Although there are several theories, it is widely believed that construction of Stonehenge began around ...

This article begins with the recent discovery and then provides background details about prior events. This is a typical structure for newspaper reporting. However, the times are clearly labeled and can be placed in a chronological list as seen below:

Mesolithic age:	Mesolithic house built.
Neolithic age:	Neolithic people arrived.
10 years ago:	David Jacques begins studying the area around Stonehenge.
Yesterday:	Mesolithic house discovered.

CULTURE NOTE

Stonehenge is a series of huge stones arranged so that they line up with the sun on the longest and shortest days of the year. The stones came from an area many miles away. How they were moved remains a mystery, but it shows that prehistoric people had technology and knowledge about the movement of the sun.

Sequencing language

When writing chronologically, it is important to show the relationship between events using time signals—relevant words and phrases and verb tenses. The following chart outlines some devices that can be used.

Device	Example
in	**In** the Mesolithic age ...
at	**At** 10:00 A.M. ...
on	**On** Tuesday ...
after	**After** the Mesolithic people built houses ...
before	**Before** the Neolithic people arrived ...
by the time	A Mesolithic community was established **by the time** Neolithic people arrived.
during	Stonehenge was built **during** the Neolithic period.
when	David Jacques was working for the University of Buckingham **when** his team discovered the site.
the following ...	The team released details of the find **the following** day.
Using verb tenses	Mesolithic people **had established** a community before people **arrived** from the continent.

The newspaper excerpt continues with a brief history of Stonehenge. The time signals are marked in bold. Can you follow the order of events?

PART 1

Glossary

Ditch: a long, narrow hole dug at the side of a field or road to hold or carry away water

Bury: to put a dead body into the ground

Although there are several theories, it is widely believed that construction of Stonehenge **began around** 3000 BCE, in the middle of the Neolithic Age, with the building of a circular ditch. **During this time**, it is believed the site was used to bury the dead as many burial sites have been found. Around 500 years **later**, two large stone circles were set up, **followed by** the building of an early road around 200 years **after that**. The road leads to a major river, so it is thought people traveled to the site by boat.

This part of the article follows the earliest-to-latest pattern of organization, with times clearly marked. The chronology is shown below:

3000 BCE:	Construction of Stonehenge begins with circular ditch. Site used for burials.
2500 BCE:	Two large stone circles were set up.
2300 BCE:	Road built.

VOCABULARY PREVIEW

These vocabulary items appear in the reading. Circle the ones you know. Put a question mark next to the ones you don't know.

legend	vast	earthquake	gradual	destruction
civilization	refer	volcano	confirm	

EXERCISE 7

A. Read the article about Akrotiri and the island of Santorini, which some people believe was the legendary Atlantis. Then answer the comprehension questions.

CULTURE NOTE

Atlantis may have been real, but was probably only a fictional island used in a story by Plato in 360 BCE. According to the story, people on the island used advanced technology and lived in luxury. However, they made the gods angry, and so the island was destroyed. Many people believe the story to have some truth and have searched for the "lost city of Atlantis." The idea of an advanced early civilization waiting to be discovered has been a favorite theme for writers and filmmakers through the ages.

Akrotiri—The Real Atlantis

1 The Aegean Museum of Maritime History is proud to unveil "The Real Atlantis: Secrets of Santorini." This exhibit focuses on items and artifacts recovered from the ancient village of Akrotiri on the island of Santorini. Also known as Thera, this island was the crown jewel of the Minoan empire, a kingdom based in Crete that controlled trade routes in the eastern Mediterranean about two thousand years ago. Modern scholars believe that the island's volcanic eruption, which destroyed the city and much of the Minoan fleet later, inspired the legend of Atlantis that Plato spoke of in the fourth century BCE. Now, you can view artwork and objects recovered from the ancient city.

2 The Minoan civilization is one of the earliest proto-empires we have record of. Evidence shows the Minoans inhabiting Crete at least as far back as 2600 BCE, forming a vast trading and commercial power predating the Mycenaeans and Phoenicians. The Minoans were early masters of the seas in an era when few people risked traveling the Mediterranean or Aegean. The trade ships of the Minoans went as far as Egypt and what is today referred to as the Levant. The Minoans traded in valuable metals like copper and minerals like emery, which some researchers believe Egyptian artisans purchased in vast quantities as a way to polish stonework.

3 The Minoans maintained outposts on many islands of the Aegean; outside of Crete, one of their most valuable cities was on the island of Thera. At that time, Thera was a single, crescent-shaped island. Thera was located at the intersection of numerous trade routes; the crescent shape of the island offered a safe harbor for trade ships. For centuries, Thera was a grand city—until a series of earthquakes and other warning signs caused residents to flee. In 1620 BCE, an underground volcano erupted, and the island, quite literally, exploded. This eruption was considerably larger than the later eruption of Pompeii—it might have been heard from as far away as Egypt, where the skies darkened from volcanic ash. There is even, in some ancient Chinese records, mention of a darkness ruining crops around this time—perhaps the volcanic ash spread as far as East Asia.

4 Modern Santorini is only part of the island that once was Thera; in ages past, modern-day Santorini and its neighbor, Thirasia, were both part of that larger island. The eruption formed a caldera, as floodwaters rushed into an impression created by the volcano. Historians used to believe that this eruption ended Minoan civilization; we now know, however, that this is not entirely true. The eruption occurred almost a century before the collapse of the Minoan civilization—but the eruption would have weakened the Minoans considerably. Tidal waves following a volcanic eruption would have decimated the Minoan fleet; the fleet was anchored on the Northern edge of Crete, facing the eruption.

5 The Minoans gradually faded from memory; Thera itself, once a bustling trading center, became a legend—before the island was resettled by people with no memory of its ancient glory. The advanced architecture and splendor of the city, though, were remembered and passed down as part of the story. By the time Plato writes about Atlantis in 360 BCE, the city was described as a place of wealth and beauty, shaken by earthquakes and swallowed by the sea. For years, explorers tried to figure out where Atlantis could have been. It would fall to one man, Spyridon Marinatos, to confirm that Santorini was the site of an ancient civilization—one that others assumed to be Atlantis.

6 Though a few archaeologists had conducted digs on Santorini in the late nineteenth and early twentieth centuries, the island had yet to be fully investigated. Marinatos had long been convinced that evidence pointed to Santorini as the site of an ancient Minoan city. In 1967, Marinatos confirmed his suspicions, leading a dig that would gradually uncover some of the most intricate and ornate buildings of the ancient world. Houses found at Akrotiri had multiple floors, support beams, and even indoor plumbing—something the Romans would not develop for another fifteen hundred years. Interior walls are covered in beautifully detailed and multicolored frescoes; the paintings show that citizens of Thera had both a love of art and the resources to create it.

7 The Akrotiri excavation is also notable for what archaeologists have not discovered; no ancient human remains have been located. Additionally, very few metal artifacts of any kind have been found in Akrotiri. This implies that the island's citizens knew that disaster was coming and were able to escape, taking their valuables with them. In fact, the only gold found so far in the Akrotiri excavation is a single, golden statue of a goat—perhaps left behind and forgotten in its hiding spot. We cannot say for certain that ancient Akrotiri was the city later referred to as Atlantis; given its wealth, beauty, and tragic destruction, though, it certainly seems the most likely candidate! Be sure to visit the exhibit later this fall for glimpses of the remnants of this ancient civilization.

Glossary

Exhibit: an object that is shown in a public place for people to look at

Artifact: an object such as a tool or weapon that was made in the past and is historically important

Eruption: when smoke, fire, and rock come out of a volcano

Fleet: a group of ships or vehicles

Crescent: a curved shape that is wider in the middle and pointed at the ends

Ash: the grey powder that is left after something has burned

1. Why was Thera so valuable to the Minoans?

....

2. What is the probable reason that no human remains were found?

....

3. What probably caused the Minoan empire to end?

....

4. Who discovered the ancient city of Thera?

....

B. Reread the article and underline all the time signals. Then discuss your findings with a partner. What method of chronological organization is used in the article, and how do the time signals help you follow the discussion?

C. Use time signals and the events in the box to complete the chronology.

Minoans inhabiting Crete	Residents flee from a series of earthquakes
Exhibit opens	Romans develop indoor plumbing
Thera was a grand city	Plato writes about Atlantis
Volcano erupts, Thera destroyed	Minoan empire ends
Digs conducted on Santorini	Tidal wave decimates Minoan fleet
Marinatos discovers Thera in Akrotiri	Chinese crops fail

	Date	Events
1.	2600 BCE	
2.	2600 BCE–1620 BCE	
3.	Just before 1620 BCE	
4.	1620 BCE	• • • •
5.	1520 BCE	
6.	360 BCE	
7.	120 BCE	
8.	Late 1800s–early 1900s	
9.	1967	
10.	This fall	

EXERCISE 8

A. Use the chronology about the *Titanic* and your own research to write a 200–300 word paragraph on the ship's fate and its discovery. Choose an appropriate method of chronological organization and use time signals to order the events.

CULTURE NOTE

The *Titanic* was an ocean liner that sank in 1912, killing 1,500 of the 2,200 passengers. Its name means "huge," and it was promoted as unsinkable. Shortly after it began its first journey, it sank in frigid water after hitting an iceberg. So many people died because it didn't have enough lifeboats. Like Atlantis, the story of the *Titanic* became a legend.

Date	Events
March 31, 1909	Work begins on the *Titanic*
April 10, 1912	The *Titanic* leaves Southampton for New York
April 14, 1912, just before midnight	The *Titanic* hits an iceberg
April 15, 1912 at 2:20 A.M.	*Titanic* sinks in the North Atlantic Ocean
April 15, 1912 at 3:40 A.M.	*Carpathia* rescues around 700 survivors
1913	New rules adopted to ensure all boats have enough lifeboats for all passengers on board
1977	First attempt by Robert Ballard to find The *Titanic*
September 1, 1985	The *Titanic* located by Robert Ballard
1993	RMS Titanic Inc. given rights to collect artifacts from the ship
1996	17-ton section raised from the ocean floor

B. Work with a partner. Read each other's paragraphs and complete the peer review form. Discuss your comments.

Questions	Yes	No	Notes
Does the writing address the task?	☐	☐	
Is the method of chronological organization clear?	☐	☐	
Can you identify the time signals?	☐	☐	
Is the vocabulary precise?	☐	☐	
Are there any grammatical errors?	☐	☐	
Are there any other comments you would like to make?	☐	☐	

C. Revise your draft, taking into account your partner's comments.

VOCABULARY CHECK

A. Review the items in the Vocabulary Preview. Write their definitions and add examples. Use a dictionary if necessary.

B. Complete the paragraph with vocabulary items from the box.

civilization	confirmed	destruction	earthquakes	gradual
legendary	referred	vast	volcano	

People began to live in Pompeii from around the seventh century BCE. The growth of the city was .... , but by 79 CE, it was .... , with a population of approximately 11,000. The .... city, located in Italy, near Naples, was destroyed by Mt. Vesuvius, a .... , in 79 CE. Tons of ash buried the city and ended the .... living there. People nearby were also affected by .... , which shook the ground and caused buildings to fall. The ash from Mt. Vesuvius caused crops to fail in many nearby areas. Before its location was .... , the only evidence that the city existed was a letter that .... to it. The letter was written by a man who watched the .... from a distance. The city was rediscovered in 1599, with many of the artifacts still in good condition.

Go to MyEnglishLab to complete a vocabulary and skill practice and to join in collaborative activities.

PART 1

LANGUAGE SKILL

USING NARRATIVE TENSES

WHY IT'S USEFUL The correct use of verb tenses when describing and contrasting time periods is essential for helping your reader to follow your narrative by understanding when events occurred.

Go to MyEnglishLab for the Language Skill presentation and practice.

VOCABULARY STRATEGY

UNDERSTANDING AFFIXES

WHY IT'S USEFUL Understanding the parts of an unfamiliar word can often help you to figure out its meaning.

Affixes are short word parts that combine with a root word to make a new word. A prefix is an affix that comes before the root word, and a suffix is an affix that comes at the end of a root word. The word *predating* shows examples of both:

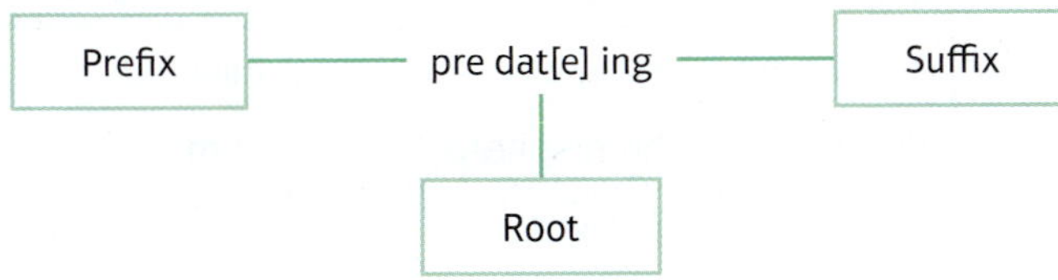

Even if we don't know this word, we can use our knowledge of the parts to make a good guess. The prefix *pre-* means "before," and we know the root word *date* has something to do with "time." The *-ing* suffix shows that the word is probably being used as a verb. We can guess the word means "to come before something." Look at the original sentence:

> Evidence shows the Minoans inhabiting Crete at least as far back as 2600 BCE, forming a vast trading and commercial power **predating** the Mycenaeans and Phoenicians.

Even if we don't know all the word parts, we can use our knowledge of affixes to make a good guess. For example, if we know that the prefix *inter-* means "between," we can use that and context clues to guess the meaning of the word in bold below. What is the likely meaning of *intersection*?

> Thera was located at the **intersection** of numerous trade routes.

Some words are made up only of affixes. For example, *archaeology* combines the prefix *archaeo-*, which means "ancient or old," with the suffix *-ology*, which means "the study of."

The most common affixes are shown below, grouped by their function:

For more on understanding word families, see Chemical Engineering, Part 1.

To give an opposite meaning

Affix	Example	Affix	Example	Affix	Example
de-	deconstruct	im-	impossible	-less	joyless
dis-	disagree	in-	invisible	mis-	misunderstand
il-	illegal	ir-	irregular	non-	nonsense
				un-	unbelievable

To show number

Meaning	Affix	Example	Affix	Example
one	mono-	monotone	uni-	unicycle
two	duo- / di-	divide	bi-	bicycle
ten	deca-	decade		
hundred	cent-	century		
thousand	kilo-	kilogram	milli-	millennium
half	hemi-	hemisphere	semi-	semiformal
many	poly-	polygon	multi-	multiply

To show a different meaning

Affix	Meaning	Example	Affix	Meaning	Example
anti-	against	anti-technology*	-ness	a condition	kindness
co-	together	cooperate	post-	after	postgraduate
counter-	against	counterclockwise	pre-	before	prehistoric
ex-	former	ex-ruler	pro-	supporting	provide
-ful	full of	careful	re-	to do again	renew
in-	into	invasive	-scope	to see	telescope
inter-	between	international	sub-	under	subconscious
-ment	action	development	tele-	far away	teleport
micro-	small	microscope	trans-	across	transport

*Note that some words use a hyphen. Check a good learner's dictionary when using affixes in your writing.

Affixes used academically

Affix	Meaning	Example	Affix	Meaning	Example
archaeo-	old	archaeology	neo-	new	Neolithic
bio-	life	biology	-ology	study of	biology
eco-	environment	ecosystem	paleo-	early	Paleolithic
-graph	write	telegraph	-phone	sound	telephone
meso-	middle	Mesolithic	photo-	light	photograph
-meter	measure	seismometer	proto-	early	prototype
			thermo-	temperature	thermometer

EXERCISE 9

A. Look at the underlined phrase in each sentence, and replace it with a word from the charts on the previous pages. Follow the example.

When I go to college, I will major in <u>the study of ancient things</u>. *archaeology*

1. Ancient humans would be amazed at the <u>thing that carries the sound of a voice over a long distance</u>. ....
2. We need to <u>work together</u> if we are going to complete this excavation. ....
3. Special sites are protected by agreements that are <u>made between different nations</u>. ....
4. Stonehenge took over a <u>one-thousand-year period</u> to build. ....
5. Archaeologists sometimes need to use <u>an instrument that can see small objects</u>. ....
6. The best way to get to the site is on a <u>two-wheeled cycle</u>. ....
7. Taking artifacts from a historical site is <u>against the law</u>. ....
8. Some people found it <u>not believable</u> when a house was found near Stonehenge. ....
9. Turn the stone <u>in the opposite direction that a clock's hands move</u>. ....
10. The Roman Empire was <u>cut into two pieces</u>. ....

B. Look at the underlined word in each sentence, and decide if the word uses the correct affix. If not, correct it.

1. Passengers on the *Titanic* wanted to be teleported from Southampton to New York.
2. Like all Assyrian kings, King Ashurbanipal was a fearless leader.
3. Excavations need to be done carelessly.
4. Researchers unagree about the location of Atlantis.
5. Understanding how people lived in posthistoric times is difficult because there are very few written records.
6. People around the world found out about the *Titanic* disaster quickly because of the telegraph.
7. Modern-day archaeologists work hard to uncode the clues they find about lost civilizations.

C. Look at the underlined word in each sentence, and guess its meaning using what you know about its affix.

1. The Aegean Museum of Maritime History is proud to unveil "The Real Atlantis: Secrets of Santorini."

   The word probably means ……………………

2. This exhibit focuses on items and artifacts recovered from the ancient village of Akrotiri on the island of Santorini.

   The word probably means ……………………

3. The Minoan civilization is one of the earliest proto-empires we have record of.

   The word probably means ……………………

4. Evidence shows the Minoans inhabiting Crete at least as far back as 2600 BCE, forming a vast trading and commercial power predating the Mycenaeans and Phoenicians.

   The word probably means ……………………

5. Tidal waves following a volcanic eruption would have decimated the Minoan fleet; the fleet was anchored on the Northern edge of Crete, facing the eruption.

   The word probably means ……………………

6. The Minoans gradually faded from memory; Thera itself, once a bustling trading center, became a legend—before the island was resettled by people with no memory of its ancient glory.

   The word probably means ……………………

7. In 1967, Marinatos confirmed his suspicions, leading a dig that would gradually uncover some of the most intricate and ornate buildings of the ancient world.

   The word probably means ....

8. Houses found at Akrotiri had multiple floors, support beams, and even indoor plumbing–something the Romans would not develop for another fifteen hundred years.

   The word probably means ....

APPLY YOUR SKILLS

WHY IT'S USEFUL By applying the skills you have learned in this unit, you will be able to write an effective narrative essay about a historical topic or a biography about a notable person. You will be able to organize your paper from a chronological perspective, using appropriate narrative tenses and other time signals to show the order of the events you are discussing.

ASSIGNMENT

Plan a 300–500 word narrative essay about Angkor Wat, discussing when it was built, how it was used, and when it was discovered by westerners.

Or

Plan a 300–500 word biography of Henri Mouhot, the explorer who made Angkor Wat famous in the West.

BEFORE YOU WRITE

A. Before you begin your assignment, discuss these questions with one or more students.

1. What ancient ruins have you read about in this unit? How did people once use these places? How were they discovered by explorers and archaeologists?
2. Where and what is Angkor Wat?
3. Who is Henri Mouhot? Where and when did he live?

B. As you consider your writing assignment, complete the tasks and answer the questions. Then share your ideas with a partner. Get feedback and revise your ideas if necessary.

1. Do some initial research on Angkor Wat and Henri Mouhot and decide which topic you would prefer to write about.

2. To help you think about the main parts of your narrative, complete the chart with information about your chosen paper topic.

Planning Questions	Answers
1. What is the story about?	
2. Who are the characters?	
3. What happened?	
4. Where did it happen?	
5. When did it happen?	
6. Why did it happen?	
7. How did it happen?	

3. How will you find out more information about Angkor Wat or Henri Mouhot? How will you organize it?

C. Review the Unit Skills Summary. As you plan the writing task, apply the skills you learned in this unit.

UNIT SKILLS SUMMARY

Use narrative writing

- Help your reader experience and understand the past by using narrative writing to tell a story focused on events at a particular historical time and place.

Write a biography

- Choose and research a biographical subject carefully and determine the main message you want to give about your subject.
- Select appropriate events and examples and details that will help your reader understand your main message.

Use chronological organization

- Use one of the three methods of chronological organization to help your reader follow the sequence of events.

Use narrative tenses

- Use narrative tenses correctly to show time sequence and add variety to your writing.

Understand affixes

- Use affixes to help figure out the meaning of unfamiliar words.

THINKING CRITICALLY

As you think about your assignment, use the information from the earlier sections of the unit to answer the questions. Discuss your answers with one or more students and revise your ideas if necessary.

1. How do archaeologists use narrative to help understand ruins and other items found at sites? Could there be multiple versions of this kind of narrative? Explain your answer.
2. Henri Mouhot is said to have "found" Angkor Wat. The people living nearby and using it each day had not lost it. In this case, what is meant by "found"? What can happen when an archaeological site is "found"?

THINKING VISUALLY

A. Look at the images and, working with a partner, create a brief narrative about each one.

Building Angkor Wat, twelfth century

Traveling to Angkor Wat, nineteenth century

THINKING ABOUT LANGUAGE

A. Read the narrative from an online site and underline the time signals, including the use of narrative verb tense contrasts. Then identify and list at least one example of each narrative past tense in the chart below.

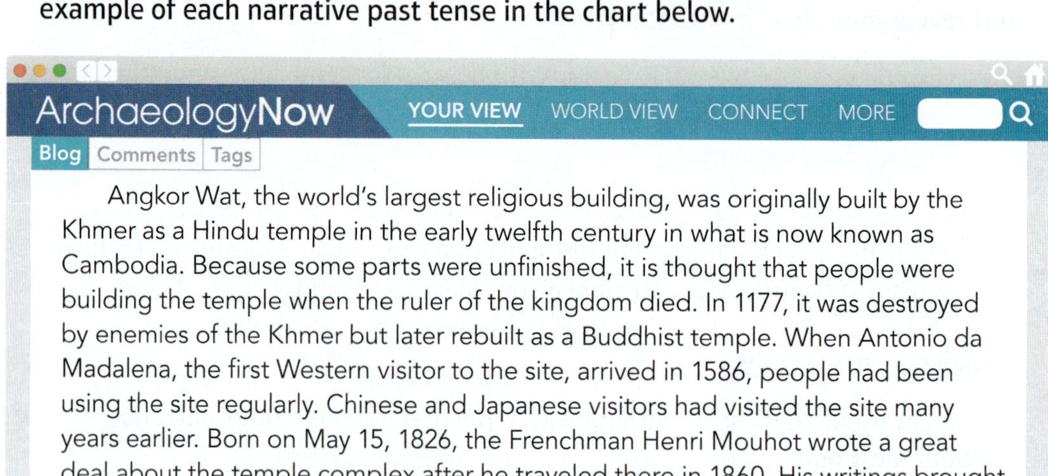

Angkor Wat, the world's largest religious building, was originally built by the Khmer as a Hindu temple in the early twelfth century in what is now known as Cambodia. Because some parts were unfinished, it is thought that people were building the temple when the ruler of the kingdom died. In 1177, it was destroyed by enemies of the Khmer but later rebuilt as a Buddhist temple. When Antonio da Madalena, the first Western visitor to the site, arrived in 1586, people had been using the site regularly. Chinese and Japanese visitors had visited the site many years earlier. Born on May 15, 1826, the Frenchman Henri Mouhot wrote a great deal about the temple complex after he traveled there in 1860. His writings brought knowledge of Angkor Wat to the Western world. Work to restore Angkor Wat began in 1908, and the site is now protected as a World Heritage Site. It is a major source of tourism and is visited by more than two million people each year.

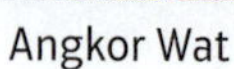

Angkor Wat

Henri Mouhot

Narrative verb tense	Example
1. Simple past	
2. Past progressive	
3. Past perfect	
4. Past perfect progressive	

B. Look again at the narrative in Exercise A and try to figure out the meaning of the following words from the narrative, using your knowledge of affixes: *unfinished*, *rebuilt*, *restore*.

WRITE

A. Look again at the writing assignment, your chart from Before You Write, your ideas from Thinking Critically, and the story you told in Thinking Visually.

B. Research your topic further and take effective notes. Discuss your notes and ideas with others and make any needed adjustments.

C. To help you organize the information you might include in this paper, create a timeline showing the major events associated with your topic.

D. Use your timeline as the basis for writing an outline of your essay.

BEYOND THE ASSIGNMENT

Write a 300–500 word narrative essay about Angkor Wat, discussing when it was built, how it was used, and when it was discovered by westerners.

Or

Write a 300–500 word biography of Henri Mouhot, the explorer who made Angkor Wat famous in the West.

Use all the skills you learned in this unit.

Go to MyEnglishLab to watch Dr. Hunt's concluding video and to complete a self-assessment.

Our everyday experiences are based on how we interact with nature

CHEMICAL ENGINEERING

Editing and Publishing

UNIT PROFILE

Earthquakes, volcanoes, tsunamis, hurricanes, and tornadoes are just some of the many terrifying and devastating natural disasters that can strike at any time. In this unit, you will learn how people prepare for such disasters—through building design, monitoring, or other types of defenses.

You will plan a 500–700 word report that explains a design solution for disaster-resistant housing in a developing country. The report should be well-presented and carefully proofread.

OUTCOMES

- Understand the visual appearance of writing
- Proofread effectively
- Write headings and subheadings
- Use prepositional phrases
- Understand word families

For more about CHEMICAL ENGINEERING, see 2 3.
See also R and OC CHEMICAL ENGINEERING 1 2 3.

GETTING STARTED

Go to MyEnglishLab to watch Professor Spakowitz's introductory video and to complete a self-assessment.

Discuss these questions with a partner or a group.

1. Why do people live in areas where natural disasters are common? What precautions do they need to take? How can authorities educate residents about natural disasters?
2. Do you think the city or the country is the safest place to be during a natural disaster? Explain your answer.
3. Professor Spakowitz suggests that safety is the most important thing to think about when designing for natural disasters. Do you agree? Why or why not?

SKILL 1

UNDERSTANDING THE VISUAL APPEARANCE OF WRITING

WHY IT'S USEFUL While producing high-quality, well-organized content is essential in academic writing, a visually appealing presentation is also very important. This creates a positive impression and makes it easy for your reader to follow your ideas.

Imagine that you have an interview for your dream job. You are qualified for the job, you have all the skills and experience required, and you have the right background knowledge. Would you dress appropriately for the job? Would you smile and look interested? Would you speak clearly when answering questions? Of course you would because you know that your appearance and manners will have a positive (or negative) effect on your interviewers. It is the same for writing. The way you present your information visually can enhance your reader's impression and understanding of your content. To help you do this, use the following design features:

Fonts

There are several things a writer can do with the text in a report. Let's start with the choice of font. As you've learned, the font is the style that letters are written in. The most common fonts you will use in academic writing are Times New Roman and Arial.

For more on understanding an assignment, see Bioethics, Part 1.

As a rule, you should use no more than two different fonts in an academic report. Often a sans-serif font, such as Arial, is used for a title, headings, or for the body text of an online document. A serif font, like Times New Roman, is used for the body paragraphs of printed text or formal assignments. Use your best judgment when deciding which font to use. Do not use Comic Sans, which is not suitable for academic writing.

Font	Example
Arial:	Surviving an Earthquake
Times New Roman:	Earthquakes can strike at any moment, like when you are having dinner or when you are asleep.

CULTURE NOTE

A serif is the small line at the bottom of each leg of this letter: A. You can see serifs on other letters, too. Many believe that a serif font is easier to read. Sans-serif fonts, like Arial, don't have serifs (*sans* means "without" in French). They stand out on the page or screen, which is why they are often used for headings..

Emphasis

Within your report, there are four things you can do to add **emphasis** to your text.

- **Boldface** type is slightly darker and heavier than standard type. It stands out to the reader, so it should be used for key details or something you want to draw attention to.
- Underlining can also add emphasis, but it is used less frequently because many documents now use an underlined word to indicate a link to a web address.
- *Italics* are generally used to show emphasis in speech, rather than content. The word or phrase that is in italics should be stressed as you read. Here's an example:

  She survived the earthquake because she had taken the correct precautions.

  She survived the earthquake *because* she had taken the correct precautions.

  She survived the earthquake because she had taken the *correct* precautions.

  The stress on the word "because" in the second sentence shows how important the precautions were. The stress on the word "correct" in the third sentence shows how important it was to take the correct precautions.
- CAPITALIZATION is often reserved for major headings. Using it in body text has the appearance of shouting. You must use capitals for acronyms, like the CEA (which stands for the California Earthquake Authority), but this is not considered the same as emphasis.

TIP

A good rule to remember about emphasis is that less is more. If you put all the words in bold, for example, nothing stands out. Only emphasize the **really important** information.

White Space

The term *white space* is used to talk about space on a page where there is no text. For many books and research papers, white space will be limited to the margins at the top, bottom, and sides of the page. However, using white space effectively in your report is also key to good presentation. If you have ever fallen asleep while reading a very long article, it's because reading is hard work. You can make it easier on your reader by writing shorter paragraphs, using bulleted lists, and adding images.

Lists

When you have a list of items, you can use bullet points instead of just listing things using commas. This approach is appropriate when you wish to draw particular attention to the points you are making or when you have a very long list. Here is an example:

> There are three things you should do in the event of an earthquake. You should
>
> - stay low to the ground,
> - find cover, and
> - hold on until the shaking stops.

Notice that the points with bullets are not as far left as the sentence above; they are indented. Notice also that the punctuation works just like in a regular list, with commas separating the items. The period comes at the end of the last item.

A numbered list is another way to list items. A numbered list is only used when the order or number of the items is important, as the following example shows:

> If you are driving when an earthquake strikes, you should
>
> 1. slow down and stop as soon as possible,
> 2. stay in your car, and
> 3. remain there until the shaking stops.

Items in a bulleted or numbered list may be complete sentences. In this case, capitalize the first letter of each item and end each sentence with a period as shown below.

> There are several ways you can prepare for an earthquake:
>
> - Put together an emergency survival pack.
> - Plan how to get out of your house safely.
> - Be informed about earthquake risks in your community.

Adding images

A well-placed image which supports or illustrates the point you are making will add information and interest and help to break up the text for your reader. The image should be connected to the main idea of the text.

Read the text from a student report and then look at the images that follow. Which image would you choose and where would you place it? (Only one of the images would be appropriate.) Discuss your ideas with your classmates.

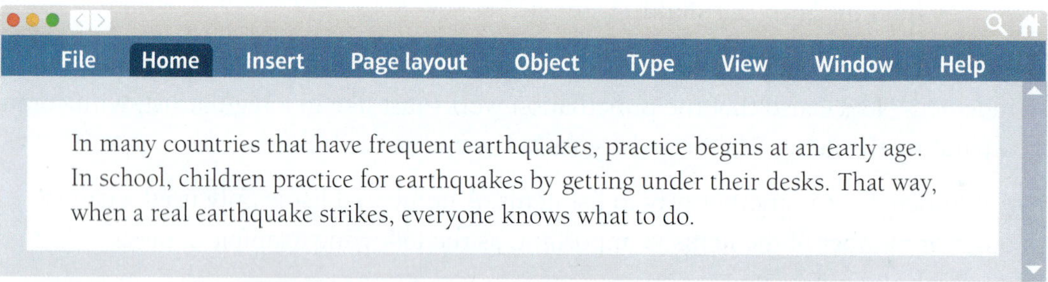

In many countries that have frequent earthquakes, practice begins at an early age. In school, children practice for earthquakes by getting under their desks. That way, when a real earthquake strikes, everyone knows what to do.

a.

b.

c.

Choose Design Features Carefully!

Each tool described in this section must be used carefully and appropriately. Using too many design features together will make your report look messy. If you think of these design features like spices that are added to food, it will help you remember that you should not add too many or too few. Only by adding the correct amount of spice will the food taste good.

VOCABULARY PREVIEW

These vocabulary items appear in the reading. Circle the ones you know. Put a question mark next to the ones you don't know.

strike (v)	secure (v)	debris	hazard (n)
item	crawl (v)	avoid	structure (n)

EXERCISE 1

A. Read this assignment and then read the writer's first draft response. Answer the questions that follow.

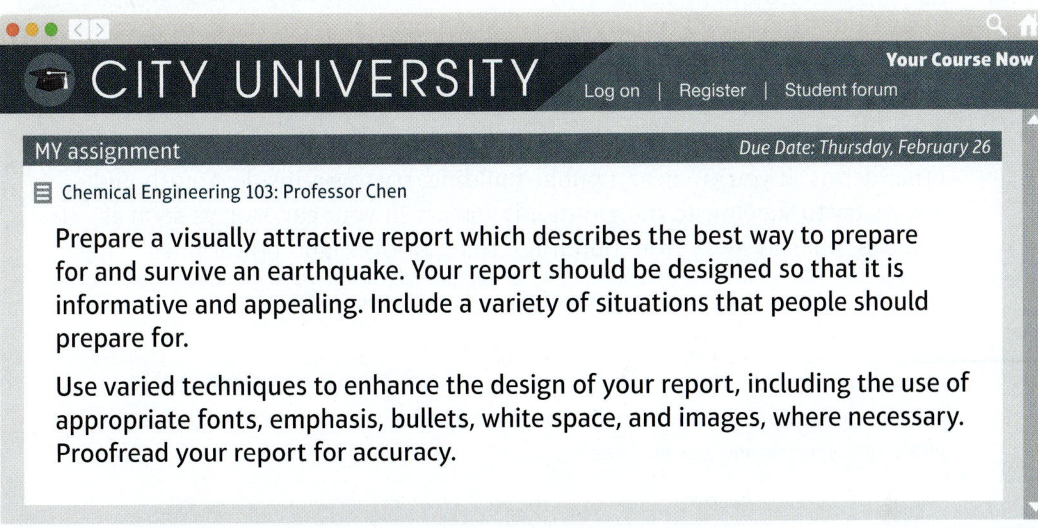

CITY UNIVERSITY

Your Course Now

Log on | Register | Student forum

MY assignment

Due Date: Thursday, February 26

Chemical Engineering 103: Professor Chen

Prepare a visually attractive report which describes the best way to prepare for and survive an earthquake. Your report should be designed so that it is informative and appealing. Include a variety of situations that people should prepare for.

Use varied techniques to enhance the design of your report, including the use of appropriate fonts, emphasis, bullets, white space, and images, where necessary. Proofread your report for accuracy.

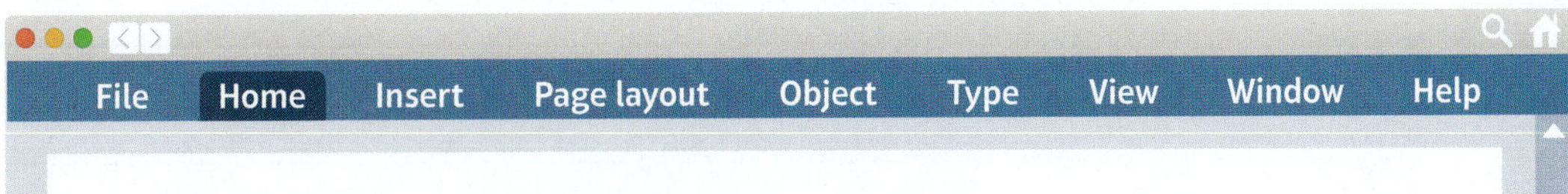

SURVIVING AN EARTHQUAKE

Earthquakes can strike at any moment, like when you are having dinner or when you are asleep. Earthquakes happen when the ground moves suddenly. Usually, this will feel like a rolling motion, or a sudden jolt.

Here are some simple steps you can take to prevent damage or loss of life if an earthquake strikes. Make sure items in your house are secured. This includes bookshelves, TV screens or lamps. Make sure that you have an emergency kit with items such as:

1. water
2. medication
3. food

Think about places in your home, like the kitchen table, that you could crawl under and that would provide protection from falling debris.

(Continued)

If you are inside your home or another building, stay there. You should not *run* outside as you risk being hit by falling power lines or streetlights. Get as low to the ground as you can and crawl under a table if possible. Stay away from windows. If you are in bed, avoiding hazards in the dark is very difficult, so you should stay where you are. Move under the bed, or cover your head with a pillow for protection.

If you are outside, try to move to an open area to avoid falling power lines, or other debris. If you are near a public building, try to get inside. You should always try to stay low to the ground. If you are in your car, stop as soon as you can, but stay away from buildings, trees, bridges, and power lines.

Once the shaking has stopped, drive **carefully** and avoid structures that may have been damaged by the earthquake.

After a big earthquake, there may be aftershocks. These are smaller earthquakes, but they can be more deadly because they shake buildings that are already damaged. If you feel an aftershock, stay low and look for cover.

1. What two types of earthquake motion are described?

   ....

2. Based on the advice given, name two other items that need to be secured in a house.

   ....

3. Why should you stay "low to the ground"?

   ....

4. During an aftershock, should you do anything differently than you would during the main earthquake?

   ....

B. Thinking about the features of a well-presented report, what could the writer of the first draft do to make the report more appealing visually? Complete the chart by making suggestions for improvements. An example has been done for you. Then compare your ideas with a partner.

Problem	Suggestion
1. The title is capitalized and in Comic Sans font.	Only capitalize the first letter of each word. Use a sans-serif font such as Arial. Bold is OK.
2. The image does not support the text.	
3. The numbered list in paragraph 2 is inappropriate.	
4. The word "run" is in italics.	
5. The word "carefully" is in bold.	
6. The final two paragraphs are a smaller font size.	
7. The final two paragraphs are in a different font.	
8.	
9.	

PART 1

EXERCISE 2

A. Based on peer feedback, the writer of the draft in Exercise 1, Part A, tried some different methods of formatting his report. Look at the two versions and complete the chart that follows by identifying the features that have been used in each text.

Text 1

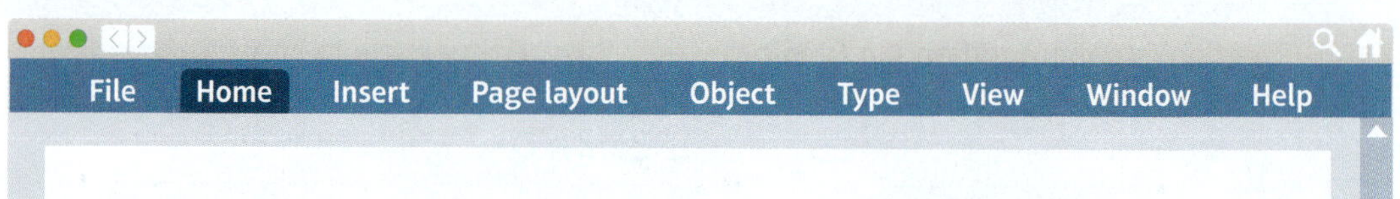

Surviving an Earthquake

Earthquakes can strike at any moment, like when you are having dinner or when you are asleep. Earthquakes happen when the ground moves suddenly. Usually, this will feel like a rolling motion, or a sudden jolt.

Being Prepared

Here are some simple steps you can take to prevent damage or loss of life if an earthquake strikes.

- Make sure items in your house are secured. This includes bookshelves, TV screens or lamps.
- Make sure that you have an emergency kit with items such as water, medication, and food.
- Think about places in your home, like the kitchen table, that you could crawl under and seek protection from falling debris.

Taking Action

If you are inside your home or another building, stay there. You should not run outside as you risk being hit by falling power lines or streetlights. Get as low to the ground as you can and crawl under a table if possible. Stay away from windows. If you are in bed, avoiding hazards in the dark is very difficult, so you should stay where you are. Move under the bed, or cover your head with a pillow for protection.

If you are outside, try to move to an open area to avoid falling power lines, or other debris. If you are near a public building, try to get inside. You should always try to stay low to the ground. If you are in your car, stop as soon as you can, but stay away from buildings, trees, bridges, or power lines. Once the shaking has stopped, drive carefully and avoid structures that may have been damaged by the earthquake.

Staying Alert

After a big earthquake, there may be aftershocks. These are smaller earthquakes, but they can be more deadly because they shake buildings that are already damaged. If you feel an aftershock, stay low and look for cover.

Text 2

File Home Insert Page layout Object Type View Window Help

Surviving an Earthquake

Earthquakes can strike at any moment, like when you are having dinner or when you are asleep.

What is an Earthquake?

Earthquakes happen when the ground moves suddenly. Usually, this will feel like a **rolling motion**, or a sudden **jolt**.

Being Prepared

Here are some simple steps you can take to prevent damage or loss of life if an earthquake strikes:

- Make sure items in your house are **secured**. This includes bookshelves, TV screens, or lamps.
- Make sure that you have an **emergency kit** with items such as water, medication, and food.
- Think about places in your home, **like the kitchen table**, that you could crawl under and seek protection from falling debris.

Taking Action

- **If you are inside your home**, or another building, stay there. You should not run outside as you risk being hit by falling power lines or streetlights. Get as low to the ground as you can and crawl under a table if possible. Stay away from windows.
- **If you are in bed**, avoiding hazards in the dark is very difficult, so you should stay where you are. Move under the bed, or cover your head with a pillow for protection.
- **If you are outside**, try to move to an open area to avoid falling power lines, or other debris. If you are near a public building, try to get inside. You should always try to stay low to the ground.
- **If you are driving,** stop as soon as you can, but stay away from buildings, trees, bridges, or power lines. Once the shaking has stopped, drive carefully and avoid structures that may have been damaged by the earthquake.

Staying Alert

After a big earthquake, there may be **aftershocks**. These are smaller earthquakes, but they can be more deadly because they shake buildings that are already damaged. If you feel an aftershock, stay low and look for cover.

	Text 1	Text 2
1. Font	Arial for title and headings	Arial for body text
2. Emphasis		
3. Bullets	Used for a list	
4. Images		

B. Referring to your analysis in Exercise A, decide which text is more visually appealing. Discuss your reasoning with a partner. Try to use the terms that have been introduced in this section.

EXERCISE 3

A. Research how to prepare for a hurricane or a flood. Go online and take notes on the best methods for survival.

B. Using your notes and the text in Exercise 2 as an example, write a 200–300 word guide to surviving one of these natural disasters. Make sure your information is useful and visually appealing. Use five words from the Vocabulary Check.

C. Work with a partner. Read each other's survival guide for a natural disaster and complete the peer review form. Discuss each other's comments and then revise your draft.

Questions	**Yes**	**No**	**Notes**
Does the writing address the assignment task?	☐	☐	
Is the structure of the writing clear?	☐	☐	
Did the writer use an appropriate font?	☐	☐	
Has emphasis been used for appropriate words?	☐	☐	
Did the writer use any: • bullets • images Were they used correctly and appropriately?	 ☐ ☐ ☐	 ☐ ☐ ☐	

D. In small groups, take turns sharing your guides with your classmates. Whose guide is the most appealing visually? Why?

VOCABULARY CHECK

A. Review the items in Vocabulary Preview. Write their definitions and add examples. Use a dictionary if necessary.

B. Complete the paragraph with a vocabulary item from the box.

avoid	debris	items	strikes (v)
crawl (v)	hazards (n)	secure (v)	structures (n)

When an earthquake .... , you should .... under a table so that you will not be injured by falling .... such as pictures, bookshelves, or lamps. If you are inside, you should .... going outside where you could encounter .... falling from damaged .... Many of these .... can be avoided by preparing for an earthquake. Be sure you live in an earthquake-proof house and .... pieces of furniture that could easily fall during an earthquake.

Go to MyEnglishLab to complete a vocabulary and skill practice and to join in collaborative activities.

SKILL 2

PROOFREADING EFFECTIVELY

WHY IT'S USEFUL Proofreading—looking for and correcting errors—is an extremely important part of academic writing that many people overlook. Proofreading every written assignment carefully can improve your grades. In addition, a carefully proofread assignment leaves your reader with a positive impression, showing that you care about the quality of your writing.

Proofreading is usually the last thing you do before you hand in an assignment. When you proofread an assignment, you are looking for mistakes in spelling, capitalization, punctuation, register, and grammar, as shown in the chart on the next page. These are often obvious mistakes that you know how to correct.

Some people like to proofread on their computers, so if they find a mistake they can fix it before printing an assignment. Others find it hard to notice mistakes on the screen. If this is true for you, consider printing your assignments on paper for proofreading.

Sometimes your eyes skip over mistakes, especially when you've spent a long time on an assignment and know what you *meant* to say. Reading your assignment out loud can help with this problem. If a sentence sounds strange, there is probably a problem with the grammar.

	Explanation	Beware...
Spelling	Spelling mistakes are easy to spot and fix, especially when you are using a computer. If you see something underlined in red, it's a good idea to look at what the software is pointing out to you.	• Names and places are especially easy to misspell; check these carefully. • Typos, errors caused by mistyping, aren't always obvious. For example, maybe you typed "an" when you meant to type "and."
Capitalization	Be sure to follow the rules of capitalization: The first word of each sentence and proper nouns need to be capitalized. The pronoun "I" is always capitalized.	Sometimes it's not clear if what you're writing needs to be capitalized or not. You can usually find out by doing a simple Internet search. However, if you're still in doubt, make a choice and be consistent.
Punctuation	Familiarize yourself with simple punctuation rules and follow them in your writing. Remember that complete sentences must be separated by periods, not commas.	Including a comma after the next-to-last item in a list is optional. This comma is called a "serial" comma. Be consistent in using—or not using—a serial comma. Choose: Do you have enough food, water and medical supplies? OR Do you have enough food, water, and medical supplies?
Academic Register	As you have learned, it is important in academic English to write in a neutral or a formal register. When you are getting your ideas down, it is easy to slip into an informal register, so be sure to look for this kind of mistake when proofreading.	Informal vocabulary can easily creep into your paper. Watch out for slang and words that you would use in everyday conversation, like "kids," and replace them with more formal alternatives, like "children."
Grammar	There are many kinds of grammar mistakes and you won't be able to find all of them when proofreading. However, you should be able to find and correct "little" mistakes. Be sure you have a good grammar book to refer to when you need to check a rule as you proofread your assignment.	• Avoid very common, careless grammar mistakes such as forgetting the "s" on third person singular verbs: for example, writing "he believe" instead of "he believes." • Other common mistakes include missing words ("under bed" instead of "under the bed"), using an incorrect word ("on bed" instead of "in bed"), or using the wrong part of speech. For instance, you might use a noun when you need an adjective, or a verb when you need a noun, saying, "scientists use many kinds of equip" instead of "scientists use many kinds of equipment."

For more on understanding register, see Bioethics, Part 1.

TIP

When using a word processing application, be sure that you have the language setting for the type of English you are using (e.g., American, British, Australian, etc.). Otherwise you may end up with an "s" where there should be a "z," or a "u" in the word "color."

Look at an early draft of two paragraphs on how to survive an earthquake. What types of mistakes did the writer highlight as she proofread her paper? Look at the chart that follows and notice how the errors were corrected.

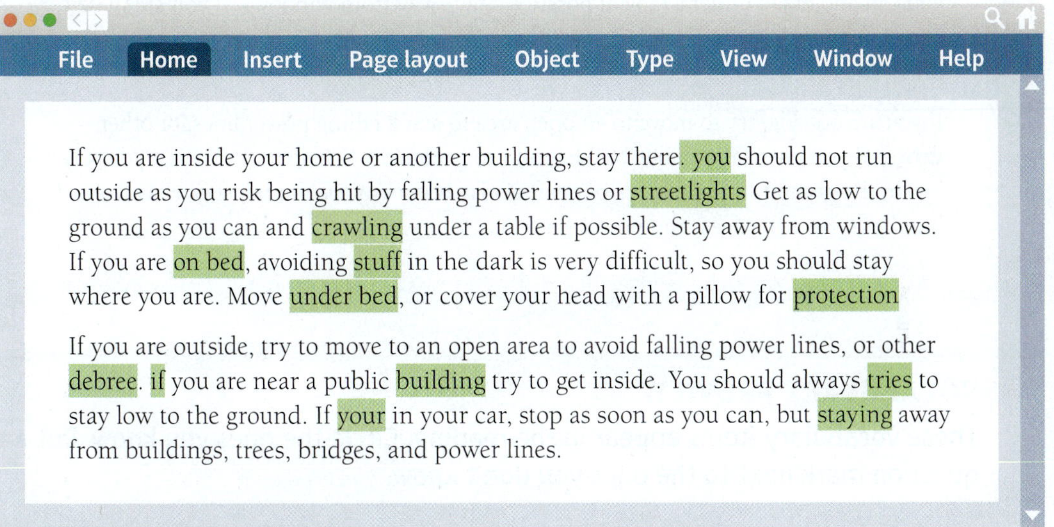

If you are inside your home or another building, stay there. you should not run outside as you risk being hit by falling power lines or streetlights Get as low to the ground as you can and crawling under a table if possible. Stay away from windows. If you are on bed, avoiding stuff in the dark is very difficult, so you should stay where you are. Move under bed, or cover your head with a pillow for protection

If you are outside, try to move to an open area to avoid falling power lines, or other debree. if you are near a public building try to get inside. You should always tries to stay low to the ground. If your in your car, stop as soon as you can, but staying away from buildings, trees, bridges, and power lines.

Error type	Example from text	Correction
Spelling	debree your	debris you are
Capitalization	you if	You If
Punctuation	streetlights protection building	streetlights. protection. building,
Academic Register	stuff	hazards
Grammar	crawling on bed under bed tries staying	crawl in bed under the bed try stay

The writer corrected her paragraphs based on the errors in punctuation, register, and grammar that she identified. The corrections are highlighted in yellow.

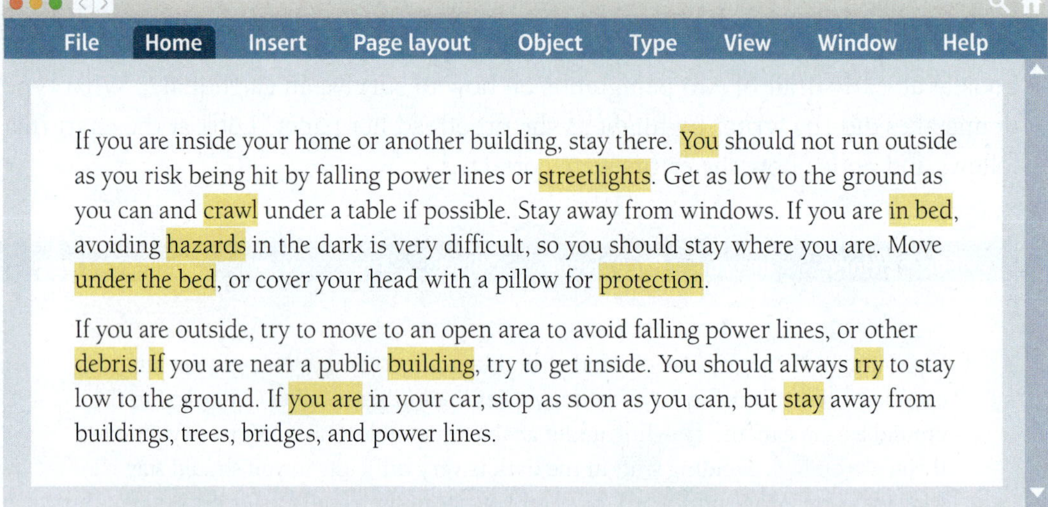

If you are inside your home or another building, stay there. You should not run outside as you risk being hit by falling power lines or streetlights. Get as low to the ground as you can and crawl under a table if possible. Stay away from windows. If you are in bed, avoiding hazards in the dark is very difficult, so you should stay where you are. Move under the bed, or cover your head with a pillow for protection.

If you are outside, try to move to an open area to avoid falling power lines, or other debris. If you are near a public building, try to get inside. You should always try to stay low to the ground. If you are in your car, stop as soon as you can, but stay away from buildings, trees, bridges, and power lines.

VOCABULARY PREVIEW

These vocabulary items appear in the reading. Circle the ones you know. Put a question mark next to the ones you don't know.

monitor (v)	equipment	erupt	analyze	pattern (n)

EXERCISE 4

A. Read the assignment and then read the writer's uncorrected response. Answer the questions that follow.

Glossary

Volcanologist: a geologist who studies how volcanoes form and their eruption patterns

A swarm of earthquakes: a group of minor earthquakes, occurring in the same area in a short amount of time

Mount: an abbreviation of *mountain*. When reading aloud, say "mount."

St.: an abbreviation of *saint*. When reading aloud, say "saint."

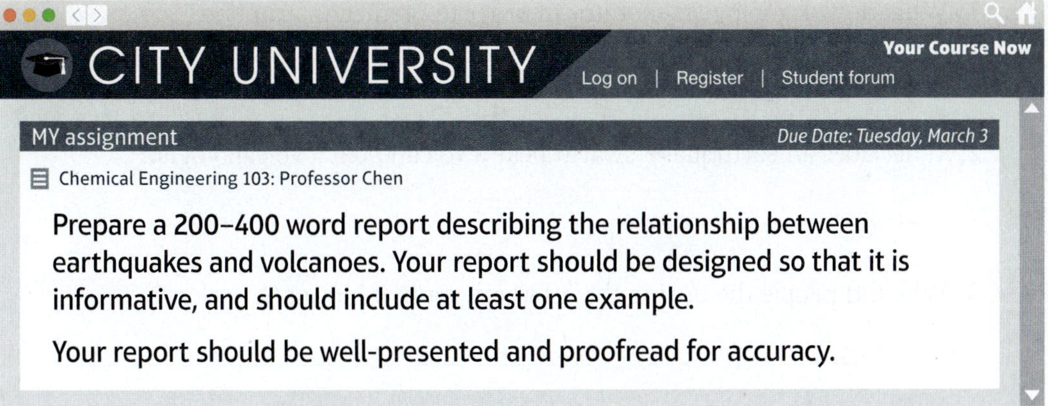

CITY UNIVERSITY

Your Course Now

Log on | Register | Student forum

MY assignment

Due Date: Tuesday, March 3

Chemical Engineering 103: Professor Chen

Prepare a 200–400 word report describing the relationship between earthquakes and volcanoes. Your report should be designed so that it is informative, and should include at least one example.

Your report should be well-presented and proofread for accuracy.

File Home Insert Page layout Object Type View Window Help

Earthquake Swarms and Volcanic Eruptions

Volcanologists, scientists who study volcanoes, use many method to monitor volcanoes activity. It is important for them to observe many things, not just the volcano, to tell when it might go boom. For example, earthquakes often occuring near volcanoes and may be too small to feel without special equipment. Volcanologists watch for swarms of earthquakes. this is when many earthquakes happen on a volcanic area in a short period of time, A swarm might mean that the volcano will erupt. however it does not always prediction an eruption. When a swarm occurs, volcanologists analyze the kinds of earthquakes careful. They learn which patterns of earthquakes will lead to an eruption.

Mount st. helens is a good example of why volcanologists should monitor volcano to save lives. In 1980, this volcano in Washington State erupts and 57 people died. Although volcanologists were monitoring the volcano they did not know how big the eruption would be. There equipment and knowledges was not advanced at the time. smaller eruptions continued until 1986 Volcanologists warned of another possible eruption in 2004 after they recorded swarms of earthquakes. The volcano erupted again and again until 2008, but these eruptions were smaller. Volcanologists learned the difference between the patterns of earthquakes before the 1980 eruption and the 2004 eruptions. In fact, volcanologists have learned lots and lots of things about earthquake swarms from Mount St. Helens because there have been millions of earthquakes in area since they started recording data.

1. What do volcanologists monitor in order to predict an eruption?

2. What does an earthquake swarm near a volcano tell a volcanologist?

3. Why did people die during the 1980 eruption of Mount St. Helens?

4. How have earthquake swarms that occurred before eruptions at Mount St. Helens helped volcanologists?

B. The writer of "Earthquake Swarms and Volcanic Eruptions" has highlighted some mistakes in the first paragraph of her text. Decide which type of error has been highlighted in each case, adding each example to the chart. With a partner, decide how the error should be corrected. An example has been done for you.

Error type	Example from text	Correction
1. Spelling		
2. Capitalization		
3. Punctuation		
4. Academic Register		
5. Grammar	method	methods

C. Now look again at the second paragraph of the text, which contains ten mistakes. With a partner, take turns reading the text out loud. When you see or hear a mistake, stop and highlight it. Then complete the chart. One example and one correction have been done for you.

Error type	Example from text	Correction
1. Spelling		
2. Capitalization	• Mount st. helens	• Mount St. Helens
3. Punctuation		
4. Academic Register		
5. Grammar		

EXERCISE 5

A. Research and write a 200–300 word report about the dangers of living near a volcano. Answer these questions: What dangers do communities located near a volcano face? How could they prepare for possible eruptions? When you are finished writing, proofread your paper, watching especially for mistakes in spelling, capitalization, punctuation, academic register, and grammar.

B. Exchange your paper with a partner and check each other's work for any remaining errors. Use the chart to help you. Discuss any points of disagreement.

Error type	Example from text	Correction
1. Spelling		
2. Capitalization		
3. Punctuation		
4. Academic Register		
5. Grammar		

C. Write a second draft of your paragraph based on the peer review and discussion.

VOCABULARY CHECK

A. Review the items in Vocabulary Preview. Write their definitions and add examples. Use a dictionary if necessary.

B. Complete each sentence with a vocabulary item from the box.

analyzes	equipment	erupt	monitor (v)	pattern (n)

1. Predicting when volcanos will .... is the job of volcanologists.
2. They .... , or watch, volcanoes to understand them better and to collect data.
3. An example of special .... that a volcanologist might use is a seismograph, an instrument to measure earthquakes.
4. A volcanologist .... , or studies carefully, the data from volcanoes to determine when there might be danger.
5. A volcanologist can recognize when a cluster of earthquakes occurs in a .... that suggests the volcano will erupt.

Go to MyEnglishLab to complete a vocabulary and skill practice and to join in collaborative activities.

INTEGRATED SKILLS

WRITING HEADINGS AND SUBHEADINGS

WHY IT'S USEFUL Headings and subheadings serve two main purposes in a paper. They divide a paper into clear and logical sections, making the organization easy for your reader to follow. They also push you as the writer to establish a clear structure and make your writing an effective communication tool.

For most academic papers that you write, you will only need a title. However, in some instances, such as reports, case studies, or very long papers, you will want to add headings. Headings divide a piece of text into clearly defined sections. If you have a long section, you may further divide it using subheadings. Headings and subheadings help a reader find key information quickly, so it is important that you place and word your headings appropriately.

It is essential to remember that headings are not needed everywhere. For example, you rarely need a heading for an introduction nor does every paragraph require a heading.

Read the following excerpt from a student report on hurricanes. How do the heading and subheadings help you determine what each section is about?

Glossary

Evaporate: to become a gas. When a liquid evaporates, it changes into a gas.

Rotate: to turn

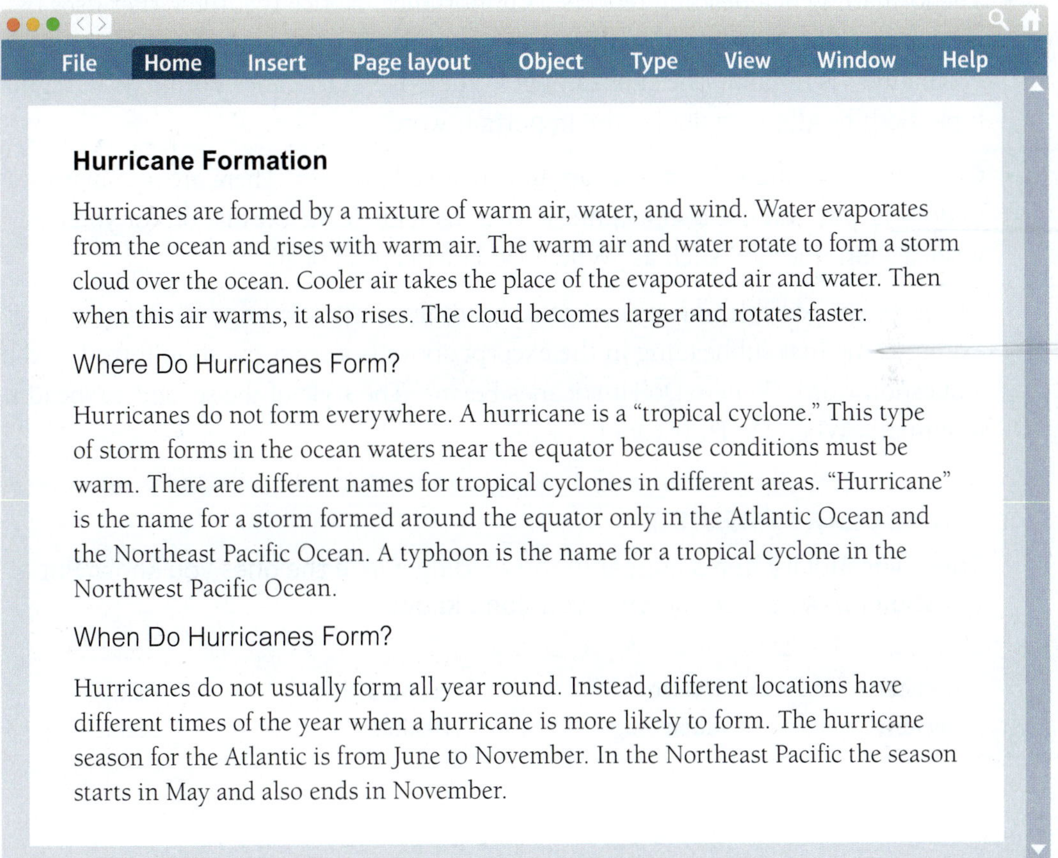

Hurricane Formation

Hurricanes are formed by a mixture of warm air, water, and wind. Water evaporates from the ocean and rises with warm air. The warm air and water rotate to form a storm cloud over the ocean. Cooler air takes the place of the evaporated air and water. Then when this air warms, it also rises. The cloud becomes larger and rotates faster.

Where Do Hurricanes Form?

Hurricanes do not form everywhere. A hurricane is a “tropical cyclone.” This type of storm forms in the ocean waters near the equator because conditions must be warm. There are different names for tropical cyclones in different areas. “Hurricane” is the name for a storm formed around the equator only in the Atlantic Ocean and the Northeast Pacific Ocean. A typhoon is the name for a tropical cyclone in the Northwest Pacific Ocean.

When Do Hurricanes Form?

Hurricanes do not usually form all year round. Instead, different locations have different times of the year when a hurricane is more likely to form. The hurricane season for the Atlantic is from June to November. In the Northeast Pacific the season starts in May and also ends in November.

Features of Good Headings

- A heading reflects the main idea of a section, but does not take the place of a topic sentence. For instance, in the example above, the main idea of the section under "Where Do Hurricanes Form?" is that hurricanes form in the warm waters of the Atlantic Ocean and Northeast Pacific Ocean. The heading reflects this idea, but is not exactly the same as the topic sentence.
- The formatting of a heading reflects its importance. Notice that the writer uses two levels of headings in the text on the previous page. The main heading, "Hurricane Formation," is in bold. The subheading, "Where Do Hurricanes Form?" is in regular type. Both headings capitalize the important words.
- Good headings and subheadings are informative but short. There are two main ways to do this. You can use a short phrase, such as "Hurricane Formation" or you can write a short question such as "Where Do Hurricanes Form?"
- To the extent possible, the style of good headings or subheadings is consistent. For example, the first subheading in the excerpt above is a short question introduced by a question word: "Where Do Hurricanes Form?" The style of the second subheading is similar: "When Do Hurricanes Form?"

VOCABULARY PREVIEW

These vocabulary items appear in the reading. Circle the ones you know. Put a question mark next to the ones you don't know.

disaster	reduce	construction	risk (n)
mystery	flood (adj)	flexible	stable

EXERCISE 6

A. Read the article about how engineering solutions can be used to help buildings survive a natural disaster. Then answer the comprehension questions.

Glossary

Tsunami: a very large wave, caused, for example, by an earthquake, which can cause a lot of damage when it reaches land

Collapse: to fall down suddenly

Seismic: a word used to describe the movements of the earth when affected by an earthquake

Minimal Impact: Science, Engineering, and the Disaster-Proof Building

1 For much of history, natural disasters were a deadly mystery. Earthquakes reduced structures to rubble. Floods and tsunamis caused water damage and even pushed buildings right off foundations. Forceful hurricane winds ripped homes to pieces.

2 Natural disasters are even more devastating in modern cities. A collapsed building can harm hundreds of people. Engineers have discovered planning and construction strategies to decrease the harm caused by natural disasters. Modern builders have a wide variety of tools and strategies available. Cities can now truly weather the storm, no matter what form it may take.

3 When it comes to constructing earthquake-resistant buildings, the solution is to reinforce a building frame's connections, both to other frames and to the foundation. Somewhat flexible steel beams result in a stronger skeleton. The steel's flexibility is a valuable attribute when seismic activity threatens to twist walls to the point of collapse.

4 Many major cities have been built near fault lines. Architects who want to build skyscrapers in these high-risk zones need all the help they can get. The construction industry has developed a new technology known as base isolation. A building's foundation is separated from the ground. The entire building sits on padding and bumpers. During a strong earthquake, this material allows the structure to safely shift back and forth at the foundation rather than whipping from side to side. This reduces swaying, and almost eliminates the risk of collapse.

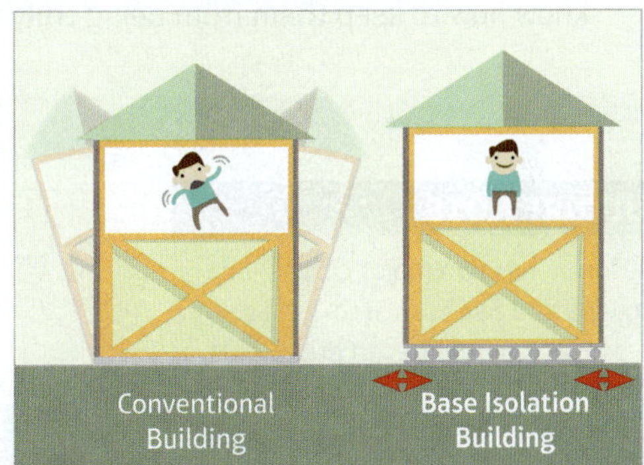

5 An earthquake can be followed by a tsunami. Even seismically stable regions often face flood risks due to bad weather. Floodwaters can destabilize the ground below a building, leading to a collapse. The safest method of prevention is to simply build only on stable ground outside of a flood zone. Geospatial research makes it easier than ever to evaluate what areas are at risk of flooding.

(Continued)

6 For already established cities, though, the latest innovations allow for rapid responses to natural disasters. Retractable floodwalls can be deployed at short notice, letting a building go from being open and inviting to closed and nearly flood proof, if the occupants have enough prior warning. Other structural innovations allow for rapid drainage. Improved foundational supports can help minimize the risk of collapse due to erosion. Despite these innovations, the most effective method is to avoid building in flood-prone areas.

7 Some cities are frequently in the path of hurricanes and typhoons. In addition to being at risk for flooding, the winds can cause significant damage. It is important to reinforce the frames of at-risk houses with strongly linked trusses and reinforced cross-beams.

8 Even buildings with sturdy frames can be torn to shreds if the wind hits at the wrong angle. Wide, flat walls and roofs with only two slopes are especially risky since these structures offer more vulnerable and exposed surface area. The solution to this problem is geometric. A roof with multiple slopes facing as many directions as possible is ideal because there is no vulnerable "long" side. This prevents large gusts of wind from easily lifting the roof.

9 It took architects and engineers years to learn how to prepare a city for natural disasters. Today, though, we know what saves lives and how to implement needed changes. New buildings are designed with natural disasters in mind; old buildings are frequently updated. It may take years to update old buildings, but the mysteries of nature are mysteries no more. We understand natural disasters, and know how to keep them from being truly disastrous.

CULTURE NOTE

California has two major cities—Los Angeles and San Francisco—that lie on the Ring of Fire, an area around the Pacific Ocean known for volcanoes and earthquakes. Both cities have building codes which require new buildings to use earthquake-resistant technology. The codes also require that older buildings be retrofitted—updated—to meet building codes. Retrofitting buildings is expensive, but financial support is available to help homeowners pay for upgrades.

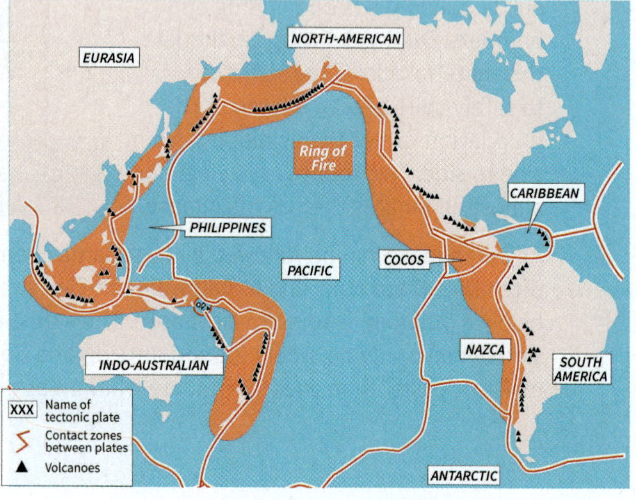

1. What kinds of natural disasters are discussed in the article?

....

2. In what ways can these disasters harm buildings?

....

3. Write *S* (shaking), *WI* (wind), or *WA* (water) beside each engineering strategy to indicate the kind of damage it prevents. There may be more than one answer. Compare your answers with a classmate. Then discuss how each strategy works.

   .... a. reinforced frames
   .... b. geospatial research
   .... c. use of flexible material, like steel
   .... d. base isolation
   .... e. retractable floodwall
   .... f. multi-sided roofs

B. Read the article again. This time decide where it would be appropriate to add headings. Discuss your ideas with a partner. Together, think of suitable academic headings for the article.

C. Working in small groups, compare your decisions about placement and wording of headings. Which seem most suited to the article? Why?

D. Write a 250–350 word report that explains three ways to wind-proof a house. Use information from the reading and at least five words from the Vocabulary Check. If necessary, go online and find additional sources to get more information. Use headings appropriately in your report.

E. Share your report with a partner. Use the peer-review questions to evaluate each other's work and to offer suggestions in the Notes column. Then rewrite your report based on the feedback you received.

Questions	**Yes**	**No**	**Notes**
Does the writing address the assignment task?	☐	☐	
Is the structure of the writing clear?	☐	☐	
Are the ideas clear, complete, and easy to understand?	☐	☐	
Did the writer use: • appropriate fonts? • sufficient emphasis? • bullets? • images?	 ☐ ☐ ☐ ☐	 ☐ ☐ ☐ ☐	
Are there any problems with: • spelling? • capitalization? • punctuation? • academic register? • grammar?	 ☐ ☐ ☐ ☐ ☐	 ☐ ☐ ☐ ☐ ☐	
Are the headings and subheadings appropriate?	☐	☐	

VOCABULARY CHECK

A. Review the items in Vocabulary Preview. Write their definitions and add examples. Use a dictionary if necessary.

B. Choose the sentence that correctly paraphrases the meaning of each underlined vocabulary item.

1. a. A natural disaster is something that causes a lot of damage and suffering.

   b. A natural disaster is something that is not understood.

2. a. How damaged a building is during a storm depends on its construction, or the way it is designed.

   b. How damaged a building is during a storm depends on its construction, or the way it is built.

3. a. Some buildings are designed to reduce, or lessen, movement during an earthquake.

   b. Some buildings are designed to reduce, or prevent, movement during an earthquake.

4. a. Flexible materials can bend.

   b. Flexible materials cannot bend.

5. a. Flood damage is caused by wind.

   b. Flood damage is caused by water.

6. a. Nowadays, weather is a mystery because people understand it.

   b. Long ago, weather was a mystery because people did not understand it.

7. a. Before climbing a ladder, be sure it is stable, or not likely to move.

   b. Before climbing a ladder, be sure it is stable, or likely to move.

8. a. Buildings in cities far away from fault lines are at higher risk of earthquake damage.

   b. Buildings in cities near fault lines are at higher risk of earthquake damage.

Go to MyEnglishLab to complete a vocabulary and skill practice and to join in collaborative activities.

LANGUAGE SKILL

USING PREPOSITIONAL PHRASES

WHY IT'S USEFUL The correct, effective use of prepositional phrases adds detail and clarity to your writing. Prepositional phrases can make your writing more interesting and provide useful information.

Go to MyEnglishLab for the Language Skill presentation and practice.

VOCABULARY STRATEGY

UNDERSTANDING WORD FAMILIES

WHY IT'S USEFUL Learning new words can be difficult and time-consuming. By learning word families, rather than just individual words, you can learn more words with only a little more effort than you need to learn single words.

English contains more words than any other language. While it is not necessary, or possible, to learn them all, it is important to know enough so that you can study and learn effectively. Research shows that students need to learn over 8,000 word families for successful university-level study.

Word families are like regular families in that the words are related in some way; they share a common root. Words in a family are simply different forms of the word—the noun, verb, adjective, and adverb forms, for example. While the different forms will be used in different ways, they often share common meanings.

Here is an example of a word family whose common root is *risk* and which has a number of forms with very similar meanings.

Noun	Verb	Adjective	Adverb
Singular: risk Plural: risks	Infinitive: to risk Present Simple: risk Present Simple (3rd person): risks Past participle: risked Present participle: risking	risky	riskily

When you learn one form of a word that is part of a word family, add all of the other forms to your vocabulary journal. When you learn *risk*, for example, you can actually record and learn nine different forms.

For more on creating a vocabulary journal, see Business and Design, Part 1.

The verb *to minimize* was used in paragraph 6 of the Integrated Skills reading. Here is an example of a word family based on that verb. Notice it has two adjective forms.

Noun	Verb	Adjective	Adverb
Singular: minimum Plural: minimums	Infinitive: to minimize Present Simple: minimize Present Simple (3rd person): minimizes Past participle: minimized Present participle: minimizing	minimal minimum	minimally

Sometimes, words in word families have different shades of meaning. It's important to understand the differences and to learn how to use the forms correctly. Here, both *minimum* and *minimal* are adjectives with the same root, but the meanings differ and the words are used in different ways.

She put in minimum effort. → She did enough to pass the class with a "C" grade.

She put in minimal effort. → She did very little in class and probably did not pass.

Minimum means "just enough" or "the required amount." *Minimal* means "very little" or "not enough." When you check meanings in a dictionary, it is important that you record examples and understand differences in usage like these.

For more on using a dictionary to expand vocabulary, see Zoology, Part 2.

Here is an example of a word family based on the word *method* used in paragraphs 5 and 6 of the Integrated Skills reading. Notice that it has two noun forms, *method* and *methodology*, which have somewhat different meanings.

Noun	Verb	Adjective	Adverb
Singular: method Plural: methods Singular: methodology Plural: methodologies		methodical	methodically

The two sentences below show how the noun forms, *method* and *methodology*, are used. A *method* is a way of doing something. A *methodology* is the set of methods used to do a job or study something.

Recording word families might be a new method of vocabulary learning for you.

When studying in another country, you will be exposed to a different educational methodology.

TIP

It is very easy to get lost in a regular dictionary when studying word families. Many words have forms that are rarely used and so would be a waste of your time to learn. A good learner's dictionary will only list members of a word family that are common and useful to learn.

EXERCISE 7

A. The following words can be found in this unit. Use a good learner's dictionary to look up members of each word family and complete the chart. An example has been done for you.

Nouns	Verbs	Adjectives	Adverbs
1. devastation	Infinitive: to devastate Present Simple: devastate Present Simple (3rd person): devastates Past participle: devastated Present participle: devastating	devastating devastated	devastatingly
2. Singular: .... Plural:	Infinitive: to monitor Present Simple: .... Present Simple (3rd person): .... Past participle: .... Present participle:	....	
3. Singular: flood Plural:	Infinitive: .... Present Simple: .... Present Simple (3rd person): .... Past participle: .... Present participle:	....	
4. Singular: disaster Plural:		....	....
5. Singular: .... Plural:		....	mysteriously

Nouns	Verbs	Adjectives	Adverbs
6. Singular: .... Plural:	Infinitive: .... Present Simple: .... Present Simple (3rd person): .... Past participle: .... Present participle:	invited	....
7. Singular: innovation Plural:	Infinitive: .... Present Simple: .... Present Simple (3rd person): .... Past participle: .... Present participle:	....	

For more on using *-ing* and *-ed* adjectives correctly, see Bioethics, Part 1.

B. Read the paragraph. Choose the best word from the box to fill in each blank. Remember to use the correct form of the word. Then compare and discuss your answers with a partner. An example has been done for you.

Noun	Verb	Adjective	Adverb
stability	to hit	frightened	expensively
result	to estimate	moving	devastatingly
occurrence			

Tsunamis are both ...devastating... and .... They usually .... after an earthquake strikes under the ocean. During the earthquake, a large amount of land can be .... This, in turn, moves the water. As the water tries to become .... again, a giant wave may form. This giant wave can travel many thousands of miles before .... land and causing great damage. In 2011, a massive earthquake occurred off the coast of Japan. The .... tsunami caused problems at the country's nuclear power plants and killed many people. The height of the tsunami waves was over 130 feet, or 40 meters, which is almost as tall as the Statue of Liberty in New York. The .... cost of the damage was over $230 billion, the most .... natural disaster in history.

C. Underline the correct word in each sentence. Then write a sentence for the word you didn't use. Check unknown words in a learner's dictionary. An example has been done for you.

The rescue workers were trying to determine the child's identity / identifiable.

New sentence: He has a birthmark that makes him easily identifiable.

1. An indestructible bridge would signify / significantly impact the building industry.
   New sentence: ....
2. Monitoring equipment must function / functional for it to save lives.
   New sentence: ....
3. What kind of equip / equipment does a volcanologist need?
   New sentence: ....
4. The builders sent an item / itemized bill for their repair work.
   New sentence: ....
5. The building has structural / structure damage from the earthquake.
   New sentence: ....
6. The construct / construction of the new stadium has been delayed due to the flood.
   New sentence: ....
7. The new building material is very flexible / flexibility.
   New sentence: ....
8. A strong foundation can stabilize / stabilization a building.
   New sentence: ....

APPLY YOUR SKILLS

WHY IT'S USEFUL By applying the skills you have learned in this unit, you will be able to effectively present a report which is free of errors, has appropriate headings, uses prepositional phrases correctly, and is visually appealing.

ASSIGNMENT

Plan a 500–700 word report that explains a design solution for disaster-resistant housing in a developing country. The report should be well-presented and carefully proofread.

BEFORE YOU WRITE

A. Before you begin your assignment, discuss these questions with one or more students.

1. How might constructing a building in a city in a developed country be different from constructing a building in a village in a developing country?
2. Why is it important to consider the climate and possible natural disasters when designing a building or house?
3. How might it be possible to use low-tech materials and methods when designing disaster-proof buildings?

B. As you consider your writing assignment, complete the tasks. Then share your ideas with a partner. Get feedback and revise your ideas, if necessary.

1. To prepare for your report, choose a developing country to research. Find out what kind of natural disasters this country deals with and what design solution for disaster-resistant housing you want to present in your report. Fill in the chart to gather ideas to include in your report.

Country	
Type of climate	
Potential natural disasters	
Local housing design	
Local building materials	
Design solution for disaster-resistant housing	

2. What techniques can you use to make your report visually appealing?

....

....

C. Review the Unit Skills Summary. As you plan the writing task, apply the skills you learned in this unit.

UNIT SKILLS SUMMARY

Understand the visual appearance of writing

- Understand that how you present your writing can have a large impact on how it is read.
- Use fonts, emphasis, bullets, indents, and images to make your reports attractive and easy to read.

Proofread effectively

- Take time and care to review your writing and check for errors of spelling, capitalization, punctuation, academic register, and grammar.
- Use peer review or reading aloud if necessary.

Write headings and subheadings

- Use headings and subheadings with groupings of similar ideas to help your reader navigate your report.
- Make sure that your headings are clear, concise, and consistent with your main idea.

Use prepositional phrases

- Use prepositional phrases to add depth and detail to your writing.
- Be alert to use the appropriate prepositions in prepositional phrases.

Understand word families

- Use the correct forms of words from word families.

THINKING CRITICALLY

As you think about your assignment, use the information from the earlier sections of the unit to answer the questions. Discuss your answers with one or more students and revise your ideas if necessary.

1. What kinds of natural disasters have you learned about in this unit? What kind of damage can these disasters do to housing?
2. What kinds of disaster-resistant housing solutions have you read about in this unit? Could any of these solutions be used in the developing country you are researching? Why or why not?

THINKING VISUALLY

A. Look at the photos and discuss the questions with a partner.

1. To what kind of climate does each type of housing seem suited?
2. What type of disaster is each house likely to resist?
3. How does each house appear suited to local materials and traditions?

a. House using straw-bale construction

b. Houses on stilts

c. House constructed from bamboo

d. House with sloped roofs

B. Find a photo that illustrates the design solution that you will present in your report.

THINKING ABOUT LANGUAGE

A. Read the Internet article about earthquake-resistant housing in Haiti. Underline the prepositional phrases. There is one grammar mistake. Find it and highlight it.

> **Glossary**
>
> Cinder block: a light brick made of cement used to build houses

Earthquake-Resistant Housing in Haiti

Haiti is a nation on an island in the Caribbean Sea. On January 12, 2010, at 4:53 P.M., a strong earthquake hit Haiti and killed many people. Estimates from some organizations say that 300,000 homes were damaged or destroyed. The homes in Haitian towns and cities were not earthquake resistant. Before the earthquake,

(Continued)

builders used cinder blocks to construct homes. This material was not strong enough and builders at the time did not reinforce walls. The roofs of this kind of house was heavy concrete. Many houses collapsed in pieces.

Some organizations are trying to rebuild homes that are earthquake resistant. They are working with local materials and local builders to construct new homes with an appropriate design. The climate of Haiti is hot and wet, so concrete is a suitable material and it is locally available in Haiti. A concrete roof on top of the house is not a good idea in earthquake-prone areas. Builders are replacing it with a metal roof. Even if these new homes are damaged in an earthquake, they should cause less harm and be easier to repair.

B. Now fill in the chart to show the word families of the words in the article above. Include only commonly used forms.

Noun	Verb	Adjective	Adverb
1. construction	....		
2.	estimate	....	
3.	reinforce	....	
4.		appropriate	....
5. design	....	....	

WRITE

A. Look back at the assignment and at the ideas you sketched out in Before You Write.

B. Research the topic and take effective notes. Discuss your notes and ideas with others and make any needed adjustments.

C. Write an outline of your report. On the basis of your outline, decide what are likely to be appropriate headings and subheadings.

BEYOND THE ASSIGNMENT

Write a 500–700 word report that explains a design solution for disaster-resistant housing in a developing country. The report should be well-presented and carefully proofread. Use all the skills you learned in this unit.

Go to MyEnglishLab to watch Professor Spakowitz's concluding video and to complete a self-assessment.

PART 2

Critical Thinking Skills

Part 2 moves from skill building to application of the skills that require critical thinking. Practice activities tied to specific learning outcomes in each unit require a deeper level of understanding of the academic content.

How advances in biosciences raise legal, social, and ethical concerns

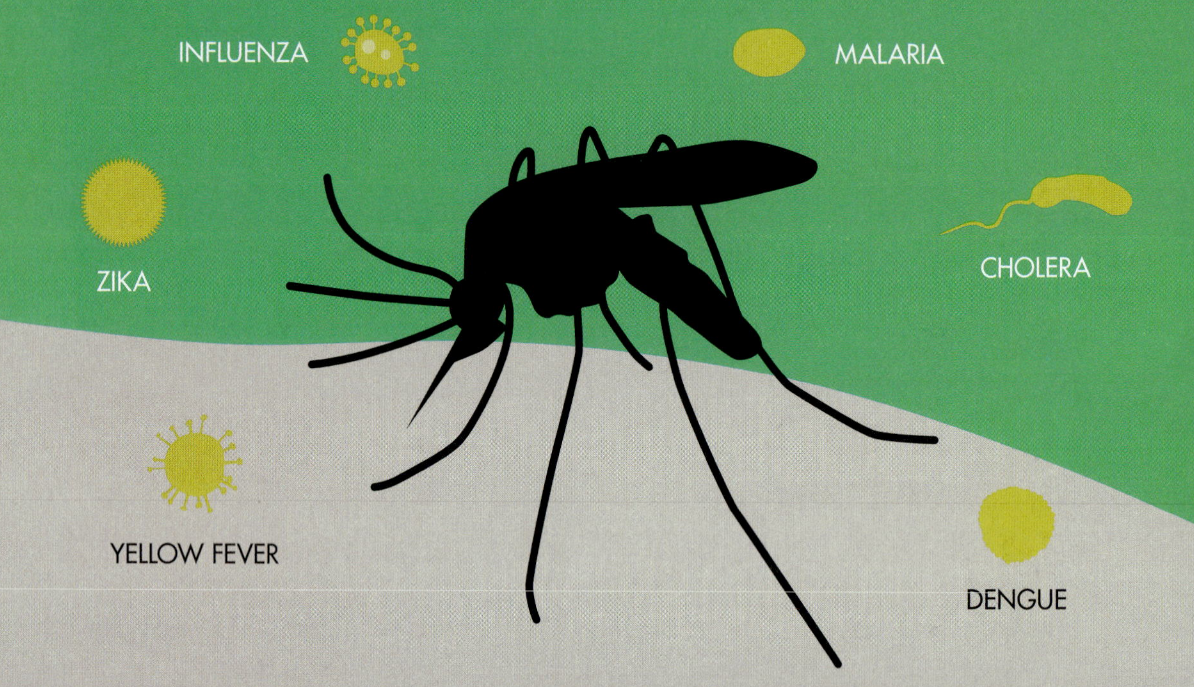

BIOETHICS

Fact and Opinion

UNIT PROFILE

If a white dog and a brown dog have puppies, about half will be brown and half will be white. Gene drive is a new technology that can force all the puppies to be brown, or to have any other genetic feature we choose. This change will force itself through all future generations, which could forever alter the characteristics of a species. Likewise, gene drive technology can be used to destroy mosquitoes carrying deadly diseases, or to wipe out an unwanted invasive species. However, this same technology could also be used to create species that can carry diseases that could cause many thousands of people to die.

OUTCOMES

- State an argument
- Support an argument with examples
- Read and respond to a persuasive essay
- Use hedging language
- Understand collocation

You will plan a 250–300 word paragraph discussing whether or not gene drive should be used outside a laboratory. Clearly state an argument, provide supporting points backed up by relevant examples, and include a counterargument with an effective refutation.

For more about **BIOETHICS**, see 1 3. See also R and OC **BIOETHICS** 1 2 3.

GETTING STARTED

Go to MyEnglishLab to watch Professor Greely's introductory video and to complete a self-assessment.

Discuss these questions with a partner or a group.

1. What diseases do mosquitoes carry? What would happen if all mosquitoes were to die out? Would this cause problems for any other animals?
2. What do you know about invasive species? How were they introduced? How can a species be invasive in one area yet protected in another? What examples do you know about from your country?
3. Professor Greely suggests that gene drive could stop the spread of malaria. Do you agree? Why or why not?

SKILL 1

STATING AN ARGUMENT

WHY IT'S USEFUL Stating an argument, or making a claim, is an important skill in academic writing. Much of the academic writing you do will have at least one argument, or claim, as the main idea. Your argument is your opinion on whatever topic you are writing about. It should be easily identifiable, both by you and your reader. When your argument is clearly stated, it is easier to develop convincing support for it.

Distinguishing facts and arguments

A good academic writer knows that an argument is an opinion, not a fact. While it is useful to use facts to support opinions, your argument should be a statement that someone could disagree with.

Fact: Gene drive is a form of gene editing.

Opinion: Gene drive is a dangerous form of gene editing.

It is not possible to disagree with the fact above. Gene drive is indeed a form of gene editing. However, it is possible to disagree with the opinion above. You might not think that gene drive is dangerous. You might think it is safe. Therefore, "Gene drive is a dangerous form of gene editing" is an argument. Look at some more examples of facts and arguments. In the chart on the next page, the boldfaced words are used to express an argument. Can you think of other language to express an argument?

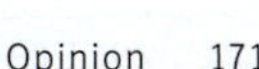

Fact	Argument
Taxpayer money is used to fund gene drive research.	Taxpayer money **should not be used** to fund gene drive research.
Gene drive research is a new trend in the biological sciences.	Gene drive research **is definitely the most promising** trend in the biological sciences.
There are no international regulations about using gene drive.	**It is possible that** making international regulations about gene drive will be difficult.
Gene drive research is not yet a top priority.	Researchers **may need** to make research on gene drive technology a top priority.
The National Academies of Sciences, Engineering, and Medicine (NASEM) is made up of members of the scientific community.	**It is clear that** the international scientific community needs to make decisions about gene drive research together.

Strong vs. tentative arguments

Glossary

Eradicate: to remove or get rid of

In order to state your argument effectively, you need to determine how strong your argument is. The strength of your argument depends on how strong your support is. To state your claim strongly, you need strong support. If you do not have strong support, you should state your claim in a more tentative way. By using certain verbs, adding phrases, and including adjectives, adverbs, and modal verbs, you can adjust the strength of your argument. Here are some examples of strong and tentative arguments, with the language highlighted. Can you think of other ways?

Strong Argument	Tentative Argument
Continuing gene drive research **is** the correct thing to do.	Continuing gene drive research **is probably** the correct thing to do.
Gene drive research **is** dangerous.	This new technology **seems to be** the best chance we have to eradicate malaria.
Research into this technology **should not be** allowed to continue.	Gene drive research **may bring** many benefits to areas affected by the Zika virus.
Gene drive **will almost certainly** benefit areas with invasive species.	**It may be possible** that a genetically modified mosquito could escape.

TIP

Personal pronouns can often be avoided when stating your argument. You do not need to say, "I think that ..." Instead, you can simply write the claim you are making. It is understood that this is your opinion.

Explaining an argument

Once you have stated an argument, the next step is to explain it. Support an argument by giving one or more reasons that explain why you hold an opinion. Your reasons should persuade your reader to agree with your argument. If your reasons are very convincing, you can express a strong argument. If your reasons are less convincing, you can express a tentative argument.

When writing an argumentative paragraph, express the argument in the topic sentence. The topic sentence also sometimes expresses one or more reasons that explain *why* you believe your argument.

For more on identifying topic sentences, see Business and Design, Part 1.

Here, a writer has provided some examples of topic sentences for an argumentative paragraph.

> Gene drive technology is beneficial because it can eradicate diseases.

In this sentence, the writer is arguing for gene drive technology. The argument is strong, rather than tentative, and provides a clear reason why gene drive technology is beneficial: because it can eradicate diseases.

In the sentence below, the writer is still arguing for gene drive, but is providing two reasons in support. This makes the argument stronger.

> Gene drive technology is beneficial because it can eradicate diseases and remove invasive species.

EXERCISE 1

A. A student has written two paragraphs about the dangers of gene drive. Underline her argument and answer the questions that follow.

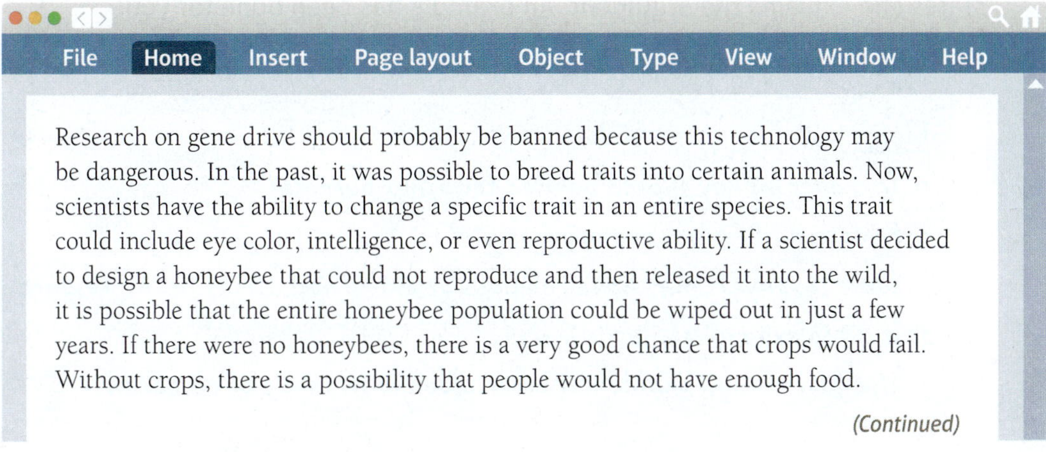

Research on gene drive should probably be banned because this technology may be dangerous. In the past, it was possible to breed traits into certain animals. Now, scientists have the ability to change a specific trait in an entire species. This trait could include eye color, intelligence, or even reproductive ability. If a scientist decided to design a honeybee that could not reproduce and then released it into the wild, it is possible that the entire honeybee population could be wiped out in just a few years. If there were no honeybees, there is a very good chance that crops would fail. Without crops, there is a possibility that people would not have enough food.

(Continued)

Security is also a concern. The facilities where much gene drive research takes place are located on university campuses. These laboratories could be easy targets for criminals. The technology may be stolen by people who want to create a deadly disease. Food shortages and biological weapons are possible dangerous outcomes of research into gene drive technology. Therefore, it should be stopped.

1. Is the argument a fact?

2. Is the writer for or against research into gene drive?

3. How strongly does the writer express the argument? How do you know?

4. What reason is given to explain why the writer holds the opinion?

5. Do you find the explanation that follows convincing? Why or why not?

6. Do you think the writer expressed the argument too strongly, too tentatively, or just right? Why?

B. Look at the arguments. Write reasons that could be used to explain each argument. Then choose the best reason(s). Write a topic sentence that clearly states and explains the argument. An example has been done for you.

1. **Argument:** Taxpayer money should not be used to fund gene drive research …

Ideas:

- Taxpayer money should be used for other purposes
- Private funds are more appropriate
- Some taxpayers may have religious or moral objections to this research
- It is too expensive
- The government should not be involved in this type of research

Topic Sentence: Taxpayer money should not be used to fund gene drive research because some taxpayers may have religious or moral objections.

2. **Argument:** Researchers may need to make research on gene drive technology a top priority …

Ideas:

- ....
- ....
- ....
- ....
- ....

Topic Sentence: Researchers may need to make research on gene drive technology a top priority because ....

....

3. **Argument:** It is clear that members of the international scientific community need to make decisions about gene drive research together …

Ideas:

- ....
- ....
- ....
- ....
- ....

Topic Sentence: It is clear that members of the international scientific community need to make decisions about gene drive research together because ....

....

C. The strength of an argument is determined by the type of explanation provided. How can you find convincing explanations for arguments? Discuss your ideas with a partner.

VOCABULARY PREVIEW

These vocabulary items appear in the reading. Circle the ones you know. Put a question mark next to the ones you don't know.

entire	population	community	accidental	release (n)	regulation

EXERCISE 2

A. In your research about gene drive, you found this article from an online science news site. Read the article and answer the questions that follow. Then discuss your responses with a partner.

Glossary

Halt: to stop something

Determine: to officially decide something

NEWS

HUMANS | BIOSCIENCE FRIDAY 12 JULY

NASEM GIVES GREEN LIGHT TO GENE DRIVE

Gene drive is a technique that scientists can use to change the genes of an entire population. This technique forces a specific trait on a population instead of leaving it to chance. The technique "drives" the change quickly through generations. A biological sciences graduate student at University of California San Diego who was doing research on fruit flies recently made a breakthrough in gene drive research. When the scientific community learned about it, there was excitement, but also hesitation. Gene drive is very powerful and an accidental release of a modified fruit fly, or another modified organism, from the lab into the real world could have serious consequences. The gene drive could change the DNA of an entire population very quickly.

The scientific community decided to halt research while the US National Academies of Sciences, Engineering, and Medicine (NASEM) weighed the risks and benefits of gene drive research. In June 2016, NASEM decided that gene drive research should continue. They also recommended that international regulations for gene drive be developed. NASEM determined that internationally agreed upon regulations are necessary because any problems that could occur from accidental release of a gene drive would not be limited by borders.

Many environmentalists are upset by NASEM's decision to continue research on gene drive. They believe that the scientific community should continue to halt this research until they have determined how to deal with possible mistakes.

1. What is NASEM?

....

2. Why was the scientific community nervous about the discovery of gene drive?

....

3. Why was gene drive research stopped?

....

4. What did NASEM decide about gene drive research?

5. Do you agree with NASEM's decision? Why or why not?

B. When preparing to write an argumentative paragraph, it is a good idea to consider all sides. First, write a sentence which shows you agree with NASEM's decision.

Compare your sentence with those written by other students in the table below. Have you stated your argument strongly or tentatively? Why?

Stating an Argument Strongly	Stating an Argument Tentatively
NASEM **made** the right decision to continue gene drive research.	NASEM **may have made** the right decision to continue gene drive research.
NASEM **definitely** made the right decision to continue gene drive research.	NASEM **perhaps** made the right decision to continue gene drive research.
It is clear that NASEM made the right decision to continue gene drive research.	**It is possible that** NASEM made the right decision to continue gene drive research.

C. Now complete the table with sentences which show that you disagree with NASEM's decision.

Stating an Argument Strongly	Stating an Argument Tentatively
1.	NASEM **may not have made** the right decision to continue gene drive research.
2.	
3. **It is clear that** NASEM made the wrong decision to continue gene drive research.	

EXERCISE 3

A. Look at the topic sentence. Does the writer agree or disagree with NASEM's decision? What reasons are given? How strong is the argument?

Topic sentence: NASEM made the right decision to continue gene drive research because the technology should be studied in a controlled way and it could help eliminate diseases.

B. Choose one topic sentence from Exercise 1, Part B on page 174, to expand into a 200–250 word paragraph. Research your topic before you begin. Provide at least two convincing reasons to support your argument. Use words from the Vocabulary Check in your paragraph.

C. Exchange your paragraph with a partner and provide a peer review using the form below. Discuss each other's ideas for improvement.

Questions	Response	Notes
Does the writing address the assignment task?	Yes ☐ No ☐	
Is the structure of the writing clear?	Yes ☐ No ☐	
Can you identify the writer's argument?	Yes ☐ No ☐	
Is the argument strong or tentative?	Strong ☐ Tentative ☐	
Can you identify the reason(s) the writer gives to explain the argument?	Yes ☐ No ☐	
Are the reasons convincing?	Yes ☐ No ☐	
Did the writer use vocabulary from the Vocabulary Check?	Yes ☐ No ☐	
Is the vocabulary precise?	Yes ☐ No ☐	
Are there any grammatical errors?	Yes ☐ No ☐	
Are there any other comments you would like to make?	Yes ☐ No ☐	

D. Write a second draft of your paragraph based on the peer review and discussion.

VOCABULARY CHECK

A. Review the items in Vocabulary Preview. Write their definitions and add examples. Use a dictionary if necessary.

B. Complete the paragraph with vocabulary items from the box.

accidentally	community	entire	population	regulations	release

The scientific .... is worried about consequences of gene drive. The possibility of an unplanned .... of an altered organism is real and could quickly change not just individual organisms, but the .... living in one area. Therefore, scientists think that international .... should be made so that if someone .... releases a gene drive, governments can act quickly together.

Go to MyEnglishLab to complete a vocabulary and a skill practice and to join in collaborative activities.

SKILL 2

SUPPORTING AN ARGUMENT WITH EXAMPLES

WHY IT'S USEFUL Most people have an opinion on a topic, but those who can support their arguments with good, relevant examples tend to be more persuasive than those who cannot.

Supporting an argument

What is your opinion of the highly controversial statement below? Are you for or against using gene drive on humans to make everyone live longer? Or, would your response be "I don't know" or "I'd rather not say"?

Gene drive should be used on humans to make everyone live longer.

Before you take a position in your academic writing, find out as much as possible about all aspects of an issue. Only by reading widely about different points of view can you form your own opinion and write a well-informed and well-supported argument.

TIP

Doing research online can often result in your finding information that is unreliable or simply untrue. Talk to your institution's library staff and learn how to use the library databases. The sources that you find in a library will be reliable and trustworthy.

Once you have taken a position, you will need to do additional research in order to be able to support it effectively. There is no "correct" number of supporting points for an argument. This depends on the topic and the length of the assignment. However, three is a good number to aim for in most circumstances.

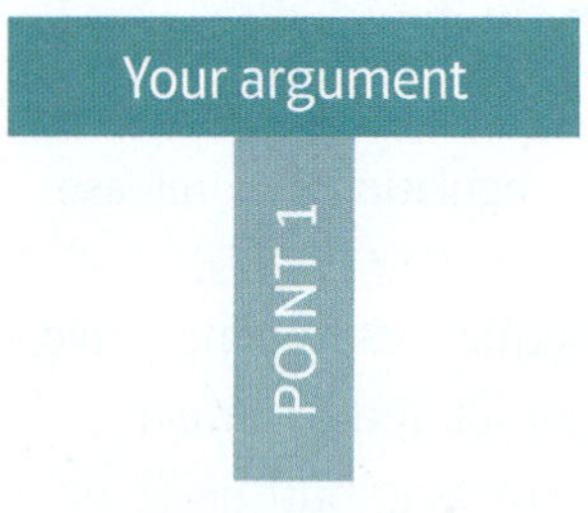

WEAK SUPPORT

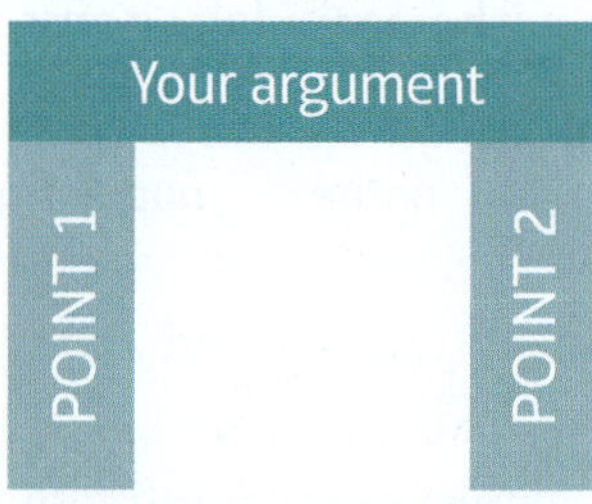

BETTER SUPPORT

STRONG SUPPORT

A student is writing a paragraph in response to the following argument about gene drive.

> Gene drive should be used to eliminate hereditary diseases like cystic fibrosis.

Look at the points that could support or oppose the argument. Do you agree or disagree with the argument? Why? Are there points you would like to add to one or both of the positions?

Glossary

Hereditary: a quality or disease that passes from a parent to a child before the child is born

Embryo: an animal or human that has just begun to develop inside its mother's body

If the student agrees with this view, he could support his argument with these points:

1. The technology to do this is currently available.
2. It would benefit many people and their families.
3. Millions of dollars would be saved on treatment of the disease.

If he disagrees with this view, he could support his argument with these points:

1. It is unethical to experiment on human embryos.
2. The technology is too new to be considered safe.
3. There may be unintended side effects of the use of gene drive.

Using examples to strengthen your support

Once the writer has his supporting points, finding specific examples will help his reader to better understand his claim and add depth to his writing. He will also demonstrate that he has done appropriate research, and he will reinforce his support, making his argument even stronger.

The student's argument					
POINT 1	EXAMPLE	POINT 2	EXAMPLE	POINT 3	EXAMPLE

In this instance, the student writer decided to agree with the argument. He found the following examples to support each point, and added the details to his outline. Notice how key information about the sources has been included. This is important because in academic writing you will need to show where you found your examples.

For more on summarizing and using reporting verbs, see Business and Design, Part 2.

These points support an agreement with the argument that gene drive should be used to eliminate hereditary diseases like cystic fibrosis:

Supporting Point 1: The technology to do this is currently available.

In 2014, a team of biologists altered unhealthy genes in the offspring of fruit flies.

Source Information*

Author: Beverly Jacobs
Date: November 21, 2015
Title: "Gene editing shows promise with fruit flies"

Supporting Point 2: It would benefit many people and their families.

Over 70,000 people suffer from cystic fibrosis.

Source Information*

Author: Cystic Fibrosis Association
Date: January 2017
Title: "Facts about cystic fibrosis"

Supporting Point 3: Millions of dollars would be saved on treatment of the disease.

Treatment costs for a cystic fibrosis patient can be around $30,000 each year.

Source Information*

Authors: Kier van Mies, HeeSun Kim, Michelle Dawson, and Samantha McKenzie
Date: 2014
Title: "Treatment costs for cystic fibrosis"

*Note: The source information is fictional and only for use in this example.

While searching for examples to support his claim, he also found examples which supported disagreement with the argument. He will be able to use these examples in his counterargument, which is covered in the Integrated Skills section.

TIP

There are a number of ways to cite sources: APA, MLA, Harvard, etc. Some institutions use the same citation methods across all courses. Others may vary by the instructor of the course. There are many online resources which can automatically generate citations, but you should always check them as part of your proofreading before handing in an assignment.

Introducing examples

Using specific phrases to introduce examples helps your reader follow your writing more easily. Phrases like *for example* and *for instance* clearly indicate an example is coming. When you want to write a short list of examples you can use *like* or *such as* but you should avoid adding *and so on* or *etc.* at the end of lists. These phrases are not generally used in academic writing.

Here is how our writer used a specific phrase to introduce an example:

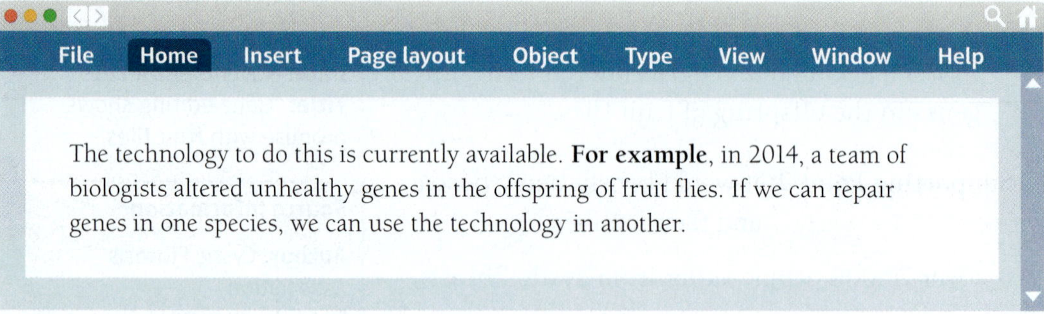

The technology to do this is currently available. **For example**, in 2014, a team of biologists altered unhealthy genes in the offspring of fruit flies. If we can repair genes in one species, we can use the technology in another.

For more on building paragraphs and connecting ideas, see Business and Design, Part 1.

VOCABULARY PREVIEW

These vocabulary items appear in the reading. Circle the ones you know. Put a question mark next to the ones you don't know.

decision	technology	terrorist	pregnant	laboratory	bacteria

EXERCISE 4

A. A student wrote a paragraph *opposing* NASEM's decision to allow more research into gene drive technology. Read her paragraph and highlight the examples. Underline the phrases used to introduce the examples. Complete the chart that follows.

Glossary

Unintentionally: not on purpose

Organism: living thing, usually a very small one

Safeguards: ways to keep something safe or protected

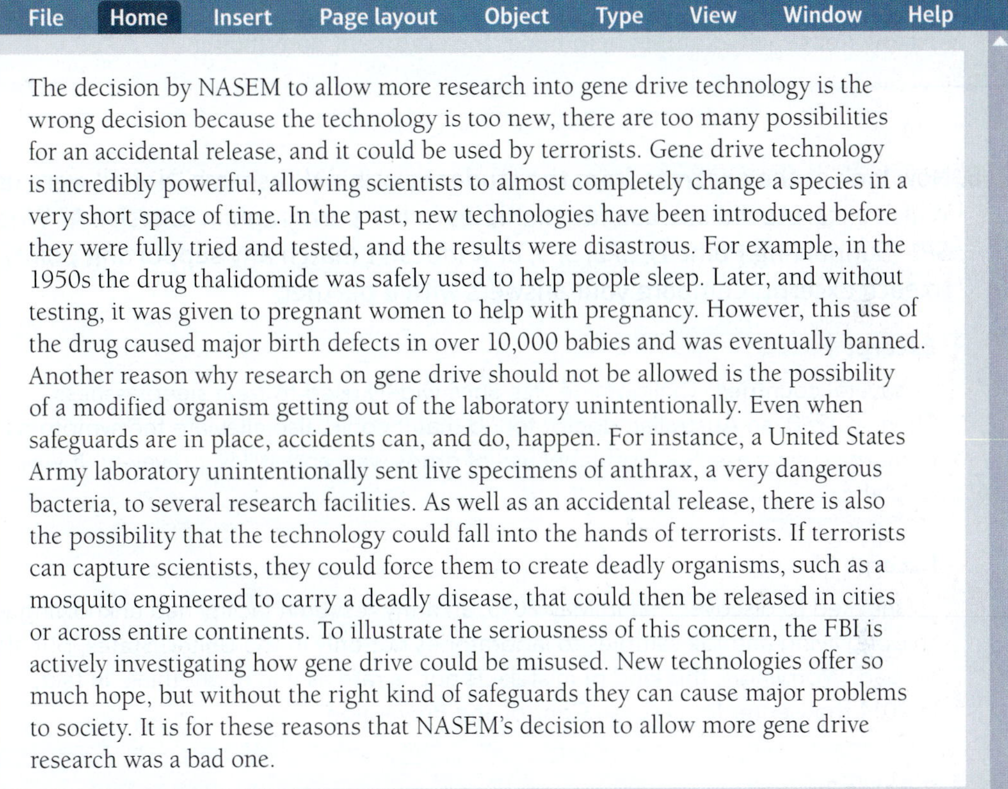

The decision by NASEM to allow more research into gene drive technology is the wrong decision because the technology is too new, there are too many possibilities for an accidental release, and it could be used by terrorists. Gene drive technology is incredibly powerful, allowing scientists to almost completely change a species in a very short space of time. In the past, new technologies have been introduced before they were fully tried and tested, and the results were disastrous. For example, in the 1950s the drug thalidomide was safely used to help people sleep. Later, and without testing, it was given to pregnant women to help with pregnancy. However, this use of the drug caused major birth defects in over 10,000 babies and was eventually banned. Another reason why research on gene drive should not be allowed is the possibility of a modified organism getting out of the laboratory unintentionally. Even when safeguards are in place, accidents can, and do, happen. For instance, a United States Army laboratory unintentionally sent live specimens of anthrax, a very dangerous bacteria, to several research facilities. As well as an accidental release, there is also the possibility that the technology could fall into the hands of terrorists. If terrorists can capture scientists, they could force them to create deadly organisms, such as a mosquito engineered to carry a deadly disease, that could then be released in cities or across entire continents. To illustrate the seriousness of this concern, the FBI is actively investigating how gene drive could be misused. New technologies offer so much hope, but without the right kind of safeguards they can cause major problems to society. It is for these reasons that NASEM's decision to allow more gene drive research was a bad one.

Supporting Point	Example	Specific Phrase Used to Introduce Example
1. Untested new technology		
2. Accidental release		
3. Terrorist uses	• •	• •

B. How can you find good examples to help support your arguments? Why is it important to note down where you found your supporting sources?

EXERCISE 5

A. Answer the questions.

1. What is the writer's argument in the paragraph cited in Exercise 4?

....

2. How does each example relate to the writer's argument?

....

3. How does each example help make the argument convincing?

....

B. Now look at the excerpts from the student's original research. Not all were used. Which excerpts did she use for examples in her paragraph in Exercise A? Write *SP1* (Supporting Point 1), *SP2*, *SP3*, or *X* (doesn't match any supporting point) next to each excerpt. Compare your answers with a partner.

Excerpt 1: ....

... several countries. Thalidomide was once widely used to treat sleeplessness. Then, in 1960, an Australian doctor found that it could also alleviate the symptoms of morning sickness. Such off-label use of drugs was, and still is, prevalent. It was only after ...

Excerpt 2: ....

... shocked to discover that in May 2015, an army research facility had unknowingly shipped living anthrax samples to laboratories not only in the United States, but also abroad. Worryingly, this kind of mistake is not as rare as you might think. In fact, in 2014 the Center for Disease Control and Prevention ...

Excerpt 3: ....

... thousands of miscarriages were caused by the misuse of thalidomide. Many babies that survived were born disabled. In fact, it is estimated that in Germany, over 10,000 babies were born with a disability. Many of these babies were ...

Excerpt 4: ....

... no laws regulating the use of gene drives inside or outside of the laboratory environment. The students were simply trying to recreate a gene drive for their science project.

Excerpt 5: ....

… problem. Officials from the FBI and other US agencies believe that gene drive technology is so easy to use that it could be used to create a deadly disease. In May …

Excerpt 6: ....

… wiped out completely. After spending billions of dollars on prevention of malaria, the Gates Foundation is very interested in the application of gene drive technology. By making the offspring of mosquitoes sterile, they won't be able to breed and the population will die out within a year. This is more progress than …

Excerpt 7: ....

… in a memo which stated that officials in the United Nations' bioweapons office are tracking gene drive research. The worry, UN officials say, is that technology of this nature could be weaponized and used in ways that are not always easy to imagine. They have been briefed by members of the National Academies of Sciences, Engineering, and Medicine who recently …

Excerpt 8: ....

… could be done. Modifying the mosquito so that it can carry dengue fever, as well as malaria, could mean trouble if mosquitoes were to be released near a large population center. They could even …

C. With a partner, look at the arguments. Research each argument online and find at least one point to support agreement and one point to support disagreement. Then find an example to strengthen each point and note down the source.

Argument 1: Gene drive experiments should only take place under strict government supervision with highly trained scientists. The technology is too dangerous to be used by just anyone.

Agree

Supporting Point 1: ....

Example: ....

Source: ....

Disagree

Supporting Point 1: ....

Example: ....

Source: ....

Argument 2: Gene drive should be used to alter mosquitoes so they cannot reproduce. Within a few years there will be no mosquitoes and no malaria.

Agree

Supporting Point 1: ....

Example: ....

Source: ....

Disagree

Supporting Point 1: ....

Example: ....

Source: ....

Argument 3: International stakeholders must agree on regulations for a future that includes genetically altered organisms. It is important to plan now for the intentional or unintentional release these organisms.

Agree

Supporting Point 1: ....

Example: ....

Source: ....

Disagree

Supporting Point 1: ....

Example: ....

Source: ....

EXERCISE 6

A. Choose one of the arguments from the previous exercise. Using your supporting point and example, expand the argument into a 250–300 word paragraph. Then do more research to provide two more supporting points and an example for each.

Begin your paragraph with an appropriate topic sentence. Use specific phrases to introduce each of your examples. Use words from the Vocabulary Check.

B. Write a first draft, then exchange your paragraph with a partner and provide feedback using the peer review form. Discuss each other's ideas for improvement.

PART 2

Questions	Yes	No	Notes
Does the writing address the assignment task?	☐	☐	
Is the structure of the writing clear?	☐	☐	
Is there a clear argument?	☐	☐	
Can you identify the writer's examples?	☐	☐	
Does the writer use appropriate phrases to introduce examples?	☐	☐	
Do the examples help make the argument convincing?	☐	☐	
Did the writer use vocabulary from the Vocabulary Check?	☐	☐	
Is the vocabulary precise?	☐	☐	
Are there any grammatical errors?	☐	☐	
Are there any other comments you would like to make?	☐	☐	

C. Write a second draft of your paragraph based on your partner's feedback and the related discussion.

VOCABULARY CHECK

A. Review the items in Vocabulary Preview. Write their definitions and add examples. Use a dictionary if necessary.

B. Complete each sentence with a vocabulary item from the box.

bacteria	decisions	laboratory	pregnant	technology	terrorist

1. A .... is a place where scientists do experiments.
2. Sometimes, scientists have to make very difficult ....
3. .... are small organisms that can be helpful or harmful.
4. Gene drive is a new kind of biological .... that is controversial.
5. If woman has an unborn baby inside of her, she is ....
6. A .... is a kind of criminal.

Go to MyEnglishLab to complete a vocabulary and skill practice and to join in collaborative activities.

INTEGRATED SKILLS

READING AND RESPONDING TO A PERSUASIVE ESSAY

WHY IT'S USEFUL In life, many people want to persuade you to do something. Whether they want you to buy their product, take some action, or agree with their opinion, you should be able to recognize the persuasive language they are using and to evaluate the argument critically. This enables you to determine whether the argument is strong and therefore convincing, or weak and not convincing. You can then decide whether you agree or disagree with the points stated and respond appropriately.

Strong vs. weak arguments

As you have learned, a well-written text clearly states an argument and then supports that argument with relevant examples. However, more than good examples are often needed to make an argument strong.

Read the three excerpts from student papers below, watching for the specific phrases used to introduce the examples. Then decide which one has the strongest argument. What makes it stronger than the others?

Excerpt 1

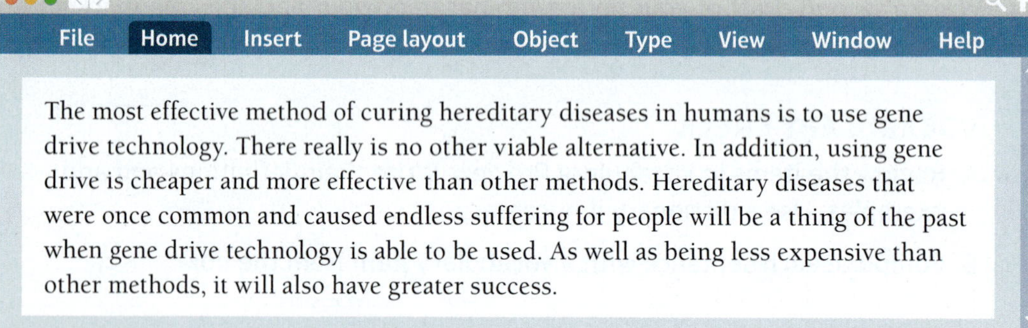

The most effective method of curing hereditary diseases in humans is to use gene drive technology. There really is no other viable alternative. In addition, using gene drive is cheaper and more effective than other methods. Hereditary diseases that were once common and caused endless suffering for people will be a thing of the past when gene drive technology is able to be used. As well as being less expensive than other methods, it will also have greater success.

Excerpt 2

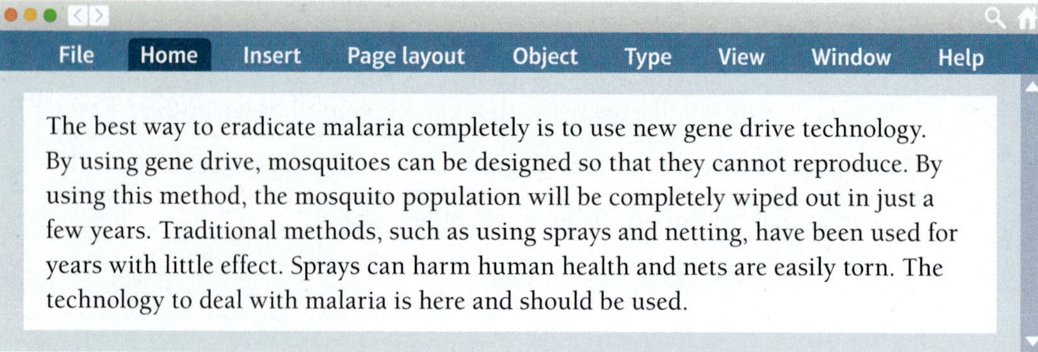

The best way to eradicate malaria completely is to use new gene drive technology. By using gene drive, mosquitoes can be designed so that they cannot reproduce. By using this method, the mosquito population will be completely wiped out in just a few years. Traditional methods, such as using sprays and netting, have been used for years with little effect. Sprays can harm human health and nets are easily torn. The technology to deal with malaria is here and should be used.

Excerpt 3

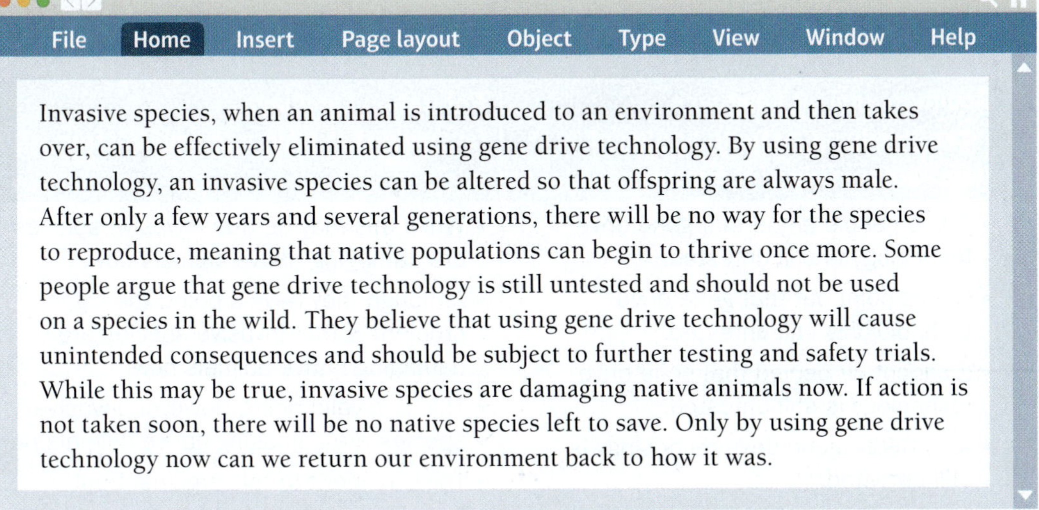

Invasive species, when an animal is introduced to an environment and then takes over, can be effectively eliminated using gene drive technology. By using gene drive technology, an invasive species can be altered so that offspring are always male. After only a few years and several generations, there will be no way for the species to reproduce, meaning that native populations can begin to thrive once more. Some people argue that gene drive technology is still untested and should not be used on a species in the wild. They believe that using gene drive technology will cause unintended consequences and should be subject to further testing and safety trials. While this may be true, invasive species are damaging native animals now. If action is not taken soon, there will be no native species left to save. Only by using gene drive technology now can we return our environment back to how it was.

As you may have noted, Excerpt 1 makes a very weak argument because it simply repeats assorted pieces of information. It does not name or discuss other methods.

Excerpt 2 provides a good argument supported by relevant examples. However, it only talks about the positive values of using gene drive technology without examining any opposing views. Are there downsides to completely eradicating a species? Will other animals that rely on mosquitoes, such as bats, lose a reliable food source and start to die out, too? Without acknowledging these alternative points of view, the argument for using gene drive technology is not entirely persuasive. It is important to show that you have considered an alternative point of view.

Excerpt 3 makes a stronger case because it contains a **counterargument** and a **refutation**. A counterargument acknowledges that there are alternative views to every opinion, and that they must be recognized, or acknowledged. After the counter-argument comes a refutation, which addresses the counterargument. It's like saying, "I understand there is an opposing argument, but I believe it is weaker than my argument—and here's why." The refutation doesn't just repeat the main argument. Instead, it addresses the concerns raised in the counterargument.

Counterargument: Some people argue that gene drive technology is still untested.

Refutation: While this may be true, invasive species are damaging native animals now.

Notice how the counterargument and refutation are introduced. In the chart below, there are examples of other phrases you can use to introduce counterarguments and refutations.

Counterargument Language (acknowledging a strong argument from another side of the issue)	**Refutation Language (showing that your argument is stronger)**
• Some people argue that gene drive technology is still untested. • Critics point out that gene drive technology is still untested. • It cannot be denied that gene drive technology is still untested. • Admittedly, gene drive technology is still untested.	• While this may be true, invasive species are damaging native animals now. • Although they have a point, the bigger problem is that invasive species are damaging native animals now. • This is a valid point. However, invasive species are damaging native animals now. • There is merit to this argument but invasive species are damaging native animals now.

TIP

A counterargument should be as strong as the main argument. Choosing a weak counterargument that is easy to refute doesn't make the main argument stronger. Choose the strongest counterargument you can find and refute that. If you can do so effectively, you are more likely to persuade someone of your point of view.

Responding to an argument

In an assignment, you may be asked to respond to a writer's argument. Begin by identifying the argument that the writer is making. Next, evaluate the argument by determining whether or not it is well supported. As we saw, the argument in Excerpt 3, on the previous page, is well supported.

Now reread Excerpt 3. Do you agree or disagree with the author's arguments and counterarguments? Discuss your reactions with a classmate and then list at least three reasons that show why you agree or disagree.

Once you have identified and evaluated the argument and decided whether you agree or disagree with it, you need to respond. You can do so by following these three steps:

Step 1: Restate the author's argument.

Step 2: Indicate whether you agree or disagree.

Step 3: Provide good, detailed reasons to explain your agreement or disagreement.

Here is a response that shows disagreement. It follows the three steps.

Step 1: Restate the author's argument.

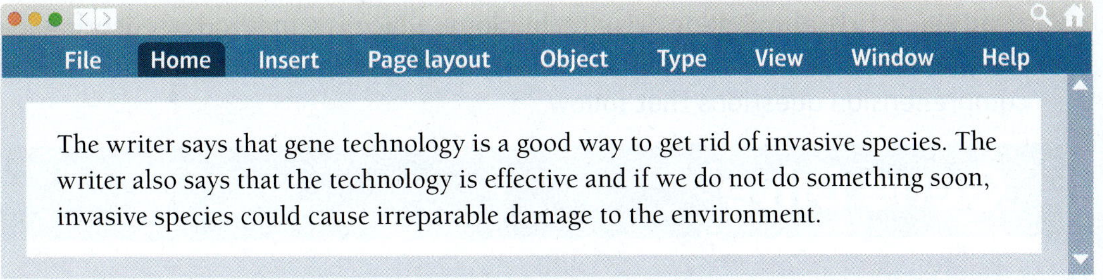

The writer says that gene technology is a good way to get rid of invasive species. The writer also says that the technology is effective and if we do not do something soon, invasive species could cause irreparable damage to the environment.

Step 2: Indicate whether you agree or disagree.

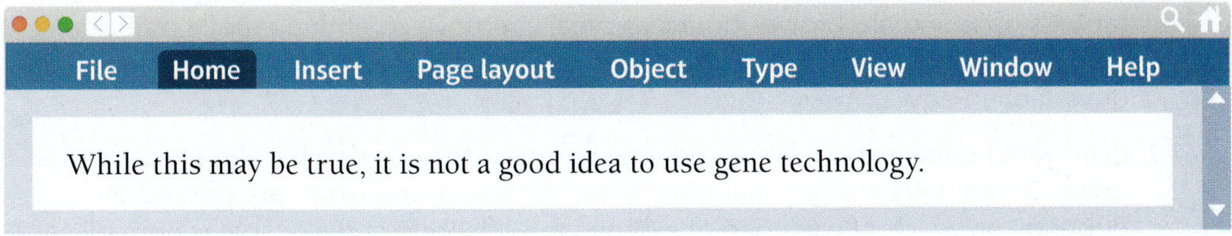

While this may be true, it is not a good idea to use gene technology.

Step 3: Provide good, detailed reasons to explain your agreement or disagreement.

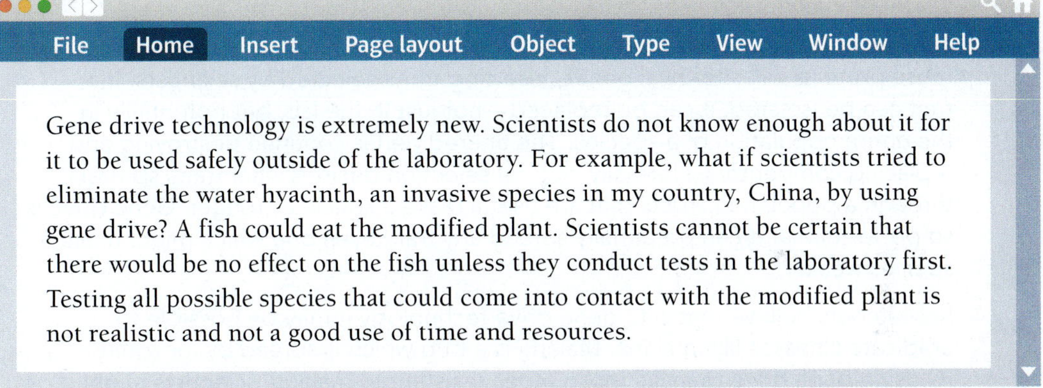

Gene drive technology is extremely new. Scientists do not know enough about it for it to be used safely outside of the laboratory. For example, what if scientists tried to eliminate the water hyacinth, an invasive species in my country, China, by using gene drive? A fish could eat the modified plant. Scientists cannot be certain that there would be no effect on the fish unless they conduct tests in the laboratory first. Testing all possible species that could come into contact with the modified plant is not realistic and not a good use of time and resources.

CULTURE NOTE

Generally, in academic writing, it is considered poor form to use the first person. However, writing an agreement or disagreement is different because you are being asked for your opinion. You should still provide good reasons based on facts or examples, rather than just how you feel.

VOCABULARY PREVIEW

These vocabulary items appear in the reading. Circle the ones you know. Put a question mark next to the ones you don't know.

generation	invasive	disrupt	aim (v)
ecosystem	fence	bat (n – animal)	method

EXERCISE 7

A. **Read the article about gene drive technology, which is a method of ensuring that genetic traits will be inherited by future generations. Then answer the comprehension questions that follow.**

Gene Drive

1 Imagine that you raise rabbits. When the rabbits are born, some are brown, some are gray, and some are a mix—all according to nature. Now, imagine that you could simply modify one rabbit and, presto—after a few generations, all that rabbit's offspring are brown. Could you really remove an entire genetic trait from a population? Genetics researchers are experimenting with just such an idea: gene drive technology.

2 Even with human manipulation, genetic heredity decides which traits are passed down. Some traits are dominant, some are recessive, and which are passed on depends on which of each parent's genes the offspring receive. That is normally a matter of chance, but gene drive technology creates "selfish" genes. These selfish genes will make certain that they are passed down—and will even alter competing genes to do so.

3 The secret is CRISPR technology, specifically the Cas9 protein. With gene drive, these proteins will alter rival genes, inserting traits selected by scientists. If a trait can be isolated, it can be replaced—not just in the lab, but potentially in the entire population of a species. The altered genes continue destroying and replacing competitors. Normally, natural selection decides what traits spread through a population. Traits that are useful make a species stronger. Gene drive is so powerful that it can potentially spread any trait, even one which might make a species weaker.

4 Researchers believe that with gene drive technology it may be possible to eradicate illnesses like malaria. Malaria is a bug which is spread by mosquitoes. By using gene drive to make mosquitoes resistant to malaria, scientists might eradicate the disease. Best of all, we would not even have to worry about vaccines, health campaigns, or taking medicine; simply release some modified mosquitoes into the wild, and the entire population's genes will be altered in a few generations.

5 Gene drive technology could also allow us to fix the mistakes of the past. Many ecosystems are suffering an imbalance due to an invasive species, a plant or animal from somewhere else which has upset the ecosystem's fragile balance. In Australia, rabbits and cane toads have been big problems; as non-native species, neither have natural predators and they can reproduce unchecked.

Glossary

Dominant: If one parent has a dominant trait, it will be passed on.

Recessive: For a recessive trait to be passed on, both parents must have it.

Eradicate: to completely remove something

Resistant: not affected by something

Imbalance: not in balance; one species is too strong in an environment and so takes over

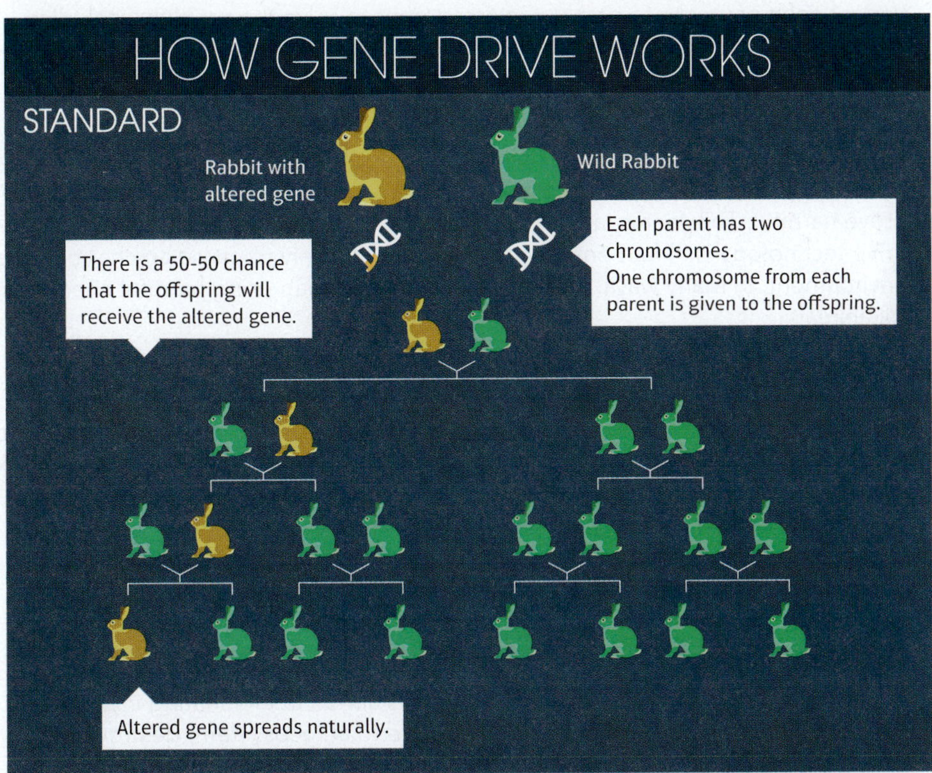
HOW GENE DRIVE WORKS
STANDARD
Rabbit with altered gene
Wild Rabbit
Each parent has two chromosomes.
One chromosome from each parent is given to the offspring.
There is a 50-50 chance that the offspring will receive the altered gene.
Altered gene spreads naturally.

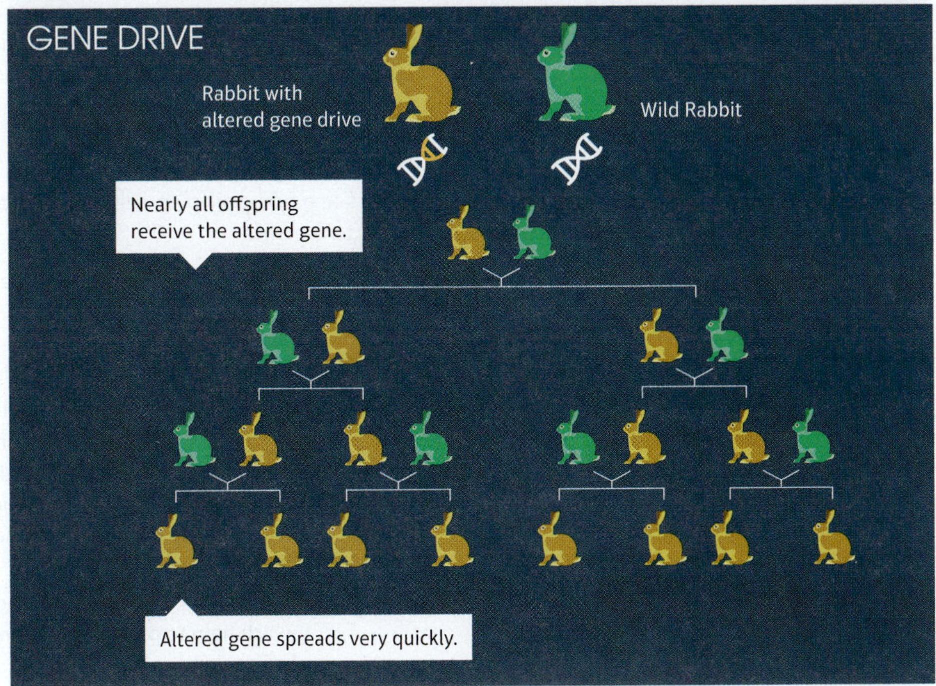
GENE DRIVE
Rabbit with altered gene drive
Wild Rabbit
Nearly all offspring receive the altered gene.
Altered gene spreads very quickly.

(Continued)

Various solutions were carried out in an attempt to solve the problem, including introducing diseases and building giant fences. Despite these measures, nothing helped. There is every hope that gene drive technology will help make these species weaker, making them easier to control.

6 Some environmental advocates have raised concerns about the use of gene drive technology. These advocates believe that the use of gene drive technology may prove harmful. This fear is largely due to past mistakes; while it seems similar, gene drive technology is in fact entirely different and unlikely to cause any harm to the environment. In many ways, it is considerably safer than using harmful chemicals to kill animals.

7 One concern some people have is that gene drive technology might lead to the eradication of a targeted species and a related disruption of the food chain. If the mosquitoes are eradicated, for example, animals like bats and birds may starve to death. After all, previous chemical-based eradication efforts caused problems like this. Although this is a valid point, thankfully modern scientists are aware of the importance of a balanced ecosystem. That is why gene drive technology, when applied to situations such as mosquito-borne illness, focuses not on eradication but on alteration. Scientists can use gene drive technology to make mosquitoes resistant to blood borne illnesses without harming them. Bats and birds will still have a steady food supply, even as we eradicate the disease.

8 Eradication is, of course, the goal of programs aimed at eliminating invasive species. Since an invasive species is not native to an ecosystem, destroying it won't disrupt the food chain. Critics worry though that the gene drive that destroys the invasive species in a non-native environment could somehow spread back to invasive species' native environment, destroying it there, too. This situation is unlikely, precisely because it would be so dangerous. Modern environmental protection measures are much better enforced today than in years past. Similar concerns about experimental genes being "accidentally released" are also unfounded. Gene drive research has been going on for years; security measures have proven to be more than adequate. Scientists are not going to release altered traits into a wild population until they are proven to be safe.

9 Other methods aimed at controlling populations, including chemicals, fences, and hunting, have had their day. The cold facts are that those other methods just don't work. If we want to use science to save the environment from invasive species and prevent the spread of harmful disease, gene editing is our best bet. If scientists continue to take all necessary precautions, gene drive offers a simple and elegant means to solve many problems.

Glossary

Advocate: someone who publicly supports someone or something

Food chain: animals and plants considered as a group, in which a plant is eaten by an insect which is then eaten by another animal and so on

Precautions: plans or processes which help to prevent bad things happening

1. How does using a gene drive differ from natural heredity?

2. What are two potential applications of gene drive technology discussed in the article?

3. What is one concern some people have about gene drive?

B. Read the text again and decide if the author is making an argument that supports the use of the technology or an argument that is against its use. Underline language that is used to introduce arguments, double-underline counterargument language and highlight refutations. Place brackets [...] around the support that is provided.

C. Looking at the arguments, decide whether you agree or disagree with the author. Discuss your assessment with a partner.

D. Based on your discussion, prepare a response. Follow the three steps presented, adding your ideas at each stage.

Step 1: Restate the author's argument.

Step 2: Show whether you agree or disagree.

Step 3: Provide good, detailed reasons to explain your agreement or disagreement.

E. Use your ideas from Part D above to draft a 200–250 word paragraph in response to the article. Include at least five of the Vocabulary Check words in your writing.

F. **Give your first draft to a partner and get feedback. Write a second draft based on the suggestions you receive.**

Questions	Yes	No	Notes
Does the writing address the assignment task?	☐	☐	
Can you identify the three steps required for a response?	☐	☐	
Are the ideas clear and easy to understand?	☐	☐	
Do the ideas fit together in an orderly, logical way?	☐	☐	
Are any ideas missing?	☐	☐	
Did the writer include at least five words from the Vocabulary Check?	☐	☐	
Are there any grammatical errors?	☐	☐	
Are there any other comments you would like to make?	☐	☐	

VOCABULARY CHECK

A. **Review the items in Vocabulary Preview. Write their definitions and add examples. Use a dictionary if necessary.**

B. **Choose the sentence that correctly expresses the meaning of the underlined vocabulary item.**

1. a. An <u>invasive</u> species is a species that is natural to an area.

   b. An <u>invasive</u> species is a species that was brought from somewhere else.

2. a. Gene drive might be the best <u>method</u>, or condition, to stop diseases like malaria.

   b. Gene drive might be the best <u>method</u>, or process, to stop diseases like malaria.

3. a. Some people believe that the use of gene drive could <u>disrupt</u>, or improve, the food chain.

   b. Some people believe that the use of gene drive could <u>disrupt</u>, or harm, the food chain.

4. a. A bat is a mammal that can fly.
   b. A bat is a reptile that can fly.
5. a. There can be problems when an animal's ecosystem, or environment, is changed.
   b. There can be problems when an animal's ecosystem, or health, is changed.
6. a. Gene drive is passed down between generations, or groups born around the same time.
   b. Gene drive is passed down between generations, or species of animals.
7. a. A fence can be used to protect animals from bad weather.
   b. A fence can be used to stop animals from getting into an area.
8. a. Scientists aim, or want, to solve problems with gene drive.
   b. Scientists aim, or intend, to solve problems with gene drive.

Go to MyEnglishLab to complete a vocabulary and skill practice and to join in collaborative activities.

LANGUAGE SKILL

USING HEDGING LANGUAGE

WHY IT'S USEFUL In academic writing, it's common to use hedging language to show there may be some doubt about an argument that you are presenting. Hedging language helps you to express a degree of uncertainty about your argument and thus avoid making claims that are too broad.

Go to MyEnglishLab for the Language Skill presentation and practice.

VOCABULARY STRATEGY

UNDERSTANDING COLLOCATION

WHY IT'S USEFUL Learning common collocations—words that are often used together—will help you as both a speaker and a writer of English. Knowing the collocations of given words enables you to use them as fluent speakers typically do.

Collocation is the way that words are used together. When we look at how language is used, we find that certain combinations of words are more common than others. It's important to learn a word's collocations because you are learning how to use the word the way it is typically used.

Another reason why it's important to learn collocations is that words go together differently in different languages.

Best of all, we would not even have to worry about vaccines, health campaigns, or *taking medicines*.

There are many kinds of collocations. Let's look at the word *medicine*, for example. In some languages you *eat* some medicine. In other languages you *drink* some medicine. In English, you usually *take* some medicine. In English, *take* is a collocation of the word *medicine*. Look at the chart below for some more examples of common collocations with the word *medicine*.

Verbs	Adjectives	Nouns
take medicine for something	a strong medicine	a medicine bottle
give someone a medicine	a powerful medicine	a medicine chest
a doctor prescribes a medicine	an over-the-counter medicine	a prescription medicine
swallow a medicine	an herbal medicine	a cough medicine

When you know a word's typical collocations, you will be more likely to use it appropriately. In the sentence below, notice that the words in bold are collocations from the chart above.

The doctor **prescribed** a **powerful** medicine **for** malaria.

Learning collocations can also help you to determine meaning. Some words have multiple meanings that change depending on the collocation(s). Look at the chart below. It shows the common verb *take* and some of its collocations. Notice how the meaning of *take* changes in each instance.

Collocation	Meaning
take a position	to have an opinion about something
take place	to happen
take action	to do something
take medicine take sugar	to eat or drink something
take notes take someone's name	to write something down
take pity on someone take pride in something	to have or cause emotions

Trying to learn the many meanings of a word such as *take* without using collocations would be very difficult. Instead, note down collocations as much as possible when learning new words.

TIP

Learner's dictionaries provide collocations. Be sure to look up new words in a learner's dictionary and note down the collocations.

EXERCISE 8

A. Find collocations for the word *trait(s)* by reading the sentences below. Write the collocations in the chart. An example has been done for you. Then check your answers with a partner and discuss any differences you may have.

- Could you really remove an entire genetic trait from a population?
- Even with human manipulation, genetic heredity decides which traits are passed down.
- Some traits are dominant, some are recessive, and which are passed on depends on which of each parents' genes the offspring receive.
- Now, scientists have the ability to change a specific trait in an entire species.
- You are going to read an article about gene drive technology, which is a method of ensuring that traits will be inherited by future generations.
- Normally, natural selection decides what traits spread through a population.

Verbs	Adjectives
1. .... a trait	a ....genetic.... trait
2. .... a trait	a .... trait
3. .... a trait	a .... trait
4. .... a trait	a .... trait
5. a trait	
6. .... a trait	

B. **Underline collocations with the word *make* in the sentences below. Then choose the meaning of *make* that is being used. You may use each meaning more than once. Some sentences may have more than one meaning.**

> **Meanings**
>
> a. to check that something is true or has been done
> b. to cause something to happen
> c. to do / create something

.... 1. The international scientific community needs to make decisions about gene drive research together.

.... 2. Scientists must make sure that the laboratory is secure.

.... 3. Pets can make a mess in the house.

.... 4. Let's make certain that the public is informed about this issue.

.... 5. Some traits make a species weaker.

.... 6. Using examples can make your argument stronger.

.... 7. Please make comments on your classmate's paragraph.

.... 8. How can we make the problem go away?

C. **The chart shows some words that can be used to form collocations with the word *population*. Write sentences using collocations on the lines. Then compare your sentences with a partner and discuss any differences you may have. An example has been done for you.**

Verbs	Nouns		Adjectives	
	Use before	**Use after**		
increase	mosquito	of something	entire	female
grow	student	levels	native	male
double	world	center	large	dense
decline	prison	size	overall	sparse
fall	increase in	map	total	working
control	areas of	density	adult	aging
reach				

1. The mosquito population is increasing.
2.
3.
4.
5.
6.
7.
8.

PART 2

APPLY YOUR SKILLS

WHY IT'S USEFUL By applying the skills you have learned in this unit, you can state an argument clearly and make it stronger by supporting it with examples. You can include a counterargument and refute it effectively to show that you understand more than one side of an issue. You can use hedging language to word your claims carefully and common collocations to make your writing sound natural and fluent.

ASSIGNMENT

Plan a 250–300 word paragraph discussing whether or not gene drive should be used outside a laboratory. Clearly state an argument, provide supporting points backed up by relevant examples, and include a counterargument with an effective refutation.

BEFORE YOU WRITE

A. Before you begin your assignment, discuss these questions with one or more students.

1. What is gene drive and what makes it different from natural selection?
2. Why is gene drive controversial?
3. How might using gene drive in a laboratory differ from using it in the real world?

B. As you consider your writing assignment, complete the tasks. Then share your ideas with a partner. Get feedback and revise your ideas, if necessary.

1. Think about the arguments you have read in support of gene drive. What arguments have you read about against gene drive? Have you found these arguments convincing? Explain why or why not.

   In support of gene drive: ....

   ....

   ....

   ....

   Against gene drive: ....

   ....

   ....

   ....

2. Decide whether you will write an argument in support of using gene drive outside a laboratory or against it.

   a. What research do you need to do to support your position?

   ....

   ....

   b. How can you use examples to strengthen your argument and what specific phrases can you use to introduce them?

   ....

   ....

   ....

   c. What counterargument will you use and how will you refute it?

   ....

   ....

3. Decide how you will express your argument. Will you express your argument in a strong or more tentative way? Why?

   ....

   ....

   ....

C. Review the Unit Skills Summary. As you plan the writing task, apply the skills you learned in this unit.

UNIT SKILLS SUMMARY

State an argument

- Find out about all aspects of an issue before taking a position.
- Clearly state your argument, or opinion, on the topic you are writing about.
- Use language that tells your reader you are expressing an opinion rather than stating facts.
- Determine how strongly you can and should express your argument.

Support an argument with examples

- Include several supporting points for your argument.
- Use examples to explain your supporting points and strengthen your argument.

Read and respond to a persuasive essay

- Identify someone else's argument.
- Agree or disagree with the argument, using reasons to support your response.
- Include a counterargument and refutation to make your argument more convincing.

Use hedging language

- Use hedging language to express an appropriate amount of uncertainty in your academic writing.
- Use modal verbs and other hedging language to express middle ground.

Understand collocation

- Learn common collocations so your writing reflects typical English usage.
- Use collocations to help you determine the meaning of words with multiple meanings.

THINKING CRITICALLY

As you think about your assignment, use the information from the earlier sections of the unit to answer the questions. Discuss your answers with one or more students and revise your ideas if necessary.

1. In what ways might a laboratory environment restrict research on gene drive? Could results from a laboratory study on gene drive turn out to be different when applied to the real world?

....

....

....

2. How could laboratories be designed to ensure security?

....

....

THINKING VISUALLY

A. This photo shows an invasive species of weed that scientists are making less resistant to herbicide. How could this photo illustrate an example that you will be using to support your argument? Write a sentence or two showing how you would use the example in your argument. Be sure to include language to introduce the example.

....

....

....

B. Find a photo that illustrates another of your examples.

THINKING ABOUT LANGUAGE

A. Read the paragraph from a student paper and insert appropriate hedging language in the blank spaces. In the spaces highlighted in yellow, insert a specific phrase to introduce an example.

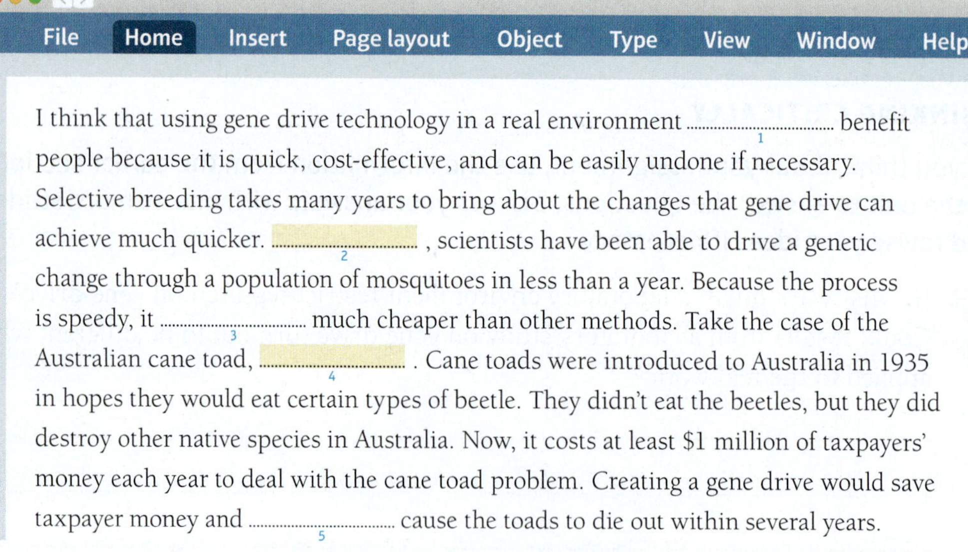

I think that using gene drive technology in a real environment __________ (1) benefit people because it is quick, cost-effective, and can be easily undone if necessary. Selective breeding takes many years to bring about the changes that gene drive can achieve much quicker. __________ (2), scientists have been able to drive a genetic change through a population of mosquitoes in less than a year. Because the process is speedy, it __________ (3) much cheaper than other methods. Take the case of the Australian cane toad, __________ (4). Cane toads were introduced to Australia in 1935 in hopes they would eat certain types of beetle. They didn't eat the beetles, but they did destroy other native species in Australia. Now, it costs at least $1 million of taxpayers' money each year to deal with the cane toad problem. Creating a gene drive would save taxpayer money and __________ (5) cause the toads to die out within several years.

Many people fear that a genetically-modified species could be accidentally released from the lab. This would cause serious problems to an ecosystem. While this .... [6] a very real risk, it is .... [7] that it would happen. Should an accidental release ever occur, there is a way to repair the damage by releasing an "undo" gene drive into the wild. This second gene drive would repair the affected species back to its original condition, much like hitting "undo" on your computer. The problems caused by malaria, Zika, and other mosquito-borne illnesses affect over 500,000 people each year. Invasive species cause untold damage to precious ecosystems. Gene drive .... [8] prevent these problems quickly, cheaply, and with very little risk. I believe that it should be used as quickly as possible.

B. Read the paragraph again and identify the writer's argument. What reasons are given for the writer's position and what examples are used in support? Discuss your responses with a partner.

....

....

....

....

....

WRITE

A. Look back at the assignment and at your ideas from Before You Write. Look for examples to strengthen your argument and for possible counterarguments.

B. Research the topic and take effective notes. Discuss your notes and ideas with others and make any needed adjustments.

C. Write an outline that shows your argument, your supporting points and examples, your counterargument, and your refutation.

BEYOND THE ASSIGNMENT

Write a 250–300 word paragraph discussing whether or not gene drive should be used outside a laboratory. Clearly state an argument, provide supporting points backed up by relevant examples, and include a counterargument with an effective refutation. Use all the skills you learned in this unit.

Go to MyEnglishLab to watch Professor Greely's concluding video and to complete a self-assessment.

BUSINESS AND DESIGN

Integrating Ideas from Sources

UNIT PROFILE

Imagine that you have designed a new product, which you think people want. How will you sell it? How will you tell people about it? What are the features of the product that will make people want to buy it? Large companies spend millions of dollars a year to answer these questions. Then they need to decide how much to charge for the product, how to advertise it, and where it will be available. The success of the marketing campaign will depend on a good strategy based on all the information available.

You will plan a 200–300 word summary of the article "Product Wars" from the Business and Design unit in Part 1.

OUTCOMES

- Identify keywords
- Paraphrase ideas
- Summarize
- Use reporting verbs
- Use synonyms

For more about **BUSINESS AND DESIGN**, see 1 3.
See also R and OC **BUSINESS AND DESIGN** 1 2 3.

GETTING STARTED

Go to MyEnglishLab to watch the instructor's introductory video and to complete a self-assessment.

Discuss these questions with a partner or group.

1. What are your favorite products and services? Which products and services do you buy regularly? Does the price affect some products more than others? What do you do if a product is not available when you need it? Do you wait, or do you go ahead and buy something similar?
2. How much does the place you buy something affect its value for you? How about the way something is advertised? What makes some products more expensive than others? Is it just the brand, or are there other elements involved? What makes a product a luxury item?
3. The instructor suggests that marketing is more than just advertising. Do you agree? Why or why not?

SKILL 1

IDENTIFYING KEYWORDS

WHY IT'S USEFUL Identifying keywords—important words—is a useful skill in academic writing that helps you find information about a research topic as completely and efficiently as possible. Using keywords enables you to gain the fullest possible understanding of your topic and to write effectively about it for your readers.

A keyword is a word that is essential to understanding the meaning of a sentence, an idea, or a topic. At the most basic level, we use the keywords of a sentence—its most important words—to understand its meaning. These words are often, but not always, nouns or noun phrases. In the example below, the keywords are underlined.

<u>Advertising</u> in the <u>digital age</u> can be a <u>challenge</u>.

At the paragraph level we use the keywords in the topic sentence to help identify the main idea. Look at the paragraph below, where a student has underlined the topic sentence. What are the keywords and what is the main idea?

Companies have many choices when it comes to advertising their products. They can promote their products using traditional forms of advertising, such as television or radio commercials. Another traditional form of advertising is print ads, and while this type of advertising isn't as popular as it once was, it still has a place in marketing. The choices don't end with print. A newer form of advertising, digital marketing, can be done in a number or ways through the Internet. Some of the many examples of digital advertising include email marketing, social media marketing, and banner advertising on websites and search engines. Finally, advertising can be done in more subtle ways than the TV commercial or Internet banner. Product placement is the advertisement of a product by placing it in a movie, TV show, or even YouTube® video. When it comes to marketing goods and services, companies are spoiled for choice in this digital age.

The main idea of the topic sentence is that companies have many choices for advertising their products. Did you identify the keywords as *choices* and *advertising*?

For more on identifying topic sentences, see Business and Design, Part 1.

Using keywords to find information

Using keywords to find meaning in single sentences or main ideas of paragraphs is not the only way that we use keywords in academic writing. We also use them with search engines to research topics. Every topic has a related set of keywords that are important words or phrases commonly associated with the topic.

Look again at the paragraph above. One of the keywords we associate with advertising is *product*. The student has highlighted this and other related keywords in yellow and added them to the list below. Can you think of any other related words?

Topic: Advertising

Keywords: product, television/radio commercials, print ads, digital marketing/advertising, product placement

These keywords describe important ideas associated with the topic of advertising. Furthermore, she has narrowed her topic to just one form of advertising, digital marketing. She has used a different color to highlight keywords related to digital marketing and added those words to her list. Can you think of any more words she could add?

Topic: Digital marketing

Keywords: email marketing, social media marketing, banner advertising

It's important to understand that there may be more than one keyword for an idea. Synonyms, words with a similar meaning, can be helpful when trying to find the best keywords for your search. For example, if you wanted to find out more about digital marketing, you could use *digital advertising* instead of *digital marketing*.

When you discover more than one search term, try each term and note any differences in the kind of information you find. One may be more common than the other and provide better search results. For example, the researcher might try out not only "digital marketing" and "digital advertising," but also "online marketing."

When our researcher used the term *digital advertising* in her search, she found there were too many results. To avoid this, she added another word, *trends*, creating the keyword *digital advertising trends*, which narrowed the search and produced fewer but more useful results. Ideally, when searching for information, you want to have just enough information to understand your topic fully and to help you write. Using the right number and combination of terms will help you achieve this. Too much information can be overwhelming and too little means you don't have enough support for your topic.

TIP

You will most likely have access to databases through your university's library. A database is an electronic index used to find articles. You use keywords, called subject headings, to find articles in a database. Using precise keywords will provide the best results when you search a database.

Using keywords in your writing

When you are exploring a topic, identifying and learning keywords will help you identify main ideas and then find additional information. As you encounter these keywords again and again, make every effort to learn their meanings and how to use them. This will enable you to write about the topic with precise, appropriate language.

EXERCISE 1

A. Complete each sentence with information about what keywords are and how they can help you.

1. Sentence keywords are ....
2. Paragraph keywords help you to identify ....
3. Topic keywords are ....
4. For your own writing, learning the meaning and appropriate use of keywords

....

B. When you start researching a new topic, do you keep track of keywords? How can you make recognizing and learning topic keywords a part of your learning routine?

VOCABULARY PREVIEW

These vocabulary items appear in the reading. Circle the ones you know. Put a question mark next to the ones you don't know.

development	target (v, adj)	locate
gather	survey (n)	observation

EXERCISE 2

A. You've been asked to write an assignment related to market research. In your research, you have found the following introductory text. Read the text and answer the questions. Then discuss your responses with a partner.

Market Research

Consumers do not often realize what happens before a new product hits the shelves. A new product is not usually just launched with the CEO crossing her fingers hoping it will be a success. Instead, long before a customer buys a new product, the marketing department has analyzed carefully collected data while researching factors that may impact its success. Data on customer behavior, such as purchasing habits and customer needs, help companies adjust a new product to better fit the market. This kind of research is called market research. No company can ever be certain that a new product will be a success. However, by conducting market research during the development of a product, a company can determine if there is room and interest in the market for it.

When doing market research, a company gathers information about its customers to determine how they might respond to the new product. However, before this information can be collected, the company first decides who the potential customer is for this new product. That means the product developer determines which demographic, or group of customers, to target. For example, perhaps the product is intended for young women, between the ages of 18 and 25, who are single and currently students or recent graduates. Once this market segment is identified, a company can begin to question them to find out if they are interested in the new product.

There are several methods that can be used to question the selected customer segment. One method is face-to-face surveys. To locate customers, a market research interviewer goes to a place where they will encounter many members of the target demographic. In the example above, a university campus would be an ideal location. Using samples of the new product, an in-person survey can produce a great deal of data and high response rates. Another method used to do market research is a focus group. A focus group is a group of people from the target demographic who are gathered together to discuss the new product. The discussion is usually led by a focus group moderator, who tries not to influence the discussion, and is recorded. Finally, a method that has been used since the beginning of market research is simple observation. This method is as simple as it sounds. Researchers watch their potential customers. A researcher counts the number of female students visiting a particular store, for example. However, observational techniques can also be done digitally. The use of computer cookies or even store loyalty cards can be a source of data for market researchers. Whatever the method, market research helps companies design products that should be successful.

1. What is market research?

....

2. What does a product developer do with market research data?

....

3. What is a demographic?

....

4. What are the different methods of market research?

....

B. Reread the article and search for keywords for each of the categories below.

Keywords related to people who work in market research:

1. product developer

2. ....

3. ....

4. ....

Keywords related to customers:

1. customer behavior
2. ....
3. ....
4. ....
5. ....
6. ....
7. ....

Keywords related to types of market research:

1. ....
2. ....
3. ....

C. Now work with a partner to provide the specified keywords.

1. Which keywords identified in Part B are synonyms of *market segment*?

   ....

   ....

2. What two keywords that appear in the article will give you more information about "digital observational techniques"?

   ....

   ....

EXERCISE 3

A. Choose a keyword from the category "keywords related to people who work in market research" in Exercise 2, Part B above. Find out more about this job by doing online research. Write a 100–150 word paragraph that explains the job. Use three words from the Vocabulary Check in your paragraph.

B. Exchange your paragraph with a partner and provide a peer review using the form below. Discuss each other's ideas for improvement.

Questions	Yes	No	Notes
Can you identify a clear topic sentence?	☐	☐	
Does the paragraph explain the job?	☐	☐	
Did the writer use vocabulary from the Vocabulary Check?	☐	☐	
Does the writer use keywords to express precise meaning?	☐	☐	

C. Write a second draft of your paragraph based on the peer review and discussion.

VOCABULARY CHECK

A. Review the items in the Vocabulary Preview. Write their definitions and add examples. Use a dictionary if necessary.

B. Complete the paragraph with vocabulary items from the box.

development	target	locate
gather	surveys (n)	observation

There are several ways that companies can .... data to help in the .... of a new product. However, before doing any kind of market research, a company must first determine which group of customers it will .... Next, the company must .... , or find, this group of customers. Then the company can conduct face-to-face .... with these potential customers or take notes from .... of their shopping habits.

Go to MyEnglishLab to complete a vocabulary and skill practice and to join in collaborative activities.

SKILL 2

PARAPHRASING IDEAS

WHY IT'S USEFUL Paraphrasing is an essential skill for academic writing that allows you to accurately include ideas from other sources in your writing without copying.

Why paraphrase?

In college-level academic writing, you are expected to include ideas from experts in your field of study. This shows your reader that you are both knowledgeable and up to date about your topic. Simply copying ideas word for word—even if you clearly identify the source—is not considered good academic form in the United States since copying does not demonstrate understanding. By paraphrasing—putting ideas into your own words—you can show that you understand what you have read while conveying important information.

CULTURE NOTE

While showing that you have read widely for your assignment is important, you must do so in a way that makes it clear where the ideas come from. Copying ideas—even by paraphrasing in your own words— without giving credit to the owner or source of the ideas is called plagiarism. Plagiarism is a form of academic misconduct that can have serious consequences for your academic career. Ideas must be credited to the specific authors or the sources where you found them. Check with your writing center about how to do this at your institution.

How to paraphrase

Generally, a paraphrase is about the same length as the original presentation but uses different words, grammar, and sentence structure. A good paraphrase must not be too close to the original in terms of its wording and structure, but it should contain all the ideas from the original source. Follow these steps when paraphrasing:

1. Read and understand the text you want to paraphrase—you can't paraphrase something you don't fully understand.
2. Move the text where you can no longer see it. Then write down the important ideas in your own words.

Let's look at an example of paraphrasing. A student has been asked to write an assignment about a famous advertising campaign. He has chosen to research the launch of the Volkswagen Beetle® in 1960. At that time, people bought large American-made cars, but the Volkswagen Beetle was a small German-built car. Nevertheless, the campaign was a success. In one article, he chose this sentence to paraphrase:

> The Volkswagen Beetle was a small car that was selling wildly in Europe and beginning to do well in America.

The writer came up with the paraphrases shown below. He decided to use Paraphrase 3 because it keeps the full meaning of the original source, while changing both the structure and wording of the original sentence. Why do you think he decided the other options were less effective?

> **Paraphrase 1:** The Volkswagen Beetle was a little car that was selling passionately in Europe and beginning to do well in the United States.
>
> **Paraphrase 2:** The Volkswagen Beetle was selling wildly in Europe, beginning to do well in America and was not a large car.
>
> **Paraphrase 3:** The Volkswagen Beetle had sold well in Europe, and was starting to make gains in America, although it was a smaller vehicle than most Americans were used to.

Changing wording in a paraphrase

Some words and phrases do not need to be changed in a paraphrase. These include proper nouns, names of events, and technical words specific to a subject. Therefore, in a paraphrase of the original sentence, the words *Volkswagen Beetle*, *Europe*, and *America* should not be changed.

On the other hand, the author-specific phrases *small car*, *selling wildly*, and *beginning to do well* should be changed. The author has used these words and phrases to add interest to the writing. To avoid plagiarism—writing paraphrases that are too close to the original—make sure you change such words. There are three types of changes you can make to words:

Use a synonym	Detail
Looking for synonyms—words with a similar meaning—is one way to change a word. However, not all synonyms have the same meaning in different contexts.	• Although *little* can be a synonym for *small*, it has a very different meaning when used with *car*, implying it is a toy car. There are no good synonyms for *small* in this context. • *Vehicle* can be used in place of *car*.
Use an antonym	
Another way is to use an antonym—a word with an opposite meaning. However, you need to use the antonym in a negative form to keep the same meaning.	• Instead of *small car*, we could say *not a large car*.
Change the word form	
Verbs can be changed into nouns, or nouns into adjectives. You can also change a singular noun to a plural, or a regular adjective into a comparative. However, you will need to adjust the grammar of your sentence to keep the same meaning.	• Instead of *small car*, we can say *a smaller car than most Americans were used to*.

TIP

Words have their own grammar. For example, some verbs are transitive and can take an object, while others are intransitive and cannot. Different nouns, adjectives, and adverbs also have rules about usage. Use a good learner's dictionary to fully understand how a word works. You cannot simply substitute a synonym without understanding the grammar specific to that word.

For more on using adjectives, see History, Part 2.

For more on using a dictionary to expand vocabulary, see Zoology, Part 2.

Changing grammar and sentence structure

To paraphrase, it is likely that you will not only change words, but also the grammatical structure of a sentence. There are many kinds of grammar and structure changes you could make. Let's look specifically at what the writer did in Paraphrase 3.

First, he changed the order of ideas. The idea of selling (highlighted in yellow) was moved to the beginning of the sentence and the idea of the size of the car (highlighted in green) was moved to the end:

Original: The Volkswagen Beetle was a small car that was selling wildly in Europe and beginning to do well in America.

Paraphrase: The Volkswagen Beetle had sold well in Europe and was starting to make gains in America, although it was a smaller vehicle than most Americans were used to.

Next, he changed the verb tenses. Instead of using the past progressive, "was selling," the writer chose to use the past perfect, "had sold," because it contrasts with the use of the past progressive "was starting to make gains."

> The Volkswagen Beetle had sold well in Europe and was starting to make gains in America, …

He also changed the sentence structure. By using the word *although*, the second idea becomes a dependent clause.

> … **although** it was a smaller vehicle than most Americans were used to.

Each paraphrase uses a different set of techniques, depending on the structure and the ideas being expressed. There is no single method, but you can develop a range of techniques with practice.

Sometimes, in order to accurately and neatly keep the idea of the original sentence, more than one sentence may be required for your paraphrase. It is also possible that a single sentence may include ideas from elsewhere in an article. In this case, to correctly paraphrase the idea, you will need to add the context, and the paraphrase may be longer than the original sentence.

VOCABULARY PREVIEW

These vocabulary items appear in the reading. Circle the ones you know. Put a question mark next to the ones you don't know.

lifestyle	campaign (n)	creativity	status
ignore	approach (n, v)	design (v)	standard (n, v)

EXERCISE 4

A. This is the full article that the student writer found in his research about a famous advertising campaign. Read the article and complete the exercises that follow. Discuss your responses with a partner.

Thinking Differently by "Thinking Small"

After World War Two, confidence was high, the American economy was booming, and automobiles were getting larger and fancier. In the late 1950s, car advertisements sold a lifestyle by showing happy families surrounded by friends in a pleasant environment. Many of the advertisements that people saw were the same, which had the effect of making people ignore them.

The reason for this state of affairs was twofold. Advertising executives liked to rely on focus groups, research, and testing. If a marketing campaign worked for one product, it should work for another. By using a template approach, ads began to have a familiar feel. Creativity was not an option. The other reason was psychology. By selling a lifestyle, advertisers believed they were getting into the subconscious of the consumer. The problem was it wasn't working.

A breakthrough came when the German car company Volkswagen approached Bill Bernbach of the advertising agency DDB. The Volkswagen Beetle was a small car that was selling wildly in Europe and beginning to do well in America. After the failure of the Edsel, the Detroit car manufacturers realized that there was a market for small cars in America, and they were getting ready to launch. The problem for DDB was that they had to sell a small, ugly, foreign-built car, which Adolf Hitler had helped design, to a public that was thought to hold status above all else.

The reason Volkswagen chose DDB was for their honesty in their ads, and it was that approach that DDB took with the Beetle. The first ad they released in 1960 featured a large white space with a car in the top left corner. The text below was laid out in three columns, but had awkward formatting and even included an oddly-placed Volkswagen logo. The designer was so worried about the ad, that he left the country to avoid the criticism. It was an instant hit. Printed in black and white, the ad stood out against the colorful pages it was placed next to. It showed honesty and simplicity—just what the American public wanted. Creativity was the new standard in advertising, all because one company chose to "Think small."

Glossary

Subconscious: the part of your mind that can affect the way you behave without your realizing it

1. Underline the two reasons that car advertisements were the same in the late 1950s.
2. Underline the reason that car manufacturers believed there was a market for small cars.
3. Underline three problems that DDB faced in advertising the Volkswagen Beetle.
4. Underline the examples that show the Volkswagen ad was different from other ads of the time.

B. Use your underlined ideas to answer the questions in your own words.

1. What were two reasons that car advertisements were the same in the late 1950s?

   ....

2. Why did car manufacturers believe there was a market for small cars?

   ....

3. What were the problems that DDB faced in advertising the Volkswagen Beetle?

   ....

4. How was the Volkswagen ad different from other ads of the time?

   ....

EXERCISE 5

A. Look at the words and phrases from the article. Using the article to help you, put each word into the appropriate category in the chart. Some examples have been done for you.

fancier	Detroit	German	World War Two
agency	~~logo~~	~~America~~	Beetle
focus groups	~~booming~~	Europe	advertisement campaign
pleasant	hit	awkward	DDB
Volkswagen	Edsel	state of affairs	Adolf Hitler
breakthrough	~~Think small~~	~~Bill Bernbach~~	subconscious
research	market	ignore	~~oddly~~
wildly	black and white	car	

Words and phrases that do not need to be changed				Words and phrases that should be changed
Events	**Places**	**Names**	**Technical vocabulary**	**Author-specific**
	America	Bill Bernbach	logo Think small	booming oddly

B. Compare your chart with another student and discuss your ideas. How did you know which words should be changed? What are possible strategies you can use to change them?

C. Look at the sentences from the article and the three paraphrases under each one. Evaluate each paraphrase. Mark the paraphrase *TC* if you feel it is too close to the original, *NQ* if you feel the paraphrase is not quite accurate, and *OK* if you feel the paraphrase is a good one. Discuss your ideas and reasoning with a partner.

1. After World War Two, confidence was high, the American economy was booming, and automobiles were getting larger and fancier.

   .... a. Following World War Two, confidence was tall, the United States economy was exploding, and cars were getting bigger and more decorative.

   .... b. After WWII, cars were larger and better than they had been before because of high confidence and a better economy.

   .... c. The increase in economic confidence following the Second World War led to the production of bigger and more stylish cars.

2. The problem was it wasn't working.

   .... a. Advertisers thought they were selling a lifestyle with their advertisements, but the consumer wasn't listening.

   .... b. The issue was that the advertising was not working.

   .... c. The old style of advertising no longer had an effect.

3. After the failure of the Edsel, the Detroit car manufacturers realized that there was a market for small cars in America, and they were getting ready to launch.

   .... a. The car manufacturers in Detroit wanted to make small cars because of the Edsel failure.

   .... b. American car manufacturers understood that a market existed for smaller cars in America after the Edsel had failed. They were ready to bring their small cars to the American market.

   .... c. After the Edsel failed, Detroit car builders knew that Americans wanted small cars, and they were ready to issue their own.

4. It was an instant hit.

   .... a. The advertisement was an immediate triumph.

   .... b. It was successful.

   .... c. The new style of advertisement was a success.

D. Look again at the sentences in Part C and answer the questions.

1. Why are the paraphrases in item 2 and item 4 longer than the original sentences?

   ....

2. Why does the second paraphrase in item 3 use two sentences?

   ....

   ....

E. Write a paraphrase for each of the sentences from the article. Some paraphrases may require more than one sentence. Compare them with a partner and discuss any differences. Decide which paraphrases are the best and why.

1. In the late 1950s, car advertisements sold a lifestyle by showing happy families surrounded by friends in a pleasant environment.

   ....

   ....

2. Advertising executives liked to rely on focus groups, research, and testing.

   ....

   ....

3. The problem for DDB was that they had to sell a small, ugly, foreign-built car, which Adolf Hitler had helped design, to a public that was thought to hold status above all else.

   ....

   ....

4. The designer was so worried about the ad that he left the country to avoid the criticism.

   ....

   ....

EXERCISE 6

A. Look back at the blog about the Ford Edsel on pages 41 and 42 of Business and Design, Part 1. Paraphrase two ideas from the article.

B. Exchange your paraphrases with a partner and provide feedback. Discuss each other's ideas for improvement.

C. Rewrite your paraphrase based on your partner's feedback and your discussion.

VOCABULARY CHECK

A. Review the items in the Vocabulary Preview. Write their definitions and add examples. Use a dictionary if necessary.

B. Choose the sentence that correctly expresses the meaning of each underlined vocabulary item.

1. a. If customers <u>ignore</u> an advertisement, they pay attention to it.
   b. If customers <u>ignore</u> an advertisement, they do not pay attention to it.

2. a. Before "Think small," marketers used the same approach, or technique, for advertising.
   b. Before "Think small," marketers used the same approach, or idea, for advertising.
3. a. Lifestyle refers to how someone lives.
   b. Lifestyle refers to where someone lives.
4. a. An advertising campaign makes the public familiar with a politician.
   b. An advertising campaign makes the public familiar with a product.
5. a. Someone who designs a car plans how it works and looks.
   b. Someone who designs a car plans where to sell it.
6. a. Some products show status, or legal position.
   b. Some products show status, or social position.
7. a. Creativity, the ability to persuade others to do something, is now valued in advertising.
   b. Creativity, the ability to use the imagination to make new things, is now valued in advertising.
8. a. "Think small" set a new standard, or level of success, for other advertisements to follow.
   b. "Think small" set a new standard, or unusual model, for other advertisements to follow.

Go to MyEnglishLab to complete a vocabulary and skill practice and to join in collaborative activities.

INTEGRATED SKILLS

SUMMARIZING

WHY IT'S USEFUL Some assignments will require you to research a topic and then summarize and use what you have learned to add support to your writing. Learning how to effectively and accurately summarize the main ideas from your classes and research will enable you to complete these types of assignments and demonstrate your understanding of the content.

What is a summary?

A summary is a brief statement or report that restates in your own words the main ideas of your reading. As in paraphrasing, you must first read and understand the text. You must also acknowledge the original author. Unlike a paraphrase, however, a summary is usually much shorter than the original text.

When writing a summary, you may need to summarize the main idea from a short text, or several ideas that are shared across multiple texts. Depending on what you are summarizing and the reason for the summary, the length of a summary can vary. It can be as short as one sentence, or cover multiple pages and include an introduction and a conclusion. Short summaries will contain only the main ideas, while longer summaries may also include supporting details. Here we will focus on longer summaries.

Regardless of length, a good summary must be objective, which means that you, as the writer, report the ideas, rather than provide your opinion. Your summary must be a complete, stand-alone text: The reader should not need to look at the original text to understand the summary.

For more on summarizing a process, see Zoology, Part 2.

For more on summarizing a table of data, see Chemical Engineering, Part 2.

Preparing to write a summary

As with paraphrasing, writing a successful summary requires you to read and fully understand the original text. Some texts, like academic papers, are well organized. Others, like magazine articles, are written with a non-academic audience in mind and may have a less clear organization. They may also have a lot of interesting, but unimportant, details. It is your task, as a summary writer, to find only the important points and understand how the text is organized. Follow these steps to get started.

Step 1: Skim the text to get a broad understanding of the main idea. Read the text again, more slowly, highlighting important parts. Identify places where topics change. If the text has headings, use them to identify different sections. Otherwise, draw a horizontal line across the text when a new topic begins.

Step 2: Give each section you've identified a heading using your own words. Within each section, paraphrase any of the important ideas you've highlighted. Ideas that cannot be paraphrased must be quoted—use quotation marks around these ideas to remind yourself later that they have been copied directly. Do not use more than one or two direct quotations in your summary.

Step 3: Using your headings and paraphrased ideas, create an outline of the summary. You may find that you need to use a different organizational style than the original text. This is OK. Group similar ideas together so that your summary is well organized and clear for your reader.

Let's follow the steps taken by a student who needs to summarize an article from the November 25, 2018, issue of *Business Review Weekly* that explains the four elements of the marketing mix known as the "Four Ps" (Product, Price, Promotion, and Place).

For more on taking effective notes, see Bioethics, Part 1.

Like the student, begin by skimming the text to get the main idea. Then read it again, looking at the sections highlighted by the student on the left and the headings and notes she made on the right. How are her headings different from the author's?

Mixing it up—the right way! John S. Riley

You already know that having the best product or service doesn't guarantee you success in the market place. Gone are the days when a company could launch a new product, advertise it on TV, and then watch sales figures tick up as buyers flocked to the store. Marketing your product or service needs a strategy, and that means finding the right balance between the elements of the marketing mix—the four Ps.

Introductory paragraph
The last sentence is useful and shows the writer's thesis.

The concept of the four Ps, also known as the 4Ps, was first defined by E. J. McCarthy in 1960 and stands for Product, Price, Promotion, and Place. By changing these elements, a marketing strategy can be adapted depending on the market conditions. As Adam Osborne, the man who first brought personal computing to the masses once said, "Money coming in says I've made the right marketing decisions."

Definition
4Ps are Product, Price, Promotion, Place— cannot change these terms, but can change the order.

Know what you're selling!

When most people think of the term marketing, they think of flashy ads they see on TV—maybe those they watch instead of the game during the Super Bowl®. However, the first consideration should be the product or service that is being offered. You may think a hotel room is just a hotel room, but it's more than that. It can be an experience, a luxury getaway, or just a cheap and convenient place to stay on the way to somewhere else. To be successful, a company needs to understand what its product does, or what need it fulfils for a customer.

Product
Companies should be aware of how their product satisfies a need.

It can be an experience or a necessity.

(Continued)

What the market will bear!

Once a company understands its product or service, it needs to figure out the right price to sell it at. For a luxury or rare item, people are often willing to pay more than they need to simply because of the added prestige. For a regular brand of cereal, this may not be an option, since customers have a choice of similar cereals in the store.

Price
luxury items can have a higher price.
Regular items (commodities) have a lower price.

Shout it out!

Promotion is more than just advertising. Offering discounts, drumming up publicity, and personal selling are all ways to inform, persuade, or remind people about the product. Again, the type of product will dictate the style of promotion. A new car, for example, is likely to be advertised nationally on TV, billboards, and online. The promotion will also be supported by salespeople in the dealerships, who are best able to explain the benefits of the new car to potential customers. A small, local store would have a very different kind of promotion, possibly using social media and discount coupons to encourage people to shop in their store.

Promotion
Personal selling, coupons, and advertisements are all ways to promote a product.
The method of promotion must fit the product.

Put it in the right place!

Another consideration for the marketing mix is the availability of your product. You can't have sales if people don't know how or where to buy your product. On the other hand, a product that is being marketed as rare, should not be widely available online. Think of a luxury sports car being sold at the local mass-market dealership. It would lose its prestige, thus reducing its price.

Place
Products need to be available, so they can be purchased.
Products need to be at a place where people expect to find them.

As we have seen, each element of the mix is unique, but also impacts other elements. Successful companies get the mix right and constantly change the mix to suit the market.

Final paragraph
Emphasis on impact.
Add to the intro.

Words: 530

As you learned to do in Skill 1, the student highlighted and used keywords and terms that she feels are important. Some of these ideas have been paraphrased using academic language rather than the informal style of the original. Likewise, she has created her own headings, which are more appropriate for an academic audience. While she will not use these headings in her own summary, they are useful for categorizing information from the text. She has also identified an idea in the final paragraph that could be placed in the introduction of her summary. Now that the student has a good grasp of the article, she can prepare an outline and then begin to write.

For more on writing headings and subheadings, see Chemical Engineering, Part 1.

PART 2

Writing a summary

Just like any piece of good academic writing, a summary needs to be well structured. Body paragraphs should have topic sentences and supporting details. However, a summary has two features that are specific to summaries—the opening sentence and attribution.

The opening sentence: The first sentence of the introduction to a summary contains four key pieces of information: the author's first and last name, the date the article was published, the title of the article, and the main idea. Look at the student's first sentence below. Notice that the verb *describes*, used to express the main idea, is in the present tense.

> In "Mixing it up—the right way!," John Riley (2018) describes a successful marketing strategy as determining how the product, place, promotion, and price are balanced.

Attribution: Since the author of the blog is John Riley, the writer must show that each idea she summarizes is his, rather than hers. This is done using the author's LAST name (Riley) along with neutral reporting verbs such as *states*, *says*, or *reports*. Using the author's last name over and over would be repetitive, so use a pronoun like *he* or *she* instead. Since John Riley is a man, the writer must use *he*.

Now, look at how the writer pulled everything together in her summary of John Riley's article. How did she use her headings to organize her summary and make it different from the original text? Can you see how the paraphrases in her notes helped her create the summary? How many times did she use attribution? How does the word count in the summary compare with the original?

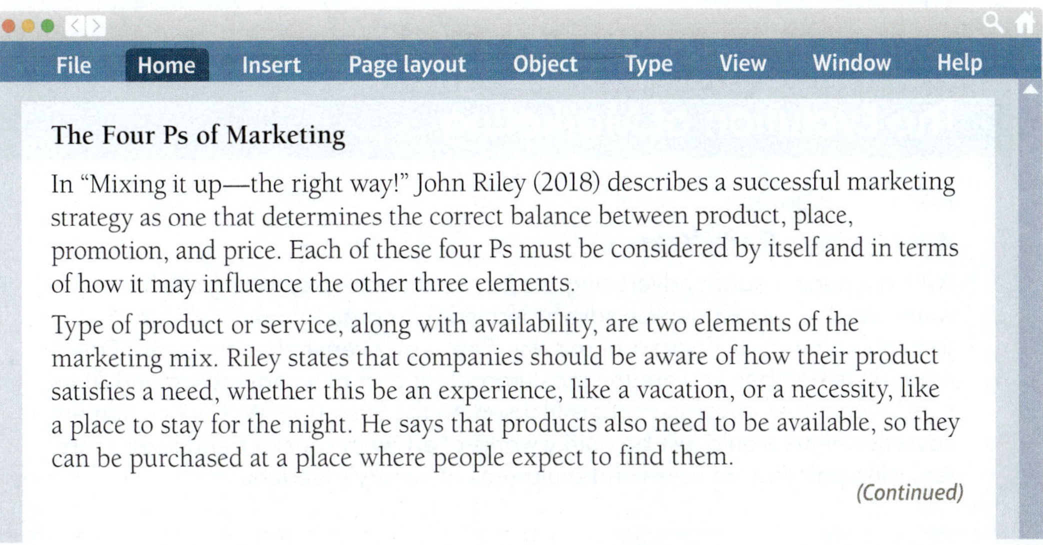

The Four Ps of Marketing

In "Mixing it up—the right way!" John Riley (2018) describes a successful marketing strategy as one that determines the correct balance between product, place, promotion, and price. Each of these four Ps must be considered by itself and in terms of how it may influence the other three elements.

Type of product or service, along with availability, are two elements of the marketing mix. Riley states that companies should be aware of how their product satisfies a need, whether this be an experience, like a vacation, or a necessity, like a place to stay for the night. He says that products also need to be available, so they can be purchased at a place where people expect to find them.

(Continued)

These factors influence the price of a product and the way it is promoted. Riley says that luxury items can be priced higher than commodities and should be promoted differently. He states that personal selling, coupons, and advertisements are all ways to promote a product, but that the method must fit the product.

Words: 177

Writing a good summary involves different skills, including notetaking, highlighting, paraphrasing, outlining, essay writing, and paying attention to detail. With practice, you will be able to combine these skills to produce accurate summaries and to incorporate them appropriately in your research essays.

VOCABULARY PREVIEW

These vocabulary items appear in the reading. Circle the ones you know. Put a question mark next to the ones you don't know.

aggressive	media	limit	specific (n, v)
sponsor (n)	appeal (n, v)	network	

EXERCISE 7

A. Read the article from the June 2017 issue of *Advertising Quarterly* about the history of marketing and brand development. Then answer the comprehension questions.

CULTURE NOTE

In the 1960s, many of the big marketing firms in the U.S. were located on Madison Avenue, in New York. The phrase Mad Men refers to the people who ran these firms. It is also the name of a TV show that focused on the lifestyles of marketing executives in the 1960s.

From Mad Men to the Digital Age: The Evolution of Marketing

Ron C. J. Bakara

Advertising's Early Years

1 Asking a person about advertising is a bit like that old joke asking a fish about water. We live surrounded by advertising; ads compete for our attention throughout nearly every part of our day. Feel a bit overwhelmed by it all? Don't! After all, remember, you are the most important part of an advertisement! At its core, every great advertisement is focused on the customer. Without customers, advertisements would just be quirky works of art, with sneakers and luxury cars replacing paintings of vases and sculptures of history's leaders.

PART 2

2 Was it always this way? If you were to flip through some magazines from the 1900s—advertising's equivalent of the Iron Age—you'd find patent medicine advertisements telling you all about the latest tonic. These ads wanted to reach the customer, true—but by our standards they were really bad at it! In the early days of advertising, businesses hoped to reach as many customers as possible with one ad. That's why many advertisements were simply long, long, long (and repetitive) lists of a product's possible benefits. Did this sort of thing actually work? Well, the products sold, and businesses made money, but everyone involved knew that something was missing—they simply weren't sure what it was.

That Special Something: Customer Segmentation

3 It turned out that the key to great marketing was a blend of two things: customer segmentation and targeted advertising. Customer segmentation divides potential customers into different categories: age, gender, cultural background, location, and many more. Companies figure out what types of people want their products and then aggressively market to them, a process called targeted advertising.

4 Targeted advertising boomed in the post-war period. Newly wealthy American consumers thought they were buying televisions, but they were really buying a fully refined advertising experience. After all, consumers didn't pay for the TV shows, sponsors did. Media writer Douglas Rushkoff put it best, saying that, "The implicit contract was that in return for this free gift, we would sit through the sponsors' ads." And those ads were some of the most innovative things ever broadcast.

5 In the 1950s, businesses began to target one of the most lucrative demographics of all: children. Branding for cereal companies, for example, used to be a simple thing: the name of the company, a description of a cereal, maybe a logo that implied trust and health. In the 1950s, though, the cereal mascot was born. Cereals were being sold by happy, excited, and appealing animated characters! Breakfast, we learned, was supposed to be FUN! Parents usually relented and bought the fun and exciting cereal that advertisers told their children to beg for.

6 Now targeted advertising wasn't new, exactly. One of the earliest innovations in magazine advertisements came in the 1920s when businesses realized just how much purchasing power women had—in many households, after all, women did most of the day-to-day shopping. It wasn't until later, though, that businesses had finally hit upon the greatest truth in marketing—the ad doesn't need to sell the product as much as the experience of buying the product. Communication expert Neil Postman put it best—"By substituting images for claims, the pictorial commercial made emotional appeal, not tests of truth, the basis of consumer decisions." You aren't buying cereal; you're buying fun. There would be bumps along the way, including legislation that limited just how aggressively companies could market towards children, but overall advertising's potential seemed limitless.

7 Growth continued through the late 1970s, but that growth no longer seemed momentous. Advertisements were still making money, but innovations were bringing in small, incremental gains in profit—not the paradigm-breaking FORTUNES they used to bring in.

(Continued)

Serving up Segments

8 The first big innovation came with cable television. When MTV® first hit the screen in the summer of 1981, companies had something unbelievably lucrative—a television network that targeted the youth demographic all day, every day. As other networks focusing on sports, food, and, yes, children's cartoons followed, advertisers could reach the most desirable customer segments better than ever. Networks built success after success on these customer segments, until the Internet came along and changed everything again.

9 For a brief period, advertisers thought it was all over. How would we reach customers now? It wasn't long before one company, Google®, had the answer. Google brought the practice of customer segmentation into the information age. Now, advertisements would target your specific interests, sending a custom assortment of ads based on not just your demographic profile but what you spent your time doing. YouTube, eventually acquired by Google, and Facebook® would build digital empires on their ability to deliver ultra-specific targeted advertisements to any business that could afford them. So, next time you click the "SKIP" button on that YouTube video you want to watch, just think about how much work went in to getting that video to you!

Glossary

Innovate: to introduce new ideas and new ways of doing things

Lucrative: to describe something that can be very successful or generate a lot of money

Demography: the study of population—the age, income, and location of people in a certain area

1. What time periods are discussed in this article?

2. In the early 1900s, "products sold and businesses made money." Why does the author believe that advertising was so bad at reaching the customer?

3. How is modern-day customer segmentation different from that used in the post-war period (after 1945)?

4. When referring to Ron C. J. Bakara, would you use *he* or *she*?

B. Prepare to summarize the article. Read the text again and highlight areas of importance. Draw a horizontal line when the topic changes and create your own headings for each section. Paraphrase important information, using attribution where appropriate.

C. There are two ways this article can be summarized: (1) using chronological organization or (2) focusing on customer segmentation and targeted advertising. Look at the areas you have highlighted and decide which approach you prefer. Create an outline, remembering that your summary doesn't need to follow the same order as the original.

D. Write the first sentence of your summary. Share and discuss it with a partner.

E. Use your outline and the first sentence you have prepared to draft a 200–300 word summary of the article.

F. Exchange the first draft of your summary with a partner and provide a peer review using the peer review form. Write a second draft based on the suggestions you receive.

Questions	**Yes**	**No**	**Notes**
Does the writing address the assignment task?	☐	☐	
Is the first sentence correct?	☐	☐	
Is there enough attribution?	☐	☐	
Do the ideas fit together in an orderly, logical way?	☐	☐	
Are any important ideas missing?	☐	☐	
Are there any other comments you would like to make?	☐	☐	

VOCABULARY CHECK

A. Review the items in the Vocabulary Preview. Write their definitions and add examples. Use a dictionary if necessary.

B. Complete each sentence with a vocabulary item from the box.

appealing	aggressively	limit (v)	media
networks (n)	specific	sponsors (n)	

1. If you work in ...., you probably have a job related to television, radio, newspapers, or magazines.
2. TV commercials make products .... to children by showing images of cartoons characters.

(Continued)

3. Cable television gives viewers a large choice of TV ....
4. Targeted advertising is when companies .... market their products to a certain group of people.
5. Your .... interests are interests that only you have.
6. .... pay in order to be allowed to advertise at an event or on television.
7. Some laws .... advertising. For example, certain products cannot be targeted at children.

Go to MyEnglishLab to complete a vocabulary and skill practice and to join in collaborative activities.

LANGUAGE SKILL

USING REPORTING VERBS

WHY IT'S USEFUL When integrating ideas from other sources into your writing, it is necessary to use reporting verbs to show that these ideas came from other people. Using these verbs accurately will help you work paraphrases, summaries, and direct quotations into your academic writing in a smooth, clear manner.

Go to MyEnglishLab for the Language Skill presentation and practice.

VOCABULARY STRATEGY

USING SYNONYMS

WHY IT'S USEFUL Learning synonyms—words that have similar meanings—will help you as both a speaker and a writer of English. Knowing synonyms expands your vocabulary and adds variety to your writing.

You have already seen how useful synonyms can be when looking for key search terms, paraphrasing, and summarizing. When used correctly, synonyms add interest to your writing and help you avoid repeating words. However, synonyms must be used correctly; otherwise, they will simply confuse your reader.

Look at the words in the box and decide which are synonyms for the word *appeal*.

application	call	influence	please
ask	charm	interest	pull
attraction	demand	petition	request
attractiveness	draw	plea	urge

In fact, all these words, and more, can be synonyms for the word *appeal*. It depends on how the word *appeal* is being used, as these examples show:

- Used as a noun to mean "charm":
  The car has a certain appeal for older customers. =
  The car has a certain charm for older customers.
- Used as a verb to mean "interest":
  The product mainly appeals to teenagers. =
  The product mainly interests teenagers.
- Used as a verb to mean "request":
  The company appealed to its customers for new product ideas. =
  The company requested new product ideas from its customers.

Notice that in the last example the grammar and sentence structure change in order to keep the original meaning.

TIP

A learner's dictionary helps you understand how synonyms function in sentences. It can show whether the synonym has certain collocations—other words commonly used with it or whether the word is followed by a specific preposition. When you learn useful synonyms, add them to your vocabulary journal, or create a word card for each one.

For more on using a dictionary to expand vocabulary, see Zoology, Part 2.

EXERCISE 8

A. Look at each sentence and the sentences that follow. Check all the sentences that have the same meaning as the original. Use a learner's dictionary to help you. The synonyms are underlined.

1. In the 1960s, the advertising agency DDB set the <u>standard</u> for other agencies to follow.

   .... a. DDB was a <u>benchmark</u> for other agencies to follow.
   .... b. DDB was a <u>flag</u> for other agencies to follow.
   .... c. DDB was a <u>norm</u> for other agencies to follow.
   .... d. DDB was a <u>measure</u> against which other agencies would be judged.

2. The main <u>innovation</u> in marketing during the twentieth century was customer segmentation.

   .... a. The main <u>novelty</u> in marketing during the twentieth century was customer segmentation.
   .... b. The main <u>revolution</u> in marketing during the twentieth century was customer segmentation.

.... c. The main <u>invention</u> in marketing during the twentieth century was customer segmentation.

.... d. The main <u>advance</u> in marketing during the twentieth century was customer segmentation.

3. Many people were excited about the product <u>launch</u>.

   .... a. Many people were excited about the product <u>takeoff</u>.

   .... b. Many people were excited about the product <u>departure</u>.

   .... c. Many people were excited about the product <u>inauguration</u>.

   .... d. Many people were excited about the product <u>unveiling</u>.

4. Volkswagen took a different <u>approach</u> to advertising in the 1960s.

   .... a. Volkswagen had a different <u>attitude</u> toward advertising in the 1960s.

   .... b. Volkswagen created a different <u>style</u> of advertising in the 1960s.

   .... c. Volkswagen used a different <u>method</u> of advertising in the 1960s.

   .... d. Volkswagen took a different <u>line</u> in their advertising in the 1960s.

B. Look at each of the sentences and create a new sentence using a synonym provided. Only one of the synonyms can be used in place of the underlined word. Use a learner's dictionary to help you.

1. The product is <u>targeted</u> at young single mothers. (leveled / aimed / trained)

   ....

2. Designing a new advertising campaign requires a great deal of <u>creativity</u> and planning. (imagination / innovation / resourcefulness)

   ....

3. Market research involves careful <u>observation</u> of a customer's buying habits. (surveillance / opinion / study)

   ....

4. The product failed because the company was unable to <u>deliver</u> the quality it had promised. (send / provide / distribute)

   ....

PART 2

C. Look at each sentence and create a new one by replacing the underlined word(s) with an appropriate synonym.

1. The company was an important <u>sponsor</u> of the event.

   ....

2. The marketing department <u>conducted</u> a <u>survey</u> in order to better understand their customers' purchasing habits.

   ....

3. An advertising campaign is <u>designed</u> around the <u>specific</u> experience that the product provides.

   ....

4. To stay ahead of its <u>rivals,</u> a company must be <u>aggressive</u> in its marketing efforts.

   ....

APPLY YOUR SKILLS

WHY IT'S USEFUL By applying the skills you have learned in this unit, you can use keywords to find essential information as you research topics. You can also use your own words to paraphrase ideas and summarize information from other sources to incorporate into your own writing. You can use synonyms to help you paraphrase and summarize other writers' ideas.

ASSIGNMENT

Plan a 200–300 word summary of the article "Product Wars" from Business and Design, Part 1, on pages 54–56.

BEFORE YOU WRITE

A. Before you begin your assignment, discuss these questions with one or more students.

1. What makes one company more successful than another in a product war?
2. What are key marketing considerations when there is a product war?
3. What happens when there is a product war, with products from two different companies competing for the same market?

B. As you consider your writing assignment, complete the tasks. Then share your ideas with another student. Get feedback and revise your ideas if necessary.

1. Go back to the article "Product Wars" and identify keywords related to the topic of the article. How do these words help you understand the topic better? Are any of these words technical words that you will need to use unchanged in your summary?

2. Reread the article and prepare to summarize it by following these steps:

   a. Identify where topics change in the article by drawing a line or by adding section headings.
   b. Highlight keywords and important ideas that you will use in your summary.
   c. Use your highlights to paraphrase the important ideas in each section.
   d. Think about how you will organize your summary. Will a chronological organization be best? Or should you organize your summary by topic? Which would be better and why?

C. Review the Unit Skills Summary. As you plan the writing task, apply the skills you learned in this unit.

UNIT SKILLS SUMMARY

Identify keywords

- Use keywords to identify meaning in sentences and paragraphs.
- Identify topic keywords to help you better understand central ideas discussed in the article.
- Use topic keywords to help you search for more information related to the topic.
- Use keywords to write accurately about the topic.

Paraphrase ideas

- Use paraphrases in your academic writing to avoid copying and quoting.
- Recognize what words to change and how to change them when paraphrasing.
- Attribute ideas to the author(s).

Summarize

- Write complete, objective summaries so your reader doesn't need to consult the original article.
- Identify topics, main ideas, and important supporting details in an article.
- Organize ideas in a way that allows for the most effective summary.
- Attribute ideas to the author(s).

Use reporting verbs

- Use neutral reporting verbs accurately to paraphrase or summarize the ideas of others.
- Use non-neutral reporting verbs carefully to add additional shades of meaning when writing about the ideas of others.

Use synonyms

- Use appropriate and accurate synonyms to match the meaning of the original idea.
- Change the grammar of the sentence as necessary, depending on the synonym you choose.

THINKING CRITICALLY

A. As you think about your assignment, use the information from the earlier sections of the unit to answer the questions. Discuss your answers with one or more students and revise your ideas if necessary.

1. How have ideas in other readings in Business and Design, Parts 1 and 2, helped shape your plans for your summary?
2. What ideas have you included in your summary outline? What ideas have you left out? How have you organized ideas from the article?

THINKING VISUALLY

With another student, discuss how the factors shown in the image relate to market segmentation. How is advertising related to market segments? How can companies find out more about market segments?

THINKING ABOUT LANGUAGE

A. Read a student's summary of an article about how online targeted advertising works. What methods are used to get the right ads to the right customer? What concerns do people have about this type of advertising? Discuss your responses with another student.

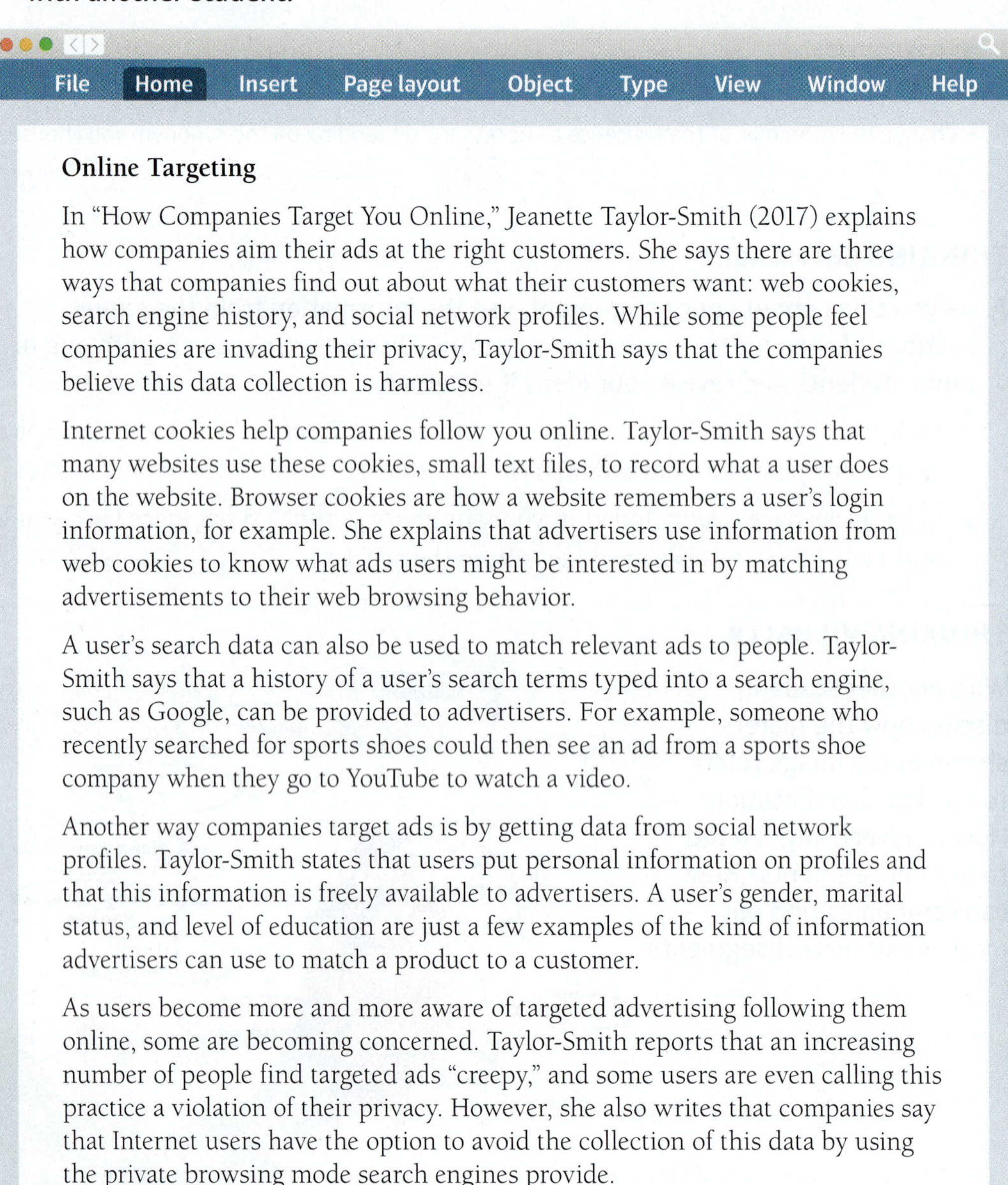

Online Targeting

In "How Companies Target You Online," Jeanette Taylor-Smith (2017) explains how companies aim their ads at the right customers. She says there are three ways that companies find out about what their customers want: web cookies, search engine history, and social network profiles. While some people feel companies are invading their privacy, Taylor-Smith says that the companies believe this data collection is harmless.

Internet cookies help companies follow you online. Taylor-Smith says that many websites use these cookies, small text files, to record what a user does on the website. Browser cookies are how a website remembers a user's login information, for example. She explains that advertisers use information from web cookies to know what ads users might be interested in by matching advertisements to their web browsing behavior.

A user's search data can also be used to match relevant ads to people. Taylor-Smith says that a history of a user's search terms typed into a search engine, such as Google, can be provided to advertisers. For example, someone who recently searched for sports shoes could then see an ad from a sports shoe company when they go to YouTube to watch a video.

Another way companies target ads is by getting data from social network profiles. Taylor-Smith states that users put personal information on profiles and that this information is freely available to advertisers. A user's gender, marital status, and level of education are just a few examples of the kind of information advertisers can use to match a product to a customer.

As users become more and more aware of targeted advertising following them online, some are becoming concerned. Taylor-Smith reports that an increasing number of people find targeted ads "creepy," and some users are even calling this practice a violation of their privacy. However, she also writes that companies say that Internet users have the option to avoid the collection of this data by using the private browsing mode search engines provide.

B. Find one or more synonyms for the following words or phrases: *cookies*, *target*, *invading privacy*.

C. What characteristics of a good summary do you see in this summary of how online targeted advertising works? Comment on the structure, the first paragraph, the presentation of the main ideas, and the use of reporting verbs.

....

....

....

....

WRITE

A. Look back at the writing assignment and your ideas from Before You Write, Thinking Critically, and Thinking Visually, and compare them with a partner.

B. Create an outline for your summary and then discuss it with your partners. Do you notice any differences in organization? Are there any changes you need to make?

C. Write your opening sentence and compare it with a partner's. Are there any differences? Did you include all the key information required?

BEYOND THE ASSIGNMENT

Write a 200–300 word summary of the article "Product Wars," from Business and Design, Part 1, on pages 54–56. Use all the skills you learned in this unit.

Go to MyEnglishLab to watch the instructor's concluding video and to complete a self-assessment.

ZOOLOGY

Process Writing

UNIT PROFILE

People communicate in a variety of ways: by writing and by speaking, and through non-verbal forms, such as using body language. Elephants, too, have different ways of communicating. They use all of their senses to send and receive messages in ways that people are only just beginning to understand.

You will plan a 150–300 word explanation of the process of one form of elephant communication: visual, tactile, or chemical. Discuss, as part of your assignment response, when and why elephants use this form of communication.

OUTCOMES

- Describe a process
- Use process language
- Summarize a process
- Use causative verbs
- Use a dictionary to expand vocabulary

For more about **ZOOLOGY**, see 1 3. See also R and OC **ZOOLOGY** 1 2 3.

GETTING STARTED

Go to MyEnglishLab to watch Professor O'Connell-Rodwell's introductory video and to complete a self-assessment.

Discuss these questions with a partner or a group.

1. Think about how many times, and in how many ways, you communicate each day. How do you do it? Who do you communicate with? Does the form of communication change depending on who you are communicating with and what the purpose is? Why?
2. How many forms of communication can you think of? What parts of your body, or anatomy, do you use? How does your anatomy help you communicate?
3. Professor O'Connell-Rodwell talks about rumbles and seismic communication. How much do you know about these forms of communication? What other methods of communication do elephants use?

SKILL 1

DESCRIBING A PROCESS

WHY IT'S USEFUL Being able to clearly and precisely describe a process will help you to explain to a reader, step by step, how something works or how something is done.

If you have ever bought a piece of furniture to assemble, you'll know that there is probably one best way to put it together. If you cook, you'll know that you need to follow the recipe for the best possible results. When you follow directions, you are following a specified procedure to complete a task. In this section, we will focus on describing a process, which is a broader concept than a procedure. A description of a process provides information and analysis, rather than directions. For instance, the way people communicate with each other is a process, not a set of instructions.

TIP

Describing a process is very common in scientific, business, and engineering fields, where difficult concepts need to be explained clearly.

Elements of a process

Before describing a process, we must first understand it. This means understanding why the process is important, what the stages of the process are, and in what order the stages occur. The following set of key questions can help.

- Why is the process important?
- What does my audience already know about the process, and what do I need to explain?

- Can I relate this process to familiar ideas?
- What are the steps, or stages, of the process, and in what order do they occur?
- Does the process require any special skills or equipment?
- What happens at the end of the process?

Let's look at an example of a process. A student has been asked to write about how people communicate, based on the diagram shown. Read the paragraph he wrote. Can you identify the stages of the process and how the student has answered each of the questions listed above?

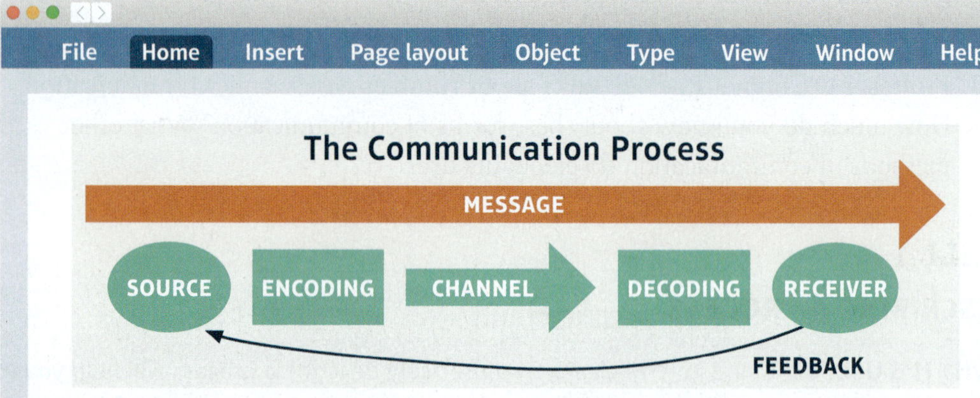

Communication is something people do every day without thinking about it. The process of communication begins when you decide you have a message to send to someone. You encode the message, which means you use language to send it. You send a message through a channel, which describes the way the language is used—think of writing and speaking as different channels. The person receiving the message must then decode it. This is a little like translation, but happens even when both speakers use the same language. It is the process of understanding the language used by the sender. Once the message is decoded, it is processed by the receiver, who then gives feedback based on the message. This feedback lets the sender know whether the message has been received accurately. If the message was a compliment, the feedback could be as simple as a smile of appreciation. An instruction should make someone do something, and a good piece of writing should result in an "A" grade on your assignment. Depending on the channel, the speed of feedback can vary. If the feedback is unexpected, the sender can send a new message, using different language to fix the problem. Humans are naturally built to communicate, but being familiar with the process can help us to understand and fix misunderstandings if they occur.

PART 2

CULTURE NOTE

Human communication is in part cultural. Different cultures have different ways to communicate with each other. For example, in some cultures, making eye contact is considered rude, whereas in the United States, eye contact shows that a person is listening. Likewise, holding your thumbs up in the United States shows approval, but, in some countries, it is an insult.

The writer has described the communication process, taking into account the questions that must be answered when a process is described. The chart below shows how he answered the questions before writing. Do you think he made the process clear?

Why is the process important?	It is something we do every day and is essential for human cooperation.
What does my audience already know about the process, and what do I need to explain?	The concept is familiar to people since it is something people do every day. The terms *encoding*, *channel*, and *decoding* may be new to many people and should be explained clearly.
Can I relate this process to familiar ideas?	This process is already familiar, but some examples will help.
What are the steps, or stages, of the process, and in what order do they occur?	source – encoding – channel – decoding – receiver – feedback
Does the process require any special skills or equipment?	Humans have all the special equipment necessary for communication.
What happens at the end of the process?	A successful act of communication can have different results based on the message sent and how it is received.

VOCABULARY PREVIEW

These vocabulary items appear in the reading. Circle the ones you know. Put a question mark next to the ones you don't know.

anatomy	measure (v)	temporary	wave (n)	focus (v)	fluid

EXERCISE 1

A. Read the assignment about human acoustic communication and a student's response. Then answer the comprehension questions.

Glossary

Acoustic: relating to sound and the way people hear things

Vocal chords: thin pieces of muscle in your throat that produce sound when you speak or sing

Vibrate: a continuous slight shaking movement

Pitch: how high or low a note or other sound is

Frequency: the number of radio waves or sound waves that go past a point each second

Eardrum: a thin piece of skin inside your ear that allows you to hear sound

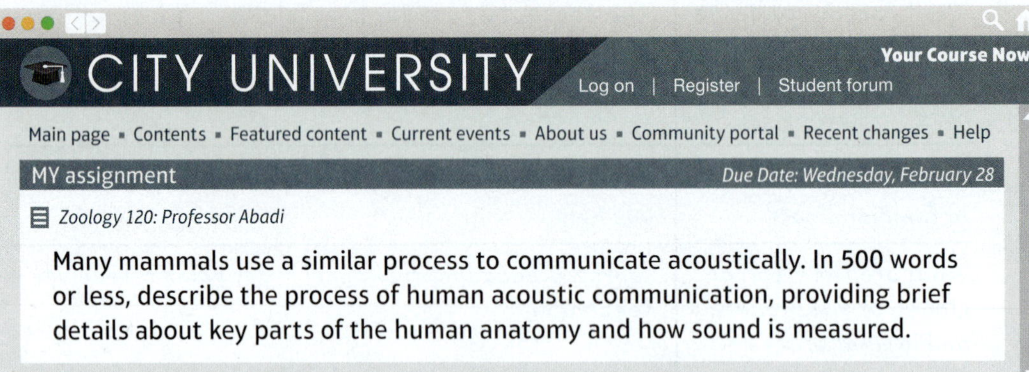

CITY UNIVERSITY

Your Course Now

Log on | Register | Student forum

Main page ▪ Contents ▪ Featured content ▪ Current events ▪ About us ▪ Community portal ▪ Recent changes ▪ Help

MY assignment *Due Date: Wednesday, February 28*

Zoology 120: Professor Abadi

Many mammals use a similar process to communicate acoustically. In 500 words or less, describe the process of human acoustic communication, providing brief details about key parts of the human anatomy and how sound is measured.

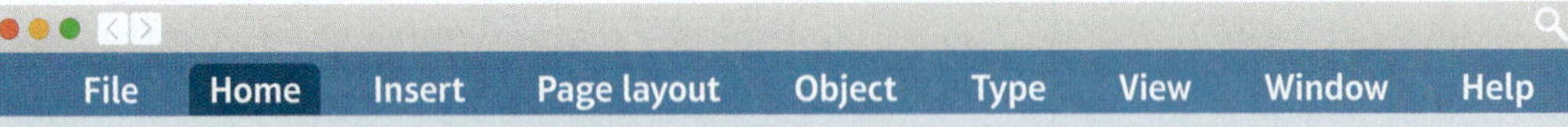

Acoustic Communication

Acoustic communication uses sound to send messages from one person to another. It is broadcast, which means it can be heard by anyone, even people who cannot be seen. It is mainly used for short, temporary, or important communication, and relies on special parts of the human anatomy to create and receive messages. To send an acoustic message, the source must first fill his or her lungs with air. This air is then moved up through the larynx, an area in the throat, to make the vocal chords vibrate. If you touch your throat and say the letter "z," you can feel this vibration. The vocal chords create sound, which can then be altered by changing the shape of the mouth and by the position of the tongue and the lips. We know this as speaking. The sound that is produced then moves through the air. How the message is received depends on the volume and pitch of the sound produced. Louder sounds are more likely to reach the receiver. The volume of sound is measured in decibels (dB), with a normal conversation measuring around 60dB. Other, louder noises can make a message hard to receive. If you have ever tried to have a conversation at a construction site, you know how hard it can be to hear another person speaking

The pitch of sound is measured by its frequency, measured in Hertz (Hz). Lower frequency sound waves travel farther than those at a higher frequency. If your neighbor is playing his music too loud, it's the booming bass you hear, rather than the rest of the tune, even though both are at the same volume. Human speech is around 85 to 180 Hz for a male, and 165 to 255 Hz for a female. When sound reaches the ear, the outer ear focuses the sound and passes it to the eardrum. The eardrum vibrates according to the frequency of the sound. The vibrations of the eardrum cause fluid and hair cells inside the cochlea, which is part of the inner ear, to move. These movements are processed by the brain, so that what is heard is meaningful. There are many moving parts in the process of acoustic communication, but they all happen naturally, and it all takes just a little more time than it takes to say, "Watch out!"

1. According to the text, what parts of human anatomy are used in acoustic communication?

....

2. Which communication is more likely to be successful: sending a quiet, high frequency message, or sending a loud, low frequency message?

....

3. It is possible for both a man and a woman to speak at a frequency of 170 Hz. Would they sound the same?

....

B. Now label each diagram with appropriate words from the text. With a partner, discuss the missing information you have supplied.

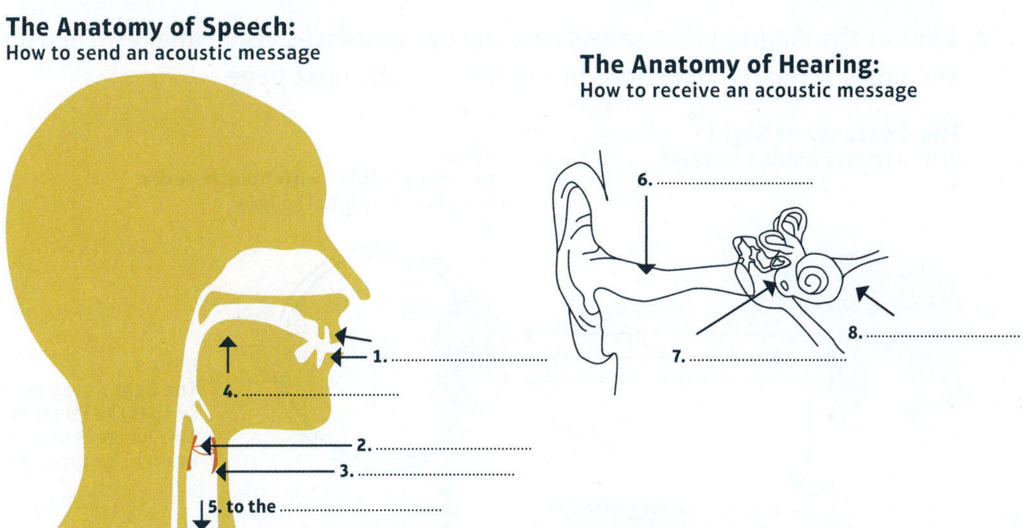

C. Before the student wrote his response to the assignment, he had to understand the process of acoustic communication. Look again at the text and answer the process-related questions. Some of them have been done for you.

1. Why is the process important?	
2. What does my audience already know about the process, and what do I need to explain?	• *There are many technical words that will need to be defined, such as:* • *larynx* • *vocal chords* • *volume* • *pitch* • *frequency* • *eardrum* • *cochlea*
3. Can I relate this process to familiar ideas?	
4. What are the steps, or stages, of the process, and in what order do they occur?	
5. Does the process require any special skills or equipment?	
6. What happens at the end of the process?	*The brain processes the sound so it is meaningful. Different sounds will be processed differently.*

EXERCISE 2

A. Look at the diagram that shows how the eye processes visual images. Then answer the process-related questions in the chart on the next page.

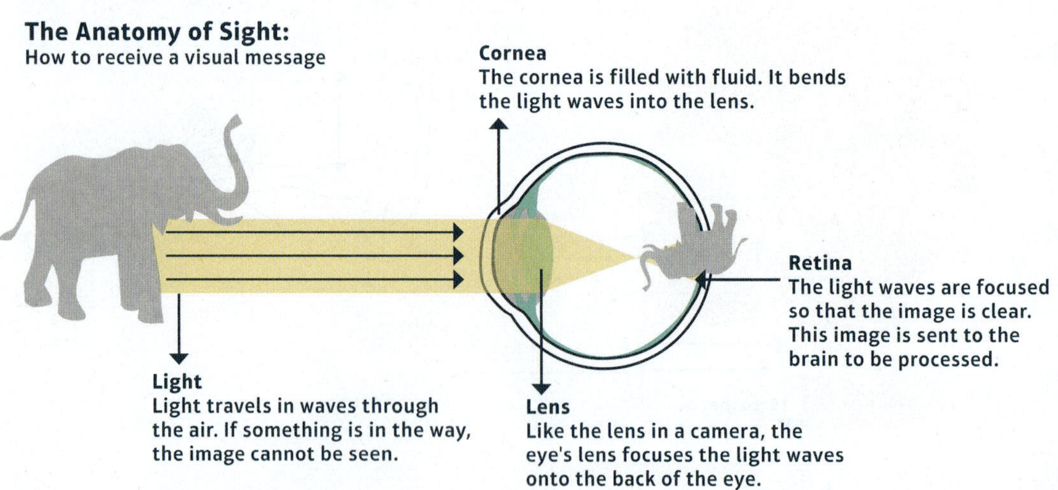

1. Why is the process important?	
2. What does my audience already know about the process, and what do I need to explain?	• There are two technical words that will need to be defined: • cornea • lens
3. Can I relate this process to familiar ideas?	
4. What are the steps, or stages, of the process, and in what order do they occur?	
5. Does the process require any special skills or equipment?	
6. What happens at the end of the process?	The brain processes the image to make it understandable. Different images will be processed differently.

B. Compare your answers with a partner and discuss any differences.

EXERCISE 3

A. Using your knowledge and the information from the diagram in Exercise 2, write a brief answer to the assignment. Include three words from the Vocabulary Check.

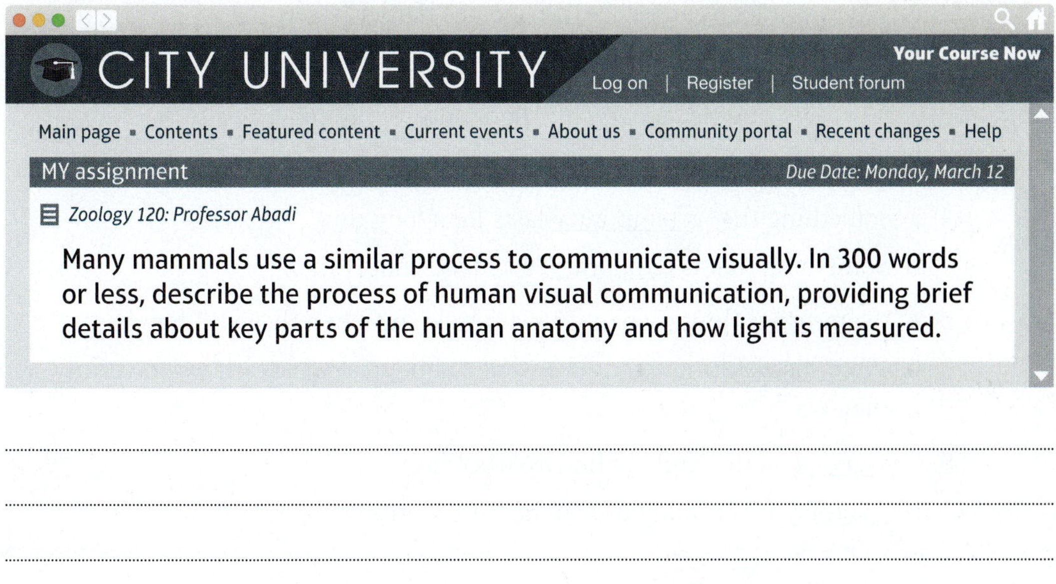

B. Work with a partner. Read each other's descriptions of the process of human visual communication and complete the peer review form. Discuss your comments.

Questions	Yes	No	Notes
Does the writer show why the process is important?	☐	☐	
Are all stages included?	☐	☐	
Are the stages in the correct order?	☐	☐	
Did the writer include three words from the Vocabulary Check?	☐	☐	

C. Revise your draft on the basis of the peer review and related discussion.

VOCABULARY CHECK

A. Review the items in the Vocabulary Preview. Write their definitions and add examples. Use a dictionary if necessary.

B. Choose the sentence that correctly shows the meaning of each underlined vocabulary item..

1. a. Water is a type of fluid.
   b. Air is a type of fluid.
2. a. When you focus an image, it becomes harder to see.
   b. When you focus an image, it becomes clearer.
3. a. A wave is the way energy, like light and sound, moves.
   b. A wave is a measurement of weight.
4. a. Something that is temporary lasts for a long time.
   b. Something that is temporary lasts for a short time.
5. a. We measure things when we want to know when they will happen.
   b. We measure things when we want to know how big or how powerful they are.
6. a. Anatomy is the study of body parts.
   b. Anatomy is the study of how hearing works.

Go to MyEnglishLab to complete a vocabulary and skill practice and to join in collaborative activities.

SKILL 2

USING PROCESS LANGUAGE

WHY IT'S USEFUL In order to describe a process clearly, you need to use process language—words and phrases used to show order—to help your reader follow the steps or stages.

Now that you learned about describing a process—and the key questions you need to ask before you begin to write—it will be helpful to look at the language you can use to clearly and precisely lay out the different steps or stages. Sequence words and adverbial clauses and phrases are very helpful for doing this. They can help you to express clearly the order in which the steps or stages occur and the cause-effect relationship between them.

Sequence words

Let's look at the following excerpt from an article on elephant acoustic communication. Notice the highlighted words and how they help you understand the order of the steps in the process.

Rumbling Elephants

Maxwell Dimka

Scientists have known for a long time that elephants talk to each other, but they have only recently determined just how talkative elephants really are. This is because elephants commonly make sounds that are infrasonic, or below the frequency which humans can hear. Generally, a sound is considered infrasonic if it is below 20 Hz. We call these low frequency sounds *rumbles*.

To send an acoustic message, an elephant first fills her lungs with air. Then she pushes the air out of the lungs and into the larynx, which contains vocal chords. When the air passes through the larynx, it causes the vocal chords to vibrate, creating sound. Finally, the sound exits the elephant's body through her mouth or trunk, which shapes the sound. The sounds that come from her trunk, the "trumpeting" many of us associate with elephants, are often higher frequency sounds. However, the sounds she makes more commonly, the rumbles, are often infrasonic.

The vocal chords in an elephant are much larger and looser than those in people, and that is one of the reasons why elephants produce much lower frequency sounds than people do. Smaller animals have shorter and tighter vocal chords, producing sounds with higher frequency. Try to imagine the difference in sound that a tightly stretched rubber band makes compared to one that is less tight. The looser rubber band makes sound at a much lower pitch, or frequency.

Glossary

Rumble: (n) a continuous low sound or (v) to make this kind of sound

In the second paragraph, a process is described. The words *first*, *then*, and *finally* are sequence words, words that show the order in which steps or events occur. In the excerpt above, the sequence word *first* helps the reader understand that this step is at the beginning of the process. When an elephant sends an acoustic message, the first step is to fill her lungs with air. The word *then* helps the reader understand that pushing air from the lungs into the larynx is next in the sequence. The word *finally* signals a step at the end of the process—in this case, the way the sound leaves the elephant's body. See the chart below for some common sequence words and phrases that you can use in your own writing.

For more on using chronological organization, see History, Part 1.

Sequence Words and Phrases		
Beginning	**Middle**	**End**
First	Second	Finally
First of all	Third	Last(ly)
At first	Then	In the end
To begin with	Next	

CULTURE NOTE

Because many elephant calls are below the frequency range of human hearing, it wasn't until the 1980s that people realized elephants communicated this way. People thought the rumbles they sometimes heard were related to digestion—they thought the elephants were hungry, rather than having a conversation with another elephant several miles away.

Adverbial clauses and phrases

One of the ways we use adverbs is to describe time relationships. Adverbial clauses and phrases are another common feature in process language. They are used to show when things happen in relation to one another. For example, in the excerpt above, the adverbial clause "when the air passes through the larynx" shows that one thing happens immediately after another: The air passes through the larynx, and immediately after that the vocal chords vibrate. Another way to think about this relationship is cause and effect. The air passing through the larynx causes the vocal chords to vibrate. The chart below shows some common adverbial clauses and further examples of how elephants communicate.

PART 2

TIP

A clause is a group of words that contains a subject and a verb. Some clauses can stand alone and are called "independent" while others need to be connected to a second clause. Adverbial clauses are "dependent," meaning they need to be connected to a second, independent clause.

Word / Phrase	Explanation	Example
When	One action follows another, often in a cause-effect relationship. The elephant makes a decision, and then she expresses it.	**When** an elephant wants to go somewhere, she uses body language and acoustic communication to express herself.
While	The two actions—making the sound and moving the ears—happen at the same time.	The elephant moves her ears back and forth **while** she makes a rumble.
Before	One action is followed by another. First, the elephant moves; then she makes the rumble.	**Before** she makes the rumble, the elephant moves to the edge of the group, facing the direction she wants to go.
After	One action is followed by another. First, the elephant positions herself, and then she lifts her foot.	She lifts her foot **after** she positions herself in the right spot.
Until	One action continues to a certain point and then stops. The rumbling stops when the elephants join her.	She will rumble repeatedly **until** other elephants join her.
As soon as	One action happens right after another. Enough elephants agree, and then they move.	**As soon as** enough elephants agree to go, they move.

A few adverbial phrases, such as *meanwhile*, *at the same time*, and *in the meantime*, can be used to show two different actions happening at the same time.

> Some elephants agree to move and join the elephant that wants to leave. **In the meantime**, elephants that do not want to move stay. Later, the groups will reunite and use body language and acoustic communication to greet one another.

TIP

Process language should not be overused. Use just enough to help your reader understand the order of the steps and the time relationship between them.

EXERCISE 4

A. Decide what each word or phrase signals when describing a process. Match each item with its meaning. You may use each letter more than once.

.... 1. When	.... 6. After	.... 11. In the meantime
.... 2. To begin with	.... 7. Then	.... 12. Next
.... 3. Last	.... 8. While	.... 13. Finally
.... 4. Meanwhile	.... 9. At first	.... 14. Until
.... 5. As soon as	.... 10. Before	.... 15. Second

a. an action at the beginning

b. an action in the middle

c. an action at the end

d. an action followed by another

e. two actions happening at the same time

B. Discuss with a partner what you can do to make sure that you are using process language appropriately in your writing.

VOCABULARY PREVIEW

These vocabulary items appear in the reading. Circle the ones you know. Put a question mark next to the ones you don't know.

greeting (n, adj)	ceremony	perform	period	separation	substance

EXERCISE 5

A. Read the assignment and a student's first draft of a response. Then answer the questions.

Glossary

Intense: extreme or very great

Gland: an organ in the body that produces a substance such as a hormone, sweat, or saliva.

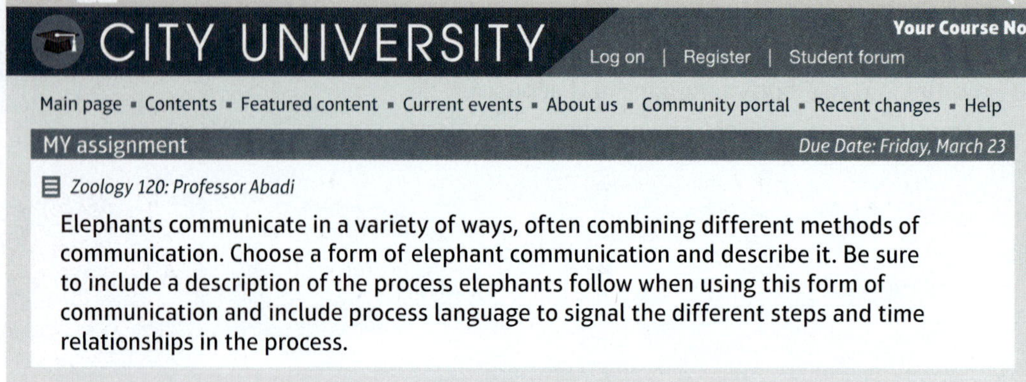

Elephants communicate in a variety of ways, often combining different methods of communication. Choose a form of elephant communication and describe it. Be sure to include a description of the process elephants follow when using this form of communication and include process language to signal the different steps and time relationships in the process.

File Home Insert Page layout Object Type View Window Help

The Elephant Greeting Ceremony

Elephants are very social animals that live in complex social groups. Creating and maintaining bonds is a very important part of an elephant's life. One way that helps elephants maintain bonds is greeting each other after being apart. Elephants perform a greeting ceremony after short periods of separation of only a few hours or longer periods of separation such as days or even weeks. Elephants that know each other well and have been separated for a longer period of time will engage in a more intense greeting ceremony.

Elephants use several methods of communication during the greeting ceremony. They rumble, using acoustic communication, and they gesture wildly, using a lot of body language to show their excitement. During this greeting ceremony, they produce a substance from glands behind their eyes, which also plays a role in communication.

Although there is variation in how elephants perform the greeting ceremony, and how intense it is, a general process is followed. ....(1) the elephants that are about to be reunited start calling to each other when they are still several hundred meters apart. ....(2) they start to move quickly toward each other, eventually running. ....(3) they see each other, they raise their heads high. ....(4) they come together, they touch each other using their trunks ....(5) flapping their ears. ....(6) they produce a substance from a gland, which can be seen running down their faces. The elephants often spin in circles ....(7) they start to settle down. ....(8) they come to rest standing next to each other, side by side.

1. When and why do elephants perform a greeting ceremony?

   ....

2. What methods of communication do they use when performing the ceremony?

   ....

3. What factors impact how intense the greeting ceremony is?

   ....

4. What is an example of body language used in the ceremony?

   ....

B. Read the assignment again. Fill in the blanks with an appropriate word or phrase to signal steps in the process.

C. Compare your answers with a partner. Notice the different ways that process language can be used.

EXERCISE 6

A. The process of an elephant reacting to a bee is illustrated below. Match each step in the process to the appropriate photo.

1. .... 2. .... 3. .... 4. ....

a. The elephant shakes his head to move the bee away.

b. A bee appears and makes a sound.

c. The elephant rumbles to warn others.

d. The elephant runs to get away from the bee.

B. Add process language to the steps in the process shown in Part A to write a brief description of how elephants respond to bees.

....

....

....

....

....

C. Compare your paragraph with a partner and discuss any areas of difference.

VOCABULARY CHECK

A. Review the items in the Vocabulary Preview. Write their definitions and add examples. Use a dictionary if necessary.

Complete the sentences with a vocabulary item from the box.

ceremony	greeting	perform	period	separation	substance

1. When elephants go through a .... , or spend time apart, they are happy to see each other again.

2. They give each other a friendly ______ by following steps in a special ______ .

3. If the elephants have been apart for a long ______ of time and know each other well, the ceremony will be intense.

4. During the ceremony, they use different methods of communication, including a chemical ______ .

5. Scientists think that elephants ______ this ceremony to strengthen bonds between family members.

Go to MyEnglishLab to complete a vocabulary and skill practice and to join in collaborative activities.

INTEGRATED SKILLS

SUMMARIZING A PROCESS

WHY IT'S USEFUL When researching a topic, you may find papers and articles that describe one or more processes. You may also encounter diagrams presenting a process. You will, at times, want to include this information in your own assignments. Being able to summarize the key process-related information accurately and objectively is essential to the clarity and quality of your writing in these instances.

As you have already learned, a summary—written in your own words—provides the main idea(s) of a text. The length of a summary depends on what you are summarizing and why you are summarizing it. A summary can be as short as one sentence that identifies the text being summarized and includes only the most important idea in the text. However, a summary can also be much longer and include supporting points and important details. Summaries are objective. You do not include your opinion or interpretation about the ideas in the text. Your goal is to present the main idea(s) of a text to your reader, so he or she does not need to refer to it.

For more on summarizing, see Business and Design, Part 2.

Your overall approach and goal in summarizing a process are similar to those for summarizing an article. You provide the main idea of the process, which is the purpose or the result of the process, and the most important steps or stages to achieve the result. As when writing a summary of an article, good highlighting and margin notes will help you decide which steps are the most important, and which are less so.

A student was asked to summarize the process of how elephants produce sound, using the article "Rumbling Elephants," by Maxwell Dimka, from Skill 2. From her highlights and notes, we can see which parts of the process she thought were important and needed to be included in a summary.

"Rumbling Elephants" – Maxwell Dimka	*Student Notes*
Scientists have known for a long time that elephants talk to each other, but they have only recently determined just how talkative elephants really are. This is because elephants commonly make sounds that are infrasonic, or below the frequency which humans can hear. Generally, a sound is considered infrasonic if it is below 20 Hz. We call these low frequency sounds "rumbles."	*Elephant speech is often "infrasonic." This is an important technical term that I'll probably need to explain in the summary.* *Elephants rumble, not talk.*
To send an acoustic message, first an elephant fills her lungs with air. Then she pushes the air out of the lungs and into the larynx, which contains vocal chords. When the air passes through the larynx, it causes the vocal chords to vibrate, creating sound. Finally, the sound exits the elephant's body through her mouth or trunk, which shapes the sound. The sounds that come from her trunk, the "trumpeting" many of us associate with elephants, are often higher frequency sounds. However, the sounds she makes more commonly, the rumbles, are often infrasonic.	*The result of the process—to communicate with sound* *Process words help me identify the key steps and how they are related to one another.* *Larynx—will my reader know this word?* *Mouth and trunk = elephant anatomy that forms the shape of the sound* *The most common sounds an elephant makes are infrasonic.*
The vocal chords in an elephant are much larger and looser than those in people, and that is one of the reasons why elephants produce much lower frequency sounds than people do. At the same time, smaller animals have shorter and tighter vocal chords, producing sounds with higher frequency. Try to imagine the difference in sound that a tightly stretched rubber band makes compared to one that is less tight. The looser rubber band makes sound at a much lower pitch, or frequency.	*This explains why the sounds are infrasonic. I can include this in the summary.* *Like a string instrument—thicker and looser strings make a lower sound (this helps me understand, but I probably won't include it).*

The writer combined highlighted elements and her notes to write the following summary in her own words:

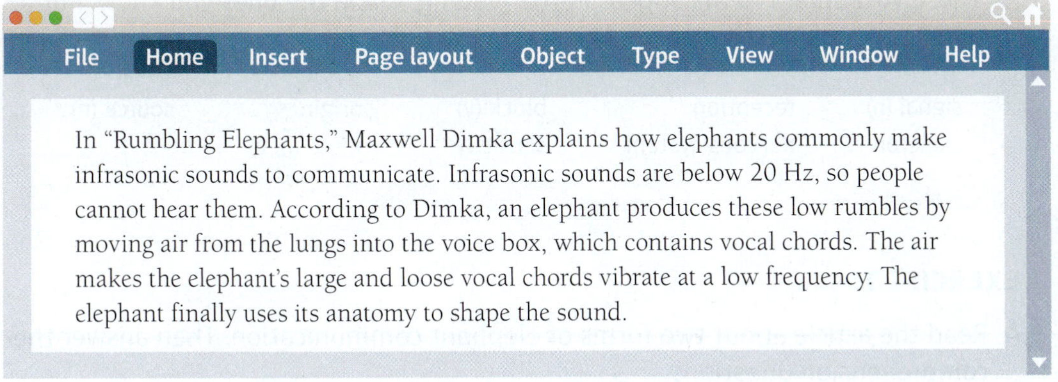

In "Rumbling Elephants," Maxwell Dimka explains how elephants commonly make infrasonic sounds to communicate. Infrasonic sounds are below 20 Hz, so people cannot hear them. According to Dimka, an elephant produces these low rumbles by moving air from the lungs into the voice box, which contains vocal chords. The air makes the elephant's large and loose vocal chords vibrate at a low frequency. The elephant finally uses its anatomy to shape the sound.

Notice how the writer used her notes to identify the important elements of the process to include in the summary. The purpose of the process—to make infrasonic sounds to communicate—is expressed in the first sentence. The writer also included the source of the information used in the summary—the title of the text and the name of the author—in the first sentence since this information comes from a single source.

For more on taking effective notes, see Bioethics, Part 1.

For more on paraphrasing ideas, see Business and Design, Part 2.

In her notes, the writer identified a technical term that she needed to use, *infrasonic*, and explained it in the summary. She found an alternative term, *voice box*, for another technical term, *larynx*. She also highlighted language to help her identify the important steps in the process. However, she actually only needed one sequence word—*finally*—in her summary because the steps were clear. She also decided to add an explanation about why elephant vocal chords produce lower sounds, and she found a good place to incorporate this information.

For more on understanding register, see Bioethics, Part 1.

Note that how you refer to source information depends on whether you are summarizing a lesser-known process from a single source, like the student has done, or if you are summarizing a well-known process, such as how human hearing works, and perhaps relying on several sources to help you understand. For the latter, you should note the sources you consulted, but your first sentence should contain only the main idea—the purpose—of the process.

By following these steps, you can write a summary of any process, however it may be presented in the original source(s)!

VOCABULARY PREVIEW

These vocabulary items appear in the reading. Circle the ones you know. Put a question mark next to the ones you don't know.

signal (n)	reception	block (v)	origin	source (n)
skeleton	nervous system	sensitive	mate (n, v)	

EXERCISE 7

A. Read the article about two forms of elephant communication. Then answer the comprehension questions.

Feeling the Earth Move

Adelaide Kamau

1 As a rule, all mammal ears work in roughly the same way: sound enters the ear, causing the eardrum to vibrate, sending sound waves through various ear bones. These bones cause hairs on the cochlea to vibrate, sending signals to the brain. The brain then interprets those signals. Recent research has shown that elephants are capable of seismic hearing, a form of hearing that lets them listen through the ground. Elephants can hear seismically using both bone conduction, which receives sound vibrations through the skeleton, and somatosensory reception, where sound is carried through the nervous system. Elephants even have the capacity to close off their ears, allowing them to better focus on seismic forms of hearing.

2 In elephants, bone conduction is the more frequently used form of seismic hearing. When an elephant wants to listen to seismic vibration, the elephant first gets into a good position. The elephant faces in the direction of the sound, moving its feet—often pointing its toes to touch the ground. This helps the elephant get more direct contact by using its toe bones. As soon as the elephant is in position, it often closes off its ears, allowing it to block out acoustic noise and focus on the seismic vibrations. From this point, vibrations in the ground are carried through the elephant's skeleton up to the skull—where the vibrations are eventually picked up like regular acoustic hearing by the cochlea.

3 This may seem like a lot of unnecessary work, but seismic hearing through bone conduction has several benefits. Since elephants can make low-pitched, low-frequency rumbling noises that travel long distances through the ground, seismic hearing lets one group of elephants find another. Elephants can split up into smaller groups and look for food, then rejoin the larger family unit later. Low-frequency, seismic rumblings also help elephants plan their day around the weather; there is a growing body of evidence that shows elephants seek out rainstorms for water using seismic hearing.

4 Unlike bone conduction, which elephants use frequently, somatosensory reception is used only when required. Somatosensory reception is often used together with bone conduction; think of it as a hearing aid. When elephants feel vibrations in the earth, they lower their head so that their trunks can touch the ground. The nerve endings in the trunk are quite sensitive; these nerves help elephants feel the vibrations in the earth. The sensory information of these vibrations is then carried up to the elephant's brain. Unlike the auditory signals an elephant listens for with acoustic hearing and bone conduction, somatosensory reception is a tactile sense. The elephants are essentially hearing through touch—something commonly seen in insects and reptiles but rare in mammals.

When another elephant trumpets, bone conduction combined with somatosensory reception helps an elephant triangulate the source of a sound.

5 By using somatosensory reception in addition to bone conduction, elephants can better triangulate a sound's point of origin. Mammals triangulate sound all the time with acoustic hearing; having two ears helps us tell where a sound is coming from, since each ear hears the sound slightly differently. By combining bone conduction and somatosensory reception, the elephant has an easier time finding the origin of a sound. Somatosensory reception is most commonly used by solitary male elephants. Female elephants are only ready to mate for a short time every year. They get males to come to them by making low and rumbling seismic mating calls. Since adult males live apart from female elephants, they need to be able to track down the source of those mating calls—sometimes from dozens of kilometers away. Solitary males can follow the calls, frequently stopping to triangulate their source using both feet and trunk. This demonstrates that, while somatosensory reception is used less frequently than bone conduction, it is still vital to the survival of elephants as a species.

Glossary

Seismic: the vibrations of the earth, often used to describe an earthquake

Hearing aid: a small thing that you put in your ear to make sounds louder if you cannot hear well

Triangulation: a way to find the source of sound using two other measurements

1. What are two processes of communication described in this text?

....

2. For what purpose do elephants usually use each form of hearing?

....

3. Why do rumbles travel long distances?

....

B. Prepare to summarize elephants' two hearing processes. Read the text again, highlight areas of importance, and take notes as needed. Paraphrase important information as necessary.

C. How would you write the first sentence of a summary for the processes in this article? Use the questions below to guide you.

1. What two pieces of information about the source of the summary would you include in the first sentence?

   a. ....

   b. ....

2. What is the main idea—the purpose or result—of bone conduction?

....

3. What is the main idea—the purpose or result—of somatosensory reception?

....

4. Use your answers to the questions above to write the first sentence of a summary for the two processes.

....

D. Use your ideas from above to draft a 150–250 word summary of how elephants use both bone conduction and somatosensory reception to hear. Use at least three words from the Vocabulary Check in your summary.

E. Give your first draft to a partner and get feedback based on the peer review form. Write a second draft based on the suggestions you receive.

Questions	Yes	No	Notes
Does the writing address the assignment task?	☐	☐	
Does the first sentence contain the correct information?	☐	☐	
Did the writer include the most important steps in the process?	☐	☐	
Are any important steps missing?	☐	☐	
Did the writer include appropriate process language?	☐	☐	
Did the writer include three or more words from the Vocabulary Check?	☐	☐	

VOCABULARY CHECK

A. Review the items in the Vocabulary Preview. Write their definitions and add examples. Use a dictionary if necessary.

B. Complete the paragraph with vocabulary items from the box.

blocks (v)	mate (v)	nervous system	origin	reception
sensitive	signal (n)	skeleton	source (n)	

An elephant uses several parts of its anatomy for seismic hearing. It uses its toes and its trunk, which is very ________ to touch. It also uses its ________ and its ________ . To get better ________ , the elephant often ________ out acoustic hearing. The elephant also faces the ________ of the sound. The message reaches the elephant's brain as either an auditory or a tactile ________ . Sometimes elephants use two forms of seismic hearing to more easily find the ________ of the sound, which is very important when a female elephant is ready to ________ .

Go to MyEnglishLab to complete a vocabulary and skill practice and to join in collaborative activities.

LANGUAGE SKILL

USING CAUSATIVE VERBS

WHY IT'S USEFUL Correct, effective use of causative verbs clearly connects actions with their results in your writing. Using causative verbs can make your academic writing more informative and useful for your reader.

Go to MyEnglishLab for the Language Skill presentation and practice.

VOCABULARY STRATEGY

USING A DICTIONARY TO EXPAND VOCABULARY

WHY IT'S USEFUL Being able to quickly and effectively use a dictionary is a vital skill for increasing both the depth and breadth of your vocabulary. This enhances all of your language skills, including your academic writing.

Research shows that language learners need to see or hear a word 30–50 times before they really know the word. Knowing a word involves understanding more than just its spelling, pronunciation, and meaning. As you develop as a language learner, you will need to use an ever greater range of vocabulary and to use the vocabulary you already know in new ways. A dictionary is an essential source of information about words you know and words that are unfamiliar. Because there are so many words in English, using a good learner's dictionary is highly recommended. A learner's dictionary only includes the most useful words and the most important information and, therefore, is easier to use when creating word cards and entries in your vocabulary journal.

For more on creating a vocabulary journal, see Business and Design, Part 1.

For more on creating word cards, see Chemical Engineering, Part 2.

To save space, a dictionary uses symbols and abbreviations to show common information. An explanation of these symbols and abbreviations is usually provided at the beginning of a dictionary. The most common information that dictionaries provide is shown in the chart below.

Meaning(s)	Some words have only one meaning, while others have many. For example, the word *aglet* has only one meaning, while *set* has over 400.
Pronunciation	Knowing how to say a word correctly is important for speaking. Your listener needs to understand the word you are saying. Some words, like *lead* can be pronounced in different ways depending on whether you are talking about the metal, or some promising information. The symbols used in a dictionary for pronunciation can look like another language. Fortunately, you can hear how to pronounce a word using a free, online dictionary.

Spelling	In writing, being able to spell a word correctly is essential for accuracy. Fortunately, many word processing applications have a spellcheck feature. Unfortunately, this doesn't help if you use a wrong word that is spelled correctly. For instance, *compliment* and *complement* are very different words that have a similar sound and only slightly different spellings.
Part of speech	Most of the words you need to learn will be nouns (n), verbs (v), adjectives (adj), or adverbs (adv). A dictionary will also tell you whether a noun is countable (c) or uncountable (u), and whether a verb is transitive (t), intransitive (i), or both.
Word use	A good learner's dictionary provides example sentences that show how a word is used. Some words collocate, or "go" with other words. Others have certain grammatical constructions. For instance, you can say *soft drink*, but you can't say *soft meat*. The correct word to describe meat in this way is *tender*. Likewise, you *get* someone *to do* something, but only *have* someone *do* it. Other information about the register of a word, whether it is academic, and any "hidden" meaning a word might have will be provided in better dictionaries.
Frequency	Some words are much more commonly used than others and should be learned before less common words. For instance, *bad* is much more common than *egregious*. A dictionary may show common words using a symbol, or a different color.

TIP

While free online dictionaries are useful sources of information when you need a quick definition, they do not include as much information as a good paper dictionary. A good learner's dictionary is a worthwhile investment in your language learning journey.

EXERCISE 8

A. Look at the dictionary entry. Using the words in the box, label the different elements. The first has been done for you.

meaning   pronunciation   spelling   part of speech   word use   ~~frequency~~

frequency

1. ....

2. ....

3. ....

4. ....

sensitive /ˈsensətɪv/ ***adjective***

1. **reacting to very small changes in light, temperature, position etc.** ***A highly sensitive alarm will activate with movement.*** ← 5. ....
2. **easily offended or upset.** ***Bobby is a sensitive child who cries when his parents argue.***
3. **easily affected or damaged by something such as a substance or temperature.** ***She can't be in the sun for very long because she has sensitive skin.***
4. **a sensitive person thinks of how other people will feel about something.** ***He was very sensitive to other people's needs.***

B. Use a learner's dictionary to complete each sentence with the correct word from the choices provided. Discuss with a partner the information you found in your dictionary that helped you decide on your answer.

1. There are .... than 500,000 elephants left in the wild. (fewer / less)
2. A big game safari park .... elephants, giraffes, and rhinos. (composes / comprises)
3. Before you hand in your paper, ask a friend to .... it. (criticize / critique)
4. Elephants are .... to bees. (averse / adverse)
5. Beehive fences .... the problem of elephants invading farms. (mitigate / militate)
6. The researchers were there to .... the farmers. (advise / advice)
7. It is hoped that new protection efforts will .... good results. (bare / bear)
8. Elephants travel .... way when they migrate. (a long / along)
9. Hunting for ivory has been .... (prescribed / proscribed)
10. Researchers often need to bring their own .... when they set up a research project overseas. (stationery / stationary)

C. Use a learner's dictionary to answer the questions.

1. What is the plural form of *ox*? Write it here: ....
2. What is the singular form of *data*? Write it here: ....
3. Is the noun *research* countable or uncountable? ....
4. Is the noun *study* countable or uncountable? ....
5. How many parts of speech is the noun *signal*? Write your own sentence for each use.

   ....

   ....

   ....

6. Is the verb *to measure* transitive or intransitive? Write your own sentence(s) to show the use(s).

   ....

   ....

   ....

7. Is the verb *to focus* transitive or intransitive? Write your own sentence(s) to show the use(s).

....

....

8. How many meanings are there for the noun *pitch*? How many of them are common? ....

9. What is the adjective form of *skeleton*? ....

10. How many meanings can you find for the noun *wave*? ....

D. Using a good learner's dictionary, look up three words from any Vocabulary Preview used in this unit. Complete the information for each word and write a sentence using each. Compare and discuss your sentences with a partner.

	Word 1:	**Word 2:**	**Word 3:**
1. What is the main meaning?			
2. How many other meanings are there?			
3. What is the part of speech?	Noun / Verb / Adjective / Adverb	Noun / Verb / Adjective / Adverb	Noun / Verb / Adjective / Adverb
4. Are there any other word forms shown?	Yes / No	Yes / No	Yes / No
5. What are they?			
6. Is the word common?	Yes / No	Yes / No	Yes / No
7. What other information did you find?			

Write your sentences here:

1. ....

....

2. ....

....

3. ....

....

APPLY YOUR SKILLS

WHY IT'S USEFUL By applying the skills you have learned in this unit, you will be able to describe or summarize a process clearly, using sequence words appropriately. You will also be able to use causative words accurately to make your academic writing informative and useful for your reader.

ASSIGNMENT

Plan a 150–300 word explanation of the process of one form of elephant communication: visual, tactile, or chemical. Discuss, as part of your assignment response, when and why elephants use this form of communication.

BEFORE YOU WRITE

A. Before you begin your assignment, discuss these questions with one or more students.

1. Does the message depend on the method of communication?
2. What kinds of messages do you write? What kinds do you say?
3. What kinds of messages do you send using body language or non-verbal communication?

B. As you consider your writing assignment, complete the tasks. Then share your ideas with a partner. Get feedback and revise your ideas if necessary.

1. Go back and look at the texts in this unit that describe forms of elephant communication. Look for information that describes how, when, and why elephants use each form of communication. Use the organizer to help you.

	Visual	Tactile	Chemical
1. How			
2. When			
3. Why			

2. Are there any forms of elephant communication that you need to learn more about? Do research online to fill in any gaps in your chart.

3. Now choose one form of elephant communication on which you will write your assignment. Use the information you have collected to (a) create a diagram that shows the steps in the process of your chosen form of communication and (b) summarize each of the key steps of the process.

C. Review the Unit Skills Summary. As you plan the writing task, apply the skills you learned in this unit.

UNIT SKILLS SUMMARY

Describe a process

- Understand and describe the steps and stages of a process in a way that your reader will be able to relate to.

Use process language

- Use sequence words and adverbial clauses and phrases accurately to help your reader understand the order of the steps or stages of a process.

Summarize a process

- Understand and summarize accurately and objectively key process-related information in your writing.

Use causative verbs

- Use causative verbs in your writing to show cause-effect relationships in an informative manner.

Use a dictionary to expand vocabulary

- Use a learner's dictionary to effectively expand and deepen your knowledge of vocabulary for use in speaking and writing.

THINKING CRITICALLY

As you think about your assignment, use the information from the earlier sections of the unit to answer the questions. Discuss your answers with one or more students and revise your ideas if necessary.

1. Think about your chosen form of communication. Do elephants use this form of communication in combination with another form? In what situations might elephants use more than one form of communication?
2. How might being in captivity influence how elephants use the form of communication you will write about?

THINKING VISUALLY

Look at the images and discuss with a partner which form of communication each one shows and why it is important. What messages could the elephants be sending or receiving?

1

2

3

THINKING ABOUT LANGUAGE

A. Read the online article about communication in male elephants. Underline the causative verb patterns.

Sarah Cadwaller

How Elephant Bulls Communicate

Researchers are learning more and more about the interaction between male, or bull, elephants. Male elephants leave the family group at around 12–15 years old. Researchers more focused on the social interaction of family groups used to think that bulls were solitary animals, living mostly alone. However, this is not the case. Bull elephants form social groups and use all forms of communication—chemical, visual, auditory, and tactile—to interact with each other and with female elephants.

One of the most striking times to see a bull elephant communicating is during a period known as musth, when he is ready to mate. This period can last several weeks in males 30 years or older. A bull in musth leaks body fluids, such as urine, almost nonstop. This form of chemical communication lets female elephants know he is healthy. The chemicals also make other bulls stay away from him. If the chemical signal doesn't work, a bull in musth uses visual communication to get other bulls to leave him alone. First, he might hold his head very high while spreading his ears. Next, he might kick the dirt which sends a cloud of dust toward another bull. Both male and female elephants that are ready to mate use auditory communication, which involves seismic hearing in elephants. These acoustic messages help the bull find a female, who may be kilometers away.

When not in musth, male elephants socialize with other males, especially at watering holes. The size of their groups depends on their environment and the amount of water available, but they can interact in groups ranging from 2 to 12 bulls. Tactile communication, or touching, is very important in all male groups. Older bulls may have younger bulls show respect by performing the trunk-to-mouth greeting. In this greeting, the younger bull extends his trunk and places it in the older bull's mouth. Other forms of tactile communication can be seen when a younger bull gets an older bull to kneel in order to play fight.

Communication is extremely important to both male and female elephants. These incredibly social animals use sight, sound, touch, and smell to send and receive complex messages.

B. Use a learner's dictionary to look up any words that you do not know. Then write a sentence for each.

....

....

....

WRITE

A. Look again at the writing assignment, your chart from Before You Write, and your answers about elephant messages in Thinking Critically and Thinking Visually.

B. Based on the type of communication you will write about, research the topic further and take effective notes. Discuss your notes and ideas with others and make any needed adjustments.

C. Write an outline of your paper, focusing both on the communication process and your explanation of when and why it is used.

BEYOND THE ASSIGNMENT

Write a 150–300 word explanation of the process of one form of elephant communication: visual, tactile, or chemical. Discuss, as part of your assignment response, when and why elephants use this form of communication. Use all the skills you learned in this unit.

Go to MyEnglishLab to watch Professor O'Connell-Rodwell's concluding video and to complete a self-assessment.

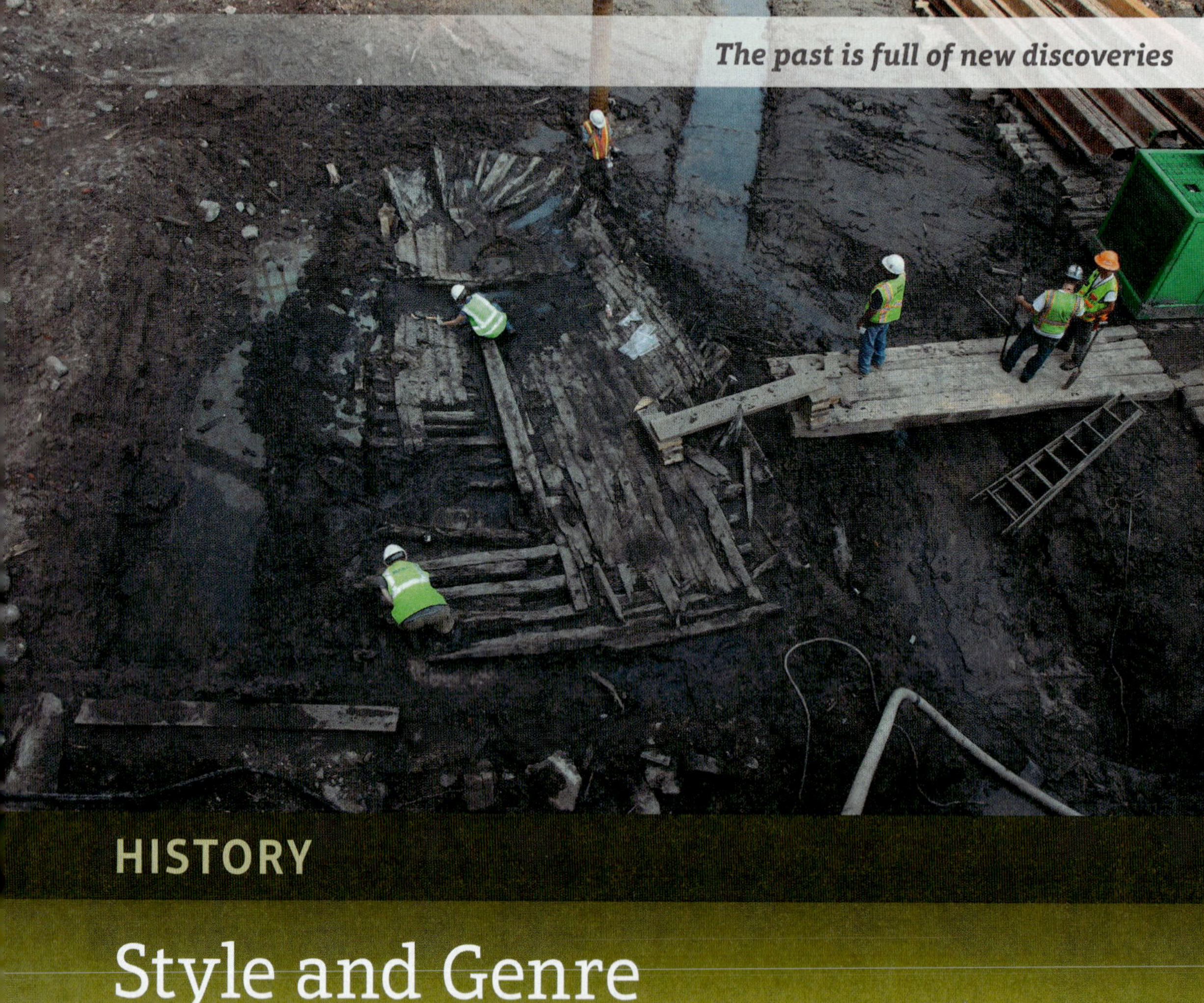

HISTORY

Style and Genre

UNIT PROFILE

Many recent important archaeological discoveries have been made by accident, including the Terracotta Army in China, the Varna Necropolis in Bulgaria, and several European caves containing early human art. In this unit, you will learn about the importance of these discoveries and how to describe the similarities and differences among them.

You will plan a well-researched 300–500 word essay comparing and contrasting the discovery, importance, and care of the Varna Necropolis and the Terracotta Army, both of which are important to our understanding of history.

OUTCOMES

- Write a descriptive paragraph
- Use compare-and-contrast organization
- Identify style and tone
- Use compare-and-contrast language
- Use adjectives

For more about **HISTORY**, see 1 3. See also R and OC **HISTORY** 1 2 3

GETTING STARTED

Go to MyEnglishLab to watch Dr. Hunt's introductory video and to complete a self-assessment.

Discuss these questions with a partner or a group.

1. Have you ever found money by accident? Can you imagine finding treasure worth millions of dollars? What would you do? Who would you tell?
2. How would you feel if you spent years looking for something, only to learn that it had been accidentally discovered by someone else?
3. Dr. Hunt talks about caves at Lascaux and Altamira, as well as a necropolis in Bulgaria. How much do you know about these places? What do you think you will learn?

SKILL 1

WRITING A DESCRIPTIVE PARAGRAPH

WHY IT'S USEFUL Effective use of descriptive writing is essential when you want to paint a vivid picture of a person, place, or object. It enables your reader to have a clear mental image of what you are describing.

Descriptive writing is one of the four broad categories of writing that you will probably need to do as a college student. The purpose of descriptive writing is to describe someone or something in a way that enables your reader to develop a clear mental picture. The chart below shows what kind of information you might include in descriptive writing about people, places, objects, or experiences. Note that not every type of information is included in each example.

Glossary

Dim: not bright, clear, or easy to see

Blink: to close and open your eyes quickly

Description	Possible types of information	Example
People	Identification of the person Physical description Likes / Dislikes Personality Feelings	Maria was an observant child, with wide eyes and long lashes that tickled her rosy cheeks when she blinked. The young adventurer liked to help her father as he explored the caves on their property, but instead of looking at the ground, her eyes ran along the cave walls and ceiling.

(Continued)

Description	Possible types of information	Example
Places	Location Sights Colors Sounds Feelings	The thick trees stood tall and straight, rising to the clouds. Their green tops were like umbrellas, shielding the forest floor from the sun. The early autumn breeze dried the sweat on her forehead. A black bird watched as a single red leaf fell silently to the ground, retiring early for the year. The bird whistled as if saying goodbye.
Objects	Shape Size Colors Texture Feelings	Wavy strips of milky wax ran down the side of the candle, like grandmother's long hair. The candle stuck out of its holder at an angle. The solid and smooth holder glowed golden in the soft light from the candle's flame, which let off a sweet scent. It was a short candle in a little round holder, perfect for a child's hand.
Experiences	Place Surroundings Actions Feelings	Drops of water dripped from the ceiling of the cave and landed on her face. Mud splashed onto her leg when she accidentally stepped in the puddle. She stopped and waited for her eyes to adjust to the dim light the candle provided. The cool air chilled her. She missed the sweater hanging over the chair at home.

There are several techniques you can use to help you write a description. These include showing rather than telling your reader about someone or something, using specific kinds of descriptive language, and giving your reader an impression or feeling about what is being described.

TIP

Descriptive writing is often used together with narrative writing to help your reader not only experience a story, but also picture it to the fullest extent.

For more on using narrative writing, see History, Part 1.

Show, don't tell

One of the guiding rules when describing is to <u>show</u> your readers something, not just <u>tell</u> them. For example, in the description of the person above, the writer does not tell the reader that Maria is pretty. Instead, the writer describes features that could help the reader imagine a pretty girl—wide eyes, long lashes, and rosy cheeks. In the second description, of a place, the writer does not tell the reader it is September. Instead, the writer gives clues about the time of year, such as "early autumn" and the red leaf that is "retiring early." Can you find other examples in the descriptions above where the writer shows the readers something, instead of giving them very brief, explicit information?

Use specific language

Another way to help your readers form clear pictures is by carefully selecting the words and phrases you use in your descriptions. There are certain kinds of language that can make your writing more descriptive.

Vivid language refers to words that give a very specific picture of something. For example, the word *breeze*, used in the description above of a place, evokes a gentle wind. Another example is use of the word *milky* to describe the candle's white color.

Language related to the five senses—sight, hearing, smell, taste, and touch—helps your reader use those senses when reading. For example, the reader can mentally feel the "tickle" of Maria's lashes and smell the candle's "sweet scent."

Figurative language is language that suggests that one thing is similar to something else. For example, when describing the trees in the forest, the writer says the tops of the trees are "umbrellas shielding the forest floor from the sun." The writer compares the trees to umbrellas and helps the reader imagine them better. Another example is the writer's comparison of the wax on the side of the candle to "grandmother's hair." Readers can easily picture white, wavy hair, which helps them "see" what the wax looks like.

TIP

Choose your words carefully to give the reader enough information to imagine what you are describing. However, do not overload—and overwhelm—your reader with descriptive words.

Give an impression

The best descriptive writing is not simply a catalogue of details. Instead, a good descriptive paragraph leaves the reader with an impression of what is being described. For example, in the description of the candle wax given above, the reader is left with an impression of comfort or safety. The candle wax is compared to the hair of the narrator's grandmother. Children usually feel comfortable with a grandparent. The light from the candle is soft, and it makes the holder glow. These are warm images, also associated with comfort or safety. Finally, the size of both the candle and its holder is a perfect fit for the child's hand. Something that is the right size is often comfortable.

In contrast, the description of the experience in the cave leaves an impression of unpleasantness and discomfort. The girl feels drips of water on her face and mud on her leg, both unpleasant feelings. She accidentally steps in a puddle, the light from the candle is dim, and she feels cold. All of these descriptions help give an impression of an unpleasant experience.

Remember that before you can write a description to give your reader a clear impression of something or someone, you must first form that impression yourself. As with all writing, careful thinking, planning, and prewriting are important first steps.

For more on using the academic writing process, see Bioethics, Part 1.

EXERCISE 1

Glossary

Vein: one of the tubes through which blood flows to your heart from other parts of your body

A. Choose one or more of the descriptions to answer each of the questions that follow.

1. The blue of the sky was almost the same as the blue of the waves. One wave was as tall as a ship and speeding toward shore. A seagull screamed before the wave crashed with a roar sending pieces of sand into the air.
2. Dried, black mud filled the lines of his hands and was trapped under his fingernails. His hands were rough from years of pushing dirt aside, looking for hidden treasures.
3. It was shaped like a leaf with lines like veins running from the middle to each edge. Attached to a long, smooth stick, the pointed tip could stab a deer running at full speed.
4. Her eyes had finally adjusted to the darkness, and she could begin to explore the room. She looked up and froze. She could hear her heart pounding in her ears, water dripping in a puddle. There were bulls on the ceiling.

.... a. Which is a description of an object?

.... b. Which is a description of a person?

.... c. Which is a description of an experience?

.... d. Which is a description of a place?

.... e. Which descriptions include color?

.... f. Which descriptions use language related to the sense of hearing?

.... g. Which descriptions use figurative language?

.... h. Which descriptions describe size and / or shape?

.... i. Which descriptions show us something, instead of telling us?

B. What impression does each short description in Part A give you? How could that impression be developed further in each instance? Discuss your responses with a partner.

VOCABULARY PREVIEW

These vocabulary items appear in the reading. Circle the ones you know. Put a question mark next to the ones you don't know.

cave	sword	muscle	approach (v)	giant
creature	royal	stretch (v)	lean (adj)	steam (n)

EXERCISE 2

A. A student has received an assignment to write a descriptive paragraph about a cave painting. Read both the assignment and the student's response. Then answer the questions.

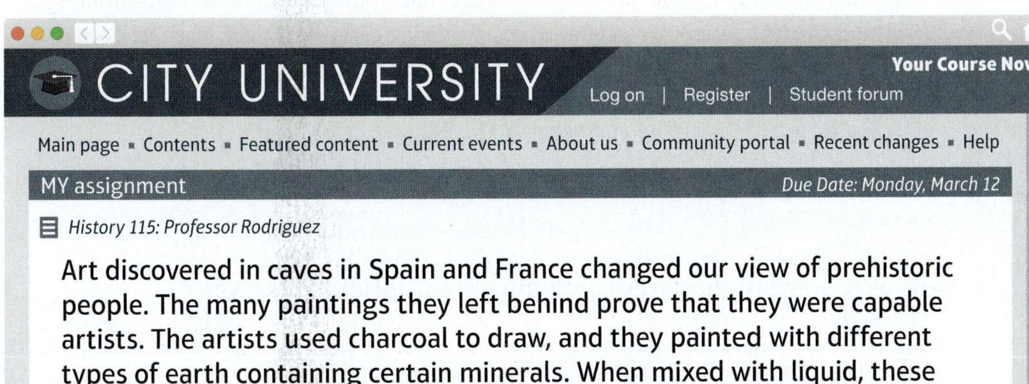

CITY UNIVERSITY

Your Course Now

Log on | Register | Student forum

Main page ▪ Contents ▪ Featured content ▪ Current events ▪ About us ▪ Community portal ▪ Recent changes ▪ Help

MY assignment *Due Date: Monday, March 12*

History 115: Professor Rodriguez

Art discovered in caves in Spain and France changed our view of prehistoric people. The many paintings they left behind prove that they were capable artists. The artists used charcoal to draw, and they painted with different types of earth containing certain minerals. When mixed with liquid, these types of earth created colors like red, brown, and yellow. The prehistoric artists painted many animals. Some of the paintings were discovered accidentally by children or teenagers. For example, Maria de Sautuola discovered the paintings in the Altamira cave when she was 8 years old, and Marcel Ravidat discovered the Lascaux cave art when he was 18 years old.

Assignment: Imagine you are Maria or Marcel describing one of the paintings you have just discovered to a friend. Choose a prehistoric cave painting and write a descriptive paragraph about it.

Glossary

Prehistoric: relating to the time in history before anything was written down

Bison: an animal that looks like a large cow with long hair on its head and shoulders

Spear: a long, pointed weapon that you can throw

File | Home | Insert | Page layout | Object | Type | View | Window | Help

The Bison

There are many animals in the cave including deer, horses, and even a rhinoceros. However, the bison is the king of the cave. This creature stares directly out from the cave wall, following anyone who walks by him. Horns come out of his head like two short swords ready to stab an enemy. Sharp black spears of hair stand out from his head, stomach, and back. Yet he is wrapped in a royal red fur coat, soft and cozy warm on winter nights. Huge muscles stand out under his coat. The bison could move a mountain or lift the world. He could certainly knock over a deer or a horse that got in his way. His slim tail stretches out from the rear, ready to whip any other creature that would dare approach him from behind. Lean legs support the giant, ready to quickly carry him away when he does not want to fight or is needed by another. Getting closer to the painting makes it easy to imagine him alive. His hot breath is steam in the cool air. It leaves a sour smell as he breathes in and out, watching his kingdom of animals on the walls of Altamira.

1. How were some of the caves containing prehistoric art discovered?

   ....

2. What kinds of materials did the prehistoric artists use?

   ....

3. The student is describing a painting from which cave and from whose point of view?

   ....

4. What other animals are depicted in the cave with the bison? Which one seems out of place?

   ....

B. Now reread the description and complete the tasks.

1. Name the type of description this is. ....
2. Showing not telling:
   a. Underline the language that describes how strong the bison is.
   b. Double underline the language that shows how fast the bison is.

3. Vivid language:

   a. Find a word that means "to look intensely at someone." ....

   b. Find a word that means "thin." ....

4. Language of the senses:

   a. What does the writer want the reader to touch? ....

   b. What does the writer want the reader to hear? ....

   c. What does the writer want the reader to smell? ....

5. Figurative language:

   a. What are the horns compared to? ....

   b. What are the black hairs compared to? ....

   c. What is his tail compared to? ....

C. What impression of the bison does the student's description give the reader? How is language used to help create the impression? Discuss your ideas with a partner.

EXERCISE 3

A. Prepare to write your own response to the assignment question. Refer to the photo of a cave painting from Lascaux, or find a different cave painting online. Then use the diagram to brainstorm ideas for your description, which you will share in your writing.

A cave painting from Lascaux

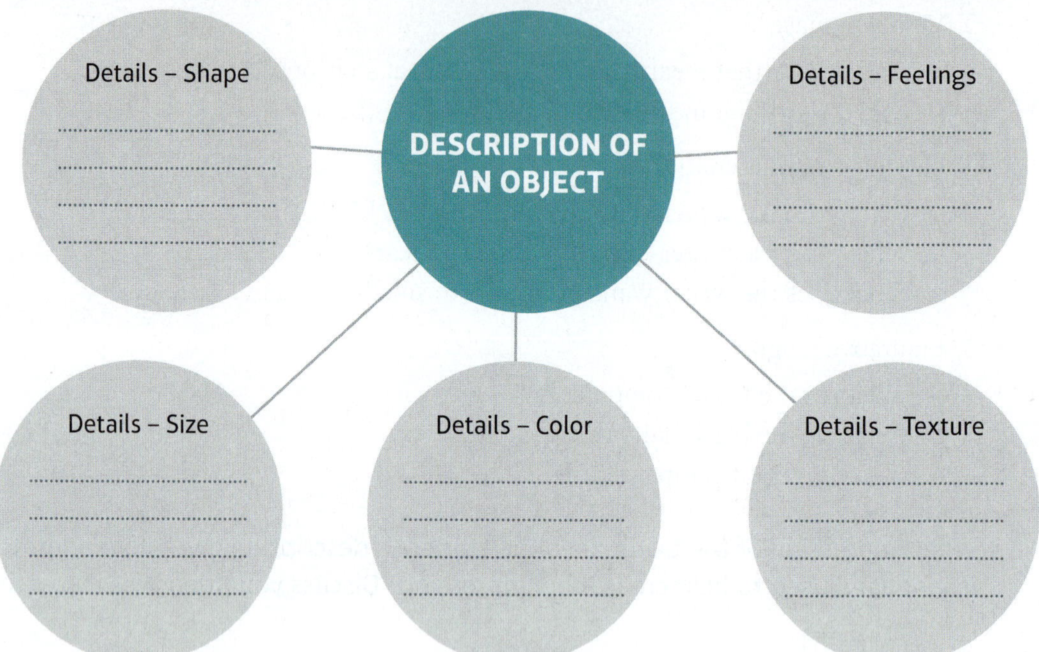

B. Now write your descriptive paragraph of the cave painting. Include three words from the Vocabulary Check.

VOCABULARY CHECK

A. Review the items in the Vocabulary Preview. Write their definitions and add examples. Use a dictionary if necessary.

B. Choose the sentence that correctly paraphrases the meaning of each underlined vocabulary item.

1. a. A <u>cave</u> is a large hole in the side of a tree.
   b. A <u>cave</u> is a large hole under the ground.
2. a. Something that is very large can be called <u>giant</u>.
   b. Something that is very far away can be called <u>giant</u>.
3. a. Someone with visible <u>muscles</u> is probably quite old.
   b. Someone with visible <u>muscles</u> is probably quite strong.
4. a. When people are <u>lean</u>, they are most likely getting enough exercise.
   b. When people are <u>lean</u>, they are probably not getting enough exercise.

5. a. When you <u>stretch</u>, you extend your arms or legs as far as possible.

   b. When you <u>stretch</u>, you bend your arms or legs.

6. a. A <u>sword</u> is a type of weapon.

   b. A <u>sword</u> is a type of art.

7. a. If something is <u>royal</u>, it is connected to a president.

   b. If something is <u>royal</u>, it is connected to a king or queen.

8. a. <u>Steam</u> is a mist that is produced from hot water.

   b. <u>Steam</u> is a kind of small river.

9. a. A <u>creature</u> is another word for an animal, fish, or insect.

   b. A <u>creature</u> is a word for something that is not real.

10. a. If you <u>approach</u> something, you walk away from it.

    b. If you <u>approach</u> something, you walk toward it.

Go to MyEnglishLab to complete a vocabulary and skill practice and to join in collaborative activities.

SKILL 2

USING COMPARE-AND-CONTRAST ORGANIZATION

WHY IT'S USEFUL Many college assignments will require that you compare and contrast two or more things, such as ideas, concepts, people, or books. Knowing how to identify relevant similarities and differences, and to effectively organize your ideas, will be essential for completing this type of writing assignment.

Comparing two things, people, or ideas involves identifying the similarities between them. Contrasting involves identifying differences. We usually compare things that are closely related and when there is a good reason. For example, two archaeological discoveries could be compared on the basis of how they were made, what objects were found, and what their significance was. However, comparing a Roman coin with gene drive would be both difficult and nonsensical because these concepts are unrelated, and there would be no reason to compare them.

When you have a compare-and-contrast writing assignment, begin by deciding how to organize your ideas. Below you will find three main ways to do this: by subject, block-style, and point-by-point.

By subject

Organizing your text by subject is the simplest form of compare-and-contrast writing. This involves writing several points about one subject, then writing about the same points with regard to another subject. For example, if a student is given an assignment to compare the caves of Altamira with those at Lascaux, he can choose to write the first section about the Lascaux cave and the second section about the Altamira cave, with one or more paragraphs in each section, as shown in the diagram below. While this type of organization is easy to follow and gives a complete overview of each subject, the reader must work harder to find the similarities and differences.

The Lascaux Cave:

- How it was discovered
- Its importance
- How it is being cared for

The Cave of Altamira:

- How it was discovered
- Its importance
- How it is being cared for

Block style

In block-style organization, the points of similarity between each subject are grouped together in one block, and then all the points of difference are placed in another block. Each block may include one or more paragraphs, as needed. If the student used this organizational style, he would first write about similarities in how the caves were discovered, how important they are, and how they are cared for. The second part of the assignment would look only at the differences. This method is a very common and useful way to group similarities and differences. However, it may seem repetitive to the reader because the topics could be discussed twice, when there are both similarities *and* differences. The layout of this style of organization is shown below:

Similarities:

- How each cave was discovered
- The importance of each cave
- How each cave is being cared for

Differences:

- How each cave was discovered
- The importance of each cave
- How each cave is being cared for

Point-by-point style

This style places importance on discussing each point in terms of both similarities and differences, before moving on to the next one. As shown in the diagram below, if the writer chooses this style of organization, he could write first about the discovery of each cave, then about the importance of each, and, finally, about how each is cared for. This style of writing is the most cohesive of the three and requires accurate use of compare-and-contrast language.

For more on building paragraphs and connecting ideas, see Business and Design, Part 1.

How each cave was discovered:

- Similarities
- Differences

How each cave is being cared for:

- Similarities
- Differences

The importance of each cave:

- Similarities
- Differences

CULTURE NOTE

Both the Altamira (in Spain) and Lascaux (in France) caves were discovered accidentally and changed the way people thought about early humans. The caves have many colorful paintings of prehistoric plants and animals. Pictures of the caves and the paintings can be seen online.

VOCABULARY PREVIEW

These vocabulary items appear in the reading. Circle the ones you know. Put a question mark next to the ones you don't know.

importance	notice (v)	recognize	discovery	damage (v)

EXERCISE 4

A. Read a student's response to the assignment to compare the Altamira and Lascaux caves. Then answer the questions that follow.

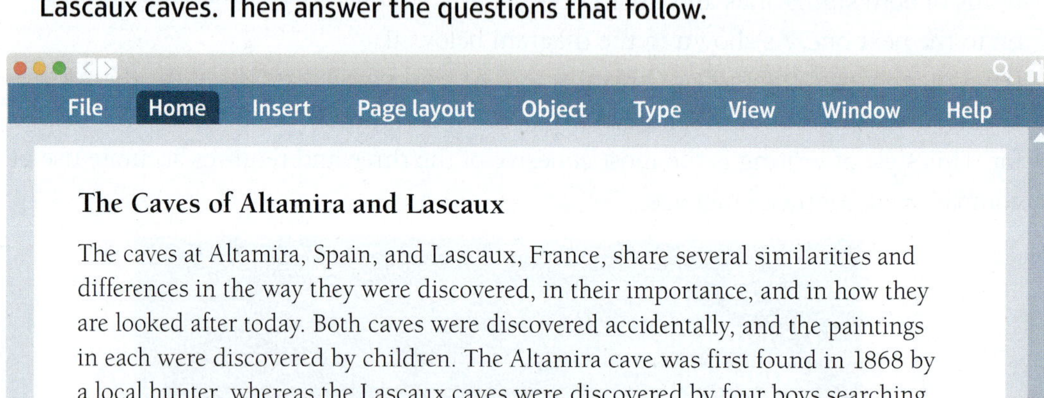

The Caves of Altamira and Lascaux

The caves at Altamira, Spain, and Lascaux, France, share several similarities and differences in the way they were discovered, in their importance, and in how they are looked after today. Both caves were discovered accidentally, and the paintings in each were discovered by children. The Altamira cave was first found in 1868 by a local hunter, whereas the Lascaux caves were discovered by four boys searching for their lost dog in 1940. The paintings in the Altamira cave were not noticed until 1879, when Marcelino Sanz de Sautuola, an amateur archaeologist, was shown them by his daughter. In contrast, the boys at Lascaux saw the paintings immediately.

Altimira Cave Art

Lascaux Cave Art

Both caves show clear examples of early Paleolithic artwork, and both are protected by UNESCO as World Heritage Sites. Before the discoveries, archaeologists did not believe that early humans had the necessary skills to paint or draw in the way they had. Altamira and Lascaux are alike in that they both led to a reevaluation of our prehistoric ancestors. However, when Altamira was discovered, many famous scientists thought that the paintings were fake. Because of the high quality of the drawings and the freshness of the paint, archaeologists at the time suggested that Sautuola had painted the images himself. Sautuola died before the cave drawings were accepted as real in 1902. On the other hand, the importance of the Lascaux caves was recognized immediately. In fact, the caves were opened to the public in 1948, just eight years after their discovery.

As more people learned about the caves, each cave became an important source of tourist income for both regions. At Lascaux, scientists began to notice that the paintings were being damaged because of the number of visitors. Similarly, at Altamira, the paintings were showing signs of wear and tear. Before they were discovered, both caves had been sealed off and preserved. With a large number of visitors and circulating air and light, action was needed to protect the caves. Both caves began to decrease the number of visitors and then closed completely. Lascaux closed in 1963, and Altamira closed in 1977. So that tourists could still enjoy the experience and the wonder of the cave, Lascaux opened a replica in 1983. In the same way, a replica of the Altamira cave was built in 2001.

Glossary

Amateur: a person who does something because he or she enjoys it, not because it is a job

Paleolithic: early stone age

Ancestor: usually, a member of your family who lived a long time ago, before your grandparents. Here it is used to talk about a human who lived many thousands of years ago.

Replica: an exact copy of something

1. How did the paintings in the caves at Altamira and Lascaux change our understanding of early people?
2. Why did people think Sautuola painted the Altamira cave himself?
3. What was damaging the paintings in both caves?

B. What type of organization did the student use in his paper comparing the Altamira and Lascaux caves? Do you feel that the organization is effective? Discuss your answers with a partner.

EXERCISE 5

A. Look again at the student's assignment and paper in Exercise 4, Part A on the previous page, and complete the chart.

The Caves of Altamira and Lascaux	
Point 1	Discovery
Similarities	
Differences	
Point 2	
Similarities	
Differences	
Point 3	
Similarities	
Differences	

B. Another student responded to the same assignment by using the block-style organization. Complete the chart to show how she probably organized her essay.

The Caves of Altamira and Lascaux	
Similarities	**Differences**

C. Based on the two outlines you have completed, which form of organization do you think is better for this topic? Discuss your ideas with a partner.

EXERCISE 6

A. Research the paintings that are found in both the Altamira and Lascaux caves. What are the similarities and differences between the types and number of paintings found in each location? Complete the chart.

The paintings in the Altamira and Lascaux caves	
Similarities	**Differences**

B. Using the information you collected in Part A, write a 300-word block-style essay that compares the paintings found in the caves at Lascaux and Altamira.

C. Work with a partner. Read each other's essay and complete the peer review form. Then discuss each other's comments.

Questions	Yes	No	Notes
Does the essay include both similarities and differences?	☐	☐	
Is the organization block style?	☐	☐	
Are the similarities and differences clear and easy to understand?	☐	☐	
Is the vocabulary precise?	☐	☐	
Are there any grammatical errors?	☐	☐	
Are there any other comments you would like to make?	☐	☐	

D. Revise your draft, taking into account your partner's comments.

VOCABULARY CHECK

A. Review the items in the Vocabulary Preview. Write their definitions and add examples. Use a dictionary if necessary.

B. Complete the paragraph with vocabulary items from the box.

damaged	discovery	importance	notice (v)	recognized

The Cueva de las Manos is located on private land in southern Argentina. The .... was made in 1972 by archaeologists who understood its .... in helping our understanding of how prehistoric humans lived. The site is underground and shows paintings of many hands, which gives the place its name—the Cave of the Hands. The paintings were made around 10,000 years ago and show more than just hands. A visitor will .... animals and hunting scenes, too. Today, because the site is .... as a UNESCO World Heritage Site and because it remains on private land—meaning there are few visitors—the paintings are not .... like those at other sites.

Go to MyEnglishLab to complete a vocabulary and skill practice and to join in collaborative activities.

INTEGRATED SKILLS

IDENTIFYING STYLE AND TONE

WHY IT'S USEFUL Identifying the style and tone of a piece of writing helps you understand the author's message and purpose. Alertness about style and tone will help you achieve consistency and the desired effect in your own writing.

Some people have a favorite movie director because they like the kind of movies the director makes. In the same way, many people have a favorite author because they like the way the author writes. When we talk about the *way* a director makes movies, or the *way* an author writes, we are talking about their style and tone. Style and tone are established by the author's purpose for writing and point of view and by the level of formality, sentence structure, vocabulary, and even punctuation the author uses.

Purpose

As you learned in Part 1, an author's purpose for writing can be to inform, persuade, describe, or narrate. Different purposes lead to different styles of writing. Examples of writing reflecting each purpose are shown below. Can you identify the differences?

Expository: The cave was by the underground river, which caused the rock to dissolve.

Persuasive: The cave should be protected because of its importance in understanding history and ourselves.

Descriptive: The cave was large, about 300 meters wide in some sections. There were more than one hundred images painted on the walls, some representing people, others, animals.

Narrative: As I looked around at the different images, I realized that the vibrant reds, yellows, and greens of the paintings were what made them come alive.

The expository sentence is factual and impersonal. The persuasive sentence, on the other hand, makes an argument about the cave, calling for action. The descriptive sentence helps the reader create an image in the mind's eye. With the narrative sentence, we share the writer's own personal experience of the cave paintings.

For more on using narrative writing, see History, Part 1.

For more on stating an argument, see Bioethics, Part 2.

Point of view

The author's point of view, whether expressed in the first, second, or third person, affects the tone of the writing. Using the first person *I* makes the writing seem much more personal than the third person *she*, *he*, or *they*. The second person *you*, often associated with describing procedures or advertising, gives the writing a sense of informality and immediacy. Do you notice these differences in the tone of the examples below?

First person: As I approached the cave's entrance, I could see that it had not been disturbed for many years. I wondered whether this would be a discovery I could use to make my name and fortune.

Second person: When you first enter the cave, you will notice the wooden ladder on your right. Since it is not safe, do not use it. Instead, turn left and use the metal ladder that has been secured to the wall of the cave.

Third person: She had been searching in the jungle for days. Stories of the cave and the treasure within had become more frequent in recent days. She knew she was close.

Sentence structure

Sentences can be long or short; they can be simple, compound, or complex; they can be active or passive; they can make a statement, issue an instruction, ask a question, or express an emotion. All of these differences affect the style and tone of a piece of writing.

A **short sentence** may be a simple sentence, which is a single independent clause, or a compound sentence, which combines two or more independent clauses. Short sentences are used a great deal in informal writing, where an idea or procedure is explained in a simple way. This can make the writing sound conversational, like spoken English. In some types of writing, short sentences can be used to show danger or fear, and they are also used for asking simple questions, giving short instructions, or showing emotions. Look at the examples below.

Statement: The cave was big, dark, and cold.

Instruction: Give money to save the cave.

Question: Should the caves be opened to the public? Is this the right thing to do?

Emotion: I felt both a sense of danger and excitement at the chance of exploring the cave.

Longer sentences tend to hold a lot of information. They are used to explain things, provide details, and move from one point to another. Longer sentences are often used in more formal academic writing. They are likely to be compound sentences, with two or more independent clauses, or complex sentences, combining one or more independent clauses with a subordinate clause.

For more on using conjunctions to connect ideas, see Business and Design, Part 1.

Statement: Although the cave was big, dark, and cold, it was also fascinating because I was the first person who had set foot inside it in more than 5,000 years.

Instruction: Give money today to save the cave, and you will receive a free movie pass for two, which can be used any time in the next year.

Question: Should the caves be opened to the public knowing that they might be damaged as a result of increased air circulation and light pollution? Is this the right thing to do, considering that the town is in desperate need of money, which can then be used to provide much-needed services for the residents?

Emotion: While I felt both a sense of danger and excitement at the chance of exploring the cave, I wondered what damage I would do in exposing my discovery to the world.

Most sentences are written in the **active voice**, with a subject followed by a verb. Using a lot of short, active sentences can make the writing seem informal and conversational, like talking to a friend. The **passive voice** is less personal and more characteristic of academic and formal writing.

For more on knowing how and when to use the passive voice, see Chemical Engineering, Part 2.

Active: The researchers studied the cave paintings.

Passive: The cave paintings were studied by the researchers.

Vocabulary choice

For more on understanding register, see Bioethics, Part 1.

For more on using synonyms, see Business and Design, Part 2.

As you have learned, ideas and concepts can be expressed in many different ways. Many words have synonyms, each of which may have a different register. The choice of words, therefore, directly affects the style and tone of the writing, making it more or less formal. The examples show the difference that word choice can make. Which one is more formal? What other differences, besides word choice, are evident?

A lot of people are going in the caves every day, and it's totally ruining them. The cash is good to have, but only part of that goes to the city. The rest goes to the people who run the place.

Because of the substantial numbers of tourists entering the caves each day, they are in danger of being extensively damaged. While the income is beneficial, only a certain percentage is returned to the city, with the remainder being kept by the owners of the site.

The second example is much more formal than the first. In addition to her more precise and formal word choices, the writer has constructed longer and more complex sentences, and she has used the passive voice. The first example is written as if the person is speaking, while the second example reads more like a serious piece of academic writing.

TIP

Use a good learner's dictionary to find out whether a word is more formal or informal. Make a note of this when you create a word card or an entry in your vocabulary journal.

Punctuation

There are only three ways to end a sentence in English: with a period, a question mark, or an exclamation point. Formal writing uses very few question marks and even fewer exclamation points. They are considered more suitable for informal and conversational writing. Look at the two example emails below. What differences in tone and style, besides differences in punctuation, do you note?

> Yo! Wassup dude! I checked out some awesome caves over the weekend! You've gotta come see them for yourself! You free Wednesday? Hows about shooting me a text when you have a sec?

> Dear Anna, I thought you would like to know about some great caves I went to see over the weekend. I really think you would enjoy seeing them. If you are available on Wednesday, please let me know so we can organize a trip.

The first example uses very informal language and reads like a text message sent to a close friend. There is a mix of punctuation and several examples of very informal vocabulary and short, active sentences. The style is conversational. The second example, an email, is more formal than the first. The vocabulary is more formal, and there are longer, more-complex sentences with no questions or exclamations. The style would not be typical of spoken English.

Recognizing style and tone will help you, as a reader, to better understand the author's context and purpose for writing. As a writer, by knowing your audience, you can use an appropriate style and tone of writing that will be most effective for sharing your ideas.

VOCABULARY PREVIEW

These vocabulary items appear in the reading. Circle the ones you know. Put a question mark next to the ones you don't know.

rare	remains (n)	routine	contain	fund (n, v)	qualified (adj)

EXERCISE 7

A. Read the letter, which supports opening a newly discovered cave to the public. Answer the questions that follow.

Glossary

Extensive: large in amount or area

Letter 1

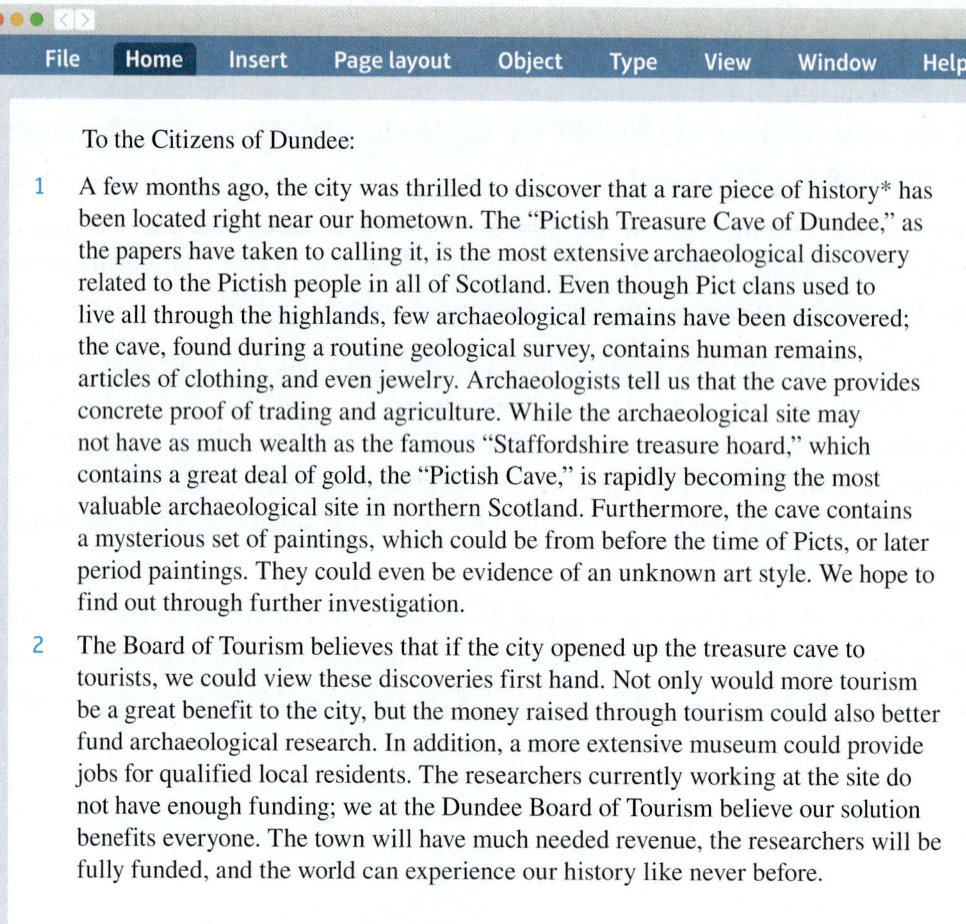

To the Citizens of Dundee:

1 A few months ago, the city was thrilled to discover that a rare piece of history* has been located right near our hometown. The "Pictish Treasure Cave of Dundee," as the papers have taken to calling it, is the most extensive archaeological discovery related to the Pictish people in all of Scotland. Even though Pict clans used to live all through the highlands, few archaeological remains have been discovered; the cave, found during a routine geological survey, contains human remains, articles of clothing, and even jewelry. Archaeologists tell us that the cave provides concrete proof of trading and agriculture. While the archaeological site may not have as much wealth as the famous "Staffordshire treasure hoard," which contains a great deal of gold, the "Pictish Cave," is rapidly becoming the most valuable archaeological site in northern Scotland. Furthermore, the cave contains a mysterious set of paintings, which could be from before the time of Picts, or later period paintings. They could even be evidence of an unknown art style. We hope to find out through further investigation.

2 The Board of Tourism believes that if the city opened up the treasure cave to tourists, we could view these discoveries first hand. Not only would more tourism be a great benefit to the city, but the money raised through tourism could also better fund archaeological research. In addition, a more extensive museum could provide jobs for qualified local residents. The researchers currently working at the site do not have enough funding; we at the Dundee Board of Tourism believe our solution benefits everyone. The town will have much needed revenue, the researchers will be fully funded, and the world can experience our history like never before.

3 The Board is aware that some researchers are concerned about this; they believe that opening the cave up to tourism presents a risk to the site. The Board of Tourism would like to point out, however, that unopened archaeological sites tend to remain unopened and unresearched. We do not believe anyone would like to visit a mound in the grass with nothing to see. An authentic discovery of Pictish artifacts is too rare to ignore. At the next meeting, we encourage people to voice their support for the opening of the Pictish Treasure Cave for all interested people to enjoy.

Sincerely,

The Dundee Board of Tourism

*Note: The cave described in this letter is fictional and has been created for pedagogical purposes.

1. Why is the cave important? What artifacts does it contain?

....

2. What reasons are given for opening the cave?

....

3. What reasons are given for not opening the cave?

....

B. Reread the letter, looking especially at the style and tone. Complete the chart with your ideas, then discuss your answers with a partner. Is the letter formal or informal? What features make it formal or informal?

1. Purpose	
2. Point of view	
3. Sentence structure	
4. Vocabulary choice	
5. Punctuation	

EXERCISE 8

A. An intern from the Consortium for the Preservation of Ancient Cave Dwellings has drafted a letter in response to the Dundee Board of Tourism. Read the letter, focusing on the style and tone. Then complete the chart that follows with your ideas and list the ways it differs from Letter 1.

Letter 2

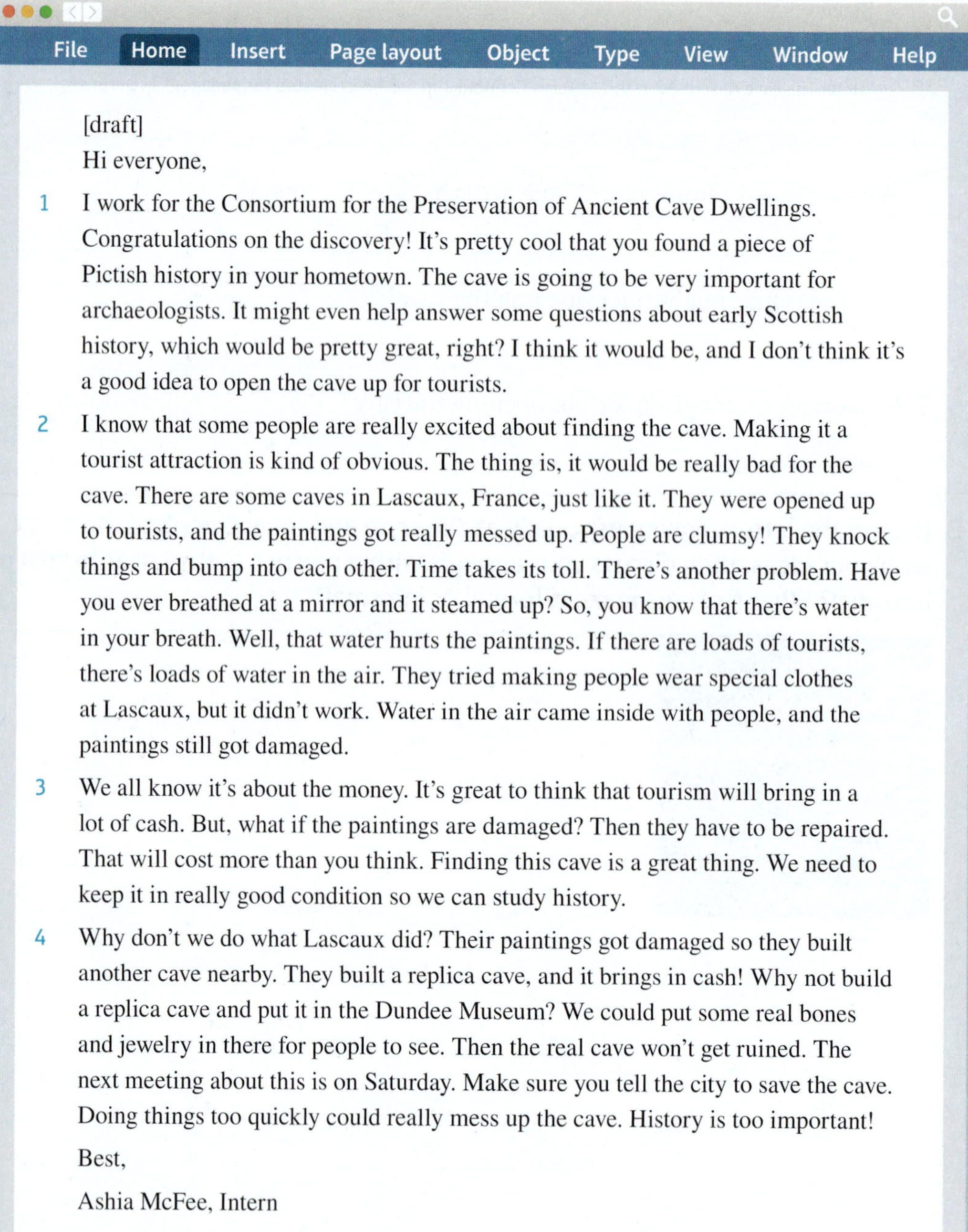

[draft]

Hi everyone,

1 I work for the Consortium for the Preservation of Ancient Cave Dwellings. Congratulations on the discovery! It's pretty cool that you found a piece of Pictish history in your hometown. The cave is going to be very important for archaeologists. It might even help answer some questions about early Scottish history, which would be pretty great, right? I think it would be, and I don't think it's a good idea to open the cave up for tourists.

2 I know that some people are really excited about finding the cave. Making it a tourist attraction is kind of obvious. The thing is, it would be really bad for the cave. There are some caves in Lascaux, France, just like it. They were opened up to tourists, and the paintings got really messed up. People are clumsy! They knock things and bump into each other. Time takes its toll. There's another problem. Have you ever breathed at a mirror and it steamed up? So, you know that there's water in your breath. Well, that water hurts the paintings. If there are loads of tourists, there's loads of water in the air. They tried making people wear special clothes at Lascaux, but it didn't work. Water in the air came inside with people, and the paintings still got damaged.

3 We all know it's about the money. It's great to think that tourism will bring in a lot of cash. But, what if the paintings are damaged? Then they have to be repaired. That will cost more than you think. Finding this cave is a great thing. We need to keep it in really good condition so we can study history.

4 Why don't we do what Lascaux did? Their paintings got damaged so they built another cave nearby. They built a replica cave, and it brings in cash! Why not build a replica cave and put it in the Dundee Museum? We could put some real bones and jewelry in there for people to see. Then the real cave won't get ruined. The next meeting about this is on Saturday. Make sure you tell the city to save the cave. Doing things too quickly could really mess up the cave. History is too important!

Best,

Ashia McFee, Intern

1. Purpose	
2. Point of view	
3. Sentence structure	
4. Vocabulary choice	
5. Punctuation	

B. With a partner, compare Letter 1 and Letter 2. What are the main differences?

C. Imagine you are a senior member of the Consortium for the Preservation of Ancient Cave Dwellings. You feel that Ashia's letter sets the wrong tone for the organization, and you would like to make it more appropriate. Use what you already know, along with the information in Ashia's letter, to draft a formal version. The first and last lines have been done for you.

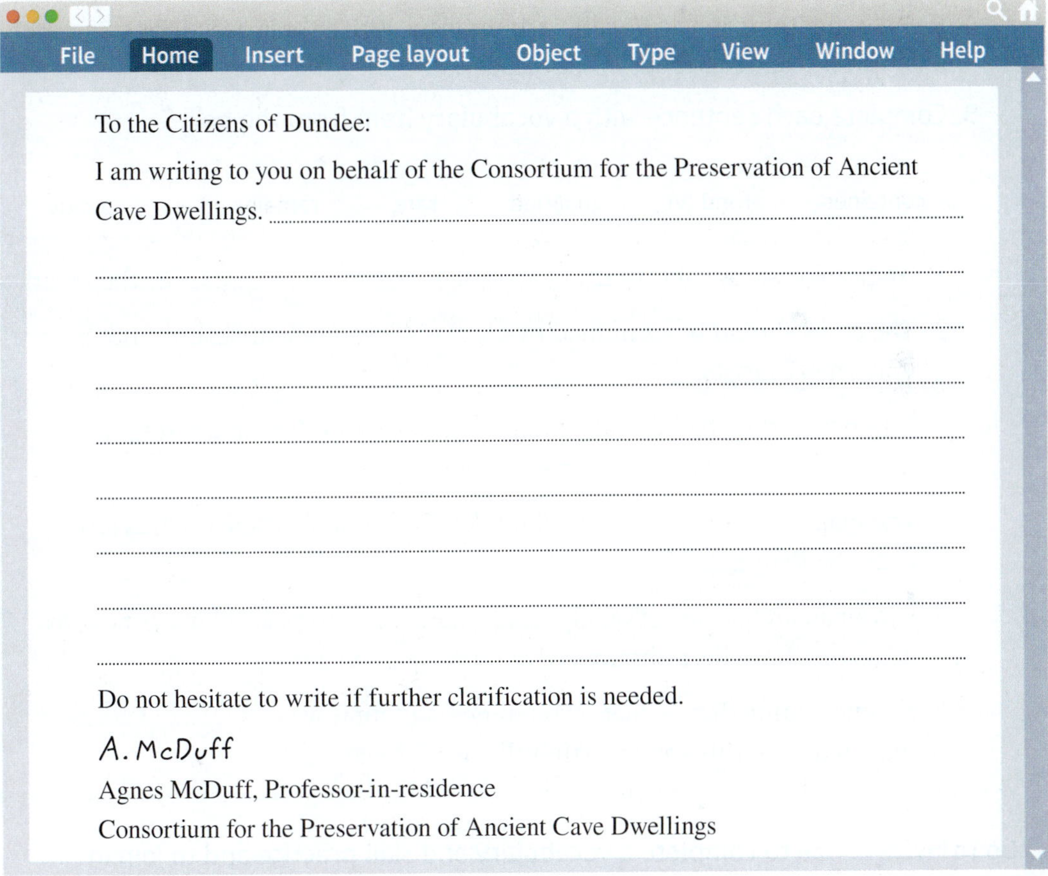

D. Work with a partner. Evaluate each other's essays, using the chart below. Then discuss your comments.

Features	Your partner's letter
1. Purpose	
2. Point of view	
3. Sentence structure	
4. Vocabulary choice	

E. Revise your draft, taking into account your partner's comments.

VOCABULARY CHECK

A. Review the items in the Vocabulary Preview. Write their definitions and add examples. Use a dictionary if necessary.

B. Complete each sentence with a vocabulary item from the box.

contained	fund (v)	qualified	rare	remains (n)	routine

1. Archaeologists are always trying to raise money to ________ their work.
2. The caves should be examined by ________ scientists only, not by untrained tourists.
3. Sam believed he had found a prehistoric cave until he came across the ________ of a half-eaten sandwich.
4. The map ________ several marks that showed where the treasure could be found.
5. Part of an archaeologist's daily ________ is to place markers next to items that have been discovered at an excavation site.
6. He knew immediately that the coin he had found was ________ and that coins like this were worth millions of dollars.

Go to MyEnglishLab to complete a vocabulary and skill practice and to join in collaborative activities.

LANGUAGE SKILL

USING COMPARE-AND-CONTRAST LANGUAGE

WHY IT'S USEFUL By using compare-and-contrast language effectively, you can help your reader gain a clear understanding of how two or more things, people, ideas, or places are similar and how they are different.

Go to MyEnglishLab for the Language Skill presentation and practice.

VOCABULARY STRATEGY

USING ADJECTIVES

WHY IT'S USEFUL Using a variety of adjectives adds interest to your writing and helps you to be precise, especially in descriptive writing. Understanding how to use adjectives in comparisons will make your writing more accurate and enable your readers to picture clearly what you are saying.

Adjectives describe nouns or pronouns. Different adjectives have different functions in writing. They can help make your writing clearer or enhance your descriptions. They can express possession or quantity or show which one you mean. We will focus on two types in this section: descriptive adjectives and adjectives of comparison.

Descriptive Adjectives

As the name suggests, descriptive adjectives are used to describe the noun or pronoun they modify. Since nouns can be described in many ways, there are many descriptive adjectives in English. One way to remember these adjectives is by putting them into different categories. The chart below shows some common descriptive adjective categories, but there are many other categories that you could add.

Category	Examples	Category	Examples
Opinion	good, beautiful, wonderful	Color	red, dark-blue, colorful
Size	giant, little, thin	Origin	French, Asian, northern
Age	young, ancient, modern	Material	metal, wooden, stone
Shape	square, round, flat	Purpose	swimming, hunting, work

Descriptive adjectives are usually placed before the noun they modify, as in the examples. Avoid placing more than two adjectives before a noun in academic writing.

The **young** archaeologist determined that the **colorful** vase was two thousand years old.

The **stone hunting** tools were buried thousands of years ago.

The **rich** collector bought a **beautiful modern** painting.

Descriptive adjectives can also be placed after certain verbs, called linking verbs, to describe nouns or pronouns that are the subject of a sentence as shown in the examples below.

The painting of the deer is **strange**.

He felt **sick** and decided to stop digging.

The students seem **interested** in the cave paintings.

Adjectives of Comparison

We often use adjectives to compare two or more people or things. Adjectives used this way are called comparative adjectives. What is being compared in the examples below?

The painting of the bison is brighter than the painting of the horse.

The paintings in Altamira are more realistic than the paintings in Lascaux.

In the first example, a painting of a bison is being compared with a painting of a horse using the adjective *bright*. Note how the ending *-er* is added to show the comparison. In the second example, the paintings in Altamira are being compared with those in Lascaux using the adjective *realistic*. Here the word *more* is used to signal the comparison. Note that the word *than* is used before the second item.

Adjectives that are used to compare three or more items are called superlative adjectives. What is being compared in the examples below?

The largest collection of rock art in the world is found in Australia.

Pompeii is one of the most preserved archaeological sites ever found.

In the first example, a collection of rock art in Australia is being compared with all other collections of rock art in the world, using the adjective *large*. Note how the ending *-est* is added to show this. In the second example, the famous site of Pompeii is being compared with all other archaeological sites using the adjective *preserved*. Here the word *most* tells us this is a comparison. Note that the word *the* is used in front of a superlative adjective in both examples.

General guidelines for forming these kinds of adjectives are explained in the chart below. However, you should consult a good grammar book for more detailed information on how to use comparative and superlative adjectives. Also, because there are many irregular forms, use a learner's dictionary to check how to form the comparative or superlative of a given adjective.

For more on using a dictionary to expand vocabulary, see Zoology, Part 2.

Word	Comparative	Superlative	Explanation
big	bigger	biggest	Add *-er* to make comparative and *-est* to make superlative adjectives for short, one-syllable words. NOTE: Spelling changes may occur.
small	smaller	smallest	
muddy	muddier	muddiest	Add *-er* to make comparative and *-est* to make superlative adjectives for two-syllable adjectives ending in *-y*, *-er*, *-ow* and *-le*. NOTE: Spelling changes may occur.
narrow	narrower	narrowest	
careful	more careful	most careful	Use the word *more* to make comparative and *most* to make superlative adjectives for other two-syllable adjectives and three-or-more-syllable adjectives.
important	more important	most important	
Irregular Forms			**Explanation**
good	better	best	The comparative and superlative forms of many adjectives do not follow the guidelines above and are irregular. You must memorize their forms. A few of the most common ones are shown here.
bad	worse	worst	
little	less	least	
far	further / farther	furthest / farthest	

EXERCISE 9

A. Put each adjective from the word box in the correct category in the chart on the next page. Then add an adjective of your own to each category. An example has been done for you.

clear	cutting	deep	digging	dirty
early	~~excellent~~	expensive	Lascaux	lean
new	old	pinkish	solar	steel
straight	straw	tall	unusual	wavy

Category	Words
Opinion	excellent,
Size	
Age	
Shape	
Color	
Origin	
Material	
Purpose	

B. Compare the items listed. Write a sentence using the adjective provided in the comparative or superlative form, depending on the number of items you are comparing. Two examples have been done for you.

1. Compare: horses, deer, and bison — Adjective: gentle

   Deer are the gentlest animal found in the cave paintings.

2. Compare: cave art and modern art — Adjective: bright

   Modern art is brighter than cave art.

3. Compare: diamonds, gold, and silver — Adjective: beautiful

4. Compare: caves and forests — Adjective: dark

5. Compare: spoons and hammers — Adjective: heavy

6. Compare: sand, soil, and mud — Adjective: light

7. Compare: red, yellow, and brown — Adjective: dull

8. Compare: archaeologists and librarians — Adjective: adventurous

C. Write two or three sentences that describe one of the pictures in each series, without naming it. Use a total of at least four adjectives in your sentences. Then read your sentences to a partner, who will guess which picture you are describing.

1. Archaeology Tools

a.

b.

c.

This tool is ....

....

2. Archaeological Sites

a.

b.

c.

This site is ....

....

3. Prehistoric weapons

a.

b.

c.

This weapon is ....

....

APPLY YOUR SKILLS

WHY IT'S USEFUL By applying the skills you have learned in this unit, you will be able to write effective compare-and-contrast essays. You will be able to provide detail using suitable descriptive adjectives and to discuss similarities and differences using appropriate organization and language.

ASSIGNMENT

Plan a well-researched 300–500 word essay comparing and contrasting the discovery, importance, and care of the Varna Necropolis and the Terracotta Army, both of which are important to our understanding of history.

BEFORE YOU WRITE

A. Before you begin your assignment, discuss these questions with one or more students.

1. What accidental discoveries have you read about in this unit? How did these discoveries change our understanding of history? How do they compare?
2. What is the Varna Necropolis? Where is it, and how was it discovered?
3. What is the Terracotta Army? Where is it, and how was it discovered?

B. As you consider your writing assignment, complete the tasks and answer the questions. Then share your ideas with a partner. Get feedback and revise your ideas if necessary.

1. How will you find out more information about the Varna Necropolis and the Terracotta Army? What points of comparison will you include?
2. What method of organization will you use? What style and tone is appropriate for this essay?
3. Depending on the method of organization you plan to use for your paper, complete one of the two charts below with information you have found.

Block Style

The Varna Necropolis and the Terracotta Army	
Similarities	**Differences**
Point 1: Discovery Found accidentally	**Point 1:** Discovery Varna found in 1972 by a construction worker Terracotta found in 1974 by a farmer
Point 2:	**Point 2:**
Point 3:	**Point 3:**

Point-by-point Style

The Varna Necropolis and the Terracotta Army	
Point 1	Discovery
Similarities	Found accidentally
Differences	Varna found in 1972 by a construction worker; Terracotta found in 1974 by a farmer
Point 2	
Similarities	
Differences	
Point 3	
Similarities	
Differences	

C. Review the Unit Skills Summary. As you plan the writing task, apply the skills you learned in this unit.

UNIT SKILLS SUMMARY

Write a descriptive paragraph

- Paint vivid verbal pictures that provide your reader with clear mental images of your subject.

Use compare-and-contrast organization

- Know how to identify relevant similarities and differences for a compare-and-contrast essay.
- Use one of the established methods of organization to help your reader understand similarities and differences.

Identify style and tone

- Identify the style and tone of a piece of writing to understand the author's message and purpose.
- Maintain a consistent and appropriate style and tone in your own writing.

Use compare-and-contrast language

- Use compare-and-contrast language effectively to show how two or more things, people, ideas, or places are similar and how they are different.

Use adjectives

- Use adjectives appropriately to add descriptive color, precision, and interest to your writing.

THINKING CRITICALLY

As you think about your assignment, use the information from the earlier sections of the unit to answer the questions. Discuss your answers with one or more students.

1. Sometimes an archaeological discovery is made in the middle of a construction project. When this happens, the construction project needs to be stopped in order to allow time to research the discovery. The delay can cause financial loss. Who should pay for the loss?
2. What can we learn from archaeological discoveries? For example, what does a tool or weapon tell us about the people who used it? What do we learn when jewelry is discovered with human remains?

THINKING VISUALLY

A. Look at the image of warriors from the Terracotta Army. Take turns with a partner describing one of the warriors. Be sure to use specific language and be aware of the order of the adjectives.

B. Now compare two or more of the warriors using comparative or superlative adjectives.

THINKING ABOUT LANGUAGE

Read a draft description of the Varna Necropolis, which has not yet been posted on the writer's blog. Identify and underline the compare-and-contrast language, including adjectives of comparison. Then highlight and rewrite the three sentences that do not fit in terms of the overall style and tone of the article.

[draft]

The Varna Necropolis

In Bulgaria, in October 1972, Raycho Marinov was operating a large excavating machine when he accidentally found the Varna Necropolis. In the same way that the Altamira caves changed our understanding of early prehistoric humans, the Varna Necropolis altered how we understood people who lived around 4600 BCE. Before the find, we knew that people had lived in the area for millennia. What we didn't know was how rich some people were! Researchers found loads of gold at the site. In fact, more gold from this time period was found in a single grave than has been found at any other site anywhere in the world.

Discoveries at the Varna Necropolis show that people were able to work with gold, a precious metal, much earlier than had been thought. The Varna settlements traded with other communities based many miles away. How did they travel? Even though this ancient civilization disappeared fairly quickly in 4200 BCE, the Varna culture may have been an early model for other European civilizations. Although the Roman empire was bigger and the Greek empire richer, the Varna empire was the earliest we know of that formed a functioning society with trade links to other cultures. Unbelievable!

Glossary

Necropolis: a large, ancient burial site

Rewrite the three sentences that do not fit:

1. ....

2. ....

3. ....

WRITE

A. Look again at the writing assignment, your chart from Before You Write, and your description in Thinking Visually.

B. Research your topic further and take effective notes. Discuss your notes and ideas with others and make any needed adjustments.

C. Write an outline of your essay.

BEYOND THE ASSIGNMENT

Write a well-researched 300–500 word essay comparing and contrasting the discovery, importance, and care of the Varna Necropolis and the Terracotta Army, both of which are important to our understanding of history. Use all the skills you learned in this unit.

Go to MyEnglishLab to watch Dr. Hunt's concluding video and to complete a self-assessment.

CHEMICAL ENGINEERING

Presenting Numerical Information

UNIT PROFILE

With every advance in technology, there is often a hidden cost. In the eighteenth century, the industrial revolution brought great wealth and prosperity to many. It also caused many hundreds of people to die prematurely because of the air pollution and difficult working conditions. Likewise, nuclear power is cheaper and cleaner than using fossil fuels. However, if a nuclear plant explodes, the surrounding environment may not be a suitable place to live for thousands of years. Despite our best efforts, such technological disasters are part of modern life.

OUTCOMES

- Create tables
- Use numbers in writing
- Summarize a table of data
- Know how and when to use the passive voice
- Create word cards

You will plan a 500-word report on the destruction of the Aral Sea. Explain what happened to the sea and why. Include at least two tables of data in your report. Your report should be typed and well-presented.

For more about **CHEMICAL ENGINEERING**, see 1 3.
See also R and OC **CHEMICAL ENGINEERING** 1 2 3.

GETTING STARTED

Go to MyEnglishLab to watch Professor Spakowitz's introductory video and to complete a self-assessment.

Discuss these questions with another partner or a group.

1. Some disasters are natural, and some are caused by people. Disasters caused by people are known as technological disasters. When you think of a technological disaster, what do you think of? Are technological disasters sudden events, or can they happen over a long period of time? Have you ever been affected by a technological disaster?
2. What technological disasters are you familiar with? What are some of the effects of these disasters? In your opinion, can technological disasters be prevented? Explain your answer.
3. Professor Spakowitz suggests that people may be able to make natural disasters less severe—or even stop them—in the future. Do you agree? Why or why not?

SKILL 1

CREATING TABLES

WHY IT'S USEFUL Tables are a visual way to present a large amount of information in a small space. Knowing when and how to use a table will help you present information to your reader in the most effective way possible.

When to use a table

A table is used to compare and contrast information, which can be in the form of numbers or text. When you have a lot of data to present, a table can be the most efficient and effective way to do so.

Read the following text. What is it about?

> There were four major smog events in the twentieth century. In 1930, the Meuse Valley smog killed approximately 60 people and the 1948 Donora smog event killed an estimated 20 people. The great smog of London in 1952 killed around 4,000 people and the New York City smog of 1966 killed roughly 170 people.

Glossary

Smog: unhealthy air in cities that contains a lot of smoke

For more on using compare-and-contrast language, see History, Part 2.

The text describes four major smog events of the twentieth century. It makes for dull, repetitive reading. For instance, the word *smog* is used five times. Each event has common related information about the year, the location, and the number of deaths.

We can therefore group this information into categories to create a clearly organized table. Here's how it might look:

Table 1: Major Smog Events in the Twentieth Century

Year	Location	Approximate number of deaths
1930	Meuse Valley, Belgium	60
1948	Donora, Pennsylvania	20
1952	London, United Kingdom	4,000
1966	New York City, New York	170

How to create a table

A table includes several key features:

- A label with a number and a title
- Columns and rows, each with their own heading
- Appropriate formatting using a word processing application

Labels and titles

Each table in your essay or report should have a label. Tables are numbered in the order they are presented. If you use three tables, the first will be labeled "Table 1," the second, "Table 2," and the last, "Table 3." Labels are placed above the table and before the title. Like Table 1, above, whose title is "Major Smog Events in the Twentieth Century," every table should have a title that clearly represents the information being presented.

Tables are used to complement your text, and you most likely will need to refer to data contained in a table. Having a label makes this easy. We could use these structures, for example, to introduce information from Table 1, above:

- **As can be seen in Table 1,** the London smog event of 1952 was the deadliest.
- **As shown in Table 1**, there were two smog events in the United States.
- **The data are presented in Table 1 and show that** smog events are rare.

Columns and rows, with headings

A table consists of **columns** and **rows**. Columns are vertical and are read from top to bottom. In Table 1 above, for example, the first column shows, in chronological order, the years when the smog events happened.

Rows are horizontal and are read from left to right. For example, reading the first row in Table 1 tells you that in 1930, approximately 60 people died in the Meuse Valley smog.

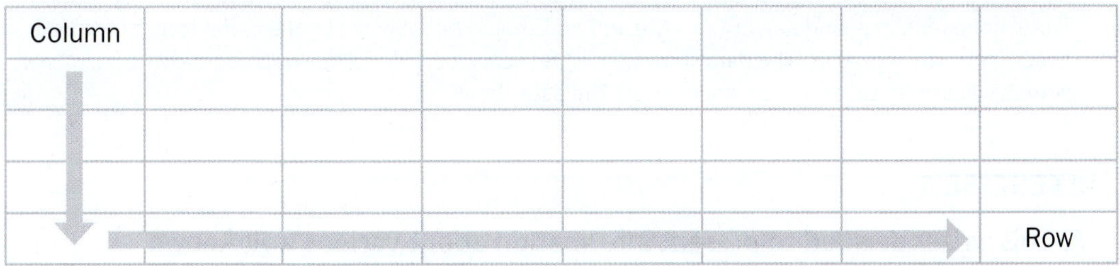

Clear and appropriate headings make your table easy to read. In order to create good headings, make sure the information you are showing within a column or row fits together. The information within each column and within each row must be consistent and of the same type. Looking again at Table 1, you see that the headings are "Year," "Location" and "Approximate number of deaths." The information contained under each heading clearly belongs in one of these three categories. Likewise, the first row is only about what happened in 1930. If your information can't be easily categorized, you will not be able to make clear headings and any table you may try to create will confuse, instead of help, your reader.

For more on writing headings and subheadings, the importance of visual presentation in writing, see Chemical Engineering, Part 1.

Appropriate format

When a table is formatted correctly, the data line up, which makes it easy to read. Good word processing applications have an "insert table" function to create grids for tables. It is important to format your table using this function so that the information in your table stays together correctly. Do not try to create a table in some other way. Using spaces or tabs may look correct on your document, but may change when printed or displayed on another person's computer as you can see below.

Table 1: Major Smog Events in the Twentieth Century

Year	Location	Approximate number of deaths
1930	Meuse Valley, Belgium	60
1948	Donora, Pennsylvania	20
1952	London United Kingdom	4,000
1966	New York City, New York	170

For more on understanding the visual appearance of writing, see Chemical Engineering, Part 1.

TIP

When inserting a table, select the number of columns and rows you need. Remember to add an extra column and / or row for the headings. Also, you can always add extra rows or columns when and as necessary.

CULTURE NOTE

Over time, words can change their meaning, or the way they are used. For example, the word *data* is a plural noun (*datum* is singular, but rarely used) and should be followed by the plural form of the verb in academic writing, as in "The data show that..." However, outside formal or academic writing, many writers will use "data" as a mass noun, as in "The data shows..."

EXERCISE 1

A. This writer decided to present information about various well-known technological disasters in a table. This is his first draft. Decide what information is missing or inconsistently formatted. Make all needed adjustments and transfer the data to the blank table. Compare your corrected table with a partner.

Table 2: Technological Disasters

July 25, 2000	Concorde Crash	France – Paris	113
19th July, 1979	The *Atlantic Empress* and *Aegean Captain* Collision	Caribbean Sea, near Tobago	27
March 12, 1928	The St. Francis Dam Disaster	LA, Cal	450*
Dec 29, 1876	Ashtabula Train Disaster	Ohio	80*
July 17th, 1981	Hyatt Regency Walkway Collapse	Kansas City, MO	114

*Approximate figures

Table 2: Technological Disasters

B. How can you make sure that a table—like Table 2, which you just worked on—is correctly formatted? Write down the features that must be included and checked, then discuss your list with a partner.

VOCABULARY PREVIEW

These vocabulary items appear in the reading. Circle the ones you know. Put a question mark next to the ones you don't know.

measure (v)	lung	compose	absorb
link (v)	breathe	fossil fuels	guideline

EXERCISE 2

A. Read the assignment and a student's first draft response that follows. Then answer the questions.

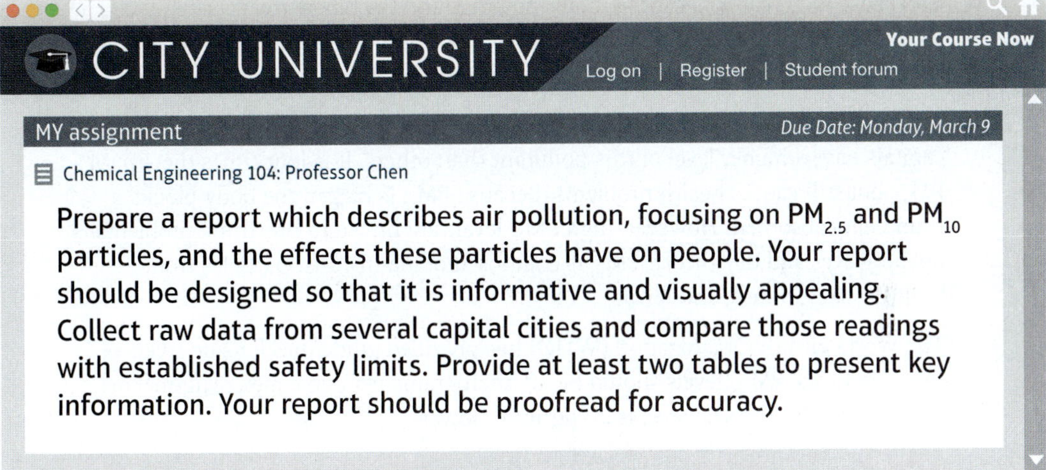

Glossary

Particle: a very small piece of something

Pollutant: something that pollutes the air, water, etc.

Micron: a unit of measurement equal to one millionth of a meter

File Home Insert Page layout Object Type View Window Help

Air Pollution in World Capitals

Although we have come a long way since the deadly smog events of the twentieth century, air pollution is a serious problem that is thought to cause over 3.3 million deaths every year. The problem with modern day air pollution is that it can be invisible. In the past, people could see the smog and knew that there was a problem. Today, air pollution may sometimes be impossible to see.

Differences between $PM_{2.5}$ and PM_{10}

Air pollution is measured in particles. These particles of pollution are tiny. $PM_{2.5}$ is the world's main air pollutant and this particle is only 2.5 microns wide. For comparison, an average human hair is about 70 microns wide. As can be seen from the data in Table 1, some cities have higher $PM_{2.5}$ levels than others. People who live in cities with high $PM_{2.5}$ levels are at greater risk for some health problems. This is because $PM_{2.5}$ can be absorbed into the lungs and the bloodstream. High $PM_{2.5}$ levels are linked to higher risk of heart attack, lower lung function and breathing problems. $PM_{2.5}$ is composed of particles produced by burning fossil fuels.

Another type of air pollutant is PM_{10}. It is clear from the data in Table 1 that some capitals have a higher level of this pollutant than others. It is four times the size of $PM_{2.5}$ but still causes health problems. Because PM_{10} is bigger, the body blocks it from being absorbed. However, high PM_{10} levels are linked to breathing problems, burning eyes and dry throat. PM_{10} is composed of mainly dust particles from building sites, mines, and farms.

The World Health Organization (WHO) has provided guidelines for safe levels of these particles. $PM_{2.5}$ levels should be 10 micrograms per cubic meter ($\mu g/m^3$) or lower. For PM_{10}, the safe level is 20 $\mu g/m^3$ or lower.

$PM_{2.5}$ and PM_{10} levels in cities around the world

$PM_{2.5}$ and PM_{10} levels for seven capital cities are presented in Table 1. However, only one of these cities meets the WHO guidelines for safe levels. According to real time data collected on one day in May, Delhi, India, was the most polluted capital city, as shown in Table 1. The $PM_{2.5}$ level was 338 $\mu g/m^3$ and the PM_{10} level was 620 $\mu g/m^3$. These levels greatly exceeded the recommended safe levels. Table 1 also shows that Moscow was the cleanest capital, reporting a $PM_{2.5}$ level of 9 $\mu g/m^3$ and a PM_{10} level of only 6 $\mu g/m^3$. These levels were below the recommended WHO levels.

Since the data were collected in real time, the levels vary depending on conditions. It is possible that the levels in Delhi are so high because it was a very busy time. Likewise, the levels in Moscow could be low because the data were collected in the middle of the night.

Table 1: Observed Particle Matter Levels in Capital Cities*

Capital cities	$PM_{2.5}$ level in µg/m³	PM_{10} level in µg/m³
Delhi, India	338	620
Beijing, China	152	83
London, United Kingdom	75	28
Seoul, South Korea	68	79
Tokyo, Japan	65	26
Mexico City, Mexico	55	26
Moscow, Russia	9	6

*All readings were taken on May 6, 2017, between 17:45 and 17:50 Central Standard Time.

1. What is the difference between air pollution today and in the past?

2. What are the two main air pollutants discussed in the article?

3. What is the difference between these two pollutants?

4. What kind of health problems can these pollutants cause?

5. Do any of the cities meet WHO guidelines for safe levels of these pollutants?

B. Look again at Table 1: Observed Particle Matter Levels in Capital Cities, featured in the preceding student report, and answer the questions.

1. What headings are provided?

 ....

2. What unit of measurement is used for the particle matter levels?

 ....

3. Why isn't the unit of measurement written after each figure?

 ....

4. In what format is the information under the heading "Capital Cities" provided? Is the format used consistently?

 ....

C. Now scan the report "Air Pollution in World Capitals" on pages 310–311 to find the phrases that are used to refer to the table. Write them below.

1. ....
2. ....
3. ....
4. ....
5. ....

D. With a partner, discuss how the table makes the report stronger. How would it be weaker without the table? Explain your answers.

Some cities, like New Delhi, battle smog, while others, like Moscow, enjoy clean air.

EXERCISE 3

To meet the assignment criteria, the student needs to create another table for the report "Air Pollution in World Capitals." Use the information provided in the report to complete Table 2 below. Follow these steps:

1. Identify common types of information about these two pollutants that could be grouped into categories for the table.
2. Make sure to add appropriate headings.
3. Fill in the missing information under each heading. Include words from Vocabulary Check where appropriate.
4. Compare your table with a partner and discuss any differences.

Table 2: ....

Particle			Composition	
PM 2.5		• • • Breathing problems		10 µg/m³
PM 10	10 microns	• • •		

VOCABULARY CHECK

A. Review the items in Vocabulary Preview. Write their definitions and add examples. Use a dictionary if necessary.

B. Complete the paragraph with a vocabulary item from the box.

absorbed	composed	guidelines	lungs
breathe	fossil fuels	linked (v)	measure (v)

Air pollution is a serious problem in many large cities around the world. People .... in very small particles which are .... of residue left after burning .... The particles are so small that they can be .... into your .... High levels of particle pollution are .... to health problems. The World Health Organization has .... for safe levels of particles. Officials in large cities around the world regularly .... the level of particles in the air.

Go to MyEnglishLab to complete a vocabulary and skill practice and to join in collaborative activities.

SKILL 2

USING NUMBERS IN WRITING

WHY IT'S USEFUL Using numbers appropriately, whether in technical or nontechnical writing, provides accuracy and clarity to your writing. Being able to express numbers consistently helps your reader and shows that you understand and can follow academic style.

It is important that you understand the conventions used at your institution, or by your class instructor, for writing numbers. Style manuals, such as APA or MLA give clear direction about how to express numerical information in a text. Consult with your instructor to see whether you need to follow one of these or another style guide. Your writing center will also be able to help.

For more on understanding an assignment, see Bioethics, Part 1.

Figures or words?

There is a wide variety of rules about how to express numerical data. Some rules apply to nontechnical writing; some apply to technical, or scientific, writing; others apply to both. As an academic writer, you need to be aware of these conventions and know when to use them.

One widely accepted rule that applies to everyday, nontechnical writing is that the numbers ten and lower are written out and that numbers greater than ten are written as figures.

Write as words	Write as figures
one	11
five	365
ten	5,520

In scientific writing, figures are generally used for all quantities, as shown below

Distances	Percentages	Other data
1 mile	1%	2 km^2
2.63 inches	5.5%	4.5 cubic miles
16 cm	10,000%	7 acres

Other important conventions for clarity in the use of numbers

Numbers at the beginning of sentences: At the beginning of sentences, always write numbers as words, rather than as figures. In both nontechnical and technical writing, a sentence must never begin with a figure.

> **Good usage:** Two hundred and twenty-two people suffered injuries as a result of the disaster.
>
> **Unacceptable usage:** 222 people suffered injuries as a result of the disaster.

Series of numbers: In both nontechnical and technical writing, numbers in a series should be written in the same style.

> **Good usage:** Overall, 2,225 people were hurt, 350 people were seriously injured, and 8 people were killed in the explosion.
>
> **Poor usage:** Overall, 2,225 people were hurt, 350 people were seriously injured, and eight people were killed in the explosion.

Combinations of numbers: In both nontechnical and technical writing, when using different types of numbers together, write them in a different way to avoid confusion.

> **Good usage:** The damaged school was home to 45 six-year-olds. OR
> The damaged school was home to forty-five 6-year-olds.
>
> **Poor usage:** The damaged school was home to 45 6-year-olds.

Punctuation of numbers: When writing large numbers in English, we use a comma to make them easier to read. If the number has more than three figures, add a comma (or commas) by counting three figures from the right, like this: 1,000; 10,000; 100,000; 1,000,000. A decimal point is indicated by a period, not a comma. For example, the average height for an American female is written as 162.05 cm. It is not written as 162,05 cm.

Money: Most currency symbols are placed before the number, with no space in between: $400, £77, ¥12,000. If the currency name is written out, you should also write out the number, and the number precedes the currency name: four hundred dollars, seventy-seven pounds, twelve thousand yen. When expressing a large number, such as a million or a billion, you can use figures followed by words: £12 billion, $9 million.

Fractions, decimals and percentages: You will often need to include decimals, percentages, or fractions in your writing.

- Always use figures for decimals in both nontechnical and scientific writing: 35.4 kilograms, $8.2 million, 145.5 meters.
- In nonscientific writing, percentages are usually expressed with a numeral and the word *percent*: 10 percent, 2.5 percent. In scientific writing, use a numeral and the "percent" sign: 10%, 2.5%.
- While decimals are preferred in scientific writing, fractions may be used in nontechnical writing. Common fractions, such as halves, thirds, quarters or fourths are usually spelled out: one-half of accidents caused by people, three-quarters of the forest. Smaller fractions are usually expressed in figures: 3/16 of a gram, 4/9 of an acre.

Dates: In academic writing in American English, dates are usually written in the following sequence: month, day, year. The month is written as a word, but the day and year are written as figures. Do not use ordinal numbers (1st, 2nd, 3rd, 4th, etc.) when writing the date in an academic paper.

Good usage: The damaged school was closed on April 3, 2003.

Poor usage: The damaged school was closed on April 3rd, 2003.

Use ordinal numbers, spelled out, when referring to centuries in academic writing.

The Grand Canal, which connects the Yangtze and the Yellow Rivers, was constructed in the seventh century.

The Panama Canal opened in the early twentieth century.

TIP

An ordinal number is a number such as first, second, or third. You might use these types of numbers in academic writing to describe steps in a process or the order of events. When using ordinal numbers in academic writing, use words (first, second, third, etc.), not figures.

EXERCISE 4

Identify the convention(s) for writing numbers observed in each sentence below. Working with a partner, write your answers on the lines provided.

The Seveso Disaster

1. On July 10, 1976, there was a chemical explosion near a small town in Italy.

....

2. The chemical plant was around 12.5 miles north of Milan.

....

3. One kilogram of a highly toxic chemical called TCDD was released into the air.

....

4. The town most affected by the disaster was Seveso, which had a population of 17,000. However, many towns were also affected by the chemical cloud including Meda, with a population of 19,000, Desio with 33,000, and Cesano Maderno with 34,000 people.

....

5. The worst affected areas contained 36.1 percent of local residents.

....

6. One month after the incident, one quarter of the people examined were found to have serious skin problems.

....

7. The Italian government spent $143.4 million on the cleanup operation.

....

8. The waste was collected into over 41 one-ton barrels.

....

9. In a study conducted at the beginning of the twenty-first century, many victims were found to have an increased risk of breast cancer.

....

VOCABULARY PREVIEW

These vocabulary items appear in the reading. Circle the ones you know. Put a question mark next to the ones you don't know.

canal	site (n)	bury	garbage	property	resident

EXERCISE 5

A. Read a student's uncorrected draft report which describes a technological disaster that happened at Love Canal, near Niagara Falls in New York State. Answer the questions that follow and then discuss your responses with a partner.

Glossary

Landfill: a place where waste is buried under the ground

Defect: a fault in the way something is made or the way it works

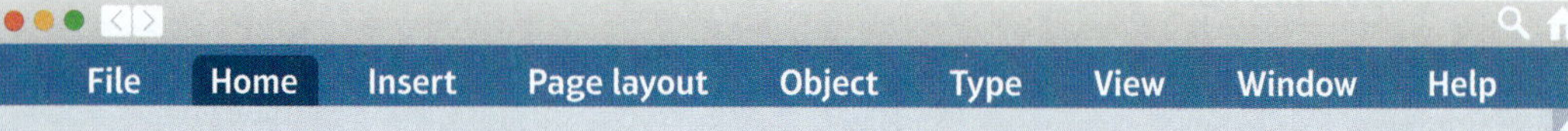

The Love Canal Disaster

Late in the nineteenth century, William T. Love, a business person, started the construction of a canal that would connect 2 parts of the Niagara River. His plan was to use the canal and the water from the river to run a power plant. Construction of the canal began, but shortly thereafter, Love ran out of money. A hole which measured 60 feet wide and three thousand feet long remained, about ¼ mile from the river.

Starting in 1920, the sixteen-acre Love Canal site was used as a landfill where the City of Niagara Falls buried garbage. About twenty years later, a company that made plastic products bought the property. For over 10 years, the company buried chemical waste in the Love Canal site before filling and covering the landfill in 1953. The company sold the property for one $ to the Niagara Falls School Board. 22,000 tons of chemical waste had been buried there before the sale. An elementary school was built on the site on top of the garbage and chemical waste. It opened in 1955. Around 400 students attended the 99th Street School each year.

People started building houses on the Love Canal site around the same time that the school opened. By the mid-1970s, about 800 1-family homes and over two hundred apartments had been built. For many years, residents of the Love Canal neighborhood complained about bad smells and waste on the ground. The situation got worse in 1975 and 1976, when it rained and snowed much more than usual. The high levels of water caused waste to leak into basements and into ponds. Finally, in 1978, the New York Department of Health acted.

It ordered that the 99th Street School close and the state bought houses from two hundred and thirty-nine families who were closest to the canal. It took an additional 2 years for the government to help the rest of the families leave Love Canal.

Studies found the Love Canal residents had increased risk of many health problems. Residents complained of health problems including asthma, migraine headaches, kidney problems and even mental health problems. One study showed that fifty-six point two five percent of the children born in Love Canal between 1974 and 1978 had a birth defect. Unfortunately, the full health impact of this technological disaster is still not known.

1. Why was a hole dug on the Love Canal site?

2. How was the hole used?

3. What did the property turn into after the chemical company sold it?

4. What kinds of health problems did Love Canal residents report?

5. What caused the health problems?

B. Now read the draft again. Underline mistakes that the writer has made with numbers while writing.

C. **With a partner, correct the mistakes you found. As you correct them, identify the guideline that helps you make the correction. An example has been done for you.**

Late in the nineteenth century, William T. Love, a business person, started the construction of a canal that would connect 2 parts of the Niagara River. *two (number is ten or lower)*

EXERCISE 6

The table presents information about three tragic technological disasters. Use the information to write two sentences about each event using a technical, academic style. Include at least two pieces of data in each sentence. An example has been done for you. Discuss your sentences with a partner, then make any needed corrections.

Glossary

Oil well: a deep hole made to get oil out of the ground

Poison: a substance that can kill or harm you if you eat it, drink it, or breathe it

Mercury: a silvery liquid metal that is poisonous

Event	Data
Kuwaiti Oil Fires: Oil wells in Kuwait were set on fire.	• 1991 • More than 600 oil wells • 1,000,000,000 barrels of oil spilled • 5% of land damaged • Lasted approximately 8 months
Bhopal Gas Tragedy: A gas leak in a chemical factory poisoned the city of Bhopal, India.	• 12/3/1984 • 45 tons of poisonous gas • 15,000 people died • 500,000 people harmed • 1989 – $470,000,000 paid by factory to victims
Minamata Disease: A plastics factory dumped mercury into Minamata Bay in Japan.	• 1932–1968 • 1784 people died from mercury poisoning • Over 10,000 people received payments • 4 parts per million (ppm) = average mercury level in people outside Minamata; 705 ppm = highest mercury level recorded in Minamata patient

1. In 1991, more than 600 oil wells burned in Kuwait and one billion barrels of oil spilled.

2. ....

3. ....

4. ....

5. ....

6. ....

PART 2

VOCABULARY CHECK

A. Review the items in Vocabulary Preview. Write their definitions and add examples. Use a dictionary if necessary.

B. Choose the sentence that correctly paraphrases the meaning of each underlined vocabulary item.

1. a. A resident is someone who lives in a particular area.
   b. A resident is someone who is traveling through a particular area.
2. a. A canal is a long, narrow area of land for cars to use.
   b. A canal is a long, narrow area of water for boats to use.
3. a. Property, or the amount of money someone owes, can be public or private.
   b. Property, or a piece of land, can be public or private.
4. a. This is a good site, or area, for the building.
   b. This is a good site, or view, of the building.
5. a. If something is garbage, it should be kept
   b. If something is garbage, it should be thrown out.
6. a. Some cities bury waste by burning it.
   b. Some cities bury waste by putting it in a hole and covering it with dirt.

Go to MyEnglishLab to complete a vocabulary and skill practice and join in collaborative activities.

INTEGRATED SKILLS

SUMMARIZING A TABLE OF DATA

WHY IT'S USEFUL When researching a topic, you will often find papers and articles that use tables to present a lot of information in a small space. You will at times need to use information from such tables for your assignments. Being able to summarize key information accurately and objectively from a table will be essential to the clarity and quality of your writing in these instances.

As you have already learned, when you write a summary, you write a brief statement or report that provides the main idea(s) of a text. The length of a summary depends on *what* you are summarizing and *why* you are summarizing it. A summary can be as short as one sentence. A single sentence summary identifies the text being summarized—the source—and includes only the most important idea of the entire article. A summary can also be several paragraphs, or even pages, long. In this case, main ideas and important supporting points are included.

Summaries are objective. You do not include your opinion or interpretation about the ideas in the text. Your goal is to present the main idea(s) of a text to your reader, so he or she does not need to refer to it.

For more on summarizing, see Business and Design, Part 2.

Your overall approach and goal in summarizing a table are similar to those for summarizing an article. You provide the main idea—the trend—that the table shows. Also, like a summary of an article, a summary of a table varies in length, depending on your purpose.

There are also some key differences between an article summary and a table summary. These are the focus of the discussion that follows.

Describing numbers

As a first step to summarizing a table, it is important to read and understand fully the information presented. Look at the title to get an initial overview of the content. Then look at the column headings to understand what information, specifically, is being presented. Are there any terms that you need to look up?

Look next at the units of measurement that have been applied to the numbers in the table. For example, in Table 1 on the next page, what are the three units of measurement used? Starting with the left column, we see that it shows complete or incomplete decades. The second and third columns contain individual numbers which relate to spills.

For example, between 1970 and 1979 there were 543 medium spills and 245 large spills. Here, the units of measurement are "medium spills" and "large spills," respectively. The final column describes the quantity of oil spilled. Which of the following sentences regarding the quantity of oil spilled is correct?

A: Between 2000 and 2009, tankers spilled 216 tons of oil.

B: Between 2000 and 2009, tankers spilled 216,000 tons of oil.

Tables sometimes combine similar units of measurement to save space. In Table 1, instead of writing out 216,000 tons, the column heading shows that each figure relates to thousands ('000) of tons. You need look at the table carefully so you do not miss this information.

Table 1: Number of Large- and Medium-Sized Tanker Spills by Decade

Decade	Number of medium spills (7.7–771 tons)	Number of large spills (>771 tons)	Quantity of oil spilled ('000 tons)
1970 – 1979	543	245	3518
1980 – 1989	360	94	1294
1990 – 1999	281	77	1248
2000 – 2009	149	32	216
2010 – 2016*	35	12	43

*Incomplete decade

Glossary

Tanker: a ship that carries oil

Describing trends when you summarize a table of data

As you have learned, tables are used to compare and contrast numerical, or other, data. By analyzing the information in tables, you can often find and reveal trends or other key details. This helps you uncover the main idea of the table, which you need to include in a summary. To describe trends, your job is to only include the important information. This will usually involve describing:

- The overall trend
- Increases and / or decreases that characterize the trend
- The largest and / or smallest numbers that describe the trend
- Any other significant information that stands out

Selecting key information to include in your summary

After you have familiarized yourself with the information presented in the table, the next step is to determine what information should be included in your summary. Look for the main idea—the overall trend as described above. This will be included in all table summaries, even the shortest. Table 2 below shows how many pipeline spills occurred between 1997 and 2003. What is the overall trend?

Table 2: Pipeline Spills, 1997–2003

Year	Number of spills
1997	161
1998	141
1999	160
2000	138
2001	128
2002	451
2003	430

Glossary

Pipeline: a line of pipes used to carry gas or oil over long distances

If your reader only needs to know the overall trend of the table, you would write one sentence that describes the type of content that the table shows and the main trend:

> Table 2 shows that there was a dramatic increase in the number of pipeline spills between 1997 and 2003.

Someone who hasn't seen Table 2 will understand that it shows the number of pipeline spills from 1997 to 2003. They will also understand that the number of spills increased dramatically—a great deal—over this time period. This is the most important information in the table.

If your reader requires more information from the table, you would move on to the other features we talked about above. Look at Table 2 again and answer the following questions:

- When did the biggest increase occur?
- When did the biggest decrease occur?
- What is the largest number on the table?
- What is the smallest number on the table?

For a longer summary, you would include some, or possibly all, of this important information provided by the table. Here is a student's summary of the information from Table 2.

Table 2 shows the number of pipeline spills between 1997 and 2003. Overall, the number of spills dramatically increased from 161 to 430 per year. In 1997, the number of pipeline spills was 161. There was a significant decrease to 128 spills in 2001. In 2002, the highest number of spills was recorded at 451. In the last year, 2003, the number of spills slightly decreased to 430. However, the number of spills in 2003 was more than double the number in 1997.

Note the specific details that the student chose to include in the longer summary. Underline the numbers of spills and the years when they occurred. Why do you think these figures have been included and other figures have not?

Using language accurately when summarizing a table

When summarizing a table, be alert to use the very precise language required to describe data and trends. Be especially careful about how you describe time periods and trends.

To describe a specific point in time we can use:

- *In* for a month or a year: In 2001, the number of pipeline incidents was 128.
- *On* for a date: On March 29, 1989, the Exxon Valdez spilled 10.8 million gallons of oil near Alaska.
- *At* for a time: At 9:45 P.M., an explosion occurred on the Deepwater Horizon oil rig.

To describe a period of time we use:

- *From … to …*: From 1997 to 2003, there was an overall increase in the number of pipeline spills from 161 to 430.
- *Between … and …*: Between 1997 and 2001, the overall number of spills decreased from 161 to 128.

To describe trends, the words *increase* and *decrease* are commonly used. However, they can be used as both nouns and verbs. It is important to know the difference and to use each form accurately.

In these sentences *increase* and *decrease* are used as a noun:

> **TIP**
>
> Be sure to look carefully at the time period shown in the table you will summarize. The tense—past, present, present perfect, or future—you use to describe trends will depend upon the time period being shown.

Between 1997 and 2002, there was a large increase in the number of spills from 161 to 451.

From 1997 to 1998, there was a small decrease from 161 to 141 spills.

In these sentences *increase* and *decrease* are used as a verb:

From 1997 to 2002, the number of incidents increased dramatically from 161 to 451.

Between 1997 and 1998, the number of spills decreased slightly from 161 to 141.

To include more precise descriptions in your summary, use adjectives and adverbs.

- Nouns can be modified by adjectives: There was a large / dramatic / significant / small / slight increase in the number of spills over the time period.
- Verbs can be modified by adverbs: The number of spills increased dramatically / significantly / substantially / slightly over the time period.

TIP

There are many other words you can use to describe trends. Sometimes this kind of vocabulary is classified as "Business English." You can consult a vocabulary reference book or search online to find additional words. Be sure you also learn how to use new vocabulary accurately!

Remain objective

Never forget the importance of objectivity when summarizing the data presented in a table. Do not include your opinion or interpretation about the data in your summary. Even though you may know, for example, that the number of pipeline spills increased because the number of pipelines increased, you can't include information in your summary that is not included in the table. Doing so would be interpreting the table, not summarizing it. Your reader trusts that you are being objective when you summarize.

VOCABULARY PREVIEW

These vocabulary items appear in the reading. Circle the ones you know. Put a question mark next to the ones you don't know.

impact (n)	frequency	incident	considerable
surrounding	occur	maintain	in operation

EXERCISE 7

A. Read the scholarly article on the trends, risks, and impacts of oil spills. Then answer the comprehension questions.

CULTURE NOTE

The largest oil spill in the United States started on April 20, 2010, when an oil rig called the *Deepwater Horizon* exploded. The explosion killed 11 people and injured many more. Two days later, the rig sank. The oil well to which the rig was attached leaked oil for 87 days before the leak was stopped. It is estimated that over 200 million gallons spilled into the Gulf of Mexico.

Oil Spills: Trends, Risks, and Impact

Abstract

1 Oil production is at an all-time high, as new technology allows for increased efficiency and volume in drilling operations. After establishing the environmental and economic impact of oil spills, the research surrounding the frequency of disasters is examined. While the occurrence of tanker spills is lower today than in previous decades, pipeline spills are occurring more frequently and modern offshore oil rigs seem to present a particularly significant, if unlikely, threat.

Introduction

2 After a few particularly disastrous incidents in the twentieth century, world governments and businesses have been committed to drilling for and transporting oil in safe, secure ways. Close examination of the data suggests that tanker spills have been significantly reduced over time. In incidents that do occur, the volume of oil spilled is much lower and response times are faster. The data surrounding pipeline spills and the risks posed by oil rigs, however, demonstrate that advances in one area do not allow those involved to ignore problems elsewhere.

Environmental Impact of Oil Spills

3 Oil spills harm the surrounding environment in several ways. Various plants and animals can be killed, decreasing the current population and creating hazardous conditions for future generations. Many kilometers of coastline and square-kilometers of ocean can be affected. Unless removed, oil and other hazardous material can remain for many years. The local environment will continue to be impacted unless a cleanup campaign is put into action.

Glossary

Drill: a piece of machinery used to make a hole in the ground

Offshore: in the sea, not far from the coast

Oil rig: a large structure with equipment for getting oil out of the ground

(Continued)

Human and Economic Impact of Oil Spills

4 The immediate loss of human life can be an issue, especially in ship or oil-rig-related incidents. Industries that depend on the surrounding area can be severely impacted; spills on land can negatively impact farming, while spills at sea can negatively impact fishing. Long term, those living near the spill can suffer serious health effects. These factors combined can harm the economy of the surrounding area. Furthermore, along with the immediate financial impact of lost oil and damaged equipment, companies will be drawn into a variety of lawsuits. Particularly bad incidents can harm the reputation and profits of all companies involved.

Findings

Better Tankers, Fewer Spills

5 In the popular imagination, the phrase "oil spill" is often associated with tanker-related disasters. Despite some high-profile incidents decades ago, the actual number of tanker-related spill incidents has decreased in recent decades, as can be seen in Table 1. Between 1970 and 2016, there has been a dramatic decrease in the tons of oil spilled from 3.5 million tons to 43,000 tons. Total cleanup of tanker related oil spills is a difficult task. Even today, there is still an unusually high amount of oil at the site of disasters which occurred decades ago. Clear and complete safety guidelines must remain the standard practice among oil companies.

Table 1: Number of Large and Medium-Sized Tanker Spills by Decade

Decade	Number of medium spills (7.7–771 tons)	Number of large spills (>771 tons)	Quantity of oil spilled ('000 tons)
1970 – 1979	543	245	3518
1980 – 1989	360	94	1294
1990 – 1999	281	77	1248
2000 – 2009	149	32	216
2010 – 2016*	35	12	43

*Incomplete decade

More Pipelines, Growing Risk

6 Pipelines were originally seen as a safer alternative to oil tankers. While much safer overall, the pipeline network must be maintained at considerable ongoing cost. As the pipeline network ages, it will become important to maintain and replace aging pipelines. As Table 2 shows, the number of incidents since 1997 has dramatically increased. The highest number of incidents occurred in 2015, when there were 458. However, it is not clear if the increase is due entirely to the increase in the length of pipelines in operation.

Table 2: Pipeline Spills, 1997–2015

Year	Number of spills	Miles of pipeline*
1997	161	—
1998	141	—
1999	160	—
2000	138	—
2001	128	—
2002	451	—
2003	430	—
2004	363	166,669
2005	345	166,760
2006	343	166,719
2007	329	169,846
2008	368	173,789
2009	336	175,965
2010	346	181,986
2011	342	183,580
2012	363	186,221
2013	400	192,412
2014	451	199,659
2015	458	208,616

*Data available from 2004

(Continued)

Oil Rigs, Big Profits, New Hazards

7 Modern rig technology now allows companies to drill to a much greater depth; oil rigs can now drill for previously unreachable oil reserves. While each rig is thoroughly inspected, there are too many factors involved to ensure total safety and problems do, occasionally, occur. While unlikely, a catastrophic failure of safety measures on an offshore rig can result in the worst kind of disaster: a damaged rig may find itself unable to stop oil from leaking on the ocean floor.

8 Not only would such an event hurt the company's profits, the environmental damage would be enormous. Particularly deep wells may be difficult to plug, allowing entire oil reservoirs to leak into the ocean. The effect on wildlife and local economies would resemble the problems of an oil tanker spill, but would likely be many times worse. Such a leak would involve not just crude oil, but gasses and other waste as well.

Conclusion

9 Due to high profile tanker spills in the 1970s, increased awareness and regulation has lessened the frequency and size of tanker-related oil spills. The large number of pipelines currently in operation has led to a comparatively high number of pipeline spills. Care must be taken in the future to ensure that the pipeline infrastructure is maintained, as the number of spills seems to be on the rise. Oil rigs, despite their safety measures, would cause massive environmental damage in the event of a catastrophic failure and must be closely monitored.

1. What is the purpose of the abstract? What kind of information does it provide?

   ....

2. What kinds of oil spills does the article discuss?

   ....

3. How can oil spills harm the environment?

   ....

4. How can oil spills harm the economy?

   ....

5. What is the overall finding from the research on oil spills?

   ....

6. What kind of spill could cause the most harm? Why?

   ....

B. Read the article again, and look specifically in paragraphs 5 and 6 for language that is used to summarize information from the tables. Underline language that shows the time period. Double underline language that shows the trend.

C. Looking at the information that has been summarized from the tables, decide why the writer chose this information to summarize. What other information could be included in a summary of each table? Discuss your ideas with a partner.

D. Choose a table from the article and write a detailed summary of it. Use your ideas from Parts B and C to determine what important information you will include. Use the questions to help you prepare your summary.

1. What is the overall trend that the table shows?
2. Are there any increases?
3. Are there any decreases?
4. What is the largest number?
5. What is the smallest number?
6. Is there any other information that stands out?

E. Use your ideas from Parts B, C, and D of this exercise to draft a 100–150 word summary of one of the tables from the article on oil spills. Try to include Vocabulary Check words in your writing.

F. Give your first draft to a partner and get feedback using the peer review form. Write a second draft based on the suggestions you receive.

Questions	Yes	No	Notes
Does the writing address the assignment task?	☐	☐	
Can you identify the overall trend shown in the table?	☐	☐	
Can you identify key details from the table?	☐	☐	
Are any key details missing?	☐	☐	
Are the ideas clear and easy to understand?	☐	☐	
Did the writer include words from the Vocabulary Check?	☐	☐	
Are there any grammatical errors?	☐	☐	
Are there any other comments you would like to make?	☐	☐	

VOCABULARY CHECK

A. Review the items in Vocabulary Preview. Write their definitions and add examples. Use a dictionary if necessary.

B. Choose the word that has a similar meaning to the underlined word.

1. Considerable (large / small) damage has been caused by oil spills.
2. The frequency (size / rate) of oil spills is decreasing.
3. Oils spills often have a negative impact (cause / effect) on the environment.
4. One of the most well-known incidents (events / examples) is the *Deepwater Horizon* explosion.
5. Pipelines must be maintained (preserved / replaced) in order to be safe.
6. Oils spills do not occur (stop / happen) as often as they did in the past.
7. There are many oil rigs in operation (working / resting) at any time.
8. Plants and animals in the environment surrounding (away from / around) an oil spill can be harmed.

Go to MyEnglishLab to complete a vocabulary and skill practice and to join in collaborative activities.

LANGUAGE SKILL

KNOWING HOW AND WHEN TO USE THE PASSIVE VOICE

WHY IT'S USEFUL The passive voice is very common in academic writing, especially when you need to describe a process or a procedure objectively. It highlights the object of an action, rather than the subject. Knowing when, and when not, to use the passive voice is a key academic skill.

Go to MyEnglishLab for the Language Skill presentation and practice.

VOCABULARY STRATEGY

CREATING WORD CARDS

WHY IT'S USEFUL Creating and using word cards is one of the most effective methods for learning a large number of vocabulary words in a short time. It allows you to combine and practice many of the vocabulary strategies you have learned.

Word cards are used for words that you have seen or heard but are not yet familiar with. When studying in college, you will see or hear many new words each day. While there will be some words that you may never see again, there will be others that will reappear in the same or in different contexts. Make an effort to become familiar with those words. While a vocabulary journal records words in the order that they come to your attention, word cards can be rearranged to suit your needs.

For more on creating a vocabulary journal, see Business and Design, Part 1.

Making word cards

Creating a word card is simple. First, you need to buy some index cards. On the front of each card write the word that you want to learn. Make sure your handwriting is large and easy to read. Here is an example using one of the words from the Integrated Skills reading:

On the back of the card, write key information about the word. Look at the example, which includes information that is relevant to verbs.

POS: Regular, transitive verb

FAM: maintenance – N

DEF: To keep something in good condition by taking care of it

SYN: conserve, preserve

PER: I need to maintain my car so that I can save money and reduce air pollution.

Let's look at each piece of information shown on the card:

Notation	Explanation
POS = Part of Speech	Though there are other types of words, *part of speech* refers mainly to nouns, verbs, adjectives, and adverbs. Here, you can include information about the grammatical behavior of the word—whether, for example, a noun is countable, or whether a verb is regular or irregular, or transitive or intransitive.
DEF = Definition	A simple definition from a good learner's dictionary is enough. Some words have more than one definition. Since it is difficult to learn more than one definition at a time, write down only the one you need to know, as some meanings are less common than others.
FAM = Word family	Many words have more than one member of a word family. Use a good learners' dictionary to find out whether there are any common family members.
SYN = Synonyms	Using a good learner's dictionary, find one or two common words—synonyms—with a meaning similar to that of your chosen word. Not all words have good synonyms.
PER = Personal sentence	This is an essential part of the word card. Copying a definition from a dictionary is easy. To better remember the word, write a sentence which uses the word in context, but which also has personal importance for you. This is also a good place to use, and underline, a common collocation—a word that is often used with your target word. Notice how the word "need" is underlined on the card.

For more on using a dictionary to expand vocabulary, see Zoology, Part 2.

TIP

Learner's dictionaries are the best place to find the information you need to make notes on your word card.

Using word cards

Once you have made your word cards, use them to test yourself when you have free time. For example, if you use public transportation to get to class each day, test yourself while you travel. If you have a few minutes between classes, take out your word cards and test yourself. You can also find a friend who uses word cards and test each other.

First look at the front of the card, the side with just a single word. Then try to recall what information is on the other side. Turn the card over and see how much you got correct. Did you remember the part of speech? The definition? The personal sentence? It may take a few times until you fully remember all the information on the card. When you do, remove the card from the pack so you can focus on words that you are less familiar with.

While you can, and should, make an electronic version of your cards, the physical cards will help you learn the words much faster. Making word cards takes time and effort, but it is worthwhile. The physical act of creating the card by looking up information and writing it down will help you better remember the words that you need to learn.

EXERCISE 8

A. A student is gathering information in order to create word cards. Use the words and phrases in the box to complete the chart that follows. Two examples have been done for you.

disastrous	catastrophe – N catastrophically – Adv	Missing the test had catastrophic consequences for my grade.
The weather was a key factor in my decision to come to California.	One of several things that influence or cause a situation.	reason
Having an extremely bad effect and causing a lot of damage, problems, suffering, etc.	Adjective	Regular countable noun

Word	Factor	Catastrophic
1. Part of speech	Regular countable noun	Adjective
2. Definition		
3. Word family		
4. Synonym		
5. Personal sentence		

B. Use the dictionary entries and your own research to prepare a word card for each word. Compare your completed word cards with a partner.

incident: *N*, Countable
An event, especially one that is unusual, important, or violent.
One man was arrested following the ***incident****.*
Adj: **incidental**, *Adv:* **incidentally**

considerable: *Adj.*
Large enough to be important or have an effect.
a ***considerable*** *amount of money*
N: **consideration**, *V:* **consider**, *Adv:* **considerably**

currently: *Adv.*
At the present time.
Standard Oil is ***currently*** *building a large pipeline.*
Adj: **current**

C. Using a learner's dictionary, create your own word cards for three of the following words from the Vocabulary Check on page 332.

- frequency (n)
- impact (n)
- impact (v)
- occur (v)
- operation (n)
- surrounding (adj)

D. Compare your word cards with a partner. Discuss any areas of difference.

APPLY YOUR SKILLS

WHY IT'S USEFUL By applying the skills you have learned in this unit, you will be able to create appropriate tables which clearly present information about your topic. By including correctly formatted tables which accurately present your numerical data, and by summarizing their content effectively, you will be able to create clear and interesting reports on many topics.

ASSIGNMENT:
Plan a 500-word report on the destruction of the Aral Sea. Explain what happened to the sea and why. Include at least two tables of data in your report. Your report should be typed and well-presented.

BEFORE YOU WRITE

A. Before you begin your assignment, discuss these questions with one or more students.

1. Where does your drinking water come from? What about the water used to grow crops?
2. Taking water from a river or sea to grow crops is known as irrigation. In California, many crops, such as rice, are grown using water from the Colorado River. Is it better to grow crops where there is water, or take water to grow crops where it is more convenient?
3. Rivers tend to run through more than one region or country. Can one region or country take the water from a river before it reaches the next? Can a river be owned by a region or country? Who should have priority when there is a shrinking water resource—the residents who need drinking water, farmers, or other commercial interests, such as fishermen?

B. As you consider your writing assignment, complete the tasks below. Then, share your ideas with a partner. Get feedback and revise your ideas, if necessary.

1. Go online and find basic information about the Aral Sea. Where is it? What happened to it? Take notes. Then compare your notes with a partner.

....

....

....

....

....

2. Think about the kind of data that is important for understanding what happened to the Aral Sea. Make a list of possible headings that you could use in the tables for this report.

....

....

....

....

....

3. Find information from an online encyclopedia to complete the table with data illustrating the decline of the Aral Sea. Add a title and appropriate column headings. Add any other elements you feel are necessary.

Title: ....

1960	
	33,800 km^2
1998	
2004	
2007	6,800 km^2

C. Review the Unit Skills Summary. As you plan the writing task, apply the skills you learned in this unit.

UNIT SKILLS SUMMARY

Create tables

- Know when, and when not, to use a table.
- Know which information to categorize.
- Format a table correctly.

Use numbers in writing

- Know when to use figures and when to use words to write numbers.
- Understand and follow the rules of using numbers in academic writing.

Summarize a table of data

- Be able to identify key trends in a table.
- Accurately describe and summarize data from a table in your writing.

Know how and when to use the passive voice

- Form the passive voice correctly.
- Know when, and when not, to express the agent.
- Use the passive voice when appropriate or necessary.

Create word cards

- Create and use word cards to help you quickly and efficiently learn important new words that you need for your college studies.

THINKING CRITICALLY

As you think about your assignment, use the information from the earlier sections of the unit to answer the questions. Discuss your answers with one or more classmates and revise your ideas if necessary.

1. What factors have probably contributed most significantly to the destruction of the Aral Sea?
2. Do you think the Aral Sea could be restored? What measures could be taken?

THINKING VISUALLY

Look at the images of the Aral Sea and discuss with a partner what they show. What caused this to happen? How do you think this situation must be affecting people living nearby and in the wider region?

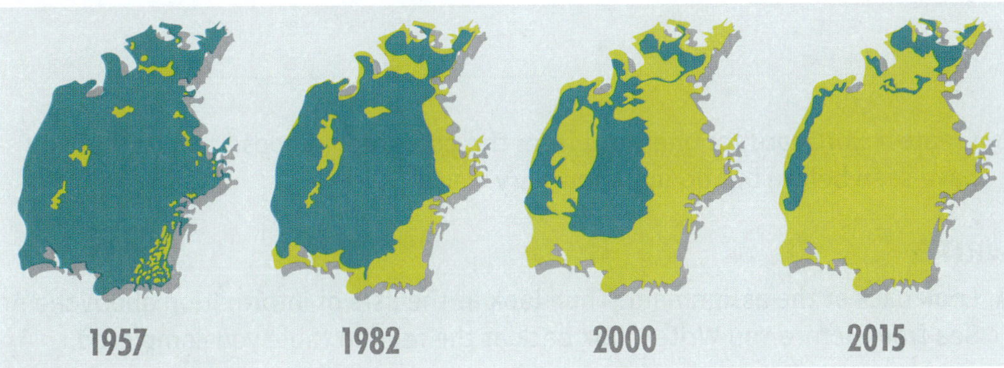

THINKING ABOUT LANGUAGE

A. Read the paragraph about the Aral Sea that has been taken from an online encyclopedia. Using information from the paragraph, write five sentences in the passive voice. Compare your sentences with a partner.

Glossary

Shrink: to become smaller

The Aral Sea was the fourth largest lake in the world until it began to shrink. In the 1960s, the government of what was then the Soviet Union redirected water from the two rivers that flowed into the Aral Sea. People call these rivers the Amu Darya and the Syr Darya. The government told farmers in the area to grow crops like cotton and rice. These crops need a lot of water. The area around the Aral Sea is a desert. Farmers relied on water from the rivers to grow these

(Continued)

water-intensive crops. Farmers used so much water that less water flowed into the Aral Sea. The amount of salt in the sea increased because there was less water. The higher level of salt killed fish and people could no longer make a living from fishing. Less water also made the sea shrink. The shrinking split the sea into several parts.

1. Water was redirected from rivers.
2. ……
3. ……
4. ……
5. ……
6. ……

B. **Create a word card for one word from the paragraph. Choose a word that you have seen before but do not know very well.**

WRITE

A. **Look back at the assignment. Then look at the lists of information about the Aral Sea from Before You Write. Look back at the related table you completed.**

B. **Do more research on the topic and take effective notes. Discuss your notes and ideas for a second, relevant table with others and make any needed adjustments. (Use the table you have already worked on as one of the required tables.)**

C. **Make an outline of your report and create the tables.**

BEYOND THE ASSIGNMENT

Write a 500-word report on the destruction of the Aral Sea. Explain what happened to the sea and why. Include at least two tables of data in your report. Your report should be typed and well-presented. Use all the skills you learned in this unit.

Go to MyEnglishLab to watch Professor Spakowitz's concluding video and to complete a self-assessment.

PART 3

Extended Writing

Part 3 presents authentic content written by university professors. Academically rigorous application and assessment activities allow for a synthesis of the skills developed in Parts 1 and 2.

How advances in biosciences raise legal, social, and ethical concerns

BIOETHICS

Writing as a Bioethicist

UNIT PROFILE

In this unit, you will watch a video interview with Professor Hank Greely, who will briefly describe how to gather ideas, explore other points of view, and become a better writer. Have you ever wondered how your professor, or an expert in the field of bioethics, develops a paper? This is your opportunity to find out more about the academic writing process.

You will write a detailed outline to plan a persuasive essay discussing whether or not people should be encouraged to have their whole genome sequenced.

For more about **BIOETHICS**, see 1 2. See also R and OC **BIOETHICS** 1 2 3.

EXTENDED WRITING

BEFORE YOU WRITE

Think about these questions before you view the interview with Professor Greely. Discuss them with a partner.

1. How do you think bioethicists get their ideas for research and writing? How do you get your own ideas?
2. What challenges do you think a bioethicist faces in organizing ideas?
3. What advice might a professor give about gathering other points of view?

THE INTERVIEW

Go to MyEnglishLab to view the interview with Professor Greely. Use the organizer to take notes while you watch. Then answer the questions in Check What You've Learned.

Glossary

Implication: something that may happen as a result of a plan, action, etc.

Branch: to divide into two or more smaller, narrower, or less important parts

Snowball: if a plan, problem, or activity snowballs, it develops or grows very quickly

Bibliography: a list of books or articles on a particular subject

Iteration: the repetition of a process

Elaborate: to give more details about something

Bias: to unfairly influence attitudes, choices, or decisions

Crucial: very important

Internalize: to make something a habit

CULTURE NOTE

Professor Greely refers to Thanksgiving dinner in his talk. In the United States, Thanksgiving occurs on the fourth Thursday in the month of November; in Canada, it occurs on the second Monday in October. The holiday began as a way of giving thanks for the blessings of the harvest. Families often gather together to share a special meal on Thanksgiving Day.

TIP

When taking notes, it often makes sense to follow the structure of the talk you are listening to. As you listen, you can leave out small words such as *a*, *an*, or *the* and use abbreviations for longer or familiar words. This allows you to capture more ideas while writing less. For example, Dvlpmts = Developments.

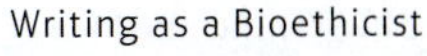

Learning from the Experts: Writing as a Bioethicist

Q1: How do you get your ideas?	Dvlpmts in sci.	
Q2: How do you get started? What brainstorming techniques do you use?	Getting started	B-storming tech.
Q3: How do you plan and organize your writing? For example, do you use outlines? Notecards?	Starts with outline	
Q4: How important is it to show more than one side of an argument?		
Q5:		
Q6:		

CHECK WHAT YOU'VE LEARNED

A. Answer the questions based on the interview with Professor Greely. Use your notes to answer the questions.

1. How does Professor Greely get most of his ideas?
   a. by reading articles about scientific developments and then asking questions
   b. by reading articles written by science journalists
   c. by reading basic articles about science
   d. all of the above

2. What brainstorming techniques does Professor Greely use in writing?
   a. He creates a detailed outline.
   b. He makes an outline using Roman numerals.
   c. He creates an outline and never changes it.
   d. He uses only four or five words.

3. How does Professor Greely plan and organize his writing?
   a. He creates a detailed initial outline and, at the same time, several smaller, less detailed ones.
   b. He uses notecards to organize all the details he wants to include in his writing.

c. He works from one outline and does not add any new information to it as he moves forward.
d. He creates an initial outline and then smaller, more detailed ones, whose information he may or may not include in the final writing.

4. How many sides of an argument does Professor Greely usually present?
   a. It depends.
   b. He only presents two.
   c. He only presents three.
   d. He typically presents five or more.

5. Why does Professor Greely present more than one side of an argument?
   a. to show that he is biased
   b. to show that he is not biased
   c. to be fair to alternative viewpoints
   d. to help him reach a conclusion

6. Why does Professor Greely believe it is important to understand opposing arguments?
   a. to test your conclusions
   b. to strengthen your conclusions
   c. to develop good counterarguments
   d. all of the above

7. What two pieces of advice does Professor Greely have for writers?
   a. Write and advise others on their writing.
   b. Write and then throw your paper away.
   c. Write and get feedback.
   d. Write one draft and hand it in.

8. What questions does Professor Greely suggest you ask if you have no one to give feedback?
   a. Is it clear? Is it relevant?
   b. Does it support my argument? Is it clear?
   c. Is it relevant? Does it support my argument?
   d. Does it support my argument? What is it doing in my paper?

B. Watch the interview again to make sure you have understood Professor Greely's comments. Then compare your answers in Part A with a partner.

Go to MyEnglishLab and use the transcript of this interview to check any answers you disagree on.

THINKING CRITICALLY

Think about the situation, keeping in mind what you learned in the interview with Professor Greely. By yourself, or with a partner, use what you know about the writing process to answer the questions.

Your assignment in your bioethics class is to write a persuasive paper on checking DNA information before hiring employees. In addition to the supporting points you have already gathered, what else do you need to include in your paper to make it as complete and persuasive as possible? How can you make your argument stronger? Explain your answers.

Go to MyEnglishLab to complete a critical thinking activity.

THINKING ABOUT LANGUAGE

UNDERSTANDING -*ING* AND -*ED* ADJECTIVES

Read the sentences from Professor Greely's essay "Whole Genome Sequencing: Uses and Challenges." Then rewrite each sentence using either the -*ing* or -*ed* form of the given adjective. An example has been done for you.

For more on using -*ing* and -*ed* adjectives correctly, see Bioethics, Part 1.

For more on paraphrasing ideas, see Business and Design, Part 2.

When whole genome sequencing (WGS) becomes sufficiently inexpensive, its medical uses will explode, bringing both benefits and challenges.

Use *worried* or *worrying.*

When whole genome sequencing (WGS) becomes more affordable, it will have more medical uses. Some of these will be beneficial, and some will be worrying.

1. At today's prices, WGS is already being used in medicine. As its price falls, its uses will grow explosively, with good and possibly bad consequences.

   Use *excited* or *exciting.*

   ....

   ....

   ....

2. WGS is being used to try to diagnose children who appear to have genetic conditions that do not fit obviously into those that are now known.

   Use *challenged* or *challenging.*

3. I expect most people with good health care to have WGS within the next 20, and possibly 10, years.

   Use *convinced* or *convincing.*

4. Today WGS reads the base sequence correctly about 99.9% of the time. That's very accurate, but making a mistake one time in a thousand in a whole genome means making 6.4 million mistakes.

   Use *troubled* or *troubling.*

5. WGS accuracy will have to improve and methods will be needed to double-check important WGS results.

   Use *improved* or *improving.*

6. If a woman mistakenly thinks having an uncertain test for a BRCA1 gene means she will get breast cancer, she may take drastic but unnecessary action.

   Use *alarmed* or *alarming.*

UNDERSTANDING HEDGING LANGUAGE

Read the sentences from Professor Greely's essay. Use appropriate hedging language to make the underlined section of each sentence more tentative. An example has been done for you.

For more on using hedging language, see Bioethics, Part 2.

When WGS becomes sufficiently inexpensive, its medical uses will explode, bringing both benefits and challenges.

When WGS becomes sufficiently inexpensive, its medical uses will probably explode, bringing both benefits and challenges.

1. But that is what is now possible for about $1,500 through WGS.

2. But each whole genome sequence will contain some important information.

3. In confusing cases, physicians will use WGS on the child, looking for something different or unusual in the child's genome that might explain the symptoms.

4. More often, it will give parents information about the child's condition and their chances of having another child with the same problems.

5. Scientists have realized that each patient's cancer has a different mix of mutations, whether the cancer started in lung, prostate, breast, or colon tissue.

6. Doctors know that certain drugs work well against cancers with particular mutations.

....

....

7. WGS will not just grow in its existing uses, but new uses will flourish.

....

....

8. WGS will soon become a routine part of a child's or adult's medical care.

....

....

9. WGS will also be used for newborn babies.

....

....

10. WGS accuracy will have to improve, and methods will be needed to double-check important WGS results.

....

....

READ

Go to MyEnglishLab to read "Whole Genome Sequencing: Uses and Challenges" for more practice reading an extended text and using your reading skills. Take notes while you read. Then answer the questions in Check What You've Learned.

For more on taking effective notes, see Bioethics, Part 1.

CHECK WHAT YOU'VE LEARNED

Answer the questions based on the essay "Whole Genome Sequencing: Uses and Challenges." Use your notes to answer the questions.

1. What is the main idea of this essay?
   a. WGS is becoming cheaper and will be used by more and more people in the future.
   b. WGS provides access to private information and should not be used.
   c. WGS can warn people about possible conditions and should be used more often.
   d. WGS is a powerful tool that has both benefits and drawbacks.

2. Which of these statements is <u>not</u> true?
   a. Professor Greely believes that having a WGS is probably a good idea.
   b. Professor Greely thinks that the cost of a WGS will continue to decrease over the next few years.
   c. Professor Greely believes that WGS will cure several different types of cancer.
   d. Professor Greely thinks that a WGS will be able to show whether babies are healthy before they are born.

3. According to Professor Greely, <u>how</u> will WGS improve newborn screening?
   a. It will be cheaper.
   b. It will test for more conditions.
   c. More states will use it.
   d. It will identify Phenylketonuria quicker.

4. Which of these statements is true about the whole genome sequence in people?
   a. The human genome sequence is very different in people, but the similarities are very important.
   b. The human genome sequence is almost the same in all people, but the differences are very important.
   c. The human genome sequence is very different in people, and the similarities are not very important.
   d. The human genome sequence is almost the same in all people, and the differences are not very important.

5. According Professor Greely, to fully understand WGS results a person needs
   a. counseling.
   b. safe storage.
   c. privacy.
   d. five hours.

6. Which of these does Professor Greely believe are concerns with regard to WGS?
   a. understanding the results, protecting the results, and paying for the results
   b. understanding the results, protecting the results, and trusting the results
   c. paying for the results, protecting the results, and trusting the results
   d. understanding the results, paying for the results, and trusting the results

7. Which of these statements is true?
   a. WGS is not accurate enough for some kinds of DNA problems.
   b. If we can read the WGS, we can understand it.
   c. WGS provides all the information people need to understand their health issues.
   d. If WGS can be stored safely, there will be no privacy issues.

8. Why does Professor Greely suggest that using WGS for non-medical use could be a problem?
   a. because it might show that a person has a mental health problem
   b. because the information could be used in a way that was not intended
   c. because it could be used by the police to solve a crime
   d. because it will show who someone is related to

GUIDED RESEARCH

ASSIGNMENT

Write a detailed outline of a persuasive essay discussing whether or not people should be encouraged to have their whole genome sequenced. In your outline, make sure you have a clearly stated position, reasons to support it, and explanatory examples. Your outline should also include a counterargument and your response to it.

A. Using Professor Greely's essay, list the benefits and challenges of using WGS.

Benefits	Challenges
1.	1.
2.	2.
3.	3.
4.	

PART 3

B. Based on what you learned about WGS in Professor Greely's essay, decide whether you are for or against people having their whole genome sequenced. Then state your position, and determine what counterargument you could include in your outline.

For more on stating an argument, see Bioethics, Part 2.

My position:

People should / should not be encouraged to have their whole genome sequenced because …

My counterargument:

Some people argue that whole genome sequencing …

C. Now, using your school's library or an online search engine, find out as much as you can about reasons that support your position. Look for examples to help you explain your reasons. Research the counterargument to understand it fully so you can develop a response. Use the questions to help with your research.

Reasons That Support My Position	My Counterargument
• What reasons can I give to support my position? • How does each reason that I am considering persuade my reader? • What examples would help someone understand each of my reasons? • Are my reasons convincing enough for me to express a strong argument? Or should I express a tentative argument?	• What reasons do people give for believing this counterargument? • What examples do people use to explain this argument? • Why don't I agree with this argument?

For more on identifying key words, see Business and Design, Part 2.

For more on using questions to guide your research, see Business and Design, Part 1.

For more on supporting an argument with examples, see Bioethics, Part 2.

WRITE

Part A

1. Based on your research, determine the reasons you will use to support your argument and persuade your reader to agree. Include specific examples you can use to add depth to your argument.

My position:

Reasons to Support My Argument	Examples to Add Depth to My Argument

2. In the same way, determine how you will handle and respond to your counterargument.

My counterargument:

Reasons People Believe My Counterargument	Refutation of My Counterargument

TIP

Your counterargument should be strong. By exploring and understanding other points of view, you can make your own arguments stronger.

Part B

1. Use your ideas from Part A and the outline template as a guide to create a detailed outline for a persuasive essay. You may modify the outline template as necessary to match your ideas.

My Position:

I. First reason to support my position
    A. Explanation
        1. Detail
        2. Detail
    B. Explanation
        1. Detail
        2. Detail

II. Second reason to support my position
    A. Explanation
        1. Detail
        2. Detail
    B. Explanation
        1. Detail
        2. Detail

III. Counterargument:
    A. Explanation
        1. Detail
        2. Detail

IV. Refutation
    A. Explanation
        1. Detail
        2. Detail

TIP

In an outline, use Roman numerals (I, II, III, etc.), letters (A, B, C, etc.), and numbers (1, 2, 3, etc.) to show the relationship between ideas. The idea expressed next to a Roman numeral should be a main idea. The idea expressed next to a letter should further explain the main idea it is under. The idea expressed with a number should be more detailed, illustrating the explanation.

PART 3

2. Work with a partner. Read each other's detailed outline and complete the peer review form. Discuss your comments and ideas.

Questions	**Yes**	**No**	**Notes**
Is the argument clearly stated?	☐	☐	
Does the writer support the argument effectively?	☐	☐	
Are examples used to help explain reasons?	☐	☐	
Is the relationship between ideas clear and easy to understand?	☐	☐	
Do the ideas fit together in an orderly, logical way?	☐	☐	
Is enough explanation provided for the counterargument?	☐	☐	
Is the refutation convincing?	☐	☐	
Are there any other comments you would like to make?	☐	☐	

3. Based on feedback from your partner, make changes to your detailed outline to improve your plan for a persuasive essay.

Go to MyEnglishLab to join in a collaborative activity.

Design principles help create business innovation

BUSINESS AND DESIGN

Writing as a Businessperson

UNIT PROFILE

In this unit, you will watch a video interview with Juli Sherry, Design Lead for Worldview Stanford, who will briefly describe how to find sources and supporting ideas. She will also talk about the importance of note-taking and how to become a better writer. Have you ever wondered how your professor, or an expert in the field of business, develops a paper? This is your opportunity to find out more about the academic writing process.

You will summarize the section about Target Corporation's business model from Juli Sherry's essay.

For more about **BUSINESS AND DESIGN**, see 1 2.
See also R and OC **BUSINESS AND DESIGN** 1 2 3.

EXTENDED WRITING

BEFORE YOU WRITE

Think about these questions before you view the interview with Juli Sherry. Discuss them with a partner.

1. How do you think businesspeople get their ideas for research or writing? How do you get your own ideas?
2. What should you do when you get stuck during the research process?
3. When do you think you should take notes, and what do you think is the most effective way to take them?

THE INTERVIEW

Go to MyEnglishLab to view the interview with Ms. Sherry. Use the organizer to take notes while you watch. Note that some of the information in the organizer is not presented in the same order as it is in the interview. Then answer the questions in Check What You've Learned.

Glossary

Subscribe: to pay to use a service or to have a newspaper or magazine sent to you regularly

Adjacent: next to something

Relational: related to how two or more ideas or people are connected

Proponent: someone who supports or argues in favor of something

Advocate: to publicly support or recommend something

TIP

Sometimes you will decide to take and organize your notes in an order that is different from the way the speaker presents the information. For example, when the speaker is talking about a process, you may choose to organize your notes in a way that most closely follows the steps of the process.

Learning From the Experts: Writing as a Businessperson

Finding sources

-
-
-
-

Finding supporting ideas

-
-
-
-

Taking notes

-
-
-
-

Getting stuck

-
-
-
-

Advice for new writers:

-
-
-
-

CHECK WHAT YOU'VE LEARNED

A. Answer the questions based on the interview with Juli Sherry. Use your notes to answer the questions.

1. How does Ms. Sherry stay informed about business news?
   a. She spends one day a week reading online business publications.
   b. She spends time each day reading business publications.
   c. She follows only one business conversation at a time.
   d. She follows the fastest moving business conversations.

2. Why does Ms. Sherry prefer online publications for staying up-to-date with business news and research?
   a. Print publications may not have the latest news.
   b. Print publications are too general.
   c. Print publications are not reliable sources.
   d. Print publications may report on only specific industries.

3. Why does she like to look "outside the box" for supporting ideas?
   a. because there are not enough business sources to find ideas
   b. because brainstorming always requires thinking "outside the box"
   c. because this is how she was trained to think as a designer
   d. because design publications are more interesting than business publications

4. According to Ms. Sherry, what is an "intersectional" publication?
   a. a publication that focuses on where two or more fields meet
   b. a publication that focuses on only one field
   c. a publication that focuses on business ideas
   d. a publication that focuses on design concepts

5. Which of these statements about the research process would she agree with?
   a. Research is an informal process in business.
   b. It is important to get feedback about your topic to help you think of new ideas.
   c. Sending emails and writing a summary is the best way to research a topic.
   d. When you get stuck in your research, change the topic.

6. When might she change a research topic?
   a. when she can't get feedback from other people
   b. when she doesn't want to brainstorm anymore
   c. when brainstorming after feedback has not worked
   d. when she is tired of the original research topic

7. Why is Ms. Sherry a big fan of note-taking?
    a. She finds that she will use notes on future projects.
    b. She relies on taking notes to help her remember what she reads.
    c. She finds that taking notes helps her organize her thoughts.
    d. She relies on taking notes to help her evaluate her sources.
8. Why does she prefer taking notes by hand?
    a. She is used to taking notes by hand.
    b. She likes old-fashioned approaches.
    c. She does not like digital note-taking systems.
    d. She remembers her notes better when she writes by hand.
9. How does Juli Sherry decide what information is relevant?
    a. If she is interested in the information, then it is relevant.
    b. If she is interested in the information, then she checks it with someone else.
    c. If she feels the information is interesting, then it is relevant.
    d. If she just keeps thinking about the information, then it is relevant.
10. Which of these pieces of advice would Ms. Sherry not agree with?
    a. Write only what you can publish.
    b. Keep practicing.
    c. Explore different writing styles online.
    d. Write short pieces.

B. Watch the interview again to make sure you have understood Ms. Sherry's comments. Then compare your answers in Part A with a partner.

Go to MyEnglishLab and use the transcript of this interview to check any answers you disagree on.

THINKING CRITICALLY

Think about the situation, keeping in mind what you learned in the interview with Ms. Sherry. By yourself, or with a partner, use what you know about the writing process to answer the question.

You have recently started a research assignment and collected several good pieces of research. However, you have decided that your chosen topic is too difficult because there is so much more information you still need to find. Other students seem to be nearly finished with their assignments, and you think they chose easier topics. Should you change your topic? Explain your answer.

Go to MyEnglishLab to complete a critical thinking activity.

THINKING ABOUT LANGUAGE

USING CONJUNCTIONS TO CONNECT IDEAS

For more on using conjunctions to connect ideas, see Business and Design, Part 1.

Read these sentence pairs, which have been paraphrased from Juli Sherry's essay "So What Is a Business Model?" Then combine both sentences in a logical way, choosing the most appropriate conjunction in parentheses. An example has been done for you.

A business model is designed to understand the operations of a business. A business model is used to understand the operations of a business. (so, but, and, even though)

A business model is used and designed to understand the operations of a business.

1. A business model describes an overall view of what makes your business successful. A business model describes the component parts of what makes your business successful. (because, whereas, and, so)

2. A business model is a part of an overall business strategy. A business model does not replace an overall business strategy. (both… and, so, but, because)

3. Describing a business model is difficult. There are many ways to approach designing one. (so, whereas, although, because)

4. Different definitions of a business model are helpful. It is useful to break a business model down into its component parts. (when, unless, and, while)

5. Target spends money on advertising through print ads in daily newspapers and TV commercials. Target spends money on online ads and billboards. (and, both… and, so, because)

6. Target Corporation manufactures products. Their main activity is working with other manufacturers to make products for their customers. (and, although, so, not only…but also)

7. Target's revenue streams come from directly selling physical products. Target's revenue streams come from a few other outlets like their sourcing services and their financial and retail services. (not only… but also, because, but, although)

8. One part of the business model changes. This means another component may also need to change. (and, if, because, as long as)

USING REPORTING VERBS

For more on using reporting verbs, see Business and Design, Part 2.

Read the statements based on Ms. Sherry's essay. Then use the reporting verb in parentheses to write a new sentence that paraphrases each statement. Indicate which reporting verbs are neutral and which are not. An example has been done for you.

A business model describes the big picture and component parts of what makes your business run and succeed. (say)

Sherry says that a business model shows not only the parts that make a business work, but also provides an overall view of the business.

PART 3

1. A business model is a tool you can use to help build a business from scratch. (state)

2. The best representations [of a business model] tend to be visual. (argue)

3. Channels are your choices about how to reach new and existing customers. (explain)

4. In order to provide this value to their customers, Target has a lot of work to do. (show)

5. The best way to start is to sit down with the Business Model Canvas and sketch out what choices you would make for each component. (claim)

6. While building your business, your model will evolve and become stronger as you grow and try different ideas. (stress)

The neutral reporting verbs are: *say,*

The non-neutral reporting verbs are:

READ

Go to MyEnglishLab to read "So What Is a Business Model?" for more practice reading an extended text and using your reading skills. Take notes while you read. Then answer the questions in Check What You've Learned.

CHECK WHAT YOU'VE LEARNED

Answer the questions based on the essay "So What Is a Business Model?" Use your notes to answer the questions.

1. What is the main idea of this essay?
   a. There are nine components of a business model.
   b. A business model guides a business as it grows.
   c. A business model cannot be described.
   d. Target has been successful in developing a business model.

2. Which of these statements about a business model is true?
   a. A business model should never change.
   b. A business model is the same as a business strategy.
   c. A business model is about understanding how a business will operate.
   d. all of the above

3. Which of these are all components of a business model?
   a. the conditions within the market, relationships with customers, and relationships with suppliers
   b. how to make money, marketing channels, and understanding the competition
   c. what the product / service is, the market conditions, and customer relationships
   d. who the customers are, how we advertise to them, and the relationship with our suppliers

4. Based on the business model in the essay, which of these people is most likely to be a customer of Target Corporation?
   a. Mr. Fred Bolger, 40 years old, and married with children
   b. Mrs. Sabrina Santiago, 38 years old, married with three children
   c. Mrs. Gina Evans, 60 years old, divorced with seven grandchildren
   d. Ms. Sonya Smith, 41 years old, single with no children

5. According to Ms. Sherry, each component of a business model should be
   a. looked at separately, in the order she has given.
   b. written on paper while sitting down.
   c. compared against other components.
   d. changed for the needs of each customer.

6. Which of these are all <u>external</u> components of a business model?
   a. channels, customer segments, and customer relationships
   b. revenue streams, cost structure, and key partners
   c. customer relationships, revenue streams, and key resources
   d. key partners, key resources, and key activities
7. Which of these statements about Target Corporation's business model is probably true?
   a. They make most of their profits through online sales.
   b. They want their customers to think of Target as a luxury brand.
   c. They believe that people still want to shop in physical stores.
   d. They aim to have the lowest price for their products.
8. If you were starting a new online ride-sharing service in your city, which of these would you probably <u>not</u> do as part of your business model?
   a. Determine how you can make sure that cars arrive on time for your customers.
   b. Look at other ride-sharing services that currently exist in your city.
   c. Find people to build an app for you so that customers can access your service.
   d. Work out how much to charge for each ride.

GUIDED RESEARCH

ASSIGNMENT

Summarize the section about Target Corporation's business model from Ms. Sherry's essay "So What Is a Business Model?"

A. Using your school's library or an online search engine, find out more about Target Corporation. Answer the questions.

1. How many stores does Target have?
2. In what countries is Target located?
3. Why does Target call their customers "guests"?
4. Who are Target's suppliers? Find 2–3 examples of Target's key partnerships.

B. Go online and find out more about the Business Model Canvas. Then complete the Business Model Canvas with the nine components of a business model. The components have been provided in the box, and first one has been inserted for you.

~~Value Proposition~~	Customer Segments	Customer Relationships
Channels	Key Activities	Key Resources
Key Partners	Cost Structure	Revenue Streams

		Value Proposition		

C. List components of the Business Model Canvas that indicate external factors affecting a business and components that indicate internal factors affecting a business.

Components indicating external factors:

....

....

Components indicating internal factors:

....

....

WRITE

PART 3

Part A

1. In preparation for your assignment, reread the section of Ms. Sherry's essay called "Target Corporation's Business Model" and highlight the important parts. Identify each place where the topic changes by creating a heading.

For more on paraphrasing ideas and summarizing, see Business and Design, Part 2.

2. List your headings in the left-hand column. Then, in the right-hand column, paraphrase the important ideas you have highlighted that are related to each heading.

My Headings	My Paraphrases

3. Use the information to help you write the opening sentence of your summary.

Author: Juli Sherry

Title: "So What Is a Business Model?"

Title of the subsection to be summarized: "Target Corporation's Business Model"

Date of publication: 2018

Main idea of the subsection to be summarized:

....

....

Your opening sentence:

....

....

Part B

1. Use your headings and paraphrases from Part A to complete the outline.

I. Introduction
- A. Opening sentence
- B. Important background information

II. Target's value proposition
- A.
- B.

III. Components indicating external factors
- A.
  1. "Minivan Mom"
  2.
- B.
  1. Physical stores
  2.
- C. Customer relationships
  1.
- D. Revenue stream
  1.

IV.
- A. Key activities
  1.
  2.
  3.
- B.
  1.
  2. Stores and equipment

PART 3

C.

1.

2. Others (architects and advertising companies)

D. Cost structure

1.

2. Write your summary. Be sure to attribute ideas to Ms. Sherry throughout the summary by using her last name, Sherry, and neutral reporting verbs.

3. Work with a partner. Read each other's summary and complete the peer review form. Discuss your comments and ideas.

TIP

Remember, you can use a pronoun to refer to the author. For example, you can refer to Ms. Sherry as "she."

TIP

Remember, a summary is an objective report of what you have read. Do not add your own opinions.

Questions	**Yes**	**No**	**Notes**
Is the first sentence correct?	☐	☐	
Is there enough attribution?	☐	☐	
Do the ideas fit together in an orderly, logical way?	☐	☐	
Are any important ideas missing?	☐	☐	

4. Based on feedback from your partner, revise your summary and prepare your final draft.

Go to MyEnglishLab to join in a collaborative activity.

ZOOLOGY

Writing as a Scientist

UNIT PROFILE

In this unit, you will watch a video interview with Professor Caitlin O'Connell-Rodwell, who will briefly describe how and when she writes her introductions and conclusions, and how she decides whether or not to use a diagram to describe a process. She also shares her advice on how to become a better writer. Have you ever wondered how your professor, or an expert in the field of zoology, develops a paper? This is your opportunity to find out more about the academic writing process.

You will write a short essay about a ritual that male elephants use to maintain social bonds. Your essay should include an introduction with a clear thesis statement, a description of the ritual process, and a conclusion.

For more about **ZOOLOGY**, see 1 2. See also R and OC **ZOOLOGY** 1 2 3.

EXTENDED WRITING

BEFORE YOU WRITE

Think about these questions before you view the interview with Professor O'Connell-Rodwell. Discuss them with a partner.

1. How do you think scientists get their ideas for research or writing? How do you get your own ideas?
2. What do you think might be the most difficult part of writing an introduction and a conclusion for a paper?
3. What do you think are the challenges in describing a process clearly?

THE INTERVIEW

Go to MyEnglishLab to view the interview with Professor O'Connell-Rodwell. Use the organizer to take notes while you watch. Then answer the questions in Check What You've Learned.

Glossary

Synthesize: to combine different things in order to produce something

Iteration: the repetition of a process

Abstract: based on ideas rather than specific examples or real events

Analogy: a way of explaining something by saying it is similar to something else

Elucidate: to explain something by providing more information

Suite: a set of matching items

Jargon: words and phrases used by people in the same profession that are difficult for other people to understand

Distill: to pull out the basic meaning of something

TIP

Often, a speaker compares and contrasts key information as part of a talk. When this happens, it is useful to lay out clearly the similarities and differences as you take notes. Also, when you go over your notes later, you can make a point of highlighting similarities and differences so they will stand out.

Learning from the Experts: Writing as a Scientist

Writing Introductions	Writing Conclusions

Describing Processes	Advice for New Writers

CHECK WHAT YOU'VE LEARNED

A. Answer the questions based on the interview with Professor O'Connell-Rodwell. Use your notes to answer the questions.

1. Why does Professor O'Connell-Rodwell compare writing a scientific paper with writing a narrative?
   a. They both introduce important characters.
   b. They both focus only on major events.
   c. They both have a long and interesting introduction.
   d. They both have a clear beginning, middle, and end.

2. What statement about introductions would Professor O'Connell-Rodwell agree with?
   a. Write your introduction first and don't change it.
   b. Write your introduction at the end of the writing process.
   c. Write your introduction first, but change it as your paper changes.
   d. Write your introduction after you understand the narrative of your paper.

3. Why does the professor write her conclusion last?
   a. She is not ready to pull all the pieces of the paper together until the end.
   b. She thinks that writing the conclusion is the hardest part.
   c. She does not like writing the conclusion and saves it for last.
   d. She thinks that the meaning of the paper is found in the conclusion.

4. Which of these statements about introductions and conclusions would she agree with?
   a. The introduction is hard, but the conclusion is easy.
   b. Writing introductions and conclusions is fun.
   c. She looks forward to writing the introduction and conclusion.
   d. The introduction is easy, but the conclusion is hard.

5. According to Professor O'Connell-Rodwell,
   a. some people only read the introduction.
   b. some people only read the conclusion.
   c. introductions and conclusions are key parts of a paper.
   d. people usually don't read the introductions and conclusions.

6. When does the professor suggest using a diagram?
   a. when people are familiar with the process
   b. when a visual will make it clearer for the reader
   c. when there is a table of behaviors
   d. all of the above

7. How does she make sure a process is easy to understand?
   a. She describes it to her neighbor and her grandmother.
   b. She uses technical language to explain science accurately.
   c. She thinks about a reader who is unfamiliar with the topic.
   d. She asks someone else to describe the process for her.

8. What advice does Professor O'Connell-Rodwell have for new writers?
   a. Read widely, and make sure you know about your subject area.
   b. Write stories with a beginning, middle, and end.
   c. Find out what your colleagues are reading.
   d. Write clearly and concisely about your topic because it is always changing.

B. Watch the interview again to make sure you have understood Professor O'Connell-Rodwell's comments. Then compare your answers in Part A with a partner.

Go to MyEnglishLab and use the transcript of this interview to check any answers you disagree on.

THINKING CRITICALLY

Think about the situation, keeping in mind what you learned in the interview with Professor O'Connell-Rodwell. By yourself, or with a partner, use what you know about the writing process to answer the question.

An assignment in your zoology class asks you to describe a complex process relating to the lifecycle of fruit flies. How can you make sure that your process description is clear and easy enough for a general audience to follow? Explain your answer.

Go to MyEnglishLab to complete a critical thinking activity.

For more on using gerunds and infinitives correctly, see Zoology, Part 1.

THINKING ABOUT LANGUAGE

USING GERUNDS AND INFINITIVES CORRECTLY

Read the sentences from Professor O'Connell-Rodwell's essay "The Role of Ritual in Male African Elephants." Then, using the pair of verbs provided, write a shorter version of each sentence. Use the gerund or infinitive form for the second verb. An example has been done for you.

When males of a species are that much larger than females, it is usually an indication of male-male competition—where adult males challenge each other physically for access to mates.

Verbs: seem / mean

A large size difference between males and females seems to mean there is competition between males.

1. Weighing an average of 250 pounds at birth, an elephant calf can stand within minutes and walk within hours, keeping up with the rest of the family.

   Verbs: learn / walk

   ....

   ....

   ....

2. In his mid-to-late teens, a male spends time with other teen and adult males, reuniting with family for some period before moving off again.

   Verbs: begin / leave

   ....

   ....

   ....

3. Male elephants have an extensive social network within which they have either a single or group of close associates of mixed ages within a larger population.

   Verbs: enjoy / have

   ....

   ....

   ....

4. Adult male elephants anticipate male-male combat by engaging in another important ritual learned at an early age—sparring.

   Verbs: learn / compete

   ....

   ....

   ....

5. These coordinated vocalizations are well documented within family groups where the matriarch initiates departure by emitting a "let's go" vocalization.

   Verbs: decide / leave

   ....

   ....

   ....

6. Even the mere presence of an older bull can affect the expression of testosterone in younger males and serve to mitigate aggressive outbursts that are often exhibited in sub-adult males, hence highlighting the importance of elders within a healthy elephant population.

   Verbs: appear / relax

   ....

   ....

   ....

USING CAUSATIVE VERBS

For more on using causative verbs, see Zoology, Part 2.

Read these sentences, which are based on Professor O'Connell-Rodwell's essay. Then use the most appropriate causative verb to combine each pair of sentences into a single sentence. An example has been done for you.

A male elephant is large. This is useful when it wants to move a large object.

Use *help someone (to) do something* or *get or have something done.*

A male elephant's size helps it to move large objects.

1. Baby elephants develop quickly. Within hours they can keep up with the rest of the family.

   Use *get someone to do something* or *let someone do something.*

   ....

   ....

2. Male elephants play fight with each other. They use signals to show they want to play fight.

   Use *get or have something done* or *get someone to do something.*

   ....

   ....

3. Male elephants use many rituals. They learn these rituals within a family.

   Use *help someone (to) do something* or *make someone do something.*

   ....

   ....

4. The trunk-to-mouth ritual is used to show respect. Smaller males have to use it to show respect to larger and stronger males.

   Use *help someone do something* or *have someone do something.*

   ....

   ....

5. Male elephants use the trunk-to-mouth ritual. It is used to strengthen social bonds between them.

   Use *make someone do something* or *have someone do something*.

   ....

   ....

6. Play fighting is useful. It is a way for male elephants to test their strength against other males.

   Use *let someone do something* or *get or have something done*.

   ....

   ....

7. The lead male elephant chooses when to leave a waterhole. Other elephants in the group have to leave.

   Use *get someone to do something* or *have someone do something*.

   ....

   ....

READ

Go to MyEnglishLab to read "The Role of Ritual in Male African Elephants" for more practice reading an extended text and using your reading skills. Take notes while you read. Then answer the questions in Check What You've Learned.

CHECK WHAT YOU'VE LEARNED

Answer the questions based on the essay "The Role of Ritual in Male African Elephants." Use your notes to answer the questions.

1. What is the main idea of this essay?
   a. Male elephants are larger than female elephants.
   b. Male elephants interact with each other in different ways.
   c. Elders are important to the development of younger males.
   d. The lifecycle of the male elephant is relatively long.

2. Which of these communication methods are discussed?
   a. tactile, visual, and acoustic
   b. acoustic, visual, and chemical
   c. visual, acoustic, and seismic
   d. chemical, tactile, and seismic

3. Compared to an average male, an average female elephant might be
    a. ten thousand pounds in weight, and seven feet tall.
    b. eight thousand pounds in weight, and twelve feet tall.
    c. twelve thousand pounds in weight, and six feet tall.
    d. nine thousand pounds in weight, and nine feet tall.
4. The trunk-to-mouth action is used for which of these reasons?
    a. departing from a watering hole
    b. challenging another male
    c. greeting each other
    d. all of the above

5. *Sparring* probably means
    a. "fighting."
    b. "playing."
    c. "play fighting."
    d. "weightlifting."
6. According to Professor O'Connell-Rodwell's essay, male elephants
    a. like to maintain a social structure within the group.
    b. fight regularly to decide who leads the group.
    c. leave the group after losing a fight.
    d. are lonely and only come together at a waterhole.
7. Which of these statements about the "let's go" rumble vocalization is true?
    a. It signals that other elephants can use the waterhole.
    b. It tells distant elephants how to find the group.
    c. It tells the group that the leader is leaving.
    d. all of the above
8. According to the essay, older male elephants
    a. are playmates for younger elephants.
    b. guide younger males as they grow up.
    c. help find good water holes.
    d. teach appropriate rituals to young males.

GUIDED RESEARCH

ASSIGNMENT

Write a short essay about a ritual that male elephants use to maintain social bonds. Your essay should include an introduction with a clear thesis statement, a description of the ritual process, and a conclusion.

A. Professor O'Connell-Rodwell describes three rituals that male elephants use to maintain social bonds. The rituals are processes. Using your school's library or an online search engine, find out as much as you can about each ritual process and complete the chart. Use the questions to guide your research.

1. Why is each ritual important?
2. Can I relate this ritual to familiar ideas?
3. What are the steps, or stages, of the ritual process, and in what order do they occur?

For more on describing a process, see Zoology, Part 2.

	The Trunk-to-Mouth Ritual	The Sparring Ritual	The Let's Go Ritual
1.			
2.			
3.			

B. Determine which of the three rituals you will write about. Then create a diagram showing the ritual process, which you can use in your essay.

WRITE

Part A

1. Determine the information you will include in the introduction of your essay. Remember, you need to give a general overview and then narrow the topic. What will your thesis statement be?

For more on writing an introduction and understanding and using thesis statements, see Zoology, Part 1.

TIP

Make sure your thesis statement provides the main idea of your essay and an outline of the points you will present in your essay.

General Overview and Narrowing of the Topic:

....

....

Thesis Statement:

....

....

2. Now think about your conclusion. Which type of final thought will you use?

....

....

TIP

Restate the main points of your essay in the conclusion. However, be sure to vary your wording. Don't simply repeat or paraphrase the thesis statement.

For more on writing a conclusion, see Zoology, Part 1.

Part B

1. Use your ideas from Part A and the outline template as a guide to create a detailed outline for your essay. You may modify the outline template as necessary to match your ideas.

I. Introduction
   A. General topic
   B. Narrowed topic
   C. Thesis statements

II. Your chosen ritual

A. How ritual maintains social bonds

B. Description of ritual process

1. ...

2. ...

3. ...

III. Conclusion

A. Restatement of main points

B. Final thought

2. Write your essay. Be sure to use your thesis statement to guide you.
3. Work with a partner. Read each other's essay and complete the peer review form. Discuss your comments and ideas.

Questions	Yes	No	Notes
Is there a general overview of the topic?	☐	☐	
Are there two or more specific sentences to narrow the topic?	☐	☐	
Is there a clear thesis statement?	☐	☐	
Did the writer use new wording in the conclusion to explain the main points again?	☐	☐	
Did the writer provide an effective final thought at the end of the paper?	☐	☐	

4. Based on feedback from your partner, revise your essay and prepare your final draft.

Go to MyEnglishLab to join in a collaborative activity.

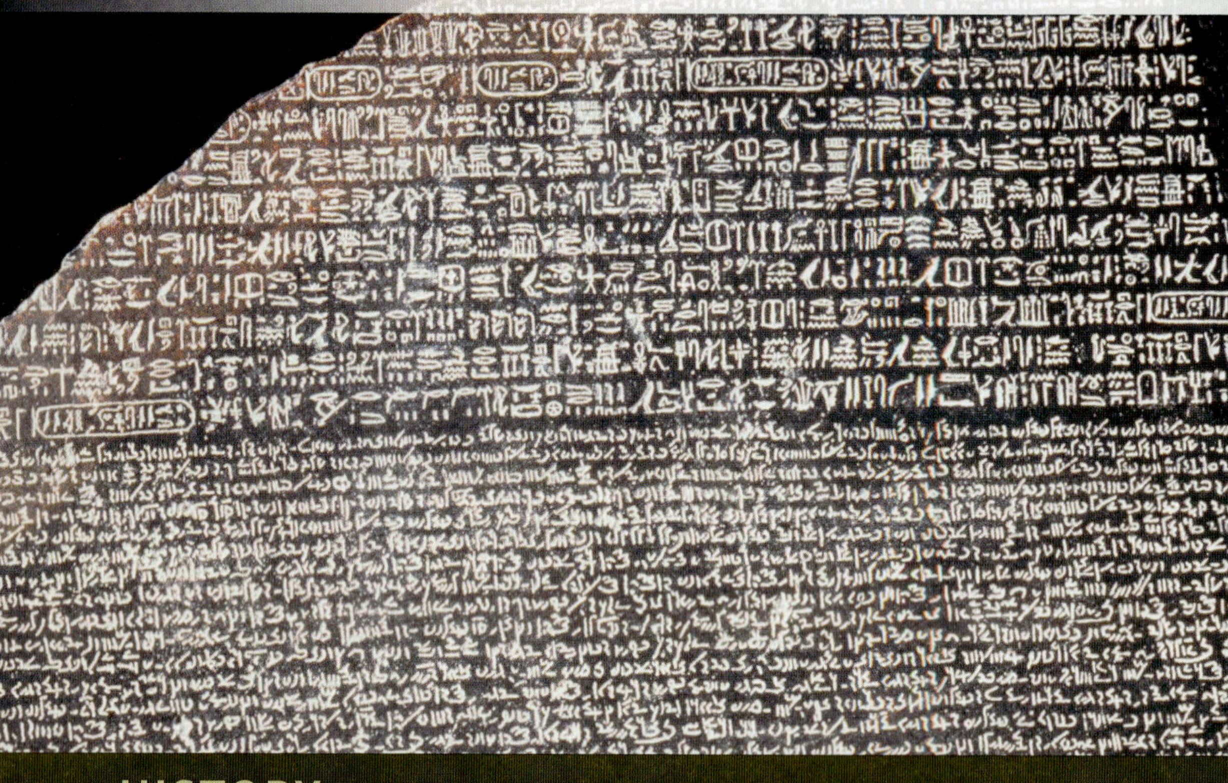

HISTORY

Writing as a Historian

UNIT PROFILE

In this unit, you will watch a video interview with Dr. Patrick N. Hunt, who will describe where to find ideas for writing, how to choose an appropriate style and tone, and what the process of getting feedback and revising is. He also gives advice for new writers in the field of history. Have you ever wondered how your professor, or an expert in the field of history, develops a paper? This is your opportunity to find out more about the academic writing process.

You will write 1–2 narrative paragraphs about the discovery of the Rosetta Stone. Be sure to include a clear chronological organization and descriptive language.

For more about **HISTORY**, see 1 2. See also R and OC **HISTORY** 1 2 3.

EXTENDED WRITING

BEFORE YOU WRITE

Think about these questions before you view the interview with Dr. Hunt. Discuss them with a partner.

1. How do you think historians get their ideas for research or writing? How do you get your own ideas?
2. How long do you wait before revising a paper?
3. Who would you ask for feedback on your writing? Why?

THE INTERVIEW

Go to MyEnglishLab to view the interview with Dr. Hunt. Use the organizer to take notes while you watch. Then answer the questions in Check What You've Learned.

Glossary

Rush to say: to say something too quickly without enough thought

Embed: to put something firmly and deeply into something else

Condescending: showing that you think you are better or more important than other people

Pithy: expressed in a brief way

Template: a document that you use as a model for producing many similar documents

Tentative: not yet certain; possible

Candid: honest, even about things that are unpleasant or embarrassing

Get rusty: to forget how to do something

CULTURE NOTE

Dr. Hunt mentions a "quasi-famous, pseudo-archaeologist" in his talk. He is referring to a quote by Indiana Jones in the 1989 movie *Indiana Jones and the Last Crusade*. Indiana Jones is a fictional adventurer who finds rare artifacts. While the movie got many people interested in archaeology, many archaeologists were upset by the character's actions, which often involved destroying a site to find the treasure.

TIP

Grouping ideas together when taking notes is a useful way to organize the ideas you hear. It will make it easier to understand your notes when you refer to them later on.

Learning from the Experts: Writing as a Historian

IDEAS FOR RESEARCH can come from:

1. ....

2. ....

3. ....

The **WRITING STYLE AND TONE** depend on:

....

Dr. Hunt **ORGANIZES HIS WRITING** by using:

....

FEEDBACK can come from:

1. ....

2. ....

3. ....

The **ADVICE FOR NEW WRITERS** includes:

1. ....

2. ....

CHECK WHAT YOU'VE LEARNED

A. Answer the questions based on the interview with Dr. Hunt. Use your notes to answer the questions.

1. Where does Dr. Hunt get ideas for his research?
   a. libraries
   b. other fields
   c. student questions
   d. all of the above

2. How does he describe his style of writing?
   a. He uses a technical style, with a lot of jargon.
   b. He writes in a way that is similar to the way he speaks.
   c. He assumes his readers know a lot about the topic.
   d. He assumes his readers do not know much about the topic.

3. Which of these best matches the style Dr. Hunt says he uses in writing?
   a. The Neolithic era is characterized by rapid agricultural advances.
   b. People learned how to be better farmers during the New Stone Age.
   c. People got better at farming during the New Stone Age.
   d. The Neolithic era, or New Stone Age, is known as a time when people advanced their knowledge of farming.

4. Which of these statements would he agree with?
   a. It's most important to match your style of writing to your audience.
   b. It's most important to be technical when writing for a general audience.
   c. It's most important to be creative when writing for a professional audience.
   d. It's most important to entertain your readers, no matter which audience.

5. How does he organize his writing?
   a. He uses an outline to begin writing.
   b. He starts writing without a plan.
   c. His hypothesis directs his writing.
   d. His conclusion directs his writing.

6. What does Dr. Hunt suggest is important when revising?
   a. getting your best ideas into the first draft
   b. working on other projects between drafts
   c. having enough time between drafts
   d. asking others to provide feedback on drafts

7. What advice would he probably give about getting feedback?
   a. Find someone you trust to say nice things about your writing.
   b. Find a good editor who will provide feedback very quickly.
   c. Get feedback from as many different types of people as possible.
   d. Read your work aloud so you can hear the mistakes you have made.

8. Why does he like to get feedback from readers who are unfamiliar with his field?
   a. They are knowledgeable about the field.
   b. They can determine if he has explained the content adequately.
   c. They can provide detailed, technical feedback on his writing.
   d. They are more honest with feedback than a professional editor.

9. What advice does Dr. Hunt have for new writers?
   a. Continue until your reader understands.
   b. Write until you can walk away.
   c. Submit your writing for publication.
   d. Keep writing every day and get feedback.

B. Watch the interview again to make sure you have understood Dr. Hunt's comments. Then compare your answers in Part A with a partner.

Go to MyEnglishLab and use the transcript of this interview to check any answers you disagree on.

THINKING CRITICALLY

Think about the situation, keeping in mind what you learned in the interview with Dr. Hunt. By yourself, or with a partner, use what you know about the writing process to answer the questions.

Your assignment in your history class is to write an essay on an important twentieth-century archaeological discovery. Your peers, students in an introductory history class, are your intended audience. What do you need to keep in mind about the style and tone of the essay you write? What should you remember about register?

For more on understanding register, see Bioethics, Part 1.

For more on identifying style and tone, see History, Part 2.

Go to MyEnglishLab to complete a critical thinking activity.

THINKING ABOUT LANGUAGE

USING NARRATIVE VERB TENSES

A. Read the sentences from Dr. Hunt's essay "Changing History by Accident: How Accidents Can Uncover Important Archaeological Finds." Look at the example, and decide on the order of events described in each sentence.

For more on using narrative tenses, see History, Part 1.

Because the Napoleonic War was unfolding in the Mediterranean, the British Navy planned to blockade French forces around the mouths of the Nile.

First: *The Napoleonic War was unfolding in the Mediterranean.*

Second: *The British Navy planned to blockade French forces around the mouths of the Nile.*

1. When his workers prized the stone out of the earth and turned it over, Bouchard suddenly noticed an unusual inscription on the side now facing up.

   First: ....

   Second: ....

2. Pompeii was a Roman city, buried and forgotten after the volcanic Mount Vesuvius erupted in AD 79.

   First: ....

   Second: ....

3. [Pompeii] was discovered accidentally around 1750 by farmers who had gradually moved back into the region, which had been completely covered by volcanic debris.

   First: ....

   Second: ....

4. While digging wells and basements in this rich soil of the old volcanic landscape above ancient Pompeii, the farmers also found large sculptures and other intact treasures, often a few meters under the surface.

   First: ....

   Second: ....

5. [The Bourbon King of Naples] hired engineers and teams of workers to bring more objects to light. Soon, the king's filling of his palace with excavated objects caught the attention of the world.

   First: ....

   Second: ....

   Third: ....

B. Read the information taken from Dr. Hunt's essay. Look at the example, and use the narrative verb tense specified to connect the ideas.

First event: Pompeii was discovered.
Second event: Archaeological methods improved.
Narrative verb tense: Past simple

Archaeological methods improved after Pompeii was discovered.

1. First event: A French officer was rebuilding a harbor.
   Second event: He discovered the Rosetta Stone.
   Narrative verb tense: Past perfect progressive

   ....

   ....

2. First event: Pierre François Xavier Bouchard discovered the Rosetta Stone.
   Second event: Thomas Young and Jean-François Champollion worked for twenty years to unlock its secrets.
   Narrative verb tense: Past perfect

3. First event: The Rosetta Stone was unlocked.
   Second event: Ancient Egyptian hieroglyphs could be understood.
   Narrative verb tense: Past simple

4. First event: Pompeii began to recover from an earthquake that struck in AD 63.
   Second event: Mount Vesuvius erupted in AD 79.
   Narrative verb tense: Past progressive

5. First event: Farmers brought the treasures they found to the Bourbon King of Naples.
   Second event: The Bourbon King of Naples ordered engineers to find more.
   Narrative verb tense: Past simple

USING COMPARE-AND-CONTRAST LANGUAGE

Read these sentences, which are based on Dr. Hunt's essay. Look at the examples, and use the most appropriate compare-and-contrast option to connect the ideas accurately.

For more on using compare-and-contrast language, see History, Part 2.

For more on using conjunctions to connect ideas, see Business and Design, Part 1.

The discovery of the Rosetta Stone was accidental.
The discovery of Pompeii was accidental.

Use *whereas* or *both*.

The discoveries of the Rosetta Stone and Pompeii were both accidental.

The discovery of the Rosetta Stone was accidental. The discovery of the Ashurbanipal Library was intentional.

Use *not only … but also* or *in contrast*.

The discovery of the Rosetta Stone was accidental. In contrast, the discovery of the Ashurbanipal Library was intentional.

1. Pompeii was discovered in Italy. The Rosetta Stone was discovered in Egypt.

   Use *likewise* or *whereas.*

2. The person who discovered the Rosetta Stone was an army officer. The people who discovered Pompeii were farmers.

   Use *but* or *in the same way.*

3. The Rosetta Stone helped historians understand Egyptian hieroglyphs. Pompeii helped historians understand ancient Rome.

   Use *similarly* or *not only...but also.*

4. The discovery of the Rosetta Stone helped improve archaeology as a science. The discovery of the Rosetta Stone helped improve the methods used in archaeology.

   Use *and* or *despite.*

5. The roads in Pompeii were built with a camber so that rain flowed to the sides. Modern roads are built with a camber.

   Use *in the same way* or *yet.*

6. Evidence at Pompeii suggests that the eruption lasted several days. The writings of Pliny the Younger suggest the eruption lasted several days.

   Use *nevertheless* or *both...and.*

READ

Go to MyEnglishLab to read "Changing History by Accident: How Accidents Can Uncover Important Archaeological Finds" for more practice reading an extended text and using your reading skills. Take notes while you read. Then answer the questions in Check What You've Learned.

CHECK WHAT YOU'VE LEARNED

Answer the questions based on the essay "Changing History by Accident: How Accidents Can Uncover Important Archaeological Finds." Use your notes to answer the questions.

1. What is the main idea of this essay?
   a. The most important archaeological discoveries are accidental.
   b. Pompeii was a large city that was destroyed in AD 79.
   c. Accidental discoveries changed our understanding of history.
   d. The Rosetta Stone unlocked the ancient Egyptian language.

2. According to Dr. Hunt, which of these statements about the Rosetta Stone and Pompeii discoveries is <u>not</u> true?
   a. They helped to improve the methods used in archaeology.
   b. They helped change archaeology from the study of books to the study of ancient remains.
   c. They were the most important accidental finds of all.
   d. They helped historians understand other discoveries.

3. According to the essay, the Rosetta Stone was found by
   a. Pierre François Xavier Bouchard.
   b. Samuel Johnson.
   c. Thomas Young.
   d. Jean-François Champollion

Pompeii, with Mt. Vesuvius in the background

4. *Decipherment* probably means
   a. "understanding a text."
   b. "understanding Greek."
   c. "understanding Egyptian hieroglyphs."
   d. "competing to read a text."

5. According to the essay, Pompeii was discovered by
   a. the Bourbon King of Naples.
   b. trained archaeologists.
   c. Samuel Johnson.
   d. none of the above

6. Why does Dr. Hunt use the word *rich* to describe the soil that covered Pompeii?
   a. because it was full of treasure
   b. because the farmers became rich after finding the treasure
   c. because it was good soil for growing crops
   d. because Pompeii was a wealthy city

7. Which of these statements about Pompeii is true?
   a. Some people survived the eruption and escaped.
   b. The roads couldn't be used when it rained.
   c. There were no street names, so you had to ask a local for directions.
   d. People left Pompeii after the earthquake in AD 63.

8. What does Dr. Hunt suggest about living in Pompeii?
   a. There were around 25,000 houses.
   b. Every house had 10 people in it.
   c. Houses came in several different shapes and sizes.
   d. All families had a few servants.

GUIDED RESEARCH

ASSIGNMENT

Write 1–2 narrative paragraphs about the discovery of the Rosetta Stone. Be sure to include clear chronological organization and descriptive language.

A. Using information from Dr. Hunt's essay, your school's library, or online sources, find out as much as you can about the discovery of the Rosetta Stone. Use the questions to help with your research.

1. Where was the Rosetta Stone discovered and whom was it discovered by?
2. Why is the Rosetta Stone such an important discovery?
3. Besides the discoverer, who else helped determine the importance of the Rosetta Stone?

B. Learn more about Egypt in 1799. Use your school's library or an online search engine. Use the questions to help with your research.

1. Who is Napoleon Bonaparte? Why was his army in Egypt in 1799?
2. Where is the town of Rosetta? How long have people lived there? What is its Arabic name?
3. Describe the climate of Rosetta.
4. What do you think life was like for a French soldier in Rosetta in 1799?

WRITE

Part A

1. Complete the chart to plan your narrative paragraph(s) about the discovery of the Rosetta Stone.

For more on using narrative writing, see History, Part 1.

Planning Questions	Answers
What is the story about?	
Who are the characters?	
What happened?	
Where did it happen?	
When did it happen?	
Why did it happen?	
How did it happen?	

2. Looking at your responses to the planning questions in Exercise 1, determine which events occurred at the beginning, in the middle, and at the end of the narrative. List them below:

For more on using chronological organization, see History, Part 1.

TIP

Since narratives should have a clear beginning, middle, and end, you will most likely use earliest to latest chronological organization in your narrative paragraph(s).

Beginning: ....

....

....

Middle: ....

....

End: ....

....

3. What descriptive language can you use to help bring your reader into this historical scene? Complete the chart, describing people, places, objects, and experiences that will be a part of your narrative, to gather ideas.

Description of	Examples of Descriptive Language
People	
Places	
Objects	
Experiences	

For more on writing a descriptive paragraph and using adjectives, see History, Part 2.

TIP

Remember, adjectives are usually placed before a noun, and it is not common to use more than two adjectives to describe the noun.

Part B

1. Using your ideas from Part A, write a first draft of your narrative paragraph(s).
2. Work with a partner. Read each other's narrative and complete the peer review form. Discuss your comments and ideas.

TIP

Remember, the best descriptions show your reader something; they do not just tell your reader. For example, instead of saying the Rosetta Stone was heavy, you could describe the effort required to lift it.

Questions	Yes	No	Notes
Did the narrator describe the character(s)?	☐	☐	
Is the setting of the narrative clear?	☐	☐	
Is there a distinct beginning, middle, and end to the narrative?	☐	☐	
Did the writer include specific descriptive language?	☐	☐	

3. Based on feedback from your partner, revise your narrative and prepare your final draft.

Go to MyEnglishLab to join in a collaborative activity.

The town of Rosetta around the time of the discovery of the Rosetta Stone

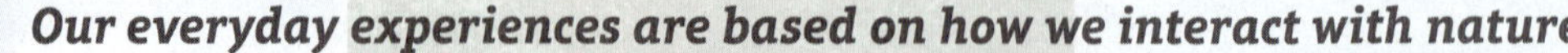

CHEMICAL ENGINEERING

Writing as a Chemical Engineer

UNIT PROFILE

In this unit, you will watch a video interview with Professor Andrew Spakowitz, who will describe how to make your academic writing more creative, interesting, and visually appealing. Have you ever wondered how your professor, or an expert in the field of chemical engineering, decides on the layout and organization of a paper? This is your opportunity to find out more about the process.

You will write 1–2 paragraphs about a synthetic material—a material that has been invented, rather than produced naturally. You will create a clear and concise heading for the section and choose a visual to support the main idea.

For more about **CHEMICAL ENGINEERING**, see 1 2.
See also R and OC **CHEMICAL ENGINEERING** 1 2 3.

EXTENDED WRITING

BEFORE YOU WRITE

Think about these questions before you view the interview with Professor Spakowitz. Discuss them with a partner.

1. How do you think chemical engineers get their ideas for research or writing? How do you get your own ideas?
2. What challenges do you think chemical engineers face in making their writing interesting?
3. How do you decide upon appropriate headings and subheadings for your writing? How do you choose visuals?

THE INTERVIEW

Go to MyEnglishLab to view the interview with Professor Spakowitz. Use the organizer to take notes while you watch. Then answer the questions in Check What You've Learned.

Glossary

Notion: an idea, belief, or opinion about something, especially one that is wrong
Endeavor: an attempt to do something new or difficult
Infusing: filling
Leverage: to use something for your benefit
Adhere: to stick firmly to something
Aesthetic: the guidelines of a kind of art
Conceptual: dealing with ideas, or based on them
Expansive: very friendly and willing to talk a lot
Delve: to research in detail
Nitty-gritty: small details

TIP

Speakers often talk about several main topics during the course of an interview. However, the details about each topic may be covered in different places. Use headings (and subheadings) in your notes to group information by topic. This way, you can add information when the speaker returns to a topic.

Learning from the Experts: Writing as a Chemical Engineer
1. Making papers interesting and effective • • • •
2. Using visual aids • • • •
3. Creating effective headings and subheadings • • • •
4. • • • •

CHECK WHAT YOU'VE LEARNED

A. Answer the questions based on the interview with Professor Spakowitz. Use your notes to answer the questions.

1. How does Professor Spakowitz make his papers more interesting?
   a. He tells stories that are interesting.
   b. He uses visuals, charts, and tables appropriately.
   c. He tries to be overly complex whenever possible.
   d. He argues that scientific writing is not very creative.

2. According to Professor Spakowitz, what should effective scientific writers be able to do?
   a. keep their writing simple
   b. add enthusiasm to their writing
   c. be creative in their writing
   d. all of the above

3. Which of these statements about visual appearance would the professor agree with?
   a. The title and the abstract are the most important.
   b. Eye-catching visual aids are the most important.
   c. Being easy for the reader to follow is the most important.
   d. The layout is the most important.
4. What does the professor say is important to remember when making a visual aid?
   a. The visual aid should be as visually appealing as possible.
   b. The chosen visual aid should be appropriate for the content.
   c. The visual aid should be simple.
   d. The visual aid should be complex.
5. What kinds of headings are effective according to the professor?
   a. simple headings that communicate the outline of the paper
   b. long headings that tell exactly what a section is about
   c. long headings that help readers understand the details
   d. simple headings that show one layer of the paper
6. According to Professor Spakowitz, why are headings and subheadings important?
   a. They help guide people who read for different reasons.
   b. They are simple and clear, and identify what the section is about.
   c. They are an alternative way for people to fully understand the paper.
   d. They provide an outline for a writer to follow.
7. What warning does he give about tables?
   a. Readers will only look at a table for a few seconds.
   b. A table should only be used to convey complex information.
   c. If the table is too complex, the reader will not understand it.
   d. Readers will look at your table, rather than read your paper.
8. Which reason does Professor Spakowitz not give for avoiding the passive voice?
   a. It is too indirect.
   b. It is too formal.
   c. It is too complex.
   d. It is often unnecessary.

9. What advice does he have for writers?
   a. Practice by writing and talking about your topics.
   b. Learn how to explain complex concepts in a simple way.
   c. Let your personality show in your writing style.
   d. all of the above

10. According to the professor, what is the biggest challenge for a writer?
    a. to convince people to read your writing
    b. to be simple and clear in your writing
    c. to practice writing about what you do
    d. to develop your own voice in your writing

B. Watch the interview again to make sure you have understood Professor Spakowitz's comments. Then compare your answers in Part A with a partner.

Go to MyEnglishLab and use the transcript of this interview to check any answers you disagree on.

THINKING CRITICALLY

Think about the situation, keeping in mind what you learned in the interview with Professor Spakowitz. By yourself, or with a partner, use what you know about the writing process to answer the questions.

An assignment in your chemical engineering class is to write a report on the behavior of molecules as they change from solids to liquids. How would you create effective and appropriate headings and subheadings for your written response? How would you make your report more visually appealing? Explain your answers.

Go to MyEnglishLab to complete a critical thinking activity.

THINKING ABOUT LANGUAGE

USING PREPOSITIONAL PHRASES

For more on using prepositional phrases, see Chemical Engineering, Part 1.

A. Look at the sentences, which are based on content in Professor Spakowitz's essay "From Molecules to Materials: The Whole Is Greater Than the Sum of the Parts." Then underline the correct preposition to introduce the prepositional phrase. An example has been done for you.

Our everyday experiences are based on how we interact with / between / on the materials around us.

1. Water is a gas below / above / between 100°C., liquid below / above / between 0°C and 100°C, and solid below / above / between 0°C.
2. The process of boiling a liquid happens on / in / at a specific temperature on / in / at a given pressure.
3. The state of a material cannot be understood on / by / for only looking at / on / in the behavior of a single molecule away to / in / from its neighbors.
4. Solid, liquids, and gases are common states in / of / for matter, but there are others that are very useful for / about / at a variety of applications.
5. The relationship in / before / between molecules and materials is often difficult to predict.

B. Use the words from the left column with one preposition from the right column to create a sentence with a prepositional phrase. You can change the form and order of the words in the first column if you need to. An example has been done for you.

Words	Prepositions
make / materials / molecules	of / in

Materials are made of molecules.

1. **Words** — 100°C / boil / water | **Prepositions** — at / in

   ....

2. **Words** — water / solid / 0°C | **Prepositions** — below / above

   ....

3. **Words** — each other / attract / molecules | **Preposition** — from / to

   ....

4. **Words** — polymers / our body / make | **Preposition** — from / at

   ....

5. **Words** — polymers / damage / recover / shape | **Preposition** — after / before

   ....

USING THE PASSIVE VOICE

For more on knowing how and when to use the passive voice, see Chemical Engineering, Part 2.

Read these sentences based on Professor Spakowitz's essay about the behavior of molecules. If the sentence is in the active voice, write it in the passive voice. If it is in the passive voice, write it in the active voice. Use the examples to help you.

Active to passive:
If I heat water over 100°C, it will turn into a gas.

If water is heated over 100°C, it will turn into a gas.

Passive to active:
Modern synthetic materials are made in the laboratory by scientists and engineers.

Scientists and engineers make modern synthetic materials in the laboratory.

1. The behavior of a material is dictated by the interactions between its molecules.

   ....

   ....

2. Modern engineering frequently focuses on design at the molecular level.

   ....

   ....

3. The boiling point can be used by engineers to fix the temperature of an object.

   ....

   ....

4. That way the chocolate is melted without burning. (Use "I" as the subject)

   ....

   ....

5. The ability of molecules to move around is characterized by a quality called entropy.

   ....

   ....

6. Many engineers perform computer simulations of molecules to predict whether a particular molecule will exist in a desired state.

   ....

   ....

7. The liquid crystal state allows the free movement of molecules.

8. Scientists and engineers must understand molecular interactions when designing liquid crystal materials.

9. Our skin is an extremely important material that influences how we experience our surroundings.

10. Our bodies rely on the behavior of the molecules in our skin to allow us to move and recover.

READ

Go to MyEnglishLab to read "From Molecules to Materials: The Whole Is Greater Than the Sum of the Parts" for more practice reading an extended text and using your reading skills. Take notes while you read. Then answer the questions in Check What You've Learned.

CHECK WHAT YOU'VE LEARNED

Answer the questions based on the essay "From Molecules to Materials: The Whole Is Greater Than the Sum of the Parts." Refer to your notes to answer the questions.

1. What is the main idea of this essay?
   a. The connection between materials—how they behave and what they are made of.
   b. Materials have three different states: solid, liquid, and gas.
   c. When materials change from one state to another, the distance between molecules changes.
   d. Materials are made of molecules, and so are our bodies.

2. Which of these statements is <u>not</u> true?

   a. Molecules in a gas are farther apart than molecules in a solid.
   b. Changing from one state to another requires a change in temperature.
   c. Our body is made of the same kinds of molecules as the clothes we wear.
   d. There are only three states: solid, liquid, and gas.

3. A state of high entropy means that the molecules are

   a. highly organized.
   b. highly disorganized.
   c. very clean.
   d. very messy.

4. Why does Professor Spakowitz use the example of melting chocolate?

   a. to show the process of melting chocolate without burning it
   b. to show that double boilers are the best way to melt certain foods
   c. to show that materials change to a liquid at different temperatures
   d. to show the process of changing a liquid to a gas

5. Which of these statements is true?

   a. Changing the atmospheric pressure can cause a material to change state.
   b. Chocolate melts at a higher temperature than water.
   c. Molecules in a solid are closer together than when they are in a gas.
   d. all of the above

6. Which of these statements about liquid crystals is true?

   a. Liquid crystals like those used in a flat screen display are not a solid, liquid, or gas.
   b. When liquid crystals are organized, it is harder for molecules to move around.
   c. The less organized the liquid crystals are, the brighter your display.
   d. Liquid crystals are just like haystacks because they can be organized very quickly.

7. Which of these can happen if we understand how molecules act at certain temperatures?

   a. We can design better building materials.
   b. We can predict how a variety of materials will act in different situations.
   c. We can develop new molecules and new materials.
   d. all of the above

8. Which of these statements about modern engineering would Professor Spakowitz probably agree with?
   a. It requires an understanding of how to construct new buildings.
   b. It requires an understanding of how the molecules in a material act.
   c. It requires an understanding of how to construct new materials.
   d. It requires an understanding of how materials change into a gas.

GUIDED RESEARCH

ASSIGNMENT

Write 1–2 paragraphs about a synthetic material—a material that has been invented, rather than produced naturally. You will create a clear and concise heading for the section and choose a visual to support the main idea.

A. Reread Professor Spakowitz's essay and determine where the essay could be divided into clearly defined sections. Then write the main topic and idea of each section you have identified in the chart. Make a heading for each section that reflects the main topic and idea. Make sure that your headings are short, and the style is consistent. An example has been done for you.

For more on writing headings and subheadings, see Chemical Engineering, Part 1.

Section Paragraph Numbers	Main Topic and Idea	Heading
2-3	Solid, liquid, and gas are universal states that dictate the behavior of molecules.	Universal States: Solid, Liquid, and Gas.

B. You are going to add another section to Professor Spakowitz's essay. Pick one of the materials from the box. Using your school's library or an online search engine, answer the questions.

Kevlar® fiber	graphene	synthetic spider silk	self-healing polymers

1. Who invented this material, and why was it invented?
2. What is special about this material?
3. How is it being used today?
4. How could this material be used in the future?

WRITE

Part A

1. Using the information you have found about your material, determine the main topic and the main idea of your section. Then create a heading for it that is short and consistent with the headings you created in Guided Research, Part A.

Main Topic:

....

....

....

Main Idea:

....

....

....

Heading:

....

2. Now determine what kind of visual you could add to support or illustrate the point you are making. Remember, the visual should be connected to the main idea of the text.

TIP

Headings should be designed so that they can guide different kinds of readers, depending on why they are reading.

....

....

TIP

Visuals should support your message, not distract the reader. Be sure you have chosen visuals that do this.

For more on understanding the visual appearance of writing, see Chemical Engineering, Part 1.

Part B

1. Using your ideas from Part A, create an outline for your paragraph(s).
2. Write your paragraph(s) and integrate your visual. Be sure to proofread your draft.
3. Work with a partner. Read each other's paragraph(s) and complete the peer review form. Discuss your comments and ideas.

For more on proofreading effectively, see Chemical Engineering, Part 1.

Questions	Yes	No	Notes
Does the heading reflect the main idea of the section?	☐	☐	
Is the heading consistent with the writer's other headings for the essay?	☐	☐	
Is the writer's idea for a visual appropriate?	☐	☐	
Did the writer effectively proofread the draft?	☐	☐	

4. Based on feedback from your partner, revise your paragraph(s) and prepare your final draft.

Go to MyEnglishLab to join in a collaborative activity.

Index

Page numbers followed by f and t indicate figures and tables, respectively. Page numbers followed by ●(LS) refer to terms found in Language Skill presentations in MyEnglishLab referenced on those pages.

Credits

Page viii (top, left): Chombosan/Shutterstock; viii (bottom, right) Pearson Education, Inc.; x: Pearson Education, Inc.; xi: Pearson Education, Inc.; Page 1: (multiple uses): Budai Romeo Gabor/Fotolia (gold coins); Nik_Merkulov/Fotolia (green leaf with drops of water); Scisetti Alfio/Fotolia (old letter); Vichly4thai/Fotolia (red molecule/DNA cell); Tobkatrina/123RF (hands holding Earth); orelphoto/Fotolia (honeycomb background); Page 2: Lightwise/123RF; 14: Geoffrey Robinson/Alamy Stock Photo; 24: Designua/Shutterstock; 34: Cartoon Resource/Alamy Stock Photo; 36: Macrovector/Shutterstock; 41: Performance Image/Alamy Stock Photo; 49 (top, left): Swill Klitch/Shutterstock; 49 (top, right): Xello/Shutterstock; 54: Cofiant Images/Alamy Stock Photo; 55 (left): MicroOne/Shutterstock; 55 (right): CkyBe/Shutterstock; 59: Top Photo Corporation/Alamy Stock Photo; 64 (top, left): Africa Studio/Shutterstock; 64 (top, right): Canadapanda/Shutterstock; 64 (bottom, left): Aleksanderdn/123RF; 64 (bottom, right): NemesisINC/Shutterstock; 66: Steffen Foerster/Shutterstock; 71: Graeme Shannon/Shutterstock; 87: Joel Sartore/National Geographic/Getty Images; 96 (top, left): Carleton Chinner/Shutterstock; 96 (top, right): Peter Mooij/123RF; 96 (bottom): Lost Horizon Images/Cultura Creative/Alamy Stock Photo; 98: Peter Horree/Alamy Stock Photo; 101 (left): www.BibleLandPictures.com/Alamy Stock Photo; 103: Classic Image/Alamy Stock Photo; 114 (left): Pictorial Press Ltd/Alamy Stock Photo; 114 (right): Paul Fearn/Alamy Stock Photo; 117: Stephen Inglis/Shutterstock; 120: Florian Trojer/Moment Open/Getty Images; 123: Emory Kristof/National Geographic Magazines/Getty Images; 131 (top): Guenter Fischer/ImageBROKER/Alamy Stock Photo; 131 (bottom): De Agostini/Biblioteca Ambrosiana/De Agostini Picture Library/Getty Images; 132 (left): Alexey Stiop/123RF; 132 (right): Paul Fearn/Alamy Stock Photo; 134: Chombosan/Shutterstock; 137: Ann Cutting/Alamy Stock Photo; 138 (left): Eddie Gerald/Alamy Stock Photo; 138 (center): Ringo Chiu/ZUMA Press Inc/Alamy Stock Photo; 138 (right): Dariusz Kantorski/123RF; 139: MBI/Alamy Stock Photo; 142: Dariusz Kantorski/123RF; 143 (top, right): Dariusz Kantorski/123RF; 143 (center, left): Alex Kosev/Shutterstock; 143 (bottom, right): Kozak Nick/Abaca/Newscom; 156: Alain Bommenel, Laurence Saubadu AFP/Newscom; 157: Mike Hill/Alamy Stock Photo; 167 (top, left): Jeff Morgan 09/Alamy Stock Photo; 167 (top, right): Piotr Pawinski/123RF; 167 (bottom, left): Nui232/Shutterstock; 167 (bottom, right): David Herraez/Alamy Stock Photo; 204: Pogonici/123RF; 206: Alexander Supertramp/Shutterstock; 217 (left): Paolo Paradiso/Shutterstock; 217 (right): VanderWolf Images/Shutterstock; 235: Arka38/Shutterstock; 238: Radius Images/Alamy Stock Photo; 251: Alta Oosthuizen/123RF; 252 (left): Felipe Duran/Shutterstock; 252 (center, left): Hans Wagemaker/Shutterstock; 252 (center, right): Michael Potter11/Shutterstock; 252 (right): Jens Siewert/EyeEm/Getty Images; 256: Michael Potter11/Shutterstock; 257 (left): Blickwinkel/Schmidbauer/Alamy Stock Photo; 257 (center): Guenter Fischer/ImageBROKER/Alamy Stock Photo; 257 (right): Tomentosaplaga/Alamy Stock Photo; 266 (left): Paul Mayall/Alamy Stock Photo; 266 (center): Sergei Uriadnikov/123RF; 266 (right): Johan W. Elzenga/Shutterstock; 268: SIPA USA/SIPA/Newscom; 274: Sergi Reboredo/Alamy Stock Photo; 275: Everett-Art/Shutterstock; 280 (left): Sergi Reboredo/Alamy Stock Photo; 280 (right): Glasshouse Images/Alamy Stock Photo; 297 (top, left): Photo one/Shutterstock; 297 (top, center): PrimaStockPhoto/Shutterstock; 297 (top, right): Siraphol/123RF; 297 (bottom, left): Memo Angeles/Shutterstock; 297 (bottom, center): Memo Angeles/Shutterstock; 297 (bottom, right): Memo Angeles/Shutterstock; 297 (middle, left): Gareth Dewar/Pearson Education Ltd; 297 (middle, center): Joakim Lloyd Raboff/Shutterstock; 297 (middle, right): Pakhnyushchy/Shutterstock; 301: Rfarrarons/123RF; 302: Edwin Baker/Alamy Stock Photo; 304: Khakimullin Aleksandr/Shutterstock; 312 (left): Chine Nouvelle/SIPA/Newscom; 312 (right): Viacheslav Lopatin/Shutterstock; 326: US Coast Guard Photo/Alamy Stock Photo; 339: Milosz Maslanka/Shutterstock; 342: Zmeel/E+/Getty Images; 356: Peshkova/Shutterstock; 370: Sonja Fowler/Alamy Stock Photo; 378: FLPA/Alamy Stock Photo; 382: Photos.com/Getty Images; 390: Katie Smith Photography/Shutterstock; 392: Photos.com/Getty Images; 395: BLM Collection/Alamy Stock Photo; 396 (left): Steve Allen/123RF; 396 (center): Don Fink/Shutterstock; 396 (right): Coleman Yuen/Pearson Education Asia Ltd.